CHARLES HANDY

THE AGE OF UNREASON

AND

THE EMPTY RAINCOAT

D1323182

ARROW

Other authors in the series

STEPHEN FRY
ROBERT HARRIS
JAMES HAWES
TIM PARKS
ANNE TYLER

Charles Handy is an independent writer, broadcaster and teacher. He has been an oil executive, an economist, a professor at the London Business School, the Warden of St George's House in Windsor Castle and the Chairman of the Royal Society for the Encouragement of Arts, Manufacture and Commerce.

He was born in Kildare in Ireland, the son of an Archdeacon, and educated in Ireland, England (Oxford University) and the USA (Massachusetts Institute of Technology).

His many books include *The Empty Raincoat*, *Understanding Organizations*, *Gods of Management*, *The Future of Work* and *Waiting for the Mountain to Move*.

He and his wife Elizabeth live in London and Norfolk.

By Charles Handy

Understanding Organizations
Understanding Schools as Organizations
Understanding Voluntary Organizations
Inside Organizations
The Age of Unreason
Waiting for the Mountain to Move
Gods of Management
The Empty Raincoat: Making Sense of the Future
Beyond Certainty: The Changing Worlds of Organizations
The Hungry Spirit

The Age of Unreason

Charles Handy

ARROW
BUSINESS BOOKS

This edition published by Arrow Books Limited 1995

5 7 9 10 8 6 4

Copyright © Charles Handy 1989, 1991

The right of Charles Handy to be identified as the author
of this work has been asserted by him in accordance
with the Copyright, Designs and Patents Act, 1988.

First published in Great Britain in 1989 by Business Books Ltd,
an imprint of Random House Group.
Arrow edition 1990. Second edition 1991
Reprinted under the Century Business imprint 1992

Arrow Books Limited
Random House
20 Vauxhall Bridge Road, London SW1V 2SA

Random House Australia (Pty) Limited
16 Dalmore Drive, Scoresby, Victoria 3179, Australia

Random House New Zealand Limited
18 Poland Road, Glenfield
Auckland 10, New Zealand

Random House South Africa (Pty) Limited
Endulini, 5a Jubilee Road, Parktown 2193, South Africa

RANDOM HOUSE UK Limited Reg. No. 954009

British Library Cataloguing Publication Data
A catalogue record for this book is available from the British Library

Papers used by Random House UK Limited
are natural, recyclable products made from wood grown in
sustainable forests. The manufacturing processes conform to
the environmental regulations of the country of origin

Printed and bound in Great Britain by
Mackays of Chatham PLC, Chatham, Kent

ISBN 0 09 954831 3

Contents

Acknowledgements

The future is not inevitable. We can influence it, if we know what we want it to be. That conviction is the reason for this book. We can and should be in charge of our own destinies in a time of change.

The book, in part, builds on my previous writings: on organizations, on the future of work, on schools and voluntary organizations, on middle-age and on religion. They all, I now realize, hang together as different parts and parcels of life. To separate them out was to collude with the besetting sin of modern life, reductionism, reducing things to their component parts and thereby too often, missing the meaning and message of the wood in a minute examination of its trees.

The book is addressed primarily to those who work in and who manage organizations or some part of them, because it is their hands that rest on the levers of change, although they may not always realize it. The changes which we are already seeing in our lives, and which we will see more of, have their origins in the changes in our workplaces. Work has always been the major influence on the way we live. It still is, but often in unexpected ways.

The ideas in the book come from many sources, only some of which I have been able to acknowledge specifically in the text. The managers, and others whom I meet in seminars, courses and conferences around the world have contributed many of them, and a group of young executives drawn together by Hay Management Consultants in 1988 to look at the world ahead of them was particularly stimulating. Peter Drucker's thoughts on the *Age of Disconti-*

nuity and Tom Peters' on *A World Turned Upside-Down* anticipated two of the major themes of the book. They were talking about organizations. I think it goes much farther than that.

Without the encouragement, and the deadlines, of my publishers, Gail Rebuck and Lucy Shankleman, this book would not have happened. I am very grateful to them for their perceptive comments and their belief in the book. Elizabeth, my wife and partner, has lived with every line of this book, on the page and in our life together. I applaud the generosity with which she has tolerated this writing through living and all the help she has given me. Writing the book was my way of beginning to take charge of my destiny: I hope that reading it will help others to do the same.

Charles Handy,
Diss, Norfolk,
England.

Preface to the second edition

I was in Dresden not so long ago, in what we must now call *Eastern* Germany. Herr Motte is the man responsible for returning to private ownership the 700 or so business corporations that were, until 1991, owned and controlled by the state in that area. He had a staff of 32 and needed to sell one or two corporations *every* day to meet his target, with many of them literally unsaleable. It is a formidable task and I asked him where he looked for guidance. 'In reshaping the business sector of Eastern Germany,' he said 'there are no models. We have to re-shape the future.'

When this book was first published that wall which divided East from West was a permanent obstacle to peace. Within six months it was gone; a dramatic example of the discontinuous change which was the excuse for the book. Herr Motte's answer to me was also the perfect summary of how we must respond, not by looking to the past but by creating something new, different and hopefully better, by being 'unreasonable' in the sense in which George Bernard Shaw meant the word, by thinking unconventionally, even upside-down.

The book is about work and about individual lives, not about politics and wars and countries, but the messages are the same and the changes just as dramatic. As this edition goes to press there are fears of widespread recession. Part of that recession will be because our organizations have become too expensive, too complicated and cumbersome. Like the centrally planned economies of the old communist world these centrally planned organizations are also discovering, rather late in the day, that the old ways which worked quite well in the past are no longer cost-effective. They will have to re-shape their futures and re-think the way they get work done if they are going to survive in an age when technology makes almost anything possible.

The answers will affect us all. All over America, on a recent trip, I saw splendid new office towers in the downtown city areas. No lights shone there, however, because no-one was in them. Recession? Or a big re-think about the need for expensive offices in the new organizations? We shall have to wait and see.

I have not changed my views since the first edition came out, about the way the world of work is heading and the ways we need to respond, although I have updated some of the numbers and the examples. Nor do many people seem to disagree, in broad principle, with these views although they may argue about the detail and the timing. For most, however, it is a depressing prospect, one of a tide of history going out carrying with it a lot of dead fish, driftwood and garbage. For me, it is a tide coming in, full of opportunities for new launches and some re-floatings. Incoming tides can also, of course, swamp the unsuspecting and the unready and I still worry about the hordes I see pouring off the commuter trains every morning who seem to think, or hope, that they live by a tideless and unchanging sea.

They don't. Nor do these tides keep to neat tables. They come in surges. It is truly an age of uncertainty and of unreason. Like it or not we shall have to live in it, and most of us, for much of our now longer lives, will live in it outside those comfortable prisons which we called organizations and which provided the structure for our days and years.

That new freedom is the most significant bit of discontinuous change for most of us. But as the new democracies of Eastern Europe are finding, freedom can be very uncomfortable. I believe that there is no choice. The old ways of work are gone; we have to re-shape our futures. A lot hinges on those who will lead and design the new organizations. They, not our politicians, are the makers of our destinies and it is to them that this book is mainly directed in the hope that they may have the vision and the courage to be sensibly unreasonable.

Charles Handy,
Diss, Norfolk,
England,
1991.

Part One: Changing

1 The Argument

The scene was the General Synod of the Church of England in the 1980s. The topic being debated was the controversial proposition that women be admitted to the priesthood. A speaker from the floor of the Chamber spoke with passion, 'In this matter,' he cried, 'as in so much else in our great country, why cannot the status quo be the way forward?'

It was the heartfelt plea not only of the traditionalists in that Church but of those in power, anywhere, throughout the ages. If change there has to be let it be more of the same, continuous change. That way, the cynic might observe, nothing changes very much.

Continuous change is comfortable change. The past is then the guide to the future. An American friend, visiting Britain and Europe for the first time wondered, 'Why is it that over here whenever I ask the reason for anything, any institution or ceremony or set of rules, they always give me an historical answer – because ..., whereas in my country we always want a functional answer – in order to ...' Europeans, I suggested, look backwards to the best of their history and change as little as they can; Americans look forward and want to change as much as they may.

Circumstances do, however, combine occasionally to discomfort the advocates of the status quo. Wars, of course, are the great discomforters, but so is technology, when it takes one of its leaps forward as it did in the Industrial Revolution, so is demography, when it throws up baby booms or busts, so is a changing set of values, like that which occurred during the student unrest of 1968, and so are economics.

Circumstances are now once again, I believe, combining in curious ways. Change is not what it used to be. The status quo will no longer be the best way forward. That way will be less comfortable and less easy but, no doubt, more interesting – a word we often use to signal an uncertain mix of danger and opportunity. If we wish to enjoy more of the opportunity and less of the risk we need to understand the changes better. Those who know why changes come waste less effort in protecting themselves or in fighting the inevitable. Those who realize where changes are heading are better able to use those changes to their own advantage. The society which welcomes change can use that change instead of just reacting to it.

George Bernard Shaw once observed that all progress depends on the unreasonable man. His argument was that the reasonable man adapts himself to the world while the unreasonable persists in trying to adapt the world to himself, therefore for any change of consequence we must look to the unreasonable man, or, I must add, to the unreasonable woman.

In that sense we are entering an Age of Unreason, when the future, in so many areas, is there to be shaped, by us and for us; a time when the only prediction that will hold true is that no predictions will hold true; a time, therefore, for bold imaginings in private life as well as public, for thinking the unlikely and doing the unreasonable.

That, then, is the purpose of this book – to understand better the changes which are already about us in order that we may, as individuals and as a society, suffer less and profit more. Change, after all, is only another word for growth, another synonym for learning. We can all do it, and enjoy it, if we want to.

The story or argument of this book rests on three assumptions:

— that the changes are different this time: they are discontinuous and not part of a pattern; that such discontinuity happens from time to time in history, although it is confusing and disturbing, particularly to those in power;

— that it is the little changes which can in fact make the biggest differences to our lives, even if these go unnoticed at the time, and that it is the changes in the way our *work* is organized which will make the biggest differences to the way we all will *live*.

— that discontinuous change requires discontinuous upside-down thinking to deal with it, even if both thinkers and thoughts appear absurd at first sight.

Change Is Not What It Used To Be

Thirty years ago I started work in a world-famous multinational company. By way of encouragement they produced an outline of my future career – 'This will be your life,' they said, 'with titles of likely jobs.' The line ended, I remember, with myself as chief executive of a particular company in a particular far-off country. I was, at the time, suitably flattered. I left them long before I reached the heights they planned for me, but already I knew that not only did the job they had picked out no longer exist, neither did the company I would have directed nor even the country in which I was to have operated.

Thirty years ago I thought that life would be one long continuous line, sloping upwards with luck. Today I know better. Thirty years ago that company saw the future as largely predictable, to be planned for and managed. Today they are less certain. Thirty years ago most people thought that change would mean more of the same, only better. That was incremental change and to be welcomed. Today we know that in many areas of life we cannot guarantee more of the same, be it work or money, peace or freedom, health or happiness, and cannot even predict with confidence what will be happening in our own lives. Change is now more chancy, but also more exciting if we want to see it that way.

Change has, of course, always been what we choose to make it, good or bad, trivial or crucial. Take, for instance, the one word 'change' and consider how we use it. Can any other word be asked to do so many things?

'Change is part of life' (a noun universal)
'There is a change in the arrangements' (a noun particular)
'Please count your change' (a noun metaphorical)
'Please change this wheel' (a verb transitive)
'I will not change' (a verb intransitive)
'Where do I change trains?' (a verb metaphorical)
'She is a clever change agent' (an adjective)

Where the same word is used to describe the trivial (a change of clothes) and the profound ('a change of life'), how can we easily distinguish whether it is heralding something important or not? When the same word can mean 'progress' and 'inconsistency', how should we know which is which? We might well ask whether the English language was devised to confuse the foreigner, or ourselves?

More of the same only better, and, if possible, for more people. It was a comfortable view of change, one which, in the growth-heady days of the sixties and seventies allowed so many to marry idealism to their personal prosperity. It allowed the big to grow bigger, the powerful to look forward to more power, and even the dispossessed to hope for some share of the action one day. It was a view of change which upset no one. The only trouble was that it did not work, it never has worked anywhere for very long, and even those societies in which it has seemed to be working, Japan, Germany and, perhaps, the USA are about to see that it does not work for ever. In each of those societies it is now increasingly relevant to ask 'what is the next trick?' because the current one shows every sign of ending.

It is not just because the pace of change has speeded up, which it has done, of course. We must all, sometime, have seen one of those graphs comparing, say, the speed of travel in 500 BC and every 100 years thereafter, with the line suddenly zooming upwards ever steeper in the last inch or two of the chart as we approached modern times, when horses are superceded by cars, then by planes and then by rockets. Faster change on its own sits quite comfortably with the 'more only better' school. It is only when the graph goes off the chart that we need to start to worry, because then things get less predictable and less manageable. Incremental change suddenly becomes discontinuous change. Catastrophe theory, they call it in mathematics, interestingly and symbolically, the study of discontinuous curves in observed phenomena, graphs that loop back on themselves or go into precipitous falls or unsuspected plateaux. Trends, after all, cannot accelerate forever on a graph paper without looping the loop.

I believe that discontinuity is not catastrophe, and that it certainly *need* not be catastrophe. Indeed, I will argue that discontinuous change is the only way forward for a tramlined society, one that has got used to its ruts and its blinkers and prefers its own ways, however dreary, to untrodden paths and new ways of looking at things. I like the story of the Peruvian Indians who, seeing the sails of their Spanish invaders on the horizon put it down to a freak of the weather and went on about their business, having no concept of sailing ships in their limited experience. Assuming continuity, they screened out what did not fit and let disaster in. I like less the story that a frog if put in cold water will not bestir itself if that water is heated up slowly and gradually and will in the end let itself be boiled alive, too comfortable with continuity to realize that continuous change at some point becomes discontinous and demands a change in behaviour. If we want to avoid the fate of the Peruvian Indians or the boiling frog we must learn to look for and embrace discontinuous change.

That is more revolutionary than it sounds. Discontinous, after all, is hardly a word to stir the multitudes; yet to embrace discontinous change means, for instance, completely re-thinking the way in which we learn things. In a world of incremental change it is sensible to ape your elders in order to take over where they leave off, in both knowledge and responsibility. But under conditions of discontinuity it is no longer obvious that their ways should continue to be your ways; we may all need new rules for new ball games and will have to discover them for ourselves. Learning then becomes the voyage of exploration, of questing and experimenting, that scientists and tiny children know it to be but which we are soon reminded, by parents, teachers and supervisors, can be time-wasting when others already know what we need to learn. It is a way of learning which can even be seen as disrespectful if not downright rebellious. Assume discontinuity in our affairs, in other words, and you threaten the authority of the holders of knowledge, of those in charge or those in power.

For those in charge continuity is comfort, and predictability ensures that they can continue in control. Instinctively, therefore, they prefer to believe that things will go on as they have before. It requires, as Mancur Olsen has argued, revolutions to unblock societies and shocks to galvanize organizations. Perhaps that is why Britain, untouched by revolution for over 300 years, seems to prefer that the status quo should be the way forward and why organizations too often learn too late.

Major change in organizations seems to follow a predictable and sad sequence:

FRIGHT	– the possibility of bankruptcy, takeover or collapse
NEW FACES	– new people are brought in at the top
NEW QUESTIONS	– questions, study groups, investigations into old ways and new options
NEW STRUCTURES	– the existing pattern is broken up and re-arranged to give new talent scope and break up old clubs
NEW GOALS & STANDARDS	– the new organization sets itself new aims and targets.

Do we always need a painful jolt to start re-thinking? Did it need the Titanic to sink before it became compulsory for ships to carry enough lifeboats for all the passengers? Did the Challenger shuttle have to explode before NASA re-organized its decision-making systems and priorities?

How many have to die before we make cars safer and less powerful?

It is the argument of this book that discontinuous change is all around us. We would be foolish to block our eyes to its signs as those Peruvian Indians did to their invaders' sails. We need not leave it too late, like the frog in boiling water, nor wait for a revolution. There are opportunities as well as problems in discontinuous change. If we change our attitudes, our habits and the ways of some of our institutions it can be an age of new discovery, new enlightenment and new freedoms, an age of true learning.

Ask people, as I have often done, to recall two or three of the most important learning experiences in their lives and they will never tell you of courses taken or degrees obtained, but of brushes with death, of crises encountered, of new and unexpected challenges or confrontations. They will tell you, in other words, of times when continuity ran out on them, when they had no past experience to fall back on, no rules or handbook. They survived, however, and came to count it as learning, as a growth experience. Discontinuous change, therefore, when properly handled, is the way we grow up.

The Beginnings Are Small

We live life on two levels. A teenager in the USA was asked to produce a list of the kinds of critical events which she saw looming in the future. It went like this:

A US/USSR alliance
A cancer cure
Test-tube babies
An accidental nuclear explosion
Spread of anarchy throughout the world
Robots holding political office in the USA

We could each provide our own such list of triumphs and disasters. When she was asked, however, to list the critical events looming in her personal life she wrote down:

Moving into my own apartment
Interior Design School
Driver's Licence
Getting a dog
Marriage
Having Children
Death

This book is about changes, but it is about the changes which will affect the *second* list more than the first. Not that a cancer cure or a nuclear war would not have an effect on the way we live our daily lives, but such mega changes belong to other books by other people. This book is written in the belief that it is often the little things in life which change things most and last the longest.

The chimney, for instance, may have caused more social change than any war. Without a chimney everyone had to huddle together in one central place around a fire with a hole in the roof above. The chimney, with its separate flues, made it possible for one dwelling to heat a variety of rooms. Small units could huddle together independently. The cohesion of the tribe in winter slipped away.

Central heating – meaning in reality *de*centralized heating – carried it even further, doing away with fireplaces altogether, making it possible to pile dwelling units on top of dwelling units into the sky and for so many people to live alone, often far above the ground, but warm.

No one would want to disinvent the chimney or central heating, but their inventors (whose names are long lost if they were ever known) could not have guessed at the changes which they would make to our social architecture. I shall argue in this book, amongst other things, that the telephone line has been and will be the modern day equivalent of the chimney, unintentionally changing the way we work and live.

I saw a man sitting in his car in the parking place I coveted. 'Are you about to move?' I asked. 'Not for a couple of hours yet,' he replied. It was then I saw the portable computer on the seat beside him and the fax connected to his car telephone line. He was using his car as a mobile office.

Rather like central heating, the telephone and its attachments make it possible today for people to work together without being together in one place. The scattered organization is now a reality. The implications, as we shall see, are considerable. It is not an unmixed blessing for being together has always been part of the fun. As Pascal once said, all the world's ills stem from the fact that a man cannot sit in a room alone. Increasingly, he, and she, may have to.

Chimneys and telephones are technology – always a

potential trigger of discontinuity. Economic reality is another. Governments can stave it off for a while but not forever. In the end countries live or die according to their comparative advantage. Comparative advantage means that there is something for which others will pay a price, be it oil and minerals, cheap labour, golden sun or brains. For Britain and the rest of the industrialized world it has, increasingly, to be brains. Clever people, making clever things or providing clever services add value, sometimes lots of value, to minimal amounts of raw material. Their sales allow the import of all the things we cannot grow and cannot afford to make. That way prosperity advances. It sounds straightforward and simple enough, but its consequences ramble everywhere. Many more clever people are now needed, for one thing, with fewer places for the less clever. Organizations making or doing clever things spend much of their time handling information in all sorts of forms. Facts, figures, words, pictures, ideas, arguments, meetings, committees, papers, conferences all proliferate. Information goes down telephone lines, so technology and economics begin to blend together to create a massive discontinuity in the shape, and skills and purposes of many of our organizations. Clever organizations do not, it seems, work the way organizations used to work, they have different shapes, different working habits, different age profiles, different traditions of authority.

Barry Jones, now an Australian Cabinet Minister, has listed the typical activities of the information sector.

teaching	creative arts & architecture
research	design
office work	music
public service	data processing
communications	computer software
the media	selling
films	accountancy

theatre	law
photography	psychiatry & psychology
post & telecommunications	social work
book publishing	management
printing	advertising
banking	church
real estate	science
administration	trade unions
museums & television	parliament

One could add to it: stockbroking, consultancy, journalism, conference organizing, secretarial work, medicine, politics and local government.

It is unlikely that anyone reading this book will not find his or her work included in this list.

Technology and economics is a potent blend. It is the premise of this book that from that blend all sorts of changes ensue. Social customs can be transformed. An information society makes it easier for more women to do satisfying jobs. Technology has turned child-bearing into an act of positive decision for most. Marriage then becomes, increasingly, a public commitment to starting a family. Relationships that do not involve the start of a family no longer need the stamp of public commitment. Women can support themselves and can in theory support a family on their own, and many will prefer to do just that. What was in former times technologically and economically impossible, and therefore socially unacceptable, becomes both possible and acceptable. Discontinuity abroad creeps unnoticed into the family.

Words are the bugles of social change. When our language changes, behaviour will not be far behind. House-husbands, single-parent families, 'dinkies' and 'telecom-muters', these and many other words were unknown ten years ago. They were not needed. Organizations used to invite men to bring their wives to functions, then it became 'spouses' in recognition of the growing number of female employees, then 'partners' as an acceptance that marriage is not the only stable relationship, and now in California it is the 'significant other' to take care of any conceivable situation.

Just Think Of It!

It is the combination of a changing technology and economics, in particular of information technology and biotechnology and the economics associated with them, which causes this discontinuity. Between them they will make the world a different place.

Information technology links the processing power of the computer with the microwaves, the satellites, and the fibre optic cables of telecommunications. It is a technology which is leaping rather than creeping into the future. It is said that if the automobile industry had developed as rapidly as the processing capacity of the computer we would now be able to buy a 400 mile-per-gallon Rolls-Royce for £1.

Biotechnology is the completely new industry that has grown out of the interpretation of DNA, the genetic code at the heart of life. It is only one generation old as a science and as an industry, and is only now becoming evident in everyday life with new types of crops, genetic fingerprinting and all the possibilities, good and bad, of what is called bio-engineering.

These two technologies are developing so fast that their outputs are unpredictable, but some of the more likely developments in the next ten to twenty years could change parts of our lives, and other peoples' lives, in a dramatic fashion. A group of young executives who were asked by their companies to contemplate 2000 AD came up with the following possibilities and probabilities.

Cordless telephones Mark 2

The next generation of cordless telephones may give everyone their own portable personal telephone to be used anywhere at affordable prices. Link it to a lap-top computer and a portable fax and a car or train seat becomes an office. More interestingly, a telephone will then belong to a person not to a place. We will call a person and not know where they are.

Monoclonal antibodies

These genetically engineered bacteria which work to prevent particular diseases already exist and will be expanded. Blood-clotting and anti-clotting agents can now be manufactured to prevent major coronary diseases. 'Scavenger Proteins' are under investigation, designed to locate undesirable substances in the bloodstream, such as excess cholesterol. Cures for most cancers, and possibly AIDS, will be available by the end of the century. Senile dementia is now understood and drugs to combat it are under development. Life could go on, if not forever, for a lot longer than before when most diseases can be cured or prevented.

The transgenic pig

The possibility of using animal organs in humans has been under investigation for some time. The pig is biologically similar to humans and experiments are under way to engineer embryos to produce the transgenic pig, an animal with organs more man-like than piglike. Pig farms may one day mean something quite different from what they do today and replacement organs could be available on demand.

Water fields

Crops can now be genetically engineered to grow on poor quality soil or even in water (without tasting like seaweed!). Under development is an idea to engineer crops which can take their nitrogen directly from the air instead of from the ground, reducing the need for fertilizer. Any country could one day grow all the food it needs.

Enzyme catalysts

Microbes can now be used as catalysts in many chemical manufacturing processes. Some microbes can even be used to extract minerals from low-grade areas which were previously uneconomic. There are bugs which can be trained to devour and break down waste materials and can even thrive on cyanide. Rubbish disposal is now part of the chemical industry. Indeed, waste can now be converted into methane as one contribution to the energy problem. We shall see, too, self-cleaning ships which will biologically repel barnacles from sticking to their hulls.

Expert G.P.s

Computers programmed with up-to-date medical knowledge will be available to all doctors. These medical expert systems will not replace the doctor but will allow every doctor to be a better doctor, to make fewer demands on specialists and so release them to be better specialists. This example of 'expert systems' to enhance the work of professionals and technicians will be copied in all types of occupations, from the solicitor's office to the supermarket purchasing department.

The hearing computer

Voice-sensitive computers which can translate the spoken word into written words on a screen will be on every executive's desk one day, turning everyone into their own typist whether they can use a keyboard or not.

Irradiated food

Irradiation, once we are convinced that it is safe, will make it possible to buy 'fresh' food from all round the world at any time of the year. There will also be appetite-reducing drugs for those who find the new foods too tempting, and even health-increasing foods for those who want it both ways.

Telecatalogues

Teleshopping, already in existence in experimental situations, will one day be commonplace. Every store will display its wares and prices on your home television teletext, with local pick-up centres available for those unwilling to pay the extra delivery charge. Personal shopping in the High Street will become a leisure activity rather than a necessity, with all the frills and fancies that go with something done for pleasure not for duty.

Smart cards

These cards, already in use in France, replace cash, keys, credit, debit and cash cards. They will not only let you into your home or your car but will automatically update all your bank account balances for you.

Genetic fingerprints

Instead of Personal Identification Numbers (PINs) which are easy to discover and replicate, we shall each have a fingerprint on our personal cards which cannot be reproduced by others.

Genetic fingerprinting can be used to detect criminals from remains of tissue left behind at the scene of a crime, and also to diagnose hereditary and latent diseases. A national data-bank of genetic fingerprints seems possible one day.

Soon, everything we know about ourselves, and somethings we do not know, will be available to anyone with the right number or fingerprint. What price privacy then, many will ask.

Windscreen Maps

Computerized autoguidance screens will become commonplace, telling you the best way to get to where you want to go and projected onto the windscreen, as in fighter aircraft, so that you need not take your eyes off the road. These systems can take weather, traffic density and roadworks into account and give you the best available route, turning the whole country, one suspects, into a constant traffic jam.

Mileage bills

Cables laid under the roads of our cities can trigger a meter inside a car programmed to charge different parts of the city at different rates, presenting you with the equivalent of a telephone bill at the end of the month for the use of your car on the city roads. Already designed for Hong Kong this system is potentially available now, although special licences for inner-city use are a more likely first step.

The technology we shall undoubtedly take in our stride. Hole-in-the-wall banking caused hardly a flutter of an eyelid when it appeared and video-recorders are now part of the furniture in many homes. It is not the technology itself that is important but the impact which, without conscious thought, it has on our lives. Microwave ovens were a clever idea, but their inventor could hardly have realized that the effect, once they were everywhere, would be to take the preparation of food out of the home and into the, increasingly automated, factory; to make cooking as it used to be into an activity of choice, not of necessity; to alter the habits of our homes, making the dining table outmoded for many, as each member of the family individually heats up his or her own meal as and when they require it; 'grazing', the advertising people call it.

Whether these developments are for good or for ill must be our choice. Technology in itself is neutral. We can use it to enrich our lives or to let them lose all meaning. What we cannot do is to pretend that nothing has changed and live in a garden of remembrance as if time had stood still. It doesn't and we can't.

Thinking Upside-Down

Discontinuous change requires discontinuous thinking. If the new way of things is going to be different from the old, not just an improvement on it, then we shall need to look at everything in a new way. The new words really will signal new ideas. Not unnaturally, discontinuous upside-down thinking has never been popular with the upholders of continuity and the status quo. Copernicus and Galileo, arch-exponents of upside-down thinking, were not thanked for their pains. Jesus Christ, with his teaching that the meek should inherit the earth, that the poor were blessed and the first should be last in the ultimate scheme of things, died an untimely and unpleasant death. Nonetheless, their ideas live on, as good ideas do, to release new energies and new possibilities. In the long perspective of history it may seem that the really influential people in the last 100 years were not Hitler or Churchill, Stalin or Gorbachev, but Freud, Marx and Einstein, men who changed nothing except the way we think, but that changed everything. Francis Crick is not today a household name, yet he, with James Watson and Maurice Wilkins, discovered the genetic code, DNA, and so created the science of microbiology and the industry of biotechnology on which much of our economic future may depend.

The creative upside-down thinking of such people is the premise on which this book is built. New ways of thinking about familiar things can release new energies and make all manner of things possible. Upside-down thinking does not have to aspire to the greatness of Einstein or the all-embracing doctrines of Marx. It has its more familiar variants. The person who decides to treat every chore as an opportunity for learning discovers that cooking can be a creative art, chopping wood a craft, childminding an educational experience and shopping a sociological expedition. The organization which treats people like assets, requiring maintenance, love and investment, can behave quite differently from the organization which looks upon them as costs, to be reduced wherever and whenever possible. Upside-down thinking changes nothing save the way we think, but that can make all the difference.

This book advocates shamrocks, doughnuts and portfolios. These new words are not intended to be humorous devices but to evoke new images of familiar things. Thirty years ago Donald Schon, an American writer on organizations and now on learning, was arguing that creativity, particularly scientific creativity, comes from the 'displacement of concepts' – from taking concepts from one field of life and applying them to another in order to bring fresh insights. Einstein's Theory of Relativity is the great example. It applies equally well, if not more so, to the field of human activities. New imagery, signalled by new words, is as important as new theory; indeed new theory without new imagery can go unnoticed. Most of what is in this book is not new, nor is it being said for the first time, but much of it has gone unnoticed.

Upside-down thinking invites one to consider the unlikely if not the absurd. If Copernicus could stand the solar system on its head and still be right nothing should be dismissed out of hand in a time of discontinuity.

— Upside-down thinking suggests that we should stop talking and thinking of employees and employment. They are words, after all, which only entered the English language some 100 years ago. If work were defined as activity, some of which is paid for, then everyone is a worker, for nearly all their natural life. If everyone were treated as self-employed during their active years then by law and logic they could not be *un*employed. They might be poor but that can be put right. The words 'retirement' and 'unemployment' used only as a contrast to 'employment' would cease to be useful.

— Upside-down thinking suggests that if we put *everyone* on welfare it would no longer be invidious to receive it. That would not mean that no one was expected to work, only that everyone, as of right, got an initial 'social dividend', to be repaid progressively as one earns.

— Upside-down thinking wonders what magic it is that determines that forty hours spread over five days should be the working week for most people. Why cannot one choose to distribute the 2000 hours per year of normal work in a wide variety of chunks?

— Upside-down thinking notices that marriages in the last century lasted fifteen years and today also for fifteen years. In the last century it was the death of a partner which ended the marriage, now it is divorce. Should all relationships as well as employment contracts have a fixed term?

— Upside-down thinking suggests that it might be desirable to reward some experts for *not* using their skills. At present dentists are paid per treatment. There is an inevitable temptation to diagnose the need for treatment. If rewards were related to the number of healthy mouths in the practise not the bad ones, we might need fewer dentists and have better teeth. Similarly, upside-down thinking observes that a national health service is run and rewarded as a national sickness service and wonders why it cannot be reversed.

— Upside-down thinking suggests that instead of a *National* Curriculum for education what is really needed is an *individual* curriculum for every child, within common guidelines maybe, but given expression in a formal contract between the home and the school.

— Upside-down thinking questions whether more money

for more effort is always the right way to reward all the people all the time, or whether at certain stages in life more time might be as welcome as more money.

— Upside-down thinking wonders why one career or one type of job should be the norm. Why not three careers, switching progressively from energy to wisdom as the years role on?

— Upside-down thinking wonders why assistants are always younger than their principals or superiors. Why could not people retrain in mid-life to be part-time assistants to doctors, teachers, social workers and lawyers, para-professionals leaving the full professionals to do the more specialized work.

— Upside-down thinking wonders why roads are free and railways expensive in most countries, and suspects that it ought to be the other way around, as it almost is in Italy.

— In organizations, upside-down thinking observes that authority now has to be earned from those people over whom it is exercised and that even formal appraisal systems are upside-down in some organizations these days, with the subordinates appraising their bosses.

— Upside-down thinking notes that before too long there will be more people working outside organizations than inside them and that, even now, organizations only employ, directly, about one-quarter of the people connected in some way with the product or service which they deliver.

— Upside-down thinking suggests, therefore, that it might be better to pay people for the work they do, not the time they spend, since that time cannot be measured if they are out of sight or out of the organization.

And so it can go on. At first sight impossible, or ludicrous, many of these ideas have already been canvased as practical possibilities in some quarters. This book will consider some of them in the wake of the changes thrown up by the new discontinuities in work.

It is a time for new imaginings, of windows opening even if some doors close. We need not stumble backwards into the future, casting longing glances at what used to be; we can turn round and face a changed reality. It is, after all, a safer posture if you want to keep moving.

Some people, however, do not want to keep moving. Change for them means sacrificing the familiar, even if it is unpleasant, for the unknown, even when it might be better. Better the hole they know rather than the one not yet dug. Sadly for them a time of discontinuous change means that standing still is not an option, for the ground is shifting underneath them. For them, more than for the movers and the shakers, it is essential that they understand what is happening, that they begin to appreciate that to move and to change is essential, and that through change we learn and grow, although not always without pain.

This book is written particularly for those who live in the midst of change and do not notice it or want it. It is not a textbook for would-be leaders, nor a political tract; more a guidebook to a new country, ending with some tips for the traveller.

It is, however, only one man's view. In an age of unreason there can be no certainty. The guidebook is a guide to a country in which few have yet travelled, a country still to be explored. It is not my purpose to convince anyone that all forecasts are inevitable or that all my prescriptions are right. Rather I am concerned to persuade people that the world around them is indeed changing, with consequences yet to be understood. An age of unreason is an age of opportunity even if it looks at first sight more like the end of all ages.

If this book helps at all to look at things in a different way, if it sometimes creates an 'Aha' effect, as when people say 'Aha, of course, that is the way it is,' if people start to think 'unreasonably' and try to shape their world the way they think it ought to be, then I shall be content.

2   The Numbers

The numbers are the key. They explain why things will
not continue as they were because they have already gone
beyond the point of no return. It is just that most of us
have not noticed. The numbers are the numbers of people,
the numbers working, numbers dying, numbers growing
up. Demography is a boring word for a mesmerizing
subject.

The New Minority

Less than half of the workforce in the industrialized world
will be in 'proper' full-time jobs in organizations by the
beginning of the 21st century. Those full-timers or insiders
will be the new minority, just when we had begun to think
that proper jobs were the norm for everyone. The others
will not be all unemployed, although in every country
there will be some who belong to this 'reserve army' as
Marx called it. More will be self-employed, more and more
every year; many will be part-timers or temporary
workers, sometimes because that is the way they want it,
sometimes because that is all that is on offer. And then
there is, everywhere, another reserve army of women in
waiting, those whom the OECD so accurately calls
'unpaid domestic workers', mothers whose talents and
energies are not totally absorbed by their families. Add all
these disparate groups together and *already* they just
about equal the numbers of those with the full-time
proper jobs.

When less than half the available workforce is in full-time employment it no longer makes sense to think of a full-time job as the norm. Continuous change will have flipped into discontinuous change and we shall begin to change our views of 'work', of 'the job' and of 'a career'.

The reason for the shift is the emergence of the shamrock organization. The shamrock organization is explained in Chapter 3. Essentially, it is a form of organization based around a core of essential executives and workers supported by outside contractors and part-time help. This is not a new way of organizing things – builders large and small have operated this way for generations, as have newspapers with their printers and their stringers, or farmers with contract harvesting and holiday labour. What is new is the growth of this way of organizing in the big businesses and in the institutions of the public sector. All organizations will soon be shamrock organizations.

It has grown because it is cheaper. Organizations have realized that while it may be convenient to have everyone around all the time, with their time at your command because you have bought all their time, it is a luxurious way of marshalling the necessary resources. It is cheaper to keep them outside the organization, employed by themselves or by specialist contractors, and to buy their services when you need them.

This is a sensible strategy when labour is plentiful, when you can pick and choose between suppliers. It is a sensible strategy when your work ebbs and flows as it tends to do in service industries. When you are manufacturing things any surplus resources of people or equipment can always be turned to good advantage by producing things for stock for the weeks of peak demand, but the *service* industries cannot, or at least should not, stockpile their customers and must therefore flex their workforce.

Both these factors currently exist. The labour supply, the potential workforce, is growing in all the industrialized countries as the boom babies of the 1960s, *and* their wives, join the workforce during the 1990s – an extra million or so in Britain, for instance. At the same time the shift to the service sector continues inexorably everywhere. Between 1960 and 1985 the share of employees in the service sector in the USA rose from 56 to 69 per cent and in Italy from 33 to 55 per cent. It is unlikely to change back. The two factors work on each other; a growing service sector offers greater opportunities to women, which increases the potential workforce, which in turn increases the potential for more flexible ways of organizing.

It has been happening slowly, so slowly that most people have not noticed the new dimensions. Like the frog in Chapter 1, the temperature changes so gradually that no reaction is called for – until it is, perhaps, too late. Before very long the full-time worker will be a minority of the working population. Our assumptions about how the world works, how taxes are collected, families supported, lives planned and corporations organized will have to change radically. The Universal Declaration of Human Rights, which in 1947 guaranteed a choice of job to everyone, will be a clear anachronism. The new minority signals a major discontinuity which will effect every family in every industrialized country within the next generation.

The New Intelligentsia

The second number is alarming in a different way. A study by McKinsey's Amsterdam office in 1986 estimated that 70 per cent of all jobs in Europe in the year 2000 would require cerebral skills rather than manual skills. In the USA the figure is expected to be 80 per cent. That would be a complete reversal of the world of work some fifty years earlier. Discontinuity indeed!

It is impossible to be precise about such things. There is, to start with, no clearcut distinction between a cerebral job, requiring brain skills, and a manual job, needing muscles. Even simple manual jobs, like gardening, now need a degree of brains to understand the proper use of fertilizers and herbicides, to distinguish plant varieties and maintain machinery. Nonetheless, looking back at the list of occupations in the information sector on pages 12–13, a sector where brain skills of some degree are essential, it is hard not to think that 70 per cent is, if anything, an underestimate.

What is more controversial and even more alarming is the estimate by McKinsey's that one half of these brain-skill jobs will require the equivalent of a higher education, or a professional qualification, to be done adequately. If that is even approximately true it means that some 35 per cent of an age group should today be entering higher education or its equivalent if the labour force is going to be adequately skilled by the year 2000. McKinsey's estimate may even be on the conservative side. If we look at the new jobs alone, the current expectation is that 60 per cent of them will be managerial or professional, graduates all, of some sort.

In spite of these trends the percentage of young people in Britain going on to higher education is currently 14 per cent, rising to 18 per cent by 1992, but only because there will be fewer teenagers in total. In the rest of Europe the overall figure is around 20 per cent, with small national differences. In France, for instance, 36 per cent pass their *baccalauréat* and are therefore entitled to enter university but nearly half leave, or are asked to leave, at the end of the first year. Only Japan, the USA, Taiwan and South Korea seem to have university populations of the right sort of size for the future, and in all these countries there are concerns about the quality if not the quantity of some of what is called higher education.

If these estimates of the required levels of education are even partly true it means that not only will we see alarming numbers of skill shortages but that, more seriously still, we may lack the skills and the wits even to create the businesses and the opportunities which will then encounter skill shortages! It will, of course, be an invisible discontinuity. We will not miss the organizations we have not had, and never thought to have. Like the frog in Chapter 1 it will just be a slow unnoticed death.

The Vanishing Generation

In the nineties there will be almost one quarter fewer young people leaving school. At first glance this seems like a timely end to the problem of youth unemployment. A second glance changes the picture because it points to even more pressure on the relatively small percentage who have the brain skills needed by today's workforce. The bulk of the new reduced cohort of young people will still be like those, 43 per cent of them in 1986, who leave British schools without a proper certificate in even one subject.

A 1988 British Report by the National Economic Development Office and the Training Commission, 'Young People and the Labour Market, A Challenge for the 1990s', pointed out that in 1987 less than twenty large employers took on half of all the 27,000 school leavers with two or more A-levels who were looking for work. The vanishing generation, therefore, is a problem because, if nothing is done, it means that the supply of brain skills, already inadequate, will be even more inadequate, and that the skills shortages referred to above will become even more severe. The competition for the more educated will intensify and the rejection of the less educated will be felt even more cruelly. Youth unemployment will *not* be solved, indeed it will be raised a notch or two.

The situation is an opportunity, however, if it makes it easier to tackle the task of educating more of our young men and women for life and work in the world of brain skills. Without doing anything, as every government has discovered, the *percentages* of those going on to higher and further education are bound to improve as the base number falls. Doing rather more will, in percentage terms, make a deal of difference and will set markers for the future.

Those markers are important because they must change a culture. There is no innate reason why Britain should be sixteenth in the OECD league table of young people in education after 16 years of age – above only Portugal and Spain. British teenagers are not innately more stupid or less educable; they are the inheritors of a tradition which held that book learning was for the few, that real life, and real money, should begin as soon as possible and that manual and pragmatic skills were best learnt on the job. The past, as so often in Europe, determines the future although, however true these beliefs might have been in the world of work as it used to be, they must be less true today.

In Japan, top of the OECD table, 98 per cent of young people stay on in formal education until 18 years of age even though that education is far from stimulating and far from being pragmatic. They are the inheritors of a different cultural tradition, one that just happens to be more attuned to the needs of the future than that of Britain and most of the rest of Europe. In America, too, the young stay on in school, but whether they learn anything there is a question of growing concern.

The information society, after all, uses information, be it in the form of numbers, words, pictures or voices, on screens, in books or in printouts and reports, as its currency. The essential requirement, therefore, of all its workers is that they are able to read, interpret and fit together the elements of this currency, irrespective, almost, of what the data actually relates to. That is a skill of the brain. It can be taught or at least developed in classrooms. It does not, for most people, happen quickly, easily or early but requires years of practice, years which are most conveniently and usefully spent at the beginning of adult life rather than inconveniently in the middle. This general skill is akin to riding a bicycle, once learnt it is never unlearnt, and having learnt it one can then go on to learn its use in particular applications.

It is this conviction that brain skills are of general use and can be developed in youth that has led places like Taiwan and South Korea, following Japan, to put such an emphasis on the formal, even scholastic, education of their youth. It has been said that every second person in Seoul has either been at university or is currently studying or teaching there, while in the 1970s Mr Goh Thock Tong, then Minister for Trade and Industry in Singapore, was arguing that Singapore needed 'to step into the shoes left behind by countries like Germany and Japan as they restructure, they from skill-intensive to knowledge-intensive and we from labour-intensive to skill-intensive'. In pursuit of these objectives Singapore proceeded to increase greatly the number of university places and lower the entry requirements. Britain, who needs to be one step ahead of Singapore, has until recently been doing the reverse.

The opportunity, however, remains and is made easier by the vanishing generation. The statistic is also good news for those who want to re-enter or enter late the work of the information society. The squeeze on qualified youth will encourage employers to turn to other sources of skill, particularly to women, many of whom have the necessary early education but have been busy working to raise their families and manage their homes. Less convenient as employees because they want and need more flexibility, they have not been wooed too assiduously in the past. In the 1990s they will be. They do, after all, represent nearly half of all university entrants (over half in 1987 in the USA for the first time). They are a neglected resource which few will be able to neglect once the vanishing generation begins to bite. The NEDO Report cited above estimates that four out of five of the 900,000 extra workers it foresees in Britain's workforce over the next eight years will be women returning to work.

Women have re-entered the workforce before, but the numbers and the conditions which they will expect in the 1990s turn this into a significant discontinuity which will change the way organizations are run, will affect family structures and living patterns quite significantly – all issues to be explored in subsequent chapters.

The Third Age

In 1988 the Social Affairs Ministers of the OECD met to contemplate the time when one person in five will be a pensioner and one in ten aged over 75, when there will be only three people of working age to support each pensioner and when old-age pensions may account for one-fifth of national income. It will be even worse for Switzerland and West Germany where there will be only two people of working age for each old person.

It will be 2040 before this scenario fully becomes a reality, but the people who will be old then are alive now and unless they quickly change their breeding habits the numbers of their children are quite predictable. This world will happen and it will start to happen before the end of this century.

Once again, there have been old people before, but never before so many of them. I knew only one grandparent – the others had died before I was born. My children knew all four. Their children will almost certainly know a great-grandparent or two. People in their sixties and retired will still be someone's children. The infrequent has become the commonplace and the world as we know it will inevitably change in some way.

It is happening because, in the richer countries, it is becoming harder to die. Each major cause of death is either diminished, like smallpox or polio and, one day, cancer, or postponed for a few more years or decades, like heart disease. Of course, nature, or man's tampering with nature, may trigger another plague and some wonder whether AIDS may not be just that plague, but such disasters excepted there seems little reason why many of today's teenagers cannot expect to live to 100, provided they do not drink, smoke or drive themselves to death.

The question is, will they want to live that long? When death as an act of God seems to be indefinitely postponed will we want to make it increasingly an act of mankind? Euthanasia, already quasi-legal in the Netherlands, may become more acceptable to more societies.

More urgent are the questions 'What will they live on?' 'What will they do?' 'Who will care for them?' By the year 2020, if nothing changes, Italy will be spending over a quarter of her national income on pensions, while Britain's health service spends ten times as much on a patient over 75 as on one of working age.

Like all discontinuities, however, this one contains opportunities as well as problems if the changes are seen coming and if everyone concerned can indulge in a little upside-down thinking.

They will not all be poor, for instance. An increasing number of them will own their own homes, an asset which can be turned into an annual income provided that they do not intend to bequeath it to the next generation (who will by then be in mid or late career with their own homes bought and paid for). Most of them will be healthy and active. That is, of course, why they are still alive. They are capable of working. One British study found that 43 per cent of over-65s regularly helped other elderly people, 25 per cent helped the disabled, 11 per cent helped neighbours. If we change our view of work to include such unpaid activity then these people are only retired in a legal or technical sense. After all, in the last century no one had heard of retirement – they worked till they dropped, or, as a farmer said once when I asked him what was the difference between farming at 75 and farming at 50, 'The same only slower!' Experience and wisdom can often compensate for energy.

So many older people will not go unnoticed, particularly when many more of them will have experienced responsibility earlier in life and will not be used to keeping quiet. If we are sensible we will want to use their talents in our organizations, but not full-time or on full pay. We shall need, then, to re-think what jobs call for part-time wisdom and experience and what work can be done at a distance by responsible people. We shall need to revise the tax rules for pensions to make it economic for such work to be done. Many people, active and healthy, will devise their own activities, organizing around their enthusiasms; we must not let too many rules from the past stand in their way. We will need to change the way we talk about them, words like 'retirement' will become as redundant as 'servant' today. Words are so often the heralds of social change, the outward signs of a discontinuity at work triggering some upside-down thinking.

Already the linguistic signposts are going up. The Third Age, the age of living, as the French would have it, which follows the first age of learning and the second of working, is already becoming a common term. There is a University of the Third Age, a network of people exchanging their skills and their knowledge. There will soon be more talk of Third Age Careers. Soon, no doubt, there will be Third Age societies and, ultimately, Ministers for the Third Age in all OECD countries! The wrinklies, as my children fondly term us, can be assets as well as liabilities, *if* we want them to be.

If words are indeed the heralds of change, then the Third Age language suggests that before too long we shall be referring to people's job-careers as we now do to their education. 'Where did you work?' for a 65-year-old with fifteen years, at least, of life ahead will sound much like 'Where did you go to school?' It would all sound strange indeed to my father who died two years after retiring, at the age of 74. For him there was no Third Age worth living and the second age, of job and career, had long been a burden before he could afford to leave it.

It will be different for us, his children, and for our children. It is change of a discontinuous sort, but it need not be change for the worse if we can see it coming and can prepare for it.

$$\frac{100,000 \ (4)}{2} = J$$

The changes which are coming to our ways of work and living, indeed the changes which are already here, are conveniently summed up by this strange equation. When it is unravelled, it will suggest that we have, for some time now, been engaged in a massive job-splitting exercise in our society and have not even noticed it.

It will work like this. Thirty years ago when I joined an international company and started my job I signed on, although I never realized it, for 100,000 hours of work during my lifetime, because I should, if I was anything like everyone else in the developed world at that time, be expected to work for 47 hours a week, including overtime paid or unpaid, for 47 weeks a year for 47 years of my life (from, on average, 18 to 65). 47 × 47 × 47 = 103, 823 or 100, 000 hours give or take a few.

My teenage son and daughter, a generation later, can

expect their *jobs* to add up, on average, to 50, 000 hours. The lifetime job will have been halved in one generation. At first sight this would imply that they would be working half as many hours per week, for half as many weeks and half as many years. But mathematics does not work like that. Just as half of 4^3 (64) is not 2^3 (8), so half of 47^3 is not 23.5^3. In fact, rather bizarrely, half of the three 47s is three 37s, for $37 \times 37 \times 37 = 50, 653$.

It is because of this statistical sleight-of-hand that we have not noticed this rather dramatic piece of discontinuous change. It is also, in part, because it is only now beginning to bite as the next generation begin their second age of jobs and careers.

The world is not so neat, however, as to switch uniformly from the three 47s to the three 37s. That is where the (4) comes in. My daughter and my son have four principal options to choose from.

In the first option they will follow in their father's footsteps and look for a full-time job, or at least a sequence of full-time jobs, in the core of an organization or perhaps as a professional of some sort. In this case their working week will not be that different from the one I knew. Statistically it will average 45 hours per week, with rather less overtime for the hourly paid and fewer Saturday mornings for office workers. Nor will their working year be much reduced; longer annual holidays bring it down to 45 weeks rather than 47.

What will change, however, is the length of their job life. To get one of those increasingly rare jobs in the core or the professions (less than half of all jobs by 2000) they will need to be both well-qualified *and* experienced. In Germany today, a six- or seven-year university course is piled on top of eighteen months of military or community service so that the average entrant into the job market is 27 years of age. In the USA, a postgraduate qualification of some sort, after a four-year degree, is increasingly becoming a prerequisite of a good job, making 24 the normal starting age in a proper job. Britain still has three-year degree courses (except in Scotland) and no military service, but employers increasingly look for further qualifications of a more vocational or professional nature *and* for relevant experience in vacations or 'gap' years. It has, after all, been the established practice in the older professions of medicine, architecture and the law for centuries – a long (seven-year) mix of education, experience and vocational training. We can expect to see it extend to many other occupations, with the result that British parents must increasingly expect to wait until the offspring are 24 or 25 before they are established in a full-time job, if that is what they want.

It is possible that the fall in the numbers of qualified young people in all industrialized countries will tempt organizations and professions to shorten their training requirements in order to get the best of a reducing supply. The form this will probably take, however, will be to finance them, perhaps under the guise of employment, during their studies. It will be education more generously funded, not a job.

The next generation of full-time core workers, therefore, be they professionals, managers, technicians or skilled workers, can expect to start their full-time careers later – and to leave them earlier. This is the crucial point. The core worker will have a harder but shorter job, with more people leaving full-time employment in their late forties or early fifties, partly because they no longer want the pressure that such jobs will increasingly entail, but mainly because there will be younger more qualified and more energetic people available for these core jobs.

It is true that early in the next century the total number of people in the workforce in every country will start to decline and the average age to rise, as the dip in the birthrate of the 1970s works its way through life, but the reducing numbers of the full-timers will continue to place a premium on youth, energy and qualifications whenever they can get them in combination. It will be a shorter life but a more furious one for the full-timers, as the new professionals in business are already discovering.

The nett result of these changes will be a full-time job which, on average, will result in 45 hours for 45 weeks for 25 years, totalling 50,000 hours. Work won't stop for such people after 50 but it will not be the same sort of work; it will not be a *job* as they have known it. They will enter their Third Age sooner than others, affluent, no doubt, but still with a good third of their lives to live.

It is happening already. One personnel manager was surprised to discover that only 2 per cent of his workforce were, as he put it, still there at the official retirement age of 62. What he had done was to look back fifteen years to all those who were then 47 and had found that only a few had stayed on with the organization for the remaining fifteen years. Some had moved to new jobs and one or two had died, but the great majority had opted for, or been persuaded into, early retirement in their fifties. 'We knew that people were leaving us early,' he said, 'but we had no idea of the scale of it all until we started counting.' An advertising agency, aware that creativity and mental energy tend to decline with the years, would like to see everyone under the age of 50. They have not, so far, been allowed by the tax authorities to make their full pension scheme applicable under the age of 55 but they are confident that it will come down to 50 within the next ten years – well in time for the generation now starting their careers.

There will always be the glorious exceptions of course, while those who control their own careers, the self-employed, the professions and, apparently, Heads of State, will buck the trend as long as the clients and their supporters will permit it. It is the bigger organizations, in which most full-timers still work, who will be most choosy about who they keep on their full-time books and they will want the energetic, the up-to-date, the committed and the flexible. Most of those will be in their thirties and forties, putting in their 50,000 hours in big annual chunks.

Full-time work in organizations will, however, be only one of the options and, if the numbers are anything like right, it will be a minority option, perhaps an élite one. Most people will have to find their place outside the organization, selling their time or their services into it, as self-employed, part-time or temporary workers.

For them the pattern of hours will be different. They may find themselves working 25 hours a week for 45 weeks of the year (part-time) or 45 hours a week for 25 weeks a year (temporary). In either case they will need to keep on working so long as they can, for 45 years if possible, because they will not be able to accumulate the savings via pension schemes or other mechanisms to live on. This will suit the organizations who will, in their temporary staff, look for experience and reliability rather than the energy and certainty of youth. Whether it is temporary work or part-time work, the sum is still $25 \times 45 \times 45 = 50,000$.

We may, therefore, see the notional retirement age going in two very different ways at the same time. Whilst for the core workers it will gradually come down towards 50 over the next twenty years, for most of the workforce it will go up. For them the questions 'What shall I do in the missing 50,000 hours, and what shall I live on?' cannot be postponed until the Third Age; they need to be answered now. For these people the future is not a generation away – it started yesterday.

My children have a fourth option. They may be able to work full-time for ten years, then take ten years out to raise a family, then return to the workforce at, say, 45 for a further ten or even fifteen years. ($45 \times 45 \times 25$ hours of paid work = 50,000.) It is an option that has traditionally been taken up by women, who have varied the pattern by going part-time for some of the intervening years, but it may increasingly be seen as an opportunity by men to vary their lifestyle and to play a bigger part in the home and family life.

Re-entry into the full-time workforce has always been difficult. It will get easier as the shortage of qualified young people begins to bite organizations in the 1990s. The organization will then turn to that reservoir of talent, the qualified women at home. In order to tempt them back, however, organizations may have to learn to be more flexible in the way they run things, more willing to recognize that they are buying the talents of someone but not necessarily all their time.

The Pressures Behind The Numbers

The $\frac{100,000 \ (4)}{2} = $ J equation is, of course, spuriously precise.

The numbers will not work out precisely like that. It is there to make a point. The world of jobs is changing. It is changing more dramatically than we realize because those sort of numbers creep up on one unexpectedly when multiplied out over a lifetime.

No one particularly wants those numbers to happen. They are not the result of any policy decisions by government or boards of directors. They are an instinctive response to a changing environment. There is now some general agreement about the nature of this changing environment and an acceptance that it is not going to change back again. Some of the main features are:

A move away from labour-intensive manufacturing
Thirty years ago nearly half of all workers in the industrialized countries were making or helping to make *things*. In another thirty years' time it may be down to 10 per cent (in the USA it is already 18 per cent).

To some extent this is because we have all had to export our factories, instead of our goods, to countries where labour is cheaper and more amenable to factory working. Even Japan has now been forced by the high price of the yen to follow suit. When Britain did not export her factories soon enough they were replicated in the newly industrialized countries and she lost out. Situations such as the rapid rise of the pound sterling in the early years of Margaret Thatcher's government only accelerated this process, leaving swathes of abandoned factories throughout Britain. It would have happened anyway. The clever thing would have been not to compete with the unbeatable but to join them by exporting the factories not the goods. Discontinuous change can always be turned to advantage with a bit of forethought.

The result is not just fewer jobs, but different organizations. Labour-intensive manufacturing was traditionally managed with a large pool of relatively cheap labour, a lot of supervision and a hierarchical management structure. There were a lot of people around, most of them full-time employees whose time was bought to be used at the discretion of the organization, subject increasingly to the agreement of the union.

It was a convenient way to run things; everything and everyone you needed was yours. If you want to control it, own it, was the message. It proved, in the end, to be a very expensive message. The Japanese always did it differently, with a small core staff, a raft of subcontractors, heavy investment in clever machines and enough clever people to instruct them and work with them. The demise of mass manufacturing has led to the end of the mass employment organization and with it a redefinition of the job.

A move towards knowledge-based organizations
The end of labour-intensive manufacturing leaves us with organizations which receive their added value from the

knowledge and the creativity they put in rather than the muscle-power. Fewer people, thinking better, helped by clever machines and computers, add more value than gangs or lines of unthinking 'human resources'. Manufacturing has gone this way. The more obviously knowledge-based businesses of consultancy, finance and insurance, advertising, journalism and publishing, television, health care, education and entertainment, have all flourished. Even agriculture and construction, the oldest of industries, have invested in knowledge and clever machines in place of muscles.

The result is not only a requirement for different people, but different organizations, organizations which recognize that they cannot do everything themselves, that they need a central group of talented and energetic people, a lot of specialist help and ancillary agencies. They are smaller, younger organizations than their predecessors, flatter and less hierarchical. We shall examine them in more detail in the following chapters, but their most immediate effect is on the numbers – fewer people inside who are better qualified, more people outside who are contracted not employed.

A move towards service

Paradoxically, rich societies seem to breed dependency. If you are poor you are forced into self-sufficiency. As you get rich it is easier and more sensible to get other people to do what you do not want to do or cannot do, be it fixing the roof or digging the garden. It makes economic sense to let others make your clothes and to buy them in the store, that way you get better clothes and more time to do what you are good at. It goes on and on. Convenience foods take the chore out of cooking, and package holidays the work out of leisure. We all of us become more specialized, better at one thing and worse at others. Like knowledge-based organizations we contract out everything we are not good at and so breed a raft of services on which we now depend.

Affluence breeds service industries and they in turn create affluence. Sometimes it seems as if everyone is taking in everyone else's metaphorical washing and making money out of it, or in my particular case, that everyone is going to everyone else's conference and being paid for it or paying for it. Affluence is a matter of mood and self-confidence as much as of economics, for dependency has its own imperatives. If you need to buy all these services you have to find something to do to pay for them, hence some competitive striving. It is a self-fulfilling prophecy which works as long as everyone believes the prophecy of continued affluence.

The service industries of affluence are therefore ephemeral creations, which could always disappear overnight. The point however, once again, is that the organizations which they spawn are of a different kind. Because they are essentially ephemeral they have to flex with every shift in demand. Small core staff and lots of part-time and temporary help has to be the rule. Many of them are not knowledge-intensive businesses, although some are, of course. Retailing, transport, cleaning, catering, leisure, are all industries with large requirements for the competent but semi-skilled. It is here that you will find most of the 30 per cent who do not have the brain skills for the knowledge-based organizations. It is here that you will find the bulk of the part-timers and the temporary workers.

It is the growth of the service sector which has transformed the working lives of so many people in Europe and the USA *because* of the kind of organization which it needs and breeds.

These shifts are irreversible. The degree of affluence may increase or wane in each country but labour-intensive manufacturing will not return to Europe, or to the USA and Japan. Knowledge-based enterprises have to be the way forward for all our countries, the more and the better the richer, whether they are manufacturing goods or providing services. The service sector will ebb and flow with local prosperity but will never now fade away.

If the shifts are irreversible so are the changes in the patterns of work which they induce, and therefore the numbers with which this chapter began. A dramatic change in the economic climate may slow things down, but it will not stop them. The world of work has changed already. We need to take notice.

3   The Theory

The message, I hope, is clear: the times are changing and we must change with them. Yes, but how? In Chapter 1 I argued that because most people do not like change, change is forced upon them by crisis and discontinuity. Thrown up against things, or into new arenas, we confront new possibilities and discover bits of ourselves we never knew were there. Discontinuity is a great learning experience, but only if we survive it.

My daughter was smitten by an unexplained viral illness earlier this year. She is 22. These illnesses knock the stuffing out of the sufferer and she had to drop everything for a year – work, friends, study, even the television. It was, for her, a massive discontinuity and profoundly depressing. Getting better slowly she went to a meeting one evening on 'Gratitude'. 'If they had asked me to speak,' she told me, 'I would have said that I was grateful for my illness. I have learnt so much.' And changed so much, I wanted to add.

Change, however, does not have to be forced on us by crisis and calamity. We can do it for ourselves. If changing is, as I have argued, only another word for learning, then the theories of learning will also be theories of changing. Those who are always learning are those who can ride the waves of change and who see a changing world as full of opportunities not damages. They are the ones most likely to be the survivors in a time of discontinuity. They are also the enthusiasts and the architects of new ways and forms and ideas. If you want to change, try learning one might say, or more precisely, if you want to be in control of your change, take learning more seriously. This chapter, therefore, is an introduction to the theory of learning, which is the theory at the heart of changing.

'A theory of learning?' the Professor of Medicine said to me when he heard what I was writing, 'I never knew there was such a thing.' It is indeed ironic that those who teach us, particularly in our universities, are so often ignorant of the basic principles of learning. The Professor had never heard of Kolb, who first convinced me that learning is a cycle of different activities, although I have used different words from his in this chapter. Nor had he heard of Bateson or of Argyris and Schon who persuaded me that learning is a double loop, that there is learning to solve a particular problem and then, more importantly, there is the habit of learning, the learning to learn to do such things, that second loop which can change the way you live. He knew not of Revans, the unsung hero of Action Learning, who showed me that the best learning happens in real life with real problems and real people and not in classrooms with know-all teachers. There were others, too, he knew not, Dewey who said, many years ago, that learning was a process of discovery and that we must each be our own discoverer, others could not do it for you; or Illich who thought that we would be better off without schools which were concerned with indoctrination not teaching. He had, sadly, heard a bit about Skinner who believes that learning is training, that teaching is producing a conditioned response as when your dog responds to your whistle.

There are many others, for learning has intrigued mankind for centuries. This chapter is my personal anthology, turned into my own images and metaphors, for reasons which will, I hope, become clear.

A Theory Of Learning

The man stood in front of the class. 'Now learn this,' he said, writing an equation on the board. We wrote it in our books. Three months later we wrote it out again in an examination paper. If the second time of writing was the same as the first, we had learnt it. I exaggerate, but only a little. That was my early concept of learning. Later on, I came to realize that I had learnt nothing at school which I now remember except only this – that all problems had already been solved, by someone, and that the answer was around, in the back of the book or the teacher's head. Learning seemed to mean transferring answers from them to me.

There was nothing about change in all of that. Nor, in fact, was there much about learning as it really is. Real learning, I came to understand, is always about answering a question or solving a problem. 'Who am I?' 'How do I do this?' 'What is the reason for ...?' 'How does this work?' 'How do I achieve this ambition?' The questions range from the immense to the trivial, but when we have no questions we need no answers, while other people's questions are soon forgotten.

It is best, I realized, to think of learning as a wheel divided into four parts:

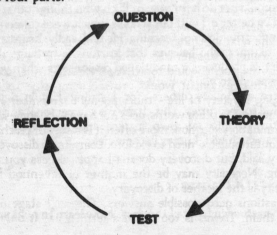

I draw it as a wheel to emphasize that it is meant to go round and round. One set of questions, duly answered and tested and reflected upon, leads on to another. It is life's special treadmill. Step off it and you ossify, and become a bore to others. The trouble is that for most of us for much of the time the wheel does *not* go round. It gets stuck or blocked.

Mankind, I am sure, is born to learn. One has only to look at little children to see that wheel turning furiously. Why, we must wonder, does it slow down for most of us as we grow older? If we knew more about that we would know more about our reluctance to change and the consequent need for crisis and calamity to budge us into action. This chapter, therefore, is really about the things in us and in our surroundings which *stop* or *block* the wheel. First, however, we need a brief introduction to the wheel itself.

The Wheel of Learning

Logically, the wheel starts with a *question*, a problem to be solved, a dilemma to be resolved, a challenge to meet. If it doesn't start there, and if it is not *our* question, we shall not push the wheel round to the stage of Reflection. It won't become part of us. I could learn a poem by heart at school to recite the next morning, but to forget by lunchtime. This was learning to answer *other* people's questions. Just occasionally the poem would touch some chord in me, some unspoken question; it would provide some clue to the emerging mystery of life – those poems I remember still. The question, in other words, does not have to be some kind of examination question, more often it is a sort of reaching for, a questioning, a need to explore. Learning is discovery, Dewey said, but discovery doesn't happen unless you are looking. Necessity may be the mother of invention but curiosity is the mother of discovery.

Questions need possible answers. The next stage provides them. *Theories* is too grand a term. I use it only to emphasize that this stage is investigating *possible* ideas. It is a stage of speculation, of free-thinking, of re-framing, of looking for clues. One way is to open the equivalent of a cookbook or, in my case, a series of cookbooks in search of that elusive formula which will produce a culinary miracle in half-an-hour from my random collection of left-overs. There are other ways to find possible answers; good friends, hired coaches, or even one's own imagination.

Ideas and Theories can never be enough. At this stage of the wheel all is still fancy. 'Dreams,' as my children used to remind me, 'give wings to fools.' The theories have to be *tested* in reality, the next stage of the wheel. Some will work, some won't. My sauce is always lumpy – why? Until I know why, which is the stage of *Reflection*, the final stage, I will not have learnt. Change only sticks when we understand why it happened. Too often have I invited chief executives to explain their philosophy only to listen to a bare record of their achievements, with no interpretation, no theory to explain them, no philosophy expounded. Such men have not changed and will not change. They have learnt nothing from their success which makes it unlikely that they will be able to repeat it.

The wheel, however, is difficult to turn. For some it never gets started. They have no questions and seek no answers. Content or dull depending on your viewpoint, they will not voluntarily learn or change.

There are those, too, who stick at the Question stage. Like small children they delight in asking why, or how, or when, or where, and as long as they get an answer, any answer, they are satisfied for it is the questions which fascinate them, not the answer. They don't learn and others don't learn much from their questions. They are life's Inspectors or Auditors; useful, no doubt, but irritating.

The next stage, Theory, has its own specialists. They are the bad Academics, full of answers to other people's questions. They teach the answer first and assume the question. Knowledge for its own sake is what motivates these people, they are fact-collectors who know a lot and have, in a fuller sense, learnt little. I have a friend who turns every conversation into a lecture, on anything. He has read a lot and forgotten nothing and is eager to share it with anyone who will listen. At last I have learnt how to enjoy his company, to come with a question to which I wanted an answer and which he could always provide.

The Testing stage has its own enthusiasts, the Action Men or Pragmatists. No time for theory or for thinking, their immediate reaction to a problem is to attack it with the tools nearest to hand. Energy conquers all, they believe, and if at first it doesn't work, try and try again. Often it does work. The trouble is they don't know why. 'I kick it, that usually does the trick' is their formula. Success without prior thought or subsequent reflection does not help you to repeat the process or to improve on it, although it does get the problem moving. They can be effective, these pragmatists, but find it hard to communicate their secret to other people because they have not gone through the other segments of the wheel.

Lastly there are those who get stuck at the Reflection stage. Endlessly they rehearse the past, seeking for better explanations of what went wrong or what went right. They are the Pundits amongst us. They have learnt because they have been round the wheel but there they have stopped. One lesson is enough; they have made up their minds and feel no need for further explanation. Busy people often have no time for more curiosity. They formed their opinions long ago and see no cause to change them. 'Consistent' we call them if we agree with them, 'bigots' if we don't.

Most of the time, most of us do not go through all the four segments of this wheel. I describe it here to emphasize how difficult true learning is and why the sort of deliberate change that goes with learning is so rare. This sort of learning, the one from experience and life, is the one that matters if we are to change. It is not to be confused with more trivial definitions of learning:

— Learning is *not* just knowing the answers. That is *Mastermind* learning at its best, rote learning at its most boring and conditioned response at its most basic. It does not help you to change or to grow, it does not move the wheel.
— Learning is *not* the same as study, nor the same as training. It is bigger than both. It is a cast of mind, a habit of life, a way of thinking about things, a way of growing.
— Learning is *not* measured by examinations, which usually only test the Theory stage, but only by a growing experience, an experience understood and tested.
— Learning is *not* automatic, it requires energy, thought, courage and support. It is easy to give up on it, to relax and to rest on one's experience, but that is to cease to grow.
— Learning is *not* only for the intellectuals, who often shine at the thinking stage, but are incurious and unadventurous and therefore add little to their experience as they go through life.
— Learning is *not* finding out what other people already know, but is solving our own problems for our own purposes, by questioning, thinking and testing until the solution is a new part of our life.

The Lubricants Of Change

The wheel of learning, I have emphasized, is difficult to start and hard to keep moving. Most of us don't succeed most of the time. We get stuck at one or other segment and only a crisis or calamity can then move us on. Luckily there are some lubricants which make it easier – 'the necessary conditions of comfortable change'. There are three of these lubricants, each of which needs some interpretation. Leave them out or screen them out and change or learning is effectively blocked.

1. *A proper selfishness*

This is a responsible selfishness. I am often tempted to observe that the Christian injunction to love one's neighbour as oneself gives the neighbour a rather poor deal since few people seem to love or even like themselves that much.

Unfortunately, however, self-hate or just a lack of some 'positive self-regard' is no way to start learning. I am not advocating a narcissistic self-indulgence. I am suggesting, on the basis of good evidence, that those who learn best and most, and change most comfortably, are those who

(a) take responsibility for themselves and for their future;
(b) have a clear view of what they want that future to be;
(c) want to make sure that they get it; and
(d) believe that they can.

It looks easy. It seldom is. Taking a view of one's future requires, first of all, that you believe that there will be a future. There are times, for all of us, when that seems doubtful. In those moods there is no learning, no changing. Then there is the question of what sort of future would we like it to be, for us. Sensibly, selfishly, it should fit our talents and our abilities, but we are sometimes the last people to know what those are. It should not be a fantasy future – that is escapism, but what *is* reality, we may well ask.

The exercises at the end of this chapter are intended as one way to focus attention on these intractable questions. We may never get the answers right but unless we take a view we shall be mere flotsam on the waves of life. Fred Hirsch, an economist and philosopher, described what happens to many people under a pervasive materialism. We end up, he suggested, not by working for what we *need* but for what we *want*, for the 'positional goods' that keep us abreast or ahead of the notional Joneses. It's a no-win situation for there will always be more Joneses to keep up with. It is unthinking, follow-my-neighbour, selfishness, not proper self-responsibility.

2. A way of re-framing

The second of the lubricants or necessary conditions is particularly useful in the second stage of the wheel of learning. Re-framing is the ability to see things, problems, situations or people in other ways, to look at them sideways, or upside-down; to put them in another perspective or another context; to think of them as opportunities not problems, as hiccups rather than disasters.

Re-framing is important because it unlocks problems. Like an unexpected move on a chessboard it can give the whole situation a new look. It is akin to lateral thinking at times, to using the right side of the brain (the creative pattern-forming side) to complement the more logical left side.

To conceive of one's life without the word 'retirement' being relevant is to re-frame it. To think of a job as 2000 hours in a year instead of 45 weeks of 5 long days is to re-frame it, and by so doing to open up new possibilities. A federal organization is a re-framing of a decentralized organization, with important consequences.

In business it has long been fashionable to ask 'What business are you in?' Is it cigarettes you are selling, or stress reducers, or social ease, or just a drug? The re-framing will have important consequences for the way the product is projected, distributed and priced.

Entrepreneurs, when they are successful, often achieve their success through intuitive re-framing, connecting what was before unconnected, putting together an opportunity and a need.

I remember the year when Britain was short of potatoes – the last year there was a drought. A friend and I went shopping for potatoes only to find there were none. Weeks later he asked me what I had done as a result.

'Bought rice instead,' I said. 'Why?'

'I rang a contact in India,' he replied, 'bought one thousand tons of potatoes to be shipped to the UK at a landed cost of £130 a ton and sold them in advance for £250 a ton.'

'But, Percy,' I said, calculating quickly, 'that's ...'

'Yes,' he interrupted, 'but don't worry, it didn't happen, the Indians refused an export permit.'

Still, his re-framing nearly made him £120,000, while I bought rice.

Businesses, at their best, re-frame all the time, re-thinking what they now call their portfolios of mini-businesses, re-defining those businesses, and their markets, checking to make sure that there are as many growing businesses as declining ones. Individuals need to do the same, looking at their portfolios of talents, recognizing that what might be a disadvantage in one situation could be an asset in another, as when Mary realized that her problem – she could only talk naturally to people when she didn't have to look at them – made her a natural for telephone selling.

Some people are natural re-framers. Most of us cannot do it alone. Other people always help. Friendly groups help one to re-think the problem or the situation. It helps if they are people outside the problem because they will bring different ideas to bear. Group-think is dangerous because like-minded groups have like-minded ideas and find it hard amongst themselves to re-frame any situation.

I am a great believer in 'Irish Education' after the Irishman who reputedly said, 'How do I know what I think until I hear what I say?' Truth, said David Hume, the Scottish philosopher, springs from argument amongst friends. Even if we don't convince the friends, we often help ourselves to see things in a new way as we look for new angles in the argument.

Metaphors and analogies help. Schon's idea of the 'displacement of concepts' mentioned in Chapter 1 as an aid to creativity is a useful discipline, to try to find other metaphors, or words from other fields, to describe the problem or the dilemma. There are other drills and disciplines to stretch the mind, most usefully in some of Edward de Bono's books.

We are all the prisoners of our past. It is hard to think of things except in the way we have always thought of them. But that way solves no problems and seldom changes anything. It is certainly no way to deal with discontinuity. We must accustom ourselves to asking 'Why?' of what already is and 'Why not?' to any possible re-framing. It can become a useful game.

For instance, why do women take their husband's name when they marry? Why not keep their own, or both choose a new common name? Why do we make marriage vows for ever, and then break them? Why not make them for shorter terms, and then renew them? Why do so many houses have their best rooms in the front, looking over the parking space? Why not put all entrances at the side? And so on ...

Upside-down thinking, re-framing, is largely a habit of mind. Those who want to learn in life, and to change comfortably, need to practise it.

3. A Negative Capability

Keats defined 'negative capability' in his letters in 1817, as 'when a man is capable of being in uncertainties, mysteries, and doubts'. I would extend the meaning to include the capacity to live with mistakes and failures without being downhearted or dismayed.

Learning and changing are never clear and never sure. Whenever we change we step out a little into the unknown.

We will never know enough about that unknown to be certain of the result. We will get it wrong some of the time. Doubt and mistakes must not be allowed to disturb us because it is from them that we learn. Theories are no good, Karl Popper argued, unless it is possible to prove them wrong. If they are bound to be right they are either tautologies, saying nothing useful, or trivial, saying nothing important.

Entrepreneurs, the successful ones, have on average nine failures for every success. It is only the successes that you will hear about, the failures they credit to experience. Oil companies expect to drill nine empty wells for every one that flows. Getting it wrong is part of getting it right. As with my friend and the potatoes, if you do not try you will not succeed and if it fails, there is always another day, another opportunity. Negative capability is an attitude of mind which learners need to cultivate, to help them to write off their mistakes as experience. It helps to get your first failures early on; the later ones are then less painful. Those who have a gilded youth, in which success leads on to success, are sometimes the least experimental and the most conservative as they grow older because the fear of failure looms larger.

We were about to appoint a new Professor. The person in question was well-known to us, a brilliant lecturer, an authority in his field, a sought-after consultant. Why then were there so many unspoken reservations in the faces around the table? Someone then captured it for us: 'The trouble is,' he said, 'Richard has no decent doubt.' Without that decent doubt there was no questioning, no learning, no deliberate change. To Richard, certainty was precious, a negative capability something he would not understand.

We learn by our mistakes, as we always tell ourselves, not from our successes; but perhaps we do not really believe it. We should, for we change by exploration not by retracing well-known paths. We start our learning with uncertainties and doubts, with questions to be resolved. We grow older wondering who we will be and what we will do. For organizations as for individuals life is a book still to be written. If we cannot live with these uncertainties we will not learn and change will always be an unpleasant surprise.

Negative capability, that capacity to live with uncertainty and mistake, is not given to everyone. Keats complained that Coleridge did not have it and missed a trick or two thereby. It helps, clearly, to have a belief that overrides the uncertainty. For some it is a feeling that their book of life is already written, that they are merely turning the pages. For others it is a belief in a superior being, a God. For myself, I have become convinced of the truth behind the Coda of Julian of Norwich, a holy lady in fourteenth century Britain: 'All will be well, and all manner of thing will be well', she said, again and again. Believe that, although one cannot know in what way all will be well, and a negative capability is easy.

The Blocks To Change

It is, unfortunately, all too easy to stop the lubricants reaching the wheel. A proper selfishness, re-framing and a negative capability are fragile. It is easier to stop them than to encourage them, often unintentionally. The principal blocks are listed here.

The 'They' syndrome

Mary was divorcing her army husband. Where would she live, I asked, when she had to leave her army apartment. 'They haven't told me yet,' she said.

'Who are they?' I asked.

'They haven't told me who they are yet, have they?' she replied, irritated at my seeming stupidity.

It is easy to laugh but once I waited outside the door of the Personnel Manager of the multinational company of my youth. A wily old Scot passed by, a veteran of that place and a wise counsellor.

'What are you waiting for, laddie?' he asked.

'I am waiting to see what they are planning for me.'

'Och, invest in yourself, my boy, don't wait for them. Invest in yourself, if you don't why should they?'

It was one of those timely triggers. Until that moment I was leaving it all to 'them', I had no sense of personal responsibility for my own future. That had been delegated to the Personnel Department. 'They' would tell me. Unfortunately, 'they' wondered why I had been so lackadaisical about my own development and did not, as Jock forecast, see any great reason to continue their investment in my future unless I also invested in it.

Too many delegate their futures and their questions to some mysterious 'they'. 'They' will set the syllabus for life just as 'they' set the syllabus for our courses at school. 'They' know what is best, 'they' must know what they are doing. 'They' are in charge, leave it to 'them'. The phrases and excuses are endless. One of the strange things about growing older is the gradual realization that 'they' don't know, that the Treasury is *not* all-wise, that 'they' are on the whole just like you, muddling through, and not very interested in you anyway.

Futility/humility

Learning starts with a belief in oneself. It is for all of us a fragile belief, easily shattered. In my early days in that big company, I found myself in Malaysia with, effectively, a license to wander through the departments. I came across what seemed to me to be some gross inefficiencies. I worked out some better options, sent them to the Operations Manager and waited – for his thanks. He sent for me.

'How long have you been out here?' he asked.

'Six months,' I replied.

'And how long has this company been successfully doing business here?'

'About fifty years, I suppose.'

'Quite so, fifty-four in fact; and do you suppose that in six months you know better than the rest of us and our predecessors in fifty-four years?'

I asked no more questions for the next three years, had no more ideas, made no more proposals. My social life prospered, I recall, but I stopped learning, and growing, and changing.

If one remark killed my belief in myself in that place, one can easily work out why it is that the unemployed or the newly redundant have little urge or energy to turn that wheel of learning. All *they* want is to turn the clock back and to have the same job again. We have made the 'job' so essential to a man's concept of himself, and now to many a woman's, that the loss of it, often through no fault of his own, can shatter his sense of identity, of personal worth, of self-esteem, for a while at least.

Self-doubt is pernicious. Humble, self-doubting people, may ask the questions but they do not press for answers or for action. 'Others need or deserve it more than I' they say, seeking always the back of the queue even if the queue is really only a huddle. John needs my help, the firm cannot spare me, my needs can wait. The selfishness is laudable, often, but the learning gets postponed. Other people become a prop for or an excuse for our lack of self-responsibility.

Self-doubters often fear success. Success puts more pressure on them to take more responsibility for even more action. Failure for some is easier to handle, particularly if you plan for it. David, his teachers noted, although a clever boy, had stopped working some months before his big exams. They tried to coax him back to work with forecasts of what he might achieve. They tried to frighten him with forecasts of what he might *not* achieve. Nothing worked. He did as badly as they feared, but he had his excuse, he had done no work. His failure was not an indictment of his ability but only of his attitude. His own conception of himself as a clever lad, was untouched. They call it a form of 'attribution theory'; it is a way of dodging failure, of not learning in order to protect a fragile sense of self. He won't start to learn again until he is strong enough in his self-confidence to take success *or* failure in his stride.

The theft of purposes

Proper, responsible selfishness, involves a purpose and a goal. It is that goal which pulls out the energy to move the wheel. Diminish that goal, displace it or, worst of all, disallow it and we remove all incentive to learn or to change. Proper selfishness, however, recognizes that the goal needs to be tuned to the goals of the group, or the organization, or society, as well as being in line with our own needs and our own talents. Only improper selfishness sets goals at odds with the bits of humanity that matter to oneself.

It is tempting to impose our goals on other people, particularly on children or our subordinates. It is tempting for society to try to impose its priorities on everybody. The strategy will however be self-defeating if our goals, or society's goals, do not fit the goals of the others. We may get our way but we don't get their learning. They may have to comply but they will not change. We have pushed out their goals with ours and stolen their purposes. It is a pernicious form of theft which kills the will to learn. The apathy and disillusion of many people in organizations, the indifference and apparent indolence of the unemployed is often due to the fact that there is no room for their purposes or goals in our scheme of things. Left goal-less, they comply, drift or rebel.

In a sensible world the goals are negotiated. The concept of the do'nut in Chapter 5 allows the organization to dictate the core and the perimeter of one's role, but allows discretion in the middle with the purposes of that discretion to be agreed. It is so, or could be so, with much of life. Responsible selfishness knows that there are core duties and necessary boundaries but also that there must be room for self-expression. Squeeze it out, as tidy-minded bureaucrats so often do, and we kill any motivation to learn.

The missing forgiveness

I asked an American the secret of his firm's obviously successful development policy. He looked me straight in the eye. 'Forgiveness,' he said. 'We give them big jobs and big responsibilities. Inevitably they make mistakes, we can't check them all the time and don't want to. They learn, we forgive, they don't make the mistake again.'

He was unusual. Too many organizations use their appraisal schemes and their confidential files to record our errors and our small disasters. They use them to chastise us with, hoping to inspire us, or to frighten us to do better. It might work once but in future we will make sure that we do not venture far enough from the beaten track to make any mistake. Yet no experiment, no test of new ideas, means no learning and no change. As in organizations, so it can be in families.

The evidence is quite consistent, if you reward the good and ignore or forgive the bad, the good will occur more frequently and the bad will gradually disappear. A concern over trouble in the classroom led to research into the way teachers allocated praise and blame. About equally, it seemed, except that all praise was for academic work and all blame was for behaviour. The teachers were coached to *only* give praise, for both academic work and good behaviour and to *ignore* the bad. It worked. Within a few weeks unruly behaviour had almost disappeared.

More difficult than forgiving others is to forgive oneself. That turns out to be one of the real blocks to change. We as individuals need to accept our past but then to turn our backs on it. Organizations often do it by changing their name, individuals by moving house, or changing spouses. It does not have to be so dramatic. Scrapbooks, I believe, are useful therapy – they are a way of putting the past to bed, decorously. Then we can move forward.

Putting The Theory To Work

If we want to change comfortably and deliberately we each have to start turning our own personal wheel of learning. The lubricants will make it easier – some proper selfishness, a constant effort to re-frame our bit of the world, and a readiness to forgive yourself.

Give yourself space, a purpose and goals to reach, questions to answer: find some friends to be your mentors, walk in other worlds, don't be afraid to be wrong.

It is, of course, easier to write or say than to do. Some exercises help, if you can organize yourself to do them and to use a partner or a friend to help you reflect upon them.

Exercise 1

Draw a line on a piece of paper to represent your life, from birth to death, and mark with a cross where you are now on that line. Think about it a bit, but not for too long; this is an impressionistic exercise not a precise one. Most people will draw a line something like the one below. Do yours before you read on.

In effect it is a line over time going up and down. What, however, do the ups and downs represent? The answer will tell you something about your real priorities in life. Where did you put the cross? The position will tell you something about the proportion of your life which you still feel is ahead of you, with time, probably, for a good Third Age. Does the line go upwards at the end or downwards? The answer will tell you something about your secret thoughts about the future. Most people feel good about it, in some modified way, and point their lines upwards.

Exercise 2

Write your own obituary to appear in your favourite paper or journal. Assume that it is written by a good friend who knows you well and understands the 'you' behind the facts. Don't write more than 200 words.

People find this difficult to do but useful if they do it and then show it to a good friend. It is difficult because it requires you to envisage your own death as a real event. To be able to do this can be a big release because it allows you to think in more concrete terms about the long period between now and your death.

The exercise forces you to stand at the end of your life and to look backwards. It puts what you are doing now into a new perspective and forces you to work out what you would like to be remembered for. It is an exercise in very personal re-framing.

Exercise 3

Imagine yourself asking ten friends to list one quality each which they liked or admired in you. List those qualities, then against each list two activities where those qualities *have* been useful in the past and one type of different activity where they *could* conceivably be useful. Better still, ask ten friends to do it for you.

It is difficult to do this objectively by yourself, but worth trying. The point is to accentuate the positive in you and to conceive of other areas where your talents might be useful. It is, in a small way, a practice in liking yourself.

Exercise 4

Now, and only now, having done the others, list five things you would like to have achieved in three years' time. Describe in a little detail how the achievement will be measured or observable and set down what practical things need to be done to start work on them.

This, of course, is putting the wheel of learning and of deliberate change into motion. It is surprising how easy it can be to do what we want to do when we know what it is that we want. Changing is exciting, fun and not too difficult if we see it as learning, learning in my sense, learning that we control and that we want.

I am more and more sure that those who are in love with learning are in love with life. For them change is never a problem, never a threat, just another exciting opportunity. It does, however, require what you might call a positive mental attitude.

Earlier this year we had to move out of our home for nine months while urgent repairs were made to the foundations. It was going to be a great nuisance and inconvenience. At first we were minded to minimize the inconvenience and camp out in makeshift accommodation next door. Then we decided to turn it into an opportunity, an opportunity to live in another part of town in a very different sort of home and community, to treat it like a foreign posting. It was more inconvenient, but now we call it exciting, fun, adventure and a bit of positive learning. Bad news became good news, change was learning.

Part Two: Working

Introduction

'He is 55 and he has just experienced his first month for 37 years without a paycheque. He is depressed, impossible to live with and I'm at my wits end.' It was a middle-class wife speaking. They were not poor because with early retirement had come an early pension, they owned their home and their children were independent. It was not even that he had enjoyed his job. He had, in fact, despised it but, masochistically, had borne his dislike of his work like a man. Remove it and, paradoxically, he began to doubt his manhood.

Later that day I ring another friend, also 55. His voice on an answerphone replies 'Anderson Associates – Paul Anderson speaking, I am contactable on 036484911.' *I* know that the Associates are he and his wife and occasional friends in his or her multifarious little enterprises, some of which make money, many of which don't. *I* know that the other telephone number is a fishing lodge belonging to some friends where he likes to spend long summer days. *I* know that his wife, a freelance journalist since the children grew up, makes more money than him, that their kitchen is their office. *I* know that for her and him, now, work and fun are inextricably intertwined, that he would never go back to working in a bank, that the telephone and the new opportunities for little service enterprises have transformed both their lives.

That evening my children, now in their early twenties, bring round some friends. The jobs they are doing did not exist in my youth – a production assistant in a small video company, a courier, a pop musician, a bond dealer in the city.

There was also the perpetual traveller and the endless student, living rather precariously off odd-jobs, a grant and the occasional cheque from the welfare office. They none of them expected their job or their lifestyle to stay that way for long. The twenties were a time of exploration, for discovering the world and themselves. Careers were middle-aged concepts, things of the 1970s. Money mattered to them, but money was earnable if you wanted it enough and if you put your mind to it, and there were other parts of life which did not depend on money. They were both more carefree and more caring for others than I was at their age; they were less bound to their jobs than I was but often put more energy into the actual work. It was loyalty to the work, not to the employer which mattered most.

But then there was the young man I had heard being interviewed on the radio that morning. He had left school at 16 and was now 23. No educational credits, no qualifications, no sense of personal talents. He had never had a job but felt let down, cheated, by a society that had seemed to promise him the right to work and to a wage. By now he was without ambition, had a child by a girl whom he had not married, was drifting with no plan for the future. When asked if he had thought of enrolling on one of the many training courses or schemes which are now available, he replied that he was no good at that sort of thing and that anyway they were only a politician's scheme for cutting down the number of unemployed.

The stories are familiar. They are happening all over Europe and in the USA. Some are those of happiness and good fortune. Some are of depression and even of hopelessness. They are the stories of discontinuous change at work, of those that adapt, even rejoice in the opportunity, and of those who lose their way and their will. Sometimes it seems that whole slices of generations have been allotted to pay the price for the mammoth change in the places of work which has taken place over the past twenty years and will continue for at least another ten. The Numbers (Chapter 2) have made clear how mammoth is that change; the next three chapters in Part Two describe and explain what it looks like.

4 The Shamrock Organization

The world of work is changing because the organizations of work are changing their ways. At the same time, however, the organizations are having to adapt to a changing world of work. It's a chicken and egg situation. One thing, at least, is clear – organizations in both private and public sectors face a tougher world – one in which they are judged more harshly than before on their effectiveness and in which there are fewer protective hedges behind which to shelter. It applies to hospitals and schools and employment offices as much as it does to businesses of all sorts.

It has been made increasingly clear, in Britain at least, that it is the organization's job to deliver; it is not its job to be everyone's alternative community, providing meaning and work for all for life; nor is its job to be another arm of the state, collecting its taxes, paying the pensions, employing the handicapped and the disadvantaged, administering an implicit incomes policy or collaborating with an exchange rate policy. They have been very convenient, these employment organizations, as the delivery instruments of government policy but now that they employ, full-time, an ever-decreasing percentage of society's adults they have become less useful. The alternative community idea has also got in the way, some people believe, of the organizations' proper job which is to deliver quality goods and services to their customers. 'My social objectives add five per cent to my costs,' one chief executive said to me recently, complainingly.

It all begs a huge question, of course. If the organizations are no longer expected to look after people, then who is? It is a question which was raised in the first chapter of this book; it will come up again. My concern in this part, however, is to examine how organizations have begun to respond to this increased pressure for results, and how their ways and their requirements of their people are now hugely different – discontinuous change has begun to happen, for good as well as for ill.

It is not just that results matter more and that there is more scope for radical change in the way they are delivered; the organizations of today are more and more places for brains not muscles. As we saw, brain skills will be required in 70 per cent of all jobs, according to one very believable forecast, and perhaps half of those brain skill jobs will require professional qualifications or education up to university degree level. These are increasingly organizations of clever people doing clever things, and clever people have to be managed rather more sensitively than in the days when factories were manned by 'hands'.

One sign of the new sorts of organization is a perceptible change in the language we use to talk about them. Organizations used to be perceived as gigantic pieces of engineering, with largely interchangeable human parts. We talked of their structures and their systems, of inputs and outputs, of control devices and of managing them, as if the whole was one large factory. Today the language is not that of engineering but of politics, with talk of cultures and networks, of teams and coalitions, of influence or power rather than control, of leadership not management. It is as if we had suddenly woken up to the fact that organizations were made up of people, after all, not just 'hands' or 'role occupants'. It is, thinking about it, a startling discontinuity even if it has crept up on most of us unnoticed.

The new thinking on organizations shows itself in several ways, in the shamrock organization, the new alliance of different types of work and worker (discussed in this chapter), in the federal organization, the new form of the organization with its interesting counterpart, the do'nut concept of management (discussed in Chapter 5), in the smart organization and the shake-up that is happening as a consequence to the careers and lives of managers (discussed in Chapter 6). Discontinuities at work do, in the end, affect what we do on Monday morning.

The Idea Of The Shamrock

The shamrock is the Irish national emblem, a small clover-like plant with three leaves to each stem. It was used by St Patrick, the patron saint of Ireland, to symbolize the three aspects of God, the Trinity. I use it, also symbolically, to make the point that the organization of today is made up of three very different groups of people, groups with different expectations, managed differently, paid differently, organized differently. The key differences were outlined earlier in the book but they need now to be described in more detail with all their implications, not least because each one of us must decide which leaf of the shamrock is for us.

The first leaf of the shamrock represents the core workers, what I prefer to call the professional core because it is increasingly made up of qualified professionals, technicians and managers. These are the people who are essential to the organization. Between them they own the organizational knowledge which distinguishes that organization from its counterparts. Lose them and you lose some of yourself. They are, therefore, precious or should be, and hard to replace. Organizations increasingly bind them to themselves with hoops of gold, with high salaries, fringe benefits and German cars. In return the organization demands of them hard work and long hours, commitment and flexibility. Not for these people are there still 40-hour weeks and 45-week years – few take all their holiday entitlements, few see their houses or their families in daylight. They are expected to go there, do this, be that, as the organization requires. In return they are increasingly well-paid.

As a consequence they are expensive, and as a further consequence there are fewer of them. Every successful organization will tell you that they have at least quadrupled their turnover in the last ten years but have halved their professional core. In three years, from 1982 to 1985, General Electric in the USA reduced its total workforce of 400,000 by 100,000 and its turnover *rose*. The people who left were mostly staffers, not factory-floor workers and were, apparently, just not necessary; they were expensive luxuries, desirable no doubt but dispensable.

They call it downsizing in the USA, or de-scaling or just re-structuring. The results are the same whatever the language. A Conference Board study in 1987 concluded that since 1979 more than a million managers and staff professionals in the USA had lost their jobs, over half of them since 1983. Many of them were, as one CEO observed, people hired just to read reports which others of them had been hired to write.

If the core is smaller, who then does the work? Increasingly, it is contracted out. It is not sensible, after all, to pay premium rates and give premium conditions to people whose work is not crucial to the organization. The old philosophy of a single-status company in which the cleaners were in principle treated to the same conditions as the directors meant that either you had rather expensive cleaners or rather cheap directors. That had to change as the directors were treated better, or the organization would go bankrupt. All non-essential work, work which could be done by someone else, is therefore sensibly contracted out to people who make a speciality of it and who should, in theory, be able to do it better for less cost. Manufacturing firms are now almost totally assembly firms, while many service organizations are, in effect, brokers, connecting the customer with a supplier with some intervening advice.

Calculations by some organizations revealed that if they broke down all the elements of their product or service, 80 per cent of the value was actually carried out by people not inside their organization. These 20/80 organizations do not always realize how large the contractual fringe has grown because it has become a way of their life. It is only recently that more individual professionals, more small businesses, more hived-off management buy-outs have shone a spotlight on a way of organizing which has, in fact, always existed. It can get exotic: smart Londoners can now get their typing done more cheaply and as quickly in Taiwan as in London using the new communications technology, while the New York Insurance Company has located its New Jersey claims office in Castleisland in Co. Kerry, Ireland, where the people are clever but also cheaper than in New Jersey.

Japan's export organizations have long depended for their efficiency on a large contractual fringe. Just-In-Time delivery means that the subcontractor carries the cost of any stocks. Subcontracts mean that the contractor carries the burden of any slowdown. It is a way of exporting uncertainty. Hence it is that only some 20 per cent of Japanese workers have the security of lifetime employment for they form the central cores of the large organizations. They are crucial, they are special, they are preferentially treated.

The *third* leaf of the shamrock is the flexible labour force, all those part-time workers and temporary workers who are the fastest growing part of the employment scene. That growth is partly a function of the switch to services, for the service industry cannot stockpile its products as a factory does. Some try to do it by putting their customers into a queue, but the more efficient and effective will always try to expand and contract their service to match the requirements of their customers. That means longer opening hours in the retail trade, it means peaks and troughs in demand. Shops now stay open for up to 70 hours a week. Airlines and airports are busier in the summer. Garden centres thrive at weekends. Of course, the full-time core staff could be asked to work the extra hours, or enough people could be employed full-time to cope with any peak and left underemployed the rest of the time. In years gone by both methods were used for they made it more convenient, easier to manage; but, today, the costs would be horrendous, given the increasingly privileged pay and conditions paid to the full-time core. It is cheaper by far, although more trouble, to bring in occasional extra labour part-time, to cope with extra hours, or temporary, to cope with peak periods. Convenience for the management has been weighed against economy and economy has won.

The Discontinuity

The three-leaved workforce has always existed in embryo. What is different today is the scale. *Each* of the leaves is now significant. It happened because it had to. The bad years of the late 1970s and early 1980s forced organizations to make significant reductions in their man-power, most of whom were still full-time employees. The threat of economic disaster forced them, in other words, to cut back their cores. When times improved managers were not going to be caught the same way twice; they did not expand the core but went instead to the other two leaves.

It makes good economic sense, but it also makes life more difficult for those who have to run the organization. Instead of one workforce there are now three, each with a different kind of commitment to the organization, a different contractual arrangement, a different set of expectations. They each have to be managed in different ways.

The core

Increasingly, the core will be composed of well-qualified people, professionals or technicians or managers. They get most of their identity and purpose from their work. They *are* the organization and are likely to be both committed to it and dependent on it. They will work long and hard, but in return they want not only proper rewards in the present but some guarantee of their future. They think in terms of careers, of advancement and of investing in the future. These, then, are not people to be ordered around. These are the new professionals who want their names to be as well-known as their roles, who want to be asked not told to do something, who see themselves in some sense as partners in the enterprise and want to be recognized as colleagues not subordinates.

Life in the core of more and more organizations is going to resemble that of consultancy firms, advertising agencies, and professional partnerships. The organizations are flat, seldom with more than four layers of rank, the top one being the assembly of partners, professors or directors. Promotion through the ranks comes quickly if you are any good (anyone of ability expects to be a partner before 40). Promotion, therefore, soon becomes an inadequate way of rewarding and recognizing people; success for those in the top rank can only mean doing the same job better and, presumably, for more money. At this level, therefore, much of the employee's pay is based on the results of the organization, the employee is in fact if not in law a 'partner'. The Japanese core will commonly take 40 per cent of their total pay in performance-related bonuses. It is the same for all top businessmen. It will soon be the same for most people in the core. It has to be.

This is because no organization can any longer guarantee that this year's pay rise can be next year's base line, not in a time of discontinuity. Therefore, this year's money has to be partly conditioned on this year's results, and next year's on next year's. With smaller cores it will no longer be possible to go in for the five-yearly cull of staff which was for many British organizations the way of reducing labour costs and counteracting the ratchet effect of the annual increment for everyone. Economic necessity, therefore, will force more organizations to re-think the way they reward their senior core people, turning them in the process into partners rather than employees, colleagues rather than bosses and subordinates, names not roles.

The contractual fringe
This is made up of both individuals and organizations. These organizations, although often smaller than the main organization, will have their own shamrocks, their own cores and their own subcontractors. It is a Chinese box type of world. The individuals will be self-employed professionals or technicians, many of them past employees of the central organization who ran out of roles in the core or who preferred the freedom of self-employment.

Whether it be organizations or individuals, however, the organizational principle remains the same – they are paid for results not for time, in fees not wages. The implications of this are important – it means that the central organization can exercise control only by specifying the results, not by overseeing the methods. If that sounds obvious and elementary it also marks a revolution in the way most managers are used to managing. 'Control the means and the methods,' the maxim used to be, 'and the results will be as they should be', or 'If they do what they should, you'll get what you want.' Of course, a proper specification of the results required does involve some investigation of the method proposed but in the end the purchaser can only accept or reject the proffered goods or services.

The management of subcontracting is well-understood in certain industries, particularly those of construction and manufacturing consumer goods. It is less well-understood elsewhere but it needs to be better appreciated.

An organization negotiated to buy back half of the work of one of their staff officers who had decided to go independent. He was their public relations adviser when they decided that they could not afford someone full-time in this role. What they meant but did not say was that they wanted to buy half his time, what they *said* was half his work. They could not control his time since he now worked from his own office and they failed, and did not try, to specify the results they expected. They felt he was now unmanageable, he felt unappreciated. They ended the contract and engaged a different full-time adviser. We often find it easier to manage someone's time than their results, but the contractual fringe does not allow us that luxury.

There are, however, opportunities as well as challenges in the contractual fringe. Fees, for example, make boring work more tolerable, and let us not deceive ourselves, much of the work in organizations *is* boring. I remember how, as a young student, I earned my extra money by printing Christmas cards and stationery on a hand-operated printing machine. There is, I can assure anyone, nothing more monotonous than taking a piece of paper, placing it in the press, pushing down the handle, taking out the paper and placing it on a pile of completed cards, and then repeating the operation 500 times in an hour. Were I doing it for a wage I would have found any excuse to break the routine; a strike, even if doomed to failure, would at least have been a change. But because each printed page placed on the pile represented another few cents of riches I found it a most tolerable form of labour. The result of my effort was immediately visible, and directly rewarded.

The shamrock organization, if it is wise, puts boring work out on contract, paying fees for results. It is piecework rediscovered, but piecework more effective than it used to be because it is no longer a dubious substitute for wages. It is also piecework made more tolerable by better equipment; one man or one woman with good machinery can now do what it once needed a group to do, making the reward more directly proportionate to the individual effort. My printing press today would be automatic, the tedium less and the quality better.

The temptation is to exploit the monopoly power of the organization, to pay minimal fees for maximum output. The challenge is to resist that temptation and to pay good fees for good work. The shamrock organization has to remember that in the contractual fringe it is money paid for work done. There is no longer a residual loyalty to be relied on, no longer any implied promise of security in return for obedient labour. Good work must, in the long run, receive good rewards or it will cease to be good work. The contract is now more explicit, and in many respects more healthy for that.

The flexible labour force

The third leaf of the shamrock is too easily seen as the hired help division, people of whom little is expected and to whom little is given. In crude terms, these people are the labour market, a market into which employers dip as they like and when they need, for as little money as they have to pay. This is a shortsighted philosophy. These people are not all pining for core jobs, marking time on the fringe, having to eke out an existence from part-time earnings until something better turns up. A lot of them are women who do not always want a demanding full-time job, but do want access to money and people, a job to supplement and to complement their other work. Many others have two or more part-time jobs, officially declared, and are therefore more properly described as full-time self-employed with a portfolio of jobs. Some of them are young, who see work as a series of apprenticeships or as pocket money opportunities.

Such people should be taken seriously because for them part-time or temporary work is a choice not just a necessity. They have skills which can be developed, commitment to give, talents and energies to offer if they are required. They do not necessarily hanker after careers or promotion, they have interests and concerns beyond the job and are not therefore susceptible to the same kinds of blandishment as the people of the core. Their commitment will be to a job and to a work group rather than to a career, or to the organization.

Treated as casual labour such people respond casually. A department store that used part-timers to staff their store on Fridays and Saturdays found that their hallowed tradition of service and politeness was visibly dented. They had not invested enough time in training these new staff, nor in persuading them of their ways, because, as they saw it, there was no guarantee that these people would be around long enough to pay back the investment through improved behaviour or better work. That way lies a self-fulfilling prophecy of the worst sort.

Organizations have to get used to the idea that not everyone wants to work for them all the time even if the jobs are available. The ways of the core cannot be and should not be the ways of the flexible labour force, for while some may hanker after full-time lifetime jobs, many will not. The new paradigm of work has begun to take hold of people's minds.

If the flexible labour force is seen to be a valuable part of the organization then the organization will be prepared to invest in them, to provide training, even training leading to qualifications, to give them some status and some privileges (including paid holidays and sick leave entitlement). Then, and only then, will the organization get the temporary or part-time help that it needs to the standard it requires.

The flexible labour force will never, however, have the commitment or the ambition of the core. Decent pay and decent conditions are what they want, fair treatment and good companions. They have jobs not careers and cannot be expected to rejoice in the organization's triumphs any more than they can expect to share in the proceeds, nor will they put themselves out for the love of it; more work, in their culture, deserves and demands more money. It is contract labour but the contract should be fair and must be honoured.

The Fourth Leaf?

There is one other category of sub-contracting which needs to be mentioned. It is the growing practice of getting the customer to do the work. Customers, however, are not paid by the organization so this fourth leaf cannot exist as part of the formal structure of the shamrock (which is just as well for the imagery since no shamrock has four leaves), but it is real all the same.

We now collect our own groceries from the shelves where my parents had shop assistants to do it for them. Our own private cars have replaced the delivery vans. Furniture makers persuade us that it is clever to assemble our own kitchens. Banks long ago worked out that if they could persuade customers to fill in their own deposit slips they, the banks not the customers, would save millions. Now we also draw out our own money from their holes in the wall and call it our convenience. We also pour our own petrol and print out our own tube tickets.

Smart restaurants may one day charge customers for cooking their own food where now they only, in fast food outlets, ask them to clear their own litter, or preferably, take it away and provide their own eating space. 'Help yourself' in clothes stores, supermarkets' pick and mix outlets, drug stores and wine shops has turned out to be a clever way of saving labour under the label of customer preference.

What is clever is that having removed the service, one can then charge extra for providing it as an optional extra, with special delivery or special fitting, or with delicatessens offering the service my parents used to take for granted but now at a premium price. It is all a way of saving labour in the core of the shamrock and reintroducing it as part of the contractual fringe. Clever.

An Interlude

At this point let me pause. Some may well be thinking – yes, I see the sense of what you're saying but is it really happening today? As one manager said to me last month, 'Who *are* all these people you call the self-employed knowledge workers – I don't see any of them on the 8.10 from Woking every morning.' No, said I, you wouldn't. These people don't need to take your trains. They have their terminals and their telephones instead. Sometimes we are so absorbed in our own surroundings that we forget to look over the fence.

This self-absorption happened to me not so long ago. When I need to compose my thoughts and write I go off to a small cottage set amid the fields of East Anglia, not a house in sight. There I can retreat to the peace of a world where nothing ever changes save the seasons. The farm in front is worked by Charlie and Jim, now into their eighties. They still pull the beet by hand for their cattle and slice off the leaves with a sickle as it used to be done 100 years ago. Jim passed by as I was writing.

'Down here for a bit of a holiday, are you?' he said.

'No, I'm working,' I replied, pointing to my papers.

'I'd call that scribbling,' he said with his gentle smile, 'not working.'

Of course, I reflected, the sons of toil have never respected the lily-white hands of the knowledge worker nor known many of them but they say that half the cottages down the lane are now owned by journalists. Perhaps things *are* changing even here. Then I reflected that until two years ago Jim used to clear his ditches with a scythe. Now young Stephen does it for him, for a fee, with his £20,000 Caterpillar digger, wearing ear muffs with walkman earphones stuffed inside – music while you work in the contractual fringe! Quite a skilled contractual fringe, too. Stephen does his own repair work and is starting a business in spare parts on the side.

Charlie grumbles about farm prices. The land is fen land, they can't grow much on it – 'I guess one day it will just go back to fen,' he says. Yet right next door, on land that 40 years ago was sold as gentlemen's rough shooting, is the biggest plant and conifer farm in Britain, indeed in Europe, plants which only need an inch or two of damp soil. Ironically they employ 200 people on 200 acres where Jim and Charlie employ no one, but then those 200 people are quite knowledgeable, at least about their plants and their cultivation. They've done what British manufacturing needs to do everywhere, change the product to a high value-added one that is knowledge-intensive and backed by research and development and in the leisure market, supporting Jonathan Gershuny's point that one person's free time is another person's job. 'That's not farming,' says Jim, 'that's gardening,' and, indeed, I would much prefer to look out at a field of ripening corn than on rows and rows of little conifers, but you don't grow rich on nostalgia.

I tell this little parable to make one point. Until we look around us with fresh eyes we often don't notice what should be obvious. There were the knowledge workers, the highly capitalized contractual workers, the move to a knowledge industry in a spot which I thought was the unchanging heart of rural England. Open your eyes and ye shall see!

Telecommuting

F International in Britain is an electronic shamrock. Francis Kinsman describes it well in his book *The Telecommuters*. It was started by Stephanie (Steve) Shirley in 1962 as a tiny business called Freelance Programmers to be run by her from her own home, writing computer programs for companies. By 1964 it was F International with four other workers and by 1988 it was the F.I. Group plc with 1,100 workers and a turnover of nearly £20 million.

The point about F International, however, is that 70 per cent of those workers work from home or from a local work centre and that over 90 per cent of them are women. F International believes that the performance of their people is 30 per cent higher than their counterparts working in offices where coffee breaks, lunches, corridor gossiping and personal phone calls tend to cut into the working day.

These women are mostly self-employed although, if they can guarantee to commit enough time to the company, they can go on the part-time or even full-time payroll; less than 200 were on salary in 1988. There is a small core staff in the Head Office, a number of small branch offices and, lately, a growing network of work centres where people can take their work if they need to meet with colleagues or to use more specialist equipment. The individual worker is linked into the organization by an electronic mail service, by a newsletter and by free-speaks, in which senior members of the core travel around the country to hold open question and answer sessions.

The women, and some men, in F International are a network built around a core, connected by telephones and computers, working from home rather than at home. They do not work alone but in shifting teams and groups built around specific projects and assignments. It is all designed, as FI's Charter puts it, 'to develop, through modern telecommunications, the unutilized intellectual energy of individuals and groups unable to work in a conventional environment'.

F International is unusual because of Steve Shirley's deliberate plan to create a culture built around the status and talents of independent people. The core grew out of the contractual fringe rather than the other way around. As a result F International invests a lot of time and energy in training its self-employed workers and in keeping in contact with them. It also pays them well.

There aren't many F Internationals around but they are an extreme example of a growing trend. Rank Xerox in Britain has its 'networkers', a group of some 60 or so specialists in marketing, finance, personnel and management services who were peeled off from the central organization and were encouraged to set up their own businesses and sell back some of their services to the parent company. ICL has two groups of high-grade part-timers (as opposed to self-employed) who are software planners and analysts and, as in F International, mainly women with young families.

These, again, are the biggest and most formal examples. It need not, however, be that organized for it to happen. There will hardly be an organization which does not get some of its typing done by someone at home, hardly an executive who has not stayed at home to work on a critical report and called in by telephone to the office. Alvin Toffler in *The Third Wave* quoted a number of eminent Company Presidents in the USA who maintain that between 25 and 75 per cent of what they do could be done at home or from home once the necessary communications are in place. Francis Kinsman quotes examples from the American companies of organized homeworker schemes, of which Freight Data systems in California is the most interesting. They let their small staff work at home when they were not needed in the office, but encouraged them to work ahead of time by means of a bonus system. They increased productivity so much that it paid for the capital cost of a terminal in each home inside five months, and the rapid growth of the company caused them no space problems and no need to move to bigger and more costly premises.

What, one might ask, is so unusual about all this, except for the electronic gadgetry? Publishers, after all, rely on authors scribbling at home for their new material. Homeworkers have knitted sweaters, addressed envelopes, marked examination papers, typed scripts, cooked pies and made quilts for centuries. The Japanese have always relied on a cottage industry tradition of small manufacturers and assemblers as the raft on which to build their huge enterprises. What is new is the higher skills, qualifications and status of the new homeworkers. The Department of Employment in Britain discovered in 1987, probably to its surprise, that some of the highest paid workers worked at home. The rate for one fifth of all the homeworkers in their survey put them in the top 10 per cent of all earnings. Homeworkers are out, telecommuters are in. It's all in the language but it is the language which signals the change, the change from freak to fashion.

Telecommuters have choice; they can choose to work before the commuter trains start running or when offices are long closed. They can commute by telephone or computer link from wherever, can move house without moving job, can revel in the occasional hour of sunshine or take time off to celebrate an anniversary with no one's permission to obtain; they can work fast or work slowly, by the fire or in the attic. It is not, however, to everyone's taste. For some it is too lonely, or the temptations of home become too great; one American lady complained that she put on two stone because of frequent trips to the fridge, and one man attributed his divorce to the fact that he was at home all the time.

Yet what today seems yuppie and freaky may be tomorrow's commonplace. The telephone has turned out to be the most user-friendly of all modern inventions and as its permutations and ramifications extend it will start to revolutionize ordinary occupations. The carphone and the cordless telephone have surprised even the most optimistic of manufacturers by their popularity. The fax is bringing handwriting back into fashion as we find that we can instantaneously reproduce our scribbled notes or diagrams half a world away. The computer and its screen, linked to a telephone cable, becomes a message box for the world, one which your local store can use to sell its wares, your friends to leave their calls, your business its memos, and now that we call it keyboard skills rather than typing (new words again!) everybody can learn to use it without loss of face or dignity.

In September 1988 the Confederation of British Industry organized a huge conference in London on 'teleworking' along with British Telecom, to celebrate an 'idea whose time has come', to quote Francis Kinsman and in recognition of their estimate that by 1995 there will be 4 million tele-workers in Britain. Four million people cannot escape notice even if they are working from home. The world is changing.

The Club Centre

One sign of the electronic shamrock will be a new concept of the central office. At present the office is an apartment house, a collection of private apartments for executives with all the attendant service functions. It is an expensive way of accommodating the work, something that became very obvious on a recent visit to one such office in central London. The chief executive was thinking of re-designing the floor layout to allow, he said, for more informal interaction between his executives, for more meeting rooms and rooms dedicated to particularly expensive pieces of electronic hardware. He showed me round to point out the disadvantages of the present layout of rooms as rows, or rather layers and layers (for it was a tall narrow building) of individual offices.

'But they are all empty,' I exclaimed.

'Of course,' he replied, 'they are all out doing business, seeing clients, attending meetings, gathering information, making deals. They only come in here to file their reports, attend departmental meetings or deal with their correspondence.

'Costed per hour of occupancy,' I said, 'you must have the most expensive rooms in London. You ought to see my friend Walter.'

'Why?' he asked, not unnaturally.

'Walter,' I explained, 'runs a design and consultancy business with a staff of around 100 professionals – quite big. He runs it from a converted warehouse, except that he hasn't converted it very much. There are no offices in it. There are meeting rooms, there is a superb farmhouse kitchen, there are drawing-boards scattered around, there are word-processors, telephones and computers abounding but no one, not even Walter himself, has any private space – except for the secretaries, who are really not secretaries as such but project co-ordinators, each assigned to work for a project rather than for an individual.'

When I asked him why he'd done this, Walter told me, 'I don't want my designers and consultants spending their time here in this very expensive space. I would rather they were out with the client or working at home where I will provide any equipment they want. They only come in here for meetings, to use some specialist equipment and, generally, to keep in touch. We lay on the best breakfasts in town in that kitchen of ours and there's always a bottle of wine open and waiting for anyone dropping in after 6.00 pm. It's a working club really.'

Indeed it was, a working club, a club being a place of privileged access to common facilities. A club not an apartment house. Turning the office into a club allows one to equip it far more lavishly and comfortably than a set of individual offices and to make sure that all the space is properly used. The idea of a club centre only works, however, if people have somewhere else to be, at home, with clients, out on business. It is the perfect facility for a network of individuals linked into a small core (in Walter's case the core was primarily the project co-ordinators).

F International, interestingly, is creating a number of regional work centres, places where their individual workers can go when they need to attend team meetings, use more specialist equipment or just want to escape from their homes and meet people. The work centres are working clubs and we shall see more of them because they are cost effective.

The shamrock organization, always there in embryo, has flourished because organizations have realized that you do not have to employ all of the people all of the time to get the work done. They are now going further and are counting the cost of having all of them around in the same place for all of the time. Offices for part-timers become common-rooms for telecommuters and, in time, clubs for everyone. The early morning crush in the commuter train will one day be a thing of the past or at least only a twice-weekly chore.

Homeworking is not, traditionally, good working - particularly for women. Men have in the past had the fun jobs, going out to work. For women, the paid work at home has been lonely, monotonous, trivial and badly paid. More homeworking, even glamorized by words like telecommuting, would not therefore seem to be good news. Times, however, may be changing.

Catherine Hakim, in Britain, has done an extensive analysis of homeworkers in Britain in 1981 for the Department of Employment. Even in 1981, she reports, the usual picture of homeworking - of work typically done by women, tied to the home with few or no skills, exploited and in poor health – was highly misleading and only applied to the small percentage doing manufacturing homework.

Her survey concluded that homeworkers are more highly qualified than most, in better health than most, and more likely to own their own homes. Many of the women in the survey were making conscious trade-offs between the flexibility of homework and the relatively low-paid job available, which probably explains why the majority of homeworkers say they are satisfied with their pay and conditions.

On the other hand, Barbara Baran in the United States studied women's work in the insurance industry and concluded that although the new technologies may be freeing women from the pink-collar assembly lines and even raising skill levels of the female workforce, there is, in the end, she says 'little cause for good cheer'. For women at the bottom end of the clerical hierarchy, jobs are simply disappearing. For skilled and particularly white clericals there will be jobs but not career opportunities. In one company one sixth of their clerical staff (mostly women) were working from home. Numbers of college-educated women may make their way into professional and managerial ranks only to find their talents, she says, under-utilized and undervalued.

Yet she also reports from companies in her study who had moved their operations from major cities to adjacent suburban areas in search of a higher quality clerical workforce – the labour pool of educated women with small children. Automation, she was told, is raising skill requirements and forcing insurance companies to relocate to be nearer high quality labour. Perhaps not all women want to be career professionals like men. If they don't then homeworking may be good news, with new types of work and new technology.

The Challenges Of The Shamrock

On the face of it the shamrock organization is logical. Logic, however, does not necessarily imply ease and these are not easy organizations to run. Meetings, planned or ad hoc, teams and committees are a familiar feature of organizations and they survive and flourish in the core, but to try to fix a quick meeting with members of the contractual fringe is a recipe for frustration and disappointment for these are the meetings that have to be negotiated weeks in advance with great comparing of diaries, inevitable absentees and compromises. Each leaf of the shamrock has to be managed differently and must yet be somehow part of the whole. The shamrock, after all, symbolizes three different aspects of one whole, three in one and one in three.

Accepting and recognizing the need for differences is only the start. The most difficult of policy decisions concerns what and who belongs in the core, what activities and which people. Too often organizations drift into this decision, gradually hiving off functions until they are left with what is inconceivable or too inconvenient to give to others. It is not an obvious choice; most organizations, if they start thinking radically enough, can justify out-sourcing, to use the current jargon, almost anything. In one organization such a brain storming exercise left only the chief executive and a car phone! A growing subsidiary business today is dedicated to answering customer complaints – on behalf of other businesses! It is a service which big companies contract out, wisely or not, getting a periodic analysis of the complaints as part of the deal.

Even more contentious can be the question of *who* belongs in the core and for how long. Smaller, flatter, more intense organizations tend to be younger. The older men cannot always stand the pace, can get out-of-date in some technologies, or become, in general, too expensive for the value which they add. The fixed-term contracts of the armed services will increasingly be a feature of the new cores. As we shall see in Chapter 6, the task of keeping the core people up-to-date and mentally alert and open is one of increasing importance to all organizations. Fewer people means better people; there is no room now for incompetence or passengers in today's cores. This pressure for quality in turn means greater selectivity on entry. More will be demanded of the aspiring executive, with more organizations tempted towards the ultimate Catch 22 of employment – 'We won't hire you unless you have previous successful experience in this area'. Rather like an actor in pursuit of an Equity card without which no acting job is possible but which you cannot apply for without an acting job, it is hard today to know where to begin.

The core is the critical hub of an organizational network. It is essential to get it right and to manage it right.

5 The Federal Organization

Alongside the emerging shamrock organization we can discern the gradual development of the federal organization. Federalism implies a variety of individual groups allied together under a common flag with some shared identity. Federalism seeks to make it big by keeping it small, or at least independent, by combining autonomy with co-operation. It is the method which businesses are slowly, and painfully, evolving for getting the best of both worlds – the size which gives them clout in the market-place and in the financial centres, as well as some economies of scale, and the small unit size which gives them the flexibility which they need, as well as the sense of community for which individuals increasingly hanker.

The Nature of Federalism

Federalism is *not* a classy word for decentralization. The differences are important and are too little understood by monarchical countries like Britain which has always regarded federalism as something more appropriate for departing colonies or vanquished enemies because, presumably, it would keep them divided and therefore weak, in spite of much historical evidence that it tends to do exactly the opposite.

Decentralization implies that the centre delegates certain tasks or duties to the outlying bits while the centre remains in overall control. The centre does the delegating, and initiates and directs. Thus it is that we have that most consistent of organizational findings, the more an organization decentralizes its operations the greater the flow of information to and from the centre. The centre may not be *doing* the work in a decentralized organization, but it makes sure that it knows how the work is going. The new technology, of course, makes it even easier for that information to flow more copiously and more immediately than ever, making it ever easier to contemplate still further decentralization, in theory at least.

Federalism is different. In federal countries states are the original founding groups, coming together because there are some things which they can do better jointly (defence is the obvious example) than individually. The centre's powers are given to it by the outlying groups, in a sort of reverse delegation. The centre, therefore, does not direct or control so much as co-ordinate, advise, influence and suggest – all words which are familiar currency in the Head Offices of multinationals, multinationals who have often been forced into federalism because of the local priorities of their subsidiaries.

Federal organizations, therefore, are reverse thrust organizations; the initiative, the drive and the energy comes mostly from the bits, with the centre an influencing force, relatively low in profile. Switzerland is a good example of the federal principle at work, a country both peaceful and prosperous, in many ways the envy of its European neighbours. Surely, one would have thought, her government would be much admired, her President's name on every lip. It is instead ironic that even when he is host to a summit conference no one readily remembers who he is, or, to be precise, who he was, because the job rotates. It is seen as a chairman's role, the chairman of a co-ordinating group who seek to guide but not direct the nation's affairs, important but low in profile.

Federal organizations are, as a result, tight-loose organizations, to use the management jargon. The centre holds some decisions very tight to itself, usually, and crucially, the choice of how to spend new money and where and when to place new people. This gives them the means to shape the long-term strategy and to influence its execution through the key executives. It is a way of working long familiar to other institutions. I once asked the Headmaster of one of England's more famous independent schools how he changed the place. 'I choose the new heads of houses and heads of departments; I allocate resources to some new facilities,' he said, 'and then I wait ten years for the results.'

Federalism, however, is not a free or willing choice for most organizations. There is, as far as I know, no example in history of any state voluntarily ceding power from the centre to its component parts. Federal constitutions arise when individual states decide to merge together, as in Australia, or when the central power is destroyed by war or revolution, as in West Germany, and no one, inside or out, wants to see so much power in the centre again.

How then, one must ask, has federalism come to organizations? Not willingly, nor in most cases deliberately or even consciously. Once again this significant piece of discontinuity has crept up on us unawares. It has happened perforce because the reduced core of the organization cannot deal with the flood of information coming in from the decentralized operations. As the shamrock took shape, as a bigger organization grew more and smaller shamrocks it tried to run them all from the core at the centre, relying on the new technologies to provide all the information needed. The new technologies did not fail, but information, to be useful, still has to be interpreted by its human masters. More information with more diversity needs more people to interpret it if it is not to lie unused in the piles of printout or in the unseen memories of the computers. Yet, paradoxically, organizations were all, as we have seen, seeking to contract their cores and cut down their staffers. In the end they have to stop asking for the information, have to stop trying to run everything from the centre, have to begin to let go. Then it is that decentralization turns into federalism, a discontinuity whose significance is not understood and not therefore developed by many a chief executive.

'How many hundreds of people do you have in that Head Office of yours?' I asked a friend of mine, a newly appointed Chief Executive of a multinational who had asked me to explain federalism. 'Fifteen, I think,' he said. 'There you are,' I said, slightly triumphantly, 'the point about federalism is small centres, with the other parts doing the real work. With federal thinking you would not need fifteen hundred people cluttering up London's airspace.'

'I said fifteen,' he replied, 'not fifteen hundred. You see,' he explained indulgently, 'all my operations are done by independent companies. At the centre we collect their surpluses and invest them in new opportunities and we watch them to see that they are producing the surpluses we think they should. If they don't we push the top people a bit and ultimately replace them. New ventures and new people, that's my concern in the centre and I only need a few wise and a few clever people to help me.'

'You don't need me,' I said, 'you have discovered organizational federalism all by yourself.'

'I would call it commonsense,' he replied.

Fifteen people cannot even begin to think of controlling in any detail the operations of perhaps thirty different companies, divisions or operating units; they would not have time to even read the information which might be available. It is better in the end that they do not even try, but concentrate instead on the things they can control and the decisions which they alone should take. Small cores make federalism ultimately inevitable and large cores make decentralization ultimately too expensive. The slow imperative of economical reality pushes larger organizations into a new kind of world.

The Role Of The Centre

A report for Britain's National Economic Development Office in 1988 was severely critical of some of the country's largest electronic businesses. They had, said the report, been growing depressingly slowly compared with their competitors in Japan, Germany and the USA. The report suggested that a major cause of this slow growth lay in the corporate structure adopted by these companies. They had broken themselves down into individual businesses and had then left those businesses to determine their own strategies. The result, too often, was short-term and parochial thinking. The implication was that it needs big organizations to think big and long-term.

If these companies had indeed devolved strategic thinking to their individual businesses then they had misunderstood corporate federalism. It would be akin to the USA letting the States decide on their individual policies for defence – no one would, in the end, be defending the USA. To see the centre only as a banker, pulling in surplus profits and dispensing funds for worthwhile projects, is to throw away most of the advantages of federalism which is a concept devised to make things big whilst keeping them small.

The centre has to be more than a banker. Only the centre can think beyond the next annual report or indeed, to quote one family business, can look beyond the grave. Only the centre can think in terms of global strategies which may link one or more of the autonomous parts. To leave these big decisions to the discretion of the parts can be a way to mortgage the future.

The centre, however, is not in full control in a federal organization. It is easy, in logic, to think of the centre taking the long-term decisions and leaving the implementation to the parts. That logic, however, reeks of the old engineering language of management, of decentralization and of delegated tasks and controls. It is not the new language of political theory, of people and communities. The federal concept requires the centre to act on behalf of the parts, if the resulting decisions are going to be self-enforcing – and they have to be because the centre does not have the manpower to control the detail.

It all requires a new image of the corporation, one in which the centre genuinely is at the middle of things and is not a polite word for the top, or even for Head Office (a term gradually disappearing from the corporate vocabulary). The centre must cling to its key functions of new people and new money, but its decisions have to be in consultation with, and on behalf of, the chiefs of the parts. In political terms this makes sense – the centre becomes an assembly of chiefs, acting in that place and time on behalf of the total federation, then returning to their own tribes to do their own bit for the whole.

Running the federal centre is not therefore the job for a monarch, someone with an overarching authority and a liking for autocratic government. It has to be a place of persuasion, of argument leading to consensus. Leadership is required but it is the leadership of ideas not of personality. It is observable how the bigger multinationals, pushed earlier than most into federalism because they have to deal with autonomous nation states, have begun to create triumvirates, even committees, to run the centre.

I asked someone who had just become Chairman of a great multinational what it felt like to be head of one of the world's biggest businesses, to be, in one sense, one of our biggest businessmen. 'It isn't like that,' he replied. 'I have just moved round the table and I'm temporarily chairing the team because someone has to.'

In 1984 Noburo Goto, the charismatic head of the Tokyo group in Japan, with 300 companies ranging from railways to property, resigned and in his place the company is run by a group. From monarchy to federalism in one move.

The centre will have its own staff in these organizations,

a staff whose concerns will largely be with the future, with plans and possibilities, scenarios and options. They will be there to advise their political seniors, many of whom will be in the part not the centre, and will have to rely increasingly on influence rather than on any formal authority or absolute power. In many organizations the centre is already becoming a training place for future chiefs, a necessary exposure to the whole before a commitment to one of the parts.

Because organizations evolve there are, as yet, few federal corporations in a pure form. The Japanese have always come close to it and, more recently, Isamu Yamashita of Mitsui was quoted (in John Naisbitt's *Reinventing the Corporation*) as saying, 'The best corporate structure today comprises a small strategic centre supported by many front-line outfits.' New words, however, are, once again, heralding new behaviours. One chief executive recently described his corporate centre as variously a 'Good Food Guide' (indicating which subsidiaries were best for what), traffic policeman, orchestra conductor, interpreter, critic or cheerleader. Asked about his own role, he replied, 'For most of my life I'm a missionary'. 'We need', he said 'to compete outside but collaborate within', a succinct description of the federal principle of interdependence, the principle that each part needs the help of the other parts, as well as the centre, in order to survive. Too much independence, after all, can lead to breakaway or to a random collection of disparate bits, a conglomerate not a federation.

Unfortunately, federalism misunderstood can be worse than no federalism. Federalism misunderstood becomes inefficient decentralization, leading to talk of the headless corporation or the hollow company and the kinds of criticisms cited in the NEDO Report of Britain's electronic businesses. A clear understanding of the role of the centre is crucial to a proper federalism, but so is an appreciation of concepts like 'subsidiarity' and 'the inverted do'nut' because structure on its own will not produce a federalist organization. The words are deliberately strange to signal that new ways of thinking are required in these organizations. More of the same will no longer work. Discontinuity demands upside-down thinking.

Subsidiarity

The federal organization is not only different in its form and shape, it is culturally different, it requires a different set of attitudes from those who seek to run it and from those who seek to manage it and from those who are managed. This is the discontinuity which matters – not the change in structure but the change in philosophy.

That philosophy is characterized by the word 'subsidiarity'. It is a word unfamiliar to most, but not to the adherents of the Roman Catholic Church where it has long been an established part of traditional doctrine. First enunciated by Pope Leo XIII, but later recalled in the papal encyclical 'Quadragesimo Anno' in 1941 at the time of Mussolini, the principal of subsidiarity holds that 'it is an injustice, a grave evil and a disturbance of right order for a large and higher organization to arrogate to itself functions which can be performed efficiently by smaller and lower bodies'. To steal people's decisions is wrong.

The choice of word is deliberate because the sense of morality implied by it is crucial to its working. Subsidiarity means giving away power. No one does that willingly in organizations, yet the federal organization will not work unless those in the centre not only *have* to let go of some of their power but actually *want* to do so, because only then will they trust the new decision-makers to take the right decisions and only then will they enable them to make them work. They have, therefore, to believe that it is an essentially *good* thing to do; they have to feel good in themselves about it because they have done the good thing.

It is only too easy in organizations to create negative self-fulfilling prophecies and to delegate with the secret knowledge that it won't work because the individual to whom you have delegated does not have the right information, or access to it, cannot mobilize the resources to implement any decisions and is inadequately trained for the new responsibilities. It would, of course, be an irresponsible manager who delegated under these circumstances but we can all act irresponsibly when we act reluctantly. To be effective, delegation requires a positive will to trust and to enable and a willingness to be trusted and enabled, a positive self-fulfilling prophecy, a moral act, subsidiarity.

Interestingly, virtue in this instance does not go unrewarded. It is the way out of one of the many Catch 22 situations in organizations. This Catch 22 starts from the observable fact that it is hard to give responsibility to someone if they are not capable of it, but how do you have any evidence of their capability if they have never been given the responsibility? Trust has to be earned, but in order to be earned it has first to be given. I must first trust my children to find their own way to school if I am to find out whether they can be trusted to get there on their own. I will do that because I am their parent, because I want them to grow and because I believe that they are capable, give or take one or two initial mistakes.

Those organizations which are forced, often because of the nature of their work, to give large responsibilities to young and junior people have a very good record of attracting a high calibre of young people, which makes it easier for those above to take the risks implied by subsidiarity. Television and journalism are both arenas which the talented young queue up to join. It cannot be the money, nor is it usually the fame; it is the chance to take responsibility publicly at an early age. It has to work this way because no one in the centre of a television company or a newspaper can specify in any detail what has to go into every programme or every page; those in power have to rely on control after the event, which can at times be embarrassing and even expensive. These are the mistakes which are an inevitable part of trust. In good organizations the mistakes are rare because the people are good, they are good because they know that they will be entrusted with big responsibilities, including the chance to make mistakes.

Practice subsidiarity, in other words, and in due course you will draw unto yourself the kinds of people whom you will need if the subsidiarity is to work. Increasingly we see subsidiarity infecting other areas of work, in the new finance houses, for example, in advertising agencies, in the more traditional fields of medicine and now of law; in places, in other words, where decisions have to move so fast that those on the spot have to be trusted. Where the young perceive it happening is where the best of them want to be. Ultimately subsidiarity is a self-justifying philosophy.

The Inverted Do'nut

An alternative analogy is that of the inverted do'nut. The do'nut is an American doughnut. It is round with a hole in the middle rather than the jam in its British equivalent. Call it a bagel if you live in New York. This, however, is an inverted American do'nut, in that it has the hole in the middle filled in and the space on the outside; like the diagram below:

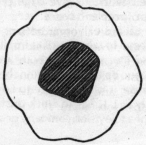

The point of the analogy begins to emerge if you think of your job, of any job. There will be a part of that job which will be clearly defined, and which, if you do not do, you will clearly be seen to have failed. That is the heart, the core, the centre of the do'nut. The tasks may be written down in a job description, or, if it's a classy organization, in a statement of objectives; the snag is that when you have done all that you have not finished, for there is more. In any job of any significance the person holding the job is expected not only to do all that is required but in some way to improve on that, to make a difference, to show responsible and appropriate initiative, to move into the empty space of the do'nut and begin to fill it up. Unfortunately, no one can tell you what you should do there because if they could they would make it part of the core. It is another organizational Catch 22. All they can tell you is the boundary of your discretion, the outer rim of the do'nut.

Some do'nuts are all core and no space. We do not want the bus driver using his initiative to leave early, take a quicker route or go for scenic detours. Some people, particularly perhaps those in the flexible labour force, want jobs which are all core; at least one knows what has to be done and when it is done. Other jobs have no rims, that of the independent entrepreneur, for instance, and some have huge areas of space as with people in the caring professions, teaching or the priesthood, where there always seems to be more that could be done were there only the time. Most people seem to like a balanced do'nut with about equal spaces of core and space.

The point is that federal organizations require large do'nuts, be they group do'nuts or individual do'nuts. That is not as it used to be. Organizational fashion used to imply that the work of most of the organization could be precisely described and defined, and therefore carefully monitored and controlled. Most jobs were all core. The changing complexity, variety and spread of reaction which is now a feature of so many organizations makes the well-cored do'nut an impossible dream today, if dream it ever was. These organizations have to be managed by specifying the essential cores of do'nuts, by being clear about boundaries or areas of discretion, and by specifying the kinds of results which are required from each do'nut, the criteria for successful initiative.

Obvious though it may sound when set down on paper, this philosophy of management marks a major discontinuity. We are not, most of us, used to running organizations by results, with large and empty do'nuts. Most managers feel more comfortable when the cores are large as well as closely defined, when they can control the methods and therefore the results, the means and not the ends. To let go, to specify success criteria, to trust people to use their own methods to achieve your ends – this can be uncomfortable. It is particularly uncomfortable when we realize that after-the-event controls, or management-by-results, means that mistakes can and will be made. It may be true that we learn more from our mistakes than from our successes but organizations have in the past been reluctant to put this theory into practice. Now they will have to, *and* they will have to learn to forgive mistakes. Not all mistakes, of course, can be forgiven but most are less critical than they seem at the time and can be the crux of important lessons.

Organizations are not by nature forgiving places. Mistakes are magnified by myth and engraved in reports and appraisals, to be neither forgotten nor forgiven. Organizational halos are for sinners as well as for saints and last for a long time. The new manager must be a different manager. He, and increasingly she, must use what, in psychological jargon, is called re-inforcement theory, applauding success and forgiving failure; he or she must use mistakes as an opportunity for learning, something only possible if the mistake is *truly* forgiven because otherwise the lesson is heard as a reprimand not an offer of help. The new manager must learn to specify the measures of success as well as the signs of failure and must then allow his or her people the space to get on with it in their own way. The new manager has to be teacher, counsellor and friend, as much as or more than he or she is commander, inspector and judge. It is a major change in our ways of managing. If we cannot do it then federalism becomes anarchy, control reverts to the centre, the centre becomes too big and too expensive, the organization is crippled, withers and can die.

The Language Of Leadership

The new organizations need to be run in new ways. As we have seen, these new ways need a new language to describe them, a language of federations and networks, of alliances and influences, as well as of shamrocks and do'nuts. The language, and the philosophy which it describes, requires us to learn new ways and new habits, to live with more uncertainty but more trust, less control but more creativity. To those of us reared in another tradition it can be a strange and a frightening language but I think that we have to recognize that it is the *right* language. No one, after all, has ever liked being managed, even if they didn't mind being the manager, for anyone who has tried to run an organization has always known that it was more like running a small country than a machine. It was only the theorists who tried to apply the hard rules of number and logic and mechanics to an essentially soft system. Maybe we were instinctively right to pay little heed to them until people like Peters and Waterman first started talking the new language in their *In Search of Excellence*, a book which obviously touched some chord.

As a result, leadership is now fashionable and the language of leadership increasingly important but, as

Warren Bennis says in his book on *Leaders*, it remains the most studied and least understood topic in all the social sciences. Like beauty, or love, we know it when we see it but cannot easily define or produce it on demand. Again, like beauty and love, the writings on it are fun, sexy even, with their pictures of heroes and stories that can be our private fantasies. To read MacGregor Burns, Maccoby, Alistair Mant, Warren Bennis, Cary Cooper or Peters and Waterman themselves is to escape into a private world of might-have-beens.

They may even do a disservice, these fun books, with their tales of heroes and their myths of the mighty, by suggesting that leadership is only for the new and the special. The significance of the new language is, I believe, that leadership has to be endemic in organizations, the fashion not the exception. Everyone with pretensions to be anyone must begin to think and act like a leader. Some will find it comes naturally and will blossom, some will not enjoy it at all, but unless you try, and are allowed to try, no one will ever know, for leadership is hard if not impossible to detect in embryo – it has to be seen in action to be recognized by oneself as much as by others.

So what is this mysterious thing and how does one acquire it? The studies agree on very little but what they do agree on is probably at the heart of things. It is this: 'A leader shapes and shares a vision which gives point to the work of others.' Would that it were as easy to do as to say! Think on these aspects of that short sentence:

— The vision must be different. A plan or a strategy which is a projection of the present or a replica of what everyone else is doing is not a vision. A vision has to 're-frame' the known scene, to re-conceptualize the obvious, connect the previously unconnected dream. Alistair Mant talks of the leader as 'builder' working with others towards a 'third corner', a goal. Those who are interested only in power or achievement for its own sake he calls 'raiders' or mere 'binary' people. MacGregor Burns talks of the 'transforming' leader as opposed to the mere 'transactional' one, the busy fixer.

— The vision must make sense to others. Ideally it should create the 'Aha Effect', which I described earlier, as when everyone says 'Aha – of course, now I see it', like wit perhaps – what often was thought but ne'er so well expressed. To make sense it must stretch people's imaginations but still be within the bounds of possibility. To give point to the work of others it must be related to their work and not to some grand design in which they feel they have no point. If 'vision' is too grand a word, try 'goal' or even 'manifesto'.

— The vision must be understandable. No one can communicate a vision that takes two pages to read, or is too full of numbers and jargon. It has to be a vision that sticks in the head. Metaphor and analogy can be keys because they provide us with vivid images with room for interpretation – low definition concepts as opposed to the more precise high definition words of engineering and management.

— The leader must live the vision. He, or she, must not only believe in it but must be seen to believe in it. It is tempting credulity to proclaim a crusade for the impoverished from a luxury apartment. Effective leaders, we are told, exude energy. Energy comes easily if you love your cause. Effective leaders, again, have integrity. Integrity, being true to yourself, comes naturally if you live for your vision. In other words, the vision cannot be something thought up in the drawing office, to be real it has to come from the deepest parts of you, from an inner system of belief. The total pragmatist cannot be a transforming leader.

— The leader must remember that it is the work of others. The vision remains a dream without that work of others. A leader with no followers is a voice in the wilderness. Leaders like to choose their teams but most inherit them and must then make them their own. Trust in others is repaid by trust from them. If it is to be *their* vision too, then their ideas should be heeded.

These six principles sound simple, obvious even, but in practice they are hard to deliver. Old-fashioned management is easier than the new leadership. Yet, if the new organizations are going to succeed, and they must succeed, our managers must think like leaders. If it happens, and in places it is happening, it will mark yet one more important discontinuity turned to advantage.

Horizontal tracking
How many leaders will one organization need? A lot, must be the answer, lots of them, all over the place and not only in the centre. Federal organizations are flat organizations and the cores of their parts will be four or five levels only.

The consequences are profound. Organizations used to look like a collection of ladders tied together at the top. A career for most people meant climbing the ladders. Success was rewarded by promotion to the next rung. Fast-moving careerists might expect to move up a rung every two years. There were some cross-over points and some general management jobs lower down, but on the whole the analogy holds for the larger organizations of Europe and the USA.

Ladder-thinking could reach bizarre extremes. I once visited an Indian organization which employed 20,000 people in a big shed in the middle of India making turbine generating equipment. The organization was suffering from bureaucratic arthritis. Nothing could be made to happen. Everyone seemed to have a power of veto over every decision. A quick look at the organization chart revealed that there were, on average, twenty rungs in each ladder in the organization, twenty levels of command. 'Well, you see,' they said, 'we are enormously taken with this British idea of an annual appraisal, but good appraisals need to be rewarded with promotion otherwise Indians lose face, therefore we have had to create all these opportunties for promotion within our factory.'

Federal organizations do not put 20,000 people in one shed. Wherever possible it will be less than 500 in each individual part, and the ladders will be short. In the core of the shamrock, as we noted in Chapter 4, success will not, cannot, mean promotion because the layers are not there. There is no god beyond the senior partner and he or she is likely to be in their forties.

What then does a career mean if it isn't always upwards? For some it will be more of the same only better. For others it will be more variety, a different job at the same level. The Japanese have a nice way of developing their high potential young people. They actually have a fast-track route for them, but instead of it being a vertical fast-track up through the organization, it is a horizontal fast-track, a succession of different jobs, real jobs with tough standards to be met, but all at the same level. The advantages are that not only does the young person get a wider view of the organization he or she gets a chance to test out their talents and skills in a wide variety of roles. Few excel at everything. Fortune favours the one who can early in life divine what they are good at. Japanese systems make it more likely that fortune will smile on the many not the few by giving them so many test beds for talents.

What works for the young in Japan can work for all ages everywhere. The horizontal fast-track can apply to seniors as well as to juniors. It is a Western notion that people's abilities and inclinations are formed in their middle to late teens, after which education and experience tend to drive them up one ladder and one ladder only. Too many people discover too late that they picked the wrong ladder. The functional organization, joined to a functional education system, can result in a one-start society. A flatter organization can offer opportunities at all ages to discover new abilities and new interests.

It is upside-down thinking again, of course; horizontal careers as a good thing. To work, it requires that the organization has faith in the ability of its people to learn and to go on learning; and believes, moreover, that learning is not linear, more of the same, but can be lateral and even discontinuous; that people, even in their forties and fifties, may have talents which even they are not aware of; that our past performance is not always the best guide to our future potential if we change our role.

Without such upside-down thinking organizations will find themselves with growing numbers of so-called 'plateaued' managers, managers who have run out of ladder and have nowhere else to go except out; organizations will spend more money and time than they want to on hiring new faces for new boxes; they will worry about the lack of motivation in some of their more senior executives, about the cultural disharmony that comes with the importing of too many new faces and about their inability to offer meaningful careers to their younger people.

Federalism is, in my view, a necessary development in the evolution of organizations. It allows individuals to work in organization villages with the advantages of big city facilities. Organizational cities no longer work unless they are broken down into villages. In their big city mode they cannot cope with the variety needed in their products, their processes and their people. On the other hand, the villages on their own have not the resources nor the imagination to grow. Some villages, of course, will be content to survive, happy in their niche, but global markets need global products and large confederations to make them or do them.

These organizational villages can also be geographical villages. Today, federalism makes it possible to bring the work to the people rather than the people to the work and to link them all together telephonically and electronically instead of in flesh and blood. In the end organizational federalism may well solve the housing problem in Britain.

It requires a little upside-down thinking, to be sure. At present, organizations in the South of Britain, and in the South of other countries too, are short of the workers and the skills they need. There are too many unemployed or underemployed in the North but they cannot afford to move house to the expensive South and, indeed, do not particularly want to. It is better to be poor in the place you know.

Instead of paying even higher salaries to attract them down, thus inflating house prices still further, organizations will increasingly see the wisdom of locating some of their work in the North. Once they realize that if they embrace federalism they do not *all* have to move North, the move will start to happen.

Nor will it just be from North to South. In the new organizations of the information society it is people who are the key assets, particularly the brainy people. Organizations always move close to their key assets or raw materials; when it was coal they went to the coalfields, now they will move to where their people want to live and their key people will often want to live near a university city and pleasant country, where there is good education to be had, good communications and a sense of space. More and more it will pay organizations to move their villages to the villages. Federalism allows them to do so and still be a city themselves.

Federalism is, however, about more than structure, as this chapter has sought to make plain. It involves a change in thinking about people and their capacities, about the way they can be asked to work and the way they are managed. They have in fact to be 'smart' as well as 'federal'. It is this requirement which the next chapter addresses.

6 The Triple I Organization

It was Wally Olins who summed it up for me. A large part of his work, and that of his successful company, involves helping organizations to discover and to express visually their strengths and their purposes. He is, therefore, in an excellent position to observe the way things are changing in organizations, and changing they are. 'Wealth in the past,' he observed, 'used to be based on the ownership of land, then, more recently on the capacity to make things. Increasingly, today, it is based on knowledge and on the ability to use that knowledge.'

The new formula for success, and for effectiveness, is $I^3 = AV$, where I stands for Intelligence, Information and Ideas, and AV means added value in cash or in kind. In a competitive information society brains on their own are not enough, they need good information to work with and ideas to build on if they are going to make value out of knowledge.

We are talking, of course, of the core of organizations, of the heart of the place. There will still be mundane jobs in these organizations; mail has to be opened, visitors looked after, offices cleaned, light bulbs replaced and meetings arranged. These things will never all be automated nor do they need budding genuises to do them. But unless the heart of the operation is a Triple I concern there will eventually be no added value to pay for the support services.

Triple I organizations are different. Not for them the organizational philosophies of the army, or the factory, or the bureacracies of government. They must look instead to some of the places where knowledge has always been key and brains more important than brawn.

'Increasingly,' I said at a conference of chief executives, 'your corporations will come to resemble universities or colleges.'

'Then God help us all,' one of them replied.

But I was serious, although I went on to agree that universities could with advantage get more like businesses.

Universities or colleges, my point was, are places where intelligent people are concerned with information and with ideas, the triple i. They use these three i's, in theory at least, to pursue truth in an atmosphere of learning.

The new organization, making added value out of knowledge, needs also to be obsessed with the pursuit of truth or, in business language, of quality. To that end the wise organization increasingly uses smart machines, with smart people to work with them. It is interesting to note how often, already, organizations talk of their 'intellectual property'. Once again, words signal the way things are going.

The wise organization also knows that their smart people are not to be easily defined as workers or as managers but as individuals, as specialists, as professionals or executives, or as leaders, (the older terms of manager and worker are dropping out of use), and that they and it need also to be obsessed with the pursuit of learning if they are going to keep up with the pace of change.

The wise organization realizes, too, that intelligent individuals can only be governed by consent and not by command, that obedience cannot be demanded and that a collegiate culture of colleagues and a shared understanding is the only way to make things happen. For intelligent, however, do not read intellectual. The words are quite different. 'He may be a great intellectual,' said my daughter of a friend, 'but intelligent he is not. He cannot run a bath, let alone a business, or even his life.'

The pursuit of quality, intelligent machines and intelligent people, a culture of individuals in search of learning and government by consent – these things hardly seem to add up to a revolution nor do they describe too many of our universities and colleges. Yet they are, as we shall see, more revolutionary concepts than they sound and if they were to be practised by more organizations then those organizations would be more truly like universities than the universities themselves.

Quality Is Truth

Quality for instance, has become the new watchword of many organizations. It is not another gimmick. For too long too many businesses were concerned with the fast buck, or the short-term bottom line of residual profit, or, more technically still, the medium-term earnings per share. Money was all. With that as your goal it made sense to treat people as costs to be minimized, to keep tight controls on everything which might cost money and to reduce as many operations as you could to a predictable routine. It works only if nothing ever changes (and so can be rigidly programmed), if people are unquestioningly obedient (and so can also be rigidly programmed), and if the cheapest is regarded as the best.

Four decades ago, inspired by two Americans, Juran and Deming, the Japanese began to think differently. In the long-term Deming argued, you stay competitive and in business by being the best there is, not necessarily the cheapest, by taking the customer seriously and giving him or her what they want and need. The product comes before the money. Quality he maintained, however, is only achieved if everyone believes in it, if everyone contributes to it and if everyone is always concerned first of all to improve their own quality at work. You get quality from quality people trusted to work positively for the good of the whole community. Eliminate mass inspection, said Deming, in what came to be his famous 'fourteen points', drive out fear, break down barriers, get rid of slogans and targets, encourage people to educate and develop themselves to work in teams, to think for themselves, and to believe that everything can be improved forever.

In a more competitive world organizations will only survive if they can guarantee quality in their goods or their services. Short-term profit at the expense of quality will lead to short-term lives. In that sense quality is, to my mind, the organizational equivalent of truth. Quality like truth will count, in the end. No one, and no organization, can live a lie for long. Hard to define, impossible to legislate for, quality like truth is an attitude of mind. It is an attitude which is now at last beginning to infect our organizations. Profit is increasingly recognized as what it always should have been, a means and not an end in itself. It is ironic that it is only now that Deming, in his eighties, has become the Western World's favourite guru, forty years after he started talking this sort of language to the Japanese, who listened and changed.

Quality, however, does not come easily. It needs the right equipment, the right people and the right environment. The effective organization, today, is learning fast to come to terms with the new machines, the new people it needs and with the new culture of consent. It is a new kind of organization in style and temperament, not an easy one to manage or to lead but one which will be increasingly necessary in the competitive knowledge-based world of the future. I call it the Triple I organization only to underline its difference from the organizations we used to know and, very occasionally, to love, but organizations in which most people were not paid to think but to do. In the Triple I organization everyone is paid to think *and* to do, including the machines. It makes a difference, a huge difference, to the way you run the place.

The Intelligent Machines

It is the age of the smart machine. Computers have revolutionized the work of organizations and will go on doing so. One person and a robot can weld a car. No person and a robot can paint it. I went around a sugar refinery worked, in rather unpleasant conditions, in Belgium, by 270 people. One year later I went again. This time it was run by shifts of five people in a carpeted control room with maintenance teams on call.

These things we know are happening. We take others in our stride; the airline can store away our reservations and our dietary requirements and produce them at the touch of a key, it can let us know, instantly, the possibility of any variations to our travel plans and their cost at the touch of a few other keys; we know that the check-out decks at the supermarket already automatically adjust the stock levels and will soon debit our bank accounts; we expect the telephone directory in every country to be computerized and the personnel records of major companies to be accessible via keyboards; we happily pull our cash out of holes in the wall; we know that sophisticated executives can review their spreadsheets on their desk-top terminals; we read of robots re-stacking the shelves in Japanese supermarkets; we ride, perhaps, in driverless trains at airports or in Lille in Northern France (and soon, everywhere?); we hear of fifth generation computers which can think for themselves (in a way), and of sixth generation ones with living cells. Technology, as such, holds few fears for most people. It is all, or it should be, in pursuit of better quality.

Smart machines, however, need smart people to work with them, or, sometimes, very dumb people. This book was written at the time when an American warship made a tragic error and shot down an Iranian passenger airline in the Gulf thinking it to be a fighter on the attack. The enquiry made it clear that the computers tracking the plane had made no mistake, but that the relatively young specialists watching the screens in the heat of a battle had misinterpreted the computers' cues. Perhaps, some said then, the smart computer should be allowed to make its own fire or not fire decisions; it might make them better on its own.

Shoshana Zuboff in her book *In the Age of the Smart Machine* describes the conversation in a large pulp mill in North America after a computer-controlled production system had been introduced: 'In fifteen years' time,' the workers said, 'there will be nothing for the workers to do. The technology will be so good it will operate itself. You will just sit there behind a desk running two or three areas of the mill yourself and get bored.'

In fact, as she goes on to demonstrate, it did not turn out like that. Once the workers got used, and it took some time, to running the mill by remote control, by reading the screens rather than by feeling the pipes and squashing the pulp, every small deviation from the norm became a mini-puzzle. The operators would gather round and test out options and possibilities until they found the cause and could put it right. As one operator said, 'Things occur to me now that would never have occurred to me before. With all this information in front of me, I begin to think about how to do the job better. And, being freed from all that manual activity, you really have time to look at things, to think about them, and to anticipate.' Or, as the plant managers said, 'We are depending on the technology to educate our people in abstract thinking ... you can no longer make a decision just based on local data ... you have to derive your decision from the inter-relationships among the variables'; you have to start thinking.

On the other hand, I have stood and watched a man watching a machine count out pills and put them in bottles – watching just in case the machine went bonkers, in which case he pressed a red button, stopped it and called for help.

Or, as one of the pulp workers said, 'Sometimes ... I realize that we stare at the screen even when it has gone down. You get in the habit and you just keep staring even if there is nothing there.'

Smart machines can reduce humans to attendant watchdogs, but smart organizations see the computers and their machines as aides to clever people. To quote one of Shoshana Zuboff's managers again, 'We never used to expect them to understand how the plant works, just to operate it. But now if they don't know the theory behind how the plant works, how can we expect them to understand all of the variables in the new computer system and how these variables interact?'

Zuboff likes to distinguish between *automating* and *informating*. Automating tends to concentrate on the smart machine and to cut out or reduce people. Informating organizations also use smart machines but in interaction with smart people. In the short-term automating pays off, but informating wins in the longer term because the organization's thinking or 'intellective' capacity has been increased. In this vision the organization is full of colleagues and co-learners, its thinking skill becomes its most precious resource and the challenge of keeping that skill upgraded the major task of the organization. It really has to be a sort of corporate university.

The hard facts of economic life mean that organizations will:

— Increasingly have to invest in smart machines if they want to be as effective as they used to be.
— Increasingly want to use skilled and thinking people to use those machines in order to get the most out of them.
— Need to pay those people more and therefore, if they can, to have fewer of them.

It all puts pressure on the core, a pressure which could be

summed up by the new equation of half the people, paid twice as much, working three times as effectively, an equation which, once you start believing it, has a built-in momentum. To get that three times improvement the smart organization will equip their people with all the technological aids they need, be it car telephones or computers in their homes or audio-printers which translate the spoken word into typescript on the screen, or expert systems which do the first analysis. It will also expect those people to be smart, to be dedicated to their work (none of the leisure age here), and to be prepared to invest enough time and energy to keep ahead of the game, to go on learning, in other words, in order that they can go on thinking.

The Intelligent People

The new organizations need new people to run them, people with new skills, new capacities and different career patterns. More of them, interestingly, are likely to be women, not from any sudden enthusiasm for equality between the sexes, but because organizations will increasingly find that there will not be enough of the skills and the capacities they need if they exclude from their recruitment half of the population.

I was being shown round one of Japan's new businesses – a women's fashion house, designing, making and marketing women's fashions worldwide, although, as it turned out, the actual making was now done in Taiwan (Japan, too, is susceptible to the price of labour). I noticed on my tour that there was an unusually high percentage of women in the offices and, particularly, in the design rooms; nor were they wearing the kind of air hostess uniforms which women in Japanese offices customarily wear. 'Are they allowed to work in jeans and tee-shirts?' I asked. My guide shook his head, scornfully almost. 'They should not,' he said, 'it is not customary, but they are our designers, we need their talent, we have to let them dress as they please.' As in Japan, that bastion of the male executive, so it will be elsewhere.

In Britain it is estimated that 800,000 additional women will join organizations in the next eight years – almost equivalent to the total net increase in the working population. Women, in other words, are poised to take up any extra jobs that are going, plus some that were not going. These will not all be the part-time counter assistants in the supermarkets. Many of them will be the well-educated, qualified women re-entering the workforce.

Organizations will be squeezed, as we have seen, by the need for all the intelligent, qualified people they can get and by the shortage of well-educated, well-qualified youngsters. They will be forced to look to less convenient sources of intelligent people. Some have suggested that the intellectual élite of Africa and China and India will be lured to the West. More obviously, however, organizations will turn first to the pool of talent on their doorstep, the married women with young families.

These women, however, as even the Japanese discovered, will not be men in skirts. They will want proper recognition of their need to raise a family while they are working. Crèches at the office are not the whole answer, although they will be a standard facility by the end of the century. A more flexible way of working is required, one which allows the woman to be at home when she has to be at home, which accepts that full-time attendance in an office is not essential for all types of work, which allows people to work in their own ways as long as the work is done on time and to standard.

The shamrock organization and the federal organization, telecommuting and work centres, are made-to-measure for the working mother. The necessity for organizations to woo more working mothers into their cores will only increase the pressures to move towards these sorts of organizations. In time, then, it will be working fathers as well as working mothers who will be living these more flexible working lives.

In my British paper today there is a picture of the Chalk family, a youngish couple with three small children. The father works from home in the country designing books and educational kits. 'There is no need, today,' he says, 'to work in cities. I like the space and the freedom of the countryside.' His wife, now that the children are starting to go to school, would like to return to the nursing she did when first she was married. Unfortunately, she says, the hours they demand do not permit it. 'Hospitals,' she says, 'have to offer me more flexible work so that I can choose the hours I work to fit in with my family.' They will, Mrs Chalk, they will – because they will have to if they want people with your skills.

The most important difference, however, in the Triple I organizations is the growing realization that everyone in the core will have to be a manager while at the same time no one can afford to be *only* a manager. Smaller numbers in the core require more flexibility and more responsibility. Everyone will increasingly be expected not only to be good at something, to have their own professional or technical expertise, but will also very rapidly acquire responsibility for money, people or projects, or all three, a managerial task, in other words. The days of British India thinking are over, the kind of thinking which boasted in the fact that 2,500 Britons ran India, with the help of technicians, foremen and workers. It was the kind of thinking that led to 'management cadres', management trainees and 'fast-tracks' to the top, for a selected few. I was once one such management trainee, and management was the only role ever expected of me; others would be the experts and the supervisors. It was a business equivalent of British India and the officer class. In future, *everyone* in the core will be an officer and will be expected to be both competent and in command.

In the newer, more hi-tech, organizations in the USA the word 'manager' has begun to disappear. People are not 'managers', they are 'team leaders', 'project heads', 'co-ordinators' or, more generally, 'executives'. They attend *executive* development programmes even though the topic is still that of management. The language is significant, once again signalling a change of attitude and a new way of looking at the world. Managers, after all, imply someone to be managed, they suggest a stratified society. An organization could not logically be staffed only by managers, but it could by executives.

The implications of this shift in thinking are considerable. Management ceases to be a definition of a status, of a class within an organization, but an *activity*, an activity which can be defined, and its skills taught, learnt and developed. The re-definition gives management a professional basis, something which, in Britain at least, it has never had. Management, after all, was held by the British to be akin to parenting, a role of great importance for which no training, preparation or qualification was required; the implication being that experience is the only possible teacher and character the only possible qualification. To study management, when it was seen as a definition of a status, was somehow to suggest that one was unworthy of that status, while 'to manage' as an activity remained a word with a very lowly pedigree in English, meaning colloquially to cope or to contrive, as when one says to one's friend 'did you manage all right today' or 'did you manage to get it working'.

The new respectability

In 1987 two reports castigated Britain's preparation and development of her managers in comparison with other leading industrial nations. The hangover of management as a class was still there. Some of the discrepancies were telling:

— In Japan and the USA some 85 per cent of top managers had degrees whilst the only available comparative figure in Britain was 24 per cent.

— Britain graduated only 1,200 MBAs in 1987 compared with 70,000 in the USA.

— Nearly half of America's 300 biggest companies provided five days off the job training each year for their managers. The comparable figure in Britain (with some noticeable exceptions) was closer to one.

— Most would-be managers in West Germany do not join their firm until the age of 27 after periods in an apprenticeship, in military service and in 6-year university degrees, whereas the well-educated Britisher joins at 22.

The two reports only confirmed what was long suspected, that British managers were amateurs, sometimes talented amateurs, by comparison with other managers in other countries. The new organizations needed something better.

The reports found ready listeners both among leaders of business and among the young. There was an explosion of interest in MBA degrees, a rush by organizations to link their development plans to some form of qualification and a general readiness to accept that at least the technical knowledge and skills of management, 'business education' as the reports termed it, could be taught and should be taught at an early age even if the human and conceptual skills needed to be honed by experience. The new activity was an outward and visible sign that management was increasingly seen to be the name for an activity and not a class of people. Another discontinuity had occurred even if not everyone perceived it this way at first.

It cannot stop, however, with business education and early qualifications. If executives in every part of the organization, any organization, are to be truly professional they must continue to build on that early base of understanding. Life for a manager, say the Japanese, should be a continual process of self-enlightenment, which is their way of saying that study and learning should never stop. In Japanese organizations, in fact, the seniors spend *more* time on thinking and study than their juniors, reading books and articles; meeting with experts; going on study tours to find out how their competitors work; sitting with their subordinates, *listening* to them not talking at them.

The Japanese are more conscious than most that the other two skills of management, as defined long ago by Professor Katz of Harvard, the human skills and the conceptual skills, are as important as the technical skills. Neither of these two skills can be taught in the classroom, although they can be discussed and debated there; both skills need to be developed by practice, improved by comment, sketched by example; they have to be worked at, for they do not come easily to most people or without effort.

The point about the new organizations is that everyone in the core will increasingly be expected to have not only the expertise appropriate to his or her particular role but will also be required to know and understand business, to have the technical skills of analysis *and* the human skills *and* the conceptual skills and to keep them up to date. Intelligence, for the manager, has three dimensions. The Japanese use mentors to make sure it happens, at least at the beginning. The Americans rely on a philosophy of individual initiative and corporate support which suits their more individualistic culture. The properly intelligent manager, they believe, will develop himself or herself. The British have hitherto relied on a Darwinian belief that the best will come through in the end, but that belief is a wasteful and a cruel philosophy in a world where good jobs are precious and talent rare. The threefold intelligence which the new organizations need in all their people does not just happen. The seeds of intelligence may have to be there in the beginning, at the recruitment stage, but those seeds will need a climate in which to germinate and careful husbandry to let them grow. The intelligent organization has to be a learning organization, at every level.

America's big corporations talk of five days off-the-job training for every executive every year. One British bank is trying to gear up its middle managers to run the kind of federal organization outlined in Chapter 5, and is currently requiring them to spend nine weeks every year on study courses. That is 20 per cent of their working time. Perhaps it should not all be spent on courses, but to expect the intelligent executive to devote one fifth (one day a week) of his or her time preparing themselves for a different and a better future would not be unreasonable in new organizations. It has, after all, long been a tradition of universities that one day a week should be reserved by their faculty for study and research. If all organizations are going to be universities of a sort, pursuing truth in their own fields, running a learning culture, growing new knowledge and new people, then 20 per cent of time devoted to these ends would not be a wasted investment.

The new careers

The new organization will seek to bind its core executives to itself for as long as it thinks it needs them. The new executives, however, will be less ready to be tied, particularly if they have some sort of qualification as a passport. It is rather like the paradox of tenure in universities; those who deserve tenure don't need it and those who need it don't deserve it. In fact, as management becomes more professional, with more professional-type qualifications, the executives will begin to think of their careers as professional careers, as a sequence of jobs which may or may not be in the same organization. Companies, too, will be reluctant to guarantee careers for life to everyone, even in the core. More contracts will be for fixed periods of years, more appointments will be tied to particular roles or jobs with no guarantee of further promotion. The appointments pages of the papers already reflect this trend: the advertisements offer a job more often than they promise a career.

To the younger new recruit a career is still promised, but the days when the booklet outlining the pension scheme arrives with the letter of appointment are now rare. Whatever they may say, neither the young applicant nor the employer today believe that the appointment is forever. Indeed, fewer and fewer organizations now promise to manage your career; instead they promise opportunities along with help to develop your capabilities to take up some of those opportunities. No longer is there the feeling that somewhere someone is thinking about your future, watching your development, planning your next steps. It probably always was an illusion, now few even pretend. It is a case of 'individual initiative and corporate support', as the Americans describe it.

This change has partly been forced on organizations by the harsher realities of competition. No longer is it possible to carry as passengers those who have failed to live up to their earlier promise or to keep people in jobs which could be done as well by others younger and, usually, cheaper. Partly, however, organizations have found out, too late, that people who have been with the organization for thirty continuous years are not always best able to cope with increasing discontinuity.

I have met too many organizations who have been religiously committed to a policy of growing their own, even recruiting them straight from school at age 15 or 16, only to end up 30 years later with a severe case of group-think at the top, with people who have only known one way of doing things, one set of people, one philosophy; who distrust outsiders, dislike conflict and expect continuity. 'Group-think', as we know from studies of historical events, most famously the 'Bay of Pigs' fiasco early in Kennedy's presidency, comes about when well-meaning people become too close and cohesive to challenge assumptions, to check out facts, to explore new options or to risk too much argument. It is often more important to agree together than to get it right. In conditions of continuity group-think in organizations made for a strong corporate culture, a sense of family, tradition and solidarity. In conditions of discontinuity it leads to falling profits, to merger or takeover, to the end of the cosy club.

Discontinuous change and the new professionalism have therefore combined to spell the end of the corporate career for all but a few. The new executive must look out for himself or herself, remembering that in this new world you are only as good as your current job – the future is not guaranteed. Education in those circumstances becomes an investment, wide experience an asset provided that it is wide and not shallow, and company loyalty something that has to be earned by the company from the individual not demanded of him or her.

Careers will therefore become more variegated. In larger companies there will still be opportunity for variety and advancement, but as these companies get more federal more decisions will be left to the separate parts with the centre left with a brokerage and counselling role. It will increasingly be the individual's responsibility to make sure that the opportunities on offer add up to a sensible career path.

Some will want to interleave their careers with periods of study. We may see an increasing number of formal sabbatical opportunities within universities and business schools to take advantage of this new market. Others, particularly but not only women, will want to interleave the career with periods of raising a family although they might be well-advised to combine this with some form of part-time or distance learning. Some will want intense and early careers allowing them the possibility of a second kind of life before they get too old to do it well. Some will use the organization as a training ground and then, in their thirties, become more independent, perhaps as entrepreneur, perhaps as consultant or professional in the contractual fringe. Most will find that their careers in the organization will in any case begin to peter out in their early or mid fifties when there will still be twenty years at least of active life ahead.

The new executives should be the fortunate ones in the new society. They should have the money and the skills to fill up the 50,000 hours of work beyond the job. They need, however, to prepare themselves for it, to realize that it is going to happen one day, and to them, to look change in the face and see it for what it is – an opportunity as well as a challenge.

One organization has recently dedicated most of its corporate advertising to proclaiming how much time and money it now invests in the education of its executives. It cannot guarantee that it will get a direct return from those who profit from this investment, for some of them will leave for richer pastures and no contract can force them to stay unwillingly, but the quality of its recruits at all levels has increased dramatically. It is a far-sighted response to the new conditions and to the growth of the intelligent organization. It is a response that other organizations need to watch.

The Culture Of Consent

Intelligent people prefer to agree rather than to obey.

In despair at the way its programmes were organized, the Business School in one university recruited as the Director of Programmes a successful businessman, who had made a modest fortune in his own business and wanted to move on to a new career. 'I will soon put some order into this place,' he thought, and said. He wrote memoranda to the academics laying down new procedures. No one read the memoranda. He called a meeting. No one came. In frustration, he asked for an explanation.

'These are independent individuals,' he was told, 'you cannot command them to come to a meeting at your convenience; you have to negotiate a time and place convenient to all of them; you had better send round a list with possible alternatives.' He did and they came, or most of them. He explained the new procedures which, he said, would be introduced next month. At that point one of the older faculty members said, gently,

'Bill, in this kind of institution you cannot *tell* us to do anything, you can only *ask* us and try to persuade us to agree.'

'Well then,' Bill said, 'let me ask you what you think we should do to put some sense into this place.'

'No, Bill,' the elder replied, 'that's what we hired *you* for, to come up with those sort of ideas. But they will only work if we agree with them. If we don't, why then you will have to persuade us or come up with some better ideas. This is, you see, an organization of consent, not of command.'

It is, however, not just because they are intelligent individuals that they cannot be commanded. There is often no one to command them. The new organization, as we have seen, will be a flat organization. Like universities they will often have no more than four layers of executives in any operation. People and groups will have large do'nuts with big areas of discretion. They will be judged increasingly by results not by the methods which they use. Everyone will have their own psychological territory or organizational space, territory which is theirs and which cannot be entered on without permission.

A university lecturer is judged on performance. He or she is in charge of their classroom or seminar. Other colleagues enter only by permission. So it will be with the new organizations.

Nor is it just the flatness of the structures. The new

intelligent machines do not respect herarchical lines of command. They can pass information to whoever needs it, in real time. Intelligent organizations do not ripple their new information systems by pushing the stuff up the ladders and then down again; they encourage the information to go straight to where it is useful. Computers jump organizational barriers and put each group or individual in effective control of their own do'nut.

Mrs Fields' Cookies, in the USA, shows how it is done at its most obvious. Each of the 600 Mrs Fields cookie stores is equipped with a cheap IBM-compatible computer. Linked up with the big computers in the organization's centre in Utah the machines:

(a) plan production. Each shop bakes its own cookies according to a schedule worked out by the computer taking into account past statistics, the weather and how many cookies have been sold in the past hour.

(b) maintain stocks. The computer tells the manager when to re-order.

(c) communicate with top managers. The computer monitors the progress of shop managers towards performance bonuses and runs an electronic mail service.

(d) carry out employee training. The computer drills employees in the knowledge needed for promotion.

(e) organize the accounting and consolidation. The computer keeps track of costs, profits and payroll and analyses them continuously for the local managers.

As a result, with 600 stores, there are only 130 people in headquarters in Park City, Utah, few to command the store managers and not much to tell them that they do not already know.

The Chief Executive of Norsk Data in Norway sums it up, 'Like Japan, we use the consensus method, when the idea is to make the decisions at the appropriate level, which is not always at the top, nor at the bottom, but at the level where the most knowledge is available and where the people are most effective. It means that we must have managers who accept that they cannot force their opinions upon their subordinates. They have to fight like everybody else with their ideas and the best ideas will win, and not necessarily the ones which come from the top or the bottom.

Tom Peters, who co-authored *In Search of Excellence*, described a visit to Johnsville Foods. A typical Johnsville work team, he says:

(a) does its own recruiting, hiring, personnel evaluation and firing;

(b) regularly acquires new skills and then conducts training for everyone;

(c) formulates and tracks its own budgets;

(d) makes capital-investment proposals as needed (with all the necessary staff-work);

(e) is responsible for all quality control, inspection and subsequent trouble-shooting;

(f) suggests and then develops prototypes of possible new products, processes and even business;

(g) works on the improvement of everything, all the time;

(h) develops its own detailed standards for productivity, quality and improvement and makes them tough standards.

This does not, says Peters, leave much for management to do, but then there is not much management, or hierarchy, at Johnsonville.

The point is that you cannot run this sort of organization or these sort of people by command. For one thing the people on the job often have more information than the would-be commander, for another their responsibility for the task is so complete that they are not going to take anyone else's word for something, they need to be convinced. Intelligent organizations have to be run by persuasion and by consent. It is hard work, and frustrating, particularly when the persuasion does not work and the consent is not forthcoming. Bill gave up the Business School in despair and went off to look after a forest, with only the trees to organize.

It is this type of organization which has given rise to what has been called the post-heroic leader. Whereas the heroic manager of the past knew all, could do all and could solve every problem, the post-heroic manager asks how every problem can be solved in a way that develops other people's capacity to handle it. It is not virtuous to do it this way, it is essential. These organizations do not work if it is left to one person. *Everyone* has to be capable or nothing happens. The post-heroic leader lives vicariously, getting kicks out of other people's successes – as old-fashioned teachers have always done.

Let us make no mistake: the cultures of consent are not easy to run, or to work in. Authority in these organizations does not come automatically with the title; it has to be earned. But the authority you need is not based on being able to do the job better yourself but on your ability to help others do the job better, by developing their skills, by liaising with the rest of the organization, by organizing their work more efficiently, by helping them to make the most of their resources, by continual encouragement and example. The job of the leader is a mixture between those of a teacher, a consultant and a trouble-shooter. Technical, human and conceptual skills, the three faces of intelligence, are all required. Some might say it is not a job for normal mortals. It isn't, unless they have grown up with it, have been trained and developed for it, then it can be a most exciting and challenging way to work. As one pulp mill worker said to Shoshana Zuboff, 'If you don't let people grow and develop and make more decisions it's a waste of human life ... Using the technology to its full potential means using the man to his full potential.' That must be good, mustn't it?

Not everyone may think so. It is often easier to be told what to do than to decide for yourself. Choice means responsibility – for failure as well as success. Full potential means full commitment. Some have other things to do. And what, some say, if my full potential is less than is required; what then? The organization of consent puts a premium on competence. There is no place for the incompetent – there are few hiding places in these organizations. Do not look to the new intelligent organizations with their intelligent machines and their cultures of consent for days of gossipy coffee breaks or for boring but untaxing jobs. The culture of consent is not, as the British would say, going to be everyone's cup of tea unless they are educated and prepared for it. There lies the challenge for our society.

Part Three: Living

Introduction

Organizations will never be the same again. That was the message of the first part of this book. It might even have been entitled 'The withering of the corporation' now that it looks as if less than one quarter of the population will have full-time jobs inside any organization.

Does it matter if organizations change or wither? Only to those who work in them, we might think. But here we'd be wrong. When work moves outside the organization, as it is doing, it affects all of us who are on the outside, the great majority. 'What do you do?' no longer means 'What is your job?' but 'How do you occupy your time?' Work has changed its meaning and its pattern. That affects our sense of identity, our families and our roles within those families; our whole way of life is changed, sometimes upside-down.

Will there then be one world and one set of rules for the intelligent and qualified people in the core of the organization and another for those on the edge or on the outside? Even those in the core will be outside for the last third of their lives. When society can no longer assume that we all have a paid job for most of our lives the old recipes for dealing with the small bits at the end (pensions) and the small bits missing (unemployment benefit) become irrelevant. The whole system of money to live on, who gets it and how they get it, needs re-thinking. Discontinuous change requires upside-down thinking by the state.

When education becomes an essential investment, whether as a passport to a core job or as a route to acquiring a saleable skill on the outside, then to ration it is absurd. It is equally absurd to try to shove it all in at the beginning of life, or to think that it can all happen in classrooms, or to ration it later on to those who were cleverest at 18 years of age, or to think that brain skills are the only skills that matter, just because a precious minority need them. A new world of work requires upside-down thinking in education.

Things need to change in the world around us if we are to make the most of the new possibilities, if we are not to keep on trying to use yesterday's answers to deal with the quite different problems of tomorrow. But we also need to change ourselves. A longer life will mean a different life. Success and achievement will have other faces than the ones they wear now. We shall describe ourselves in different ways, live in different ways, have new values and priorities. If we do not, then our children and their children will. Changing has to become a part of our life. We know something about the process of changing, what helps it and what hinders it, how to make it a plus and not a minus, more like learning than losing.

A World To Worry About

If most jobs for the next generation are only going to occupy 50,000 hours (or the equivalent of 25 years) instead of 100,000 hours, there is going to be a lot of space for all of us, sometime, outside the formal jobs, especially since we are all going to live longer. This compression of the job is going to happen, is already happening, *not* because of some miraculous rationing system but because organizations everywhere are learning how to make do with smaller bits of our time. Organizations could once wallow in our time, waste it even, when it was cheap or when everyone around them wasted it as well. A more competitive world and more expensive people demands a more careful use of time. The new technology and new types of organization make it possible to be more careful. Half the people paid double, working twice as hard and producing three times as much, has to be good sense.

Good sense, indeed, but the immediate results could be bizarre, if we are not thoughtful enough in time enough. Half the people working twice as hard while the other half have not enough to do is a worrying prospect. The new rich will not have the time or the energy to enjoy their riches; the leisured class will be those at the bottom of the heap rather than those at the top. An upside-down world.

It is worrying from many points of view. It could be a society obsessed with wealth creation with too little regard to the way that wealth is either spent or distributed. In the end, all societies are remembered more for the way they spend their wealth, than for how they made it. The great civilizations of the past are remembered today for what they did with their wealth, for the monuments they left behind them, for their great buildings, major public works, great art or great conquests, for great education or great social reforms. The pursuit of efficiency and effectiveness in our organizations has got to be a means to something even greater, but if those with the wealth have no time or no thought for its proper spending then we could end up with a society preoccupied only with getting and never with giving or creating.

It could also be a new servant society, with a whole class of people cooking, gardening, driving and maintaining for the busy rich. They might call themselves mini-businesses but their dependency on their new masters is no less because they are now called clients instead of masters. Indeed, because these new servants will be independent and not employees there will be no obligation on the part of the new masters to take any care for their future.

It could become a very divided society; a privileged exclusive world inside the organization for some and a more perilous, exploited and lonely life outside for most; a world in which, if it were dominated by the organization, the educated middle-class professional would have it good and the less-educated would be condemned to be forever the outsider.

Instead of getting more flexible, organizations could react to the shortage of qualified people by becoming *less* flexible, locking in their chosen few with big salaries and bonuses and turning their backs on the freelance or the part-time mother. It would be expensive and, ultimately therefore, dangerous but it would be easier and so may, in the short-term, be more tempting. Such a strategy would only increase the differences between the insiders and the outsiders for a time. The organizations which adapt do best but not all organizations adapt.

It could be a world in which to be old was to be useless because you were not needed by the organization, and old might come to mean over 50. Rich but useless is only marginally better than being poor and useless, particularly if the transition has been from 110 per cent involvement to zero over one weekend.

The divided society could be a mutually envious society, one in which the poor but leisured resent the rich and busy, while the rich and busy resent the drain on their incomes needed to support the new leisured class who have the time they say that they would like to have but not the money.

Maureen Duffy in her book Gor-Saga, a science fiction novel about genetic experimentation, sets the story in a Britain divided between the professional workers, all living in smart urban ghettoes with their own entry controls and pass-cards and working in campus-like offices and laboratories surrounded by high wire fences, and the rest, the 'nons' who, supported by the state, exist in a dreary monotone world of controls and regulations, with no-go areas in the cities and the countryside where guerilla groups hold sway.

I thought it was all fiction until I drove down to dinner one night in the rhododendron belt in Surrey. On turning into the private estate where my hosts lived I found my way barred by a gate. I had to identify myself before I was allowed in. At dinner, later on, discussing possible futures the lady on my right said, 'Of course, the world will inevitably be divided into alphas and gammas and you and I,' she said, politely including me amongst the alphas, 'must be prepared to pay for the gammas to have their fortnight each year on the Costa Brava.' Perhaps, I reflected, driving home, the world of science fiction may not be so fictional after all.

This divided society, this monotone world dedicated to efficiency, this world made for the professional class to dominate, will happen only if we allow the organization to dominate our lives, if all meaning, all status and all money, continue to stem from the 'job', if the 50,000 hours become the only hours that matter, if the first half of this book is the only half which really counts.

Organizations, good organizations, effective organizations, are essential. Jobs, reduced perhaps to 50,000 hours or 25 years, are important to people and to society. The re-shaped organization could, however, enslave us or free us. We shall miss a great opportunity if we do not look beyond the formal organization and beyond the 50,000 hours. Now, for the first time in the human experience, we have a chance to shape our work to suit the way we live instead of our lives to fit our work. We would be mad to miss the chance.

A World That Might Be

Shaping work to suit our lives means, first of all, taking more of the job outside the organization, so that the job is more in our control. That, as we have seen, is already happening. It is still unusual. It is more difficult for the organization to manage the contractual fringe, the independents. It is often a strange experience for the individual. Somehow we have grown used to the fact that organizations should have their own homes. People often like, it seems, to live in two places at once, the office and the family, even if it is not strictly necessary. One small business, exclusively concerned with telephone selling, still insists that the telephone sellers come in to the office to do their telephoning. They happily agree. It is, after all, what everyone does. The cost, however, of all that office space, of the time for coffee and for gossiping, of the inconvenience of the absentees, is making the bosses think again.

The world of work was not always so separate. I grew up in rural Ireland where organizations with their own homes hardly existed other than the local bank and the mill. I hardly knew anyone, as I recall, who went out to work. They lived above the shop they owned, beside the school they taught in, on their farm, above their surgery, next door to their church if they were a priest, or in the same house as their office if a solicitor. Work and life were intertwined. There was one life, not two; one community for each, not two. They were their own men and their own women, not someone else's role occupants. Villages then were places where people lived not just slept at night or relaxed on Sunday.

There will be more like them again. By some estimates one quarter of the working population will be working from home by the end of the century. *From* home is different from *at* home. The home is the base not the prison. We can leave it. There will be organizational work clubs, work centres, meeting rooms and conference centres. We shall not be confined to our terminal in our little back room; there will be people to meet, places to go to, team projects and group assignments. I work from home myself. I go out from it nearly every day, but almost always to a different place. It is not a lonely life.

By taking the job, physically, outside the organization we make it more our own. We have more control over when and how we do it. If we go one step farther and take it contractually outside the organization, becoming in some way self-employed, we make it even more our own. The organization has retreated. It is less dominant, more a helper now than an owner. Jobs do not necessarily belong in organizations any more. It is, when one thinks about it, a significant discontinuity, a change which makes a difference.

It will happen because it will be more economical for the organization. It is therefore, in my view, inevitable. It is up to us to turn the inevitable into an opportunity by seizing the chance to shape our work to suit the way we want to live instead of always living to fit in with our work. It is not always easy. Suddenly we have choice and choice requires decisions. Do you get up now or linger one hour longer in bed? It is a lovely day; should you or should you not take the afternoon off? Do you or do you not labour late into the night to make that piece of work even better still, because there is no one to tell you that it is already good enough? Can one ever dare to take a holiday?

With choice always comes responsibility. The individual gets more freedom but can choose to abuse that freedom by poor quality work, by cheating or by laziness. The organization gets more flexibility but can abuse that flexibility by exploiting the outsider, by tightening its conditions and reducing the rewards. If this world outside the organization is going to be a better world everyone must be conscious of their responsibility as well as of their choices. They may not. That is always the risk in the opportunity and why it is still only a world that might be.

Taking more jobs outside the organization is one part of the opportunity. To take more of our life outside the organization is the other part. It is going to happen, whether we wish it to or not because we are, as I have demonstrated, in the process of splitting the lifetime job in half. Where our fathers thought it normal to spend 100,000 hours, or nearly 50 years, in their organization our children will spend only half of that, whether they cram it into 25 years or spread it out more thinly.

We are taking away 50,000 hours of the job. What will happen in those hours? That is our challenge, and our opportunity. To spend them lying on the beach or sitting in front of endless television serials is one option. Few will take it, partly because they will not be able to afford it, mainly because they will not want it. Endless, mindless leisure has other names – unemployment or imprisonment. Leisure as recreation only makes sense when it is the other side of work, when it is re-creation for more work. Work I am sure, is what we will want to do, work re-discovered, work re-defined to mean more than selling your time to someone else, work that is more in tune with the rest of life, work that is more personal, more creative, more fun than most jobs can ever be.

Those unused 50,000 hours can be our opportunity to discover the missing bits of ourselves, to explore new talents, to add variety to ordinary weeks, to meet new people and to learn new skills. Those unusual hours can add up to a huge new resource for society rather than a pile of unwanted people *if* we start thinking positively, if we find a way to pay for it all, and if, first of all, we start redefining 'work' so that it no longer means only a job. It is not the devil who finds work for idle hands to do, it is our own human instincts which make us want to contribute to our world, to be useful and to matter in some way to other people; to have a reason to get up in the morning.

Put that way, work is the purpose of life, it also gives us a pattern or structure for our days and a chance to meet new people. Purpose, pattern and people, the three Ps at the heart of life. It is odd, then, and sad too, that work has had such a bad press in recent times so that people can even talk of a world without work as some sort of paradise.

It happened, that bad press, because work came to mean only the 'job', and too many jobs were full of toil for others with little sense of mattering, and not much obvious purpose even if the organization, intricate as it is, becomes our great opportunity to put work back into the heart of life. It needs a bit of upside-down thinking to re-invent work, to make it, perhaps, the best of the four-letter words.

7 Portfolios

The Work Portfolio

To re-invent work in its fullest sense we need another
word. 'Portfolio' might be that word. It is not, of course, a
new word. There are artists' portfolios, architects' portfolios, share portfolios. A portfolio is a collection of different
items, but a collection which has a theme to it. The whole is
greater than the parts. A share portfolio has balance to it,
mixing risk and security, income and long-term gain in
proper proportions, an artist's portfolio shows how one
talent has more than one way of displaying itself.

A work portfolio is a way of describing how the different
bits of work in our life fit together to form a balanced whole.
'Flat people' as E.M. Forster called them, were those who
had only one dimension to their lives. He preferred rounded
people. I would now call them portfolio people, the sort of
people who, when you ask them what they do, reply, 'It will
take a while to tell you it all, which bit would you like?'
Sooner or later, thanks to the re-shaping of the organization we shall all be portfolio people. It is good news.

The categories of the portfolio
There are five main categories of work for the portfolio:
wage work and **fee work**, which are both forms of **paid
work**; **homework, gift work** and **study work**, which are all
free work.

The definitions and the differences are obvious but
important – the most important being the difference

between paid work and free work. It is free work which has been the missing part of the portfolio in recent times.

Wage (or salary) work represents money paid for time given. **Fee work** is money paid for results delivered. Employees do wage work; professionals, craftspeople and freelancers do fee work. Fee work is increasing as jobs move outside the organization. Even some insiders now get fees (bonuses) as well as wages.

Homework includes that whole catalogue of tasks that go on in the home, from cooking and cleaning, to children and caring, from carpentry to shopping. Done willingly or grudgingly, it is all work.

Gift work is work done for free outside the home, for charities and local groups, for neighbours or for the community.

Study work done seriously and not frivolously is, to me, a form of work not recreation. Training for a sport or a skill is study work, so is the learning of a new language or a new culture, so are the long days I spend reading other peoples' books in preparation for writing my own.

In the past, for most of us, our work portfolio has had only one item in it, at least for men. It was their job or, more grandiosely, their career. This was, when you think about it, a risky strategy. Few would these days put all their money into one asset, yet that is what a lot of us have been doing with our lives. That one asset, that one job, has had to work overtime for we have looked to it for so many things at once – for interest or satisfaction in the work itself, for interesting people and good company, for security and money, for the chance of development and reality. The list of things which people say that they want from their jobs has been consistent over the years; the problem has always been that we looked for the whole list from one job – no wonder, in retrospect, that so many have been disappointed.

For some, for those in the core of the shamrock, things will not change noticeably. Indeed, because work in the core will be more pressured, more consuming and more involving, the job will fill the whole portfolio to bursting point with just one item. There will be room for nothing more, even at times for family and fun as long as they remain in that core.

The message of the 50,000 hours, however, is clear. These busy busy jobs in the core will not last for ever or for as long as they used to, or even for as long as their occupants would like them to. It will be called age discrimination, no doubt, but we shall come to realize that high energy jobs in the knowledge-based organizations of the future do require younger people. Swimmers fade in their late teens, tennis players in their late twenties, chess-players in their thirties, journalists in their forties, and who knows what happens to money-dealers after thirty? We shall become used to the idea that the full-time executive or skilled worker fades in his or her late forties, in most occupations, and, if you believe any of the earlier chapters, *everyone* in the role will be either an executive or a skilled worker.

There will be glorious exceptions, and there will be some who will fade into different glories, becoming coaches or mentors or managers to the newer stars, swapping energy for wisdom. But wisdom is a part-time role. As his partner said to my friend, 'We value your wisdom greatly, John, and would love to have you around, but only on Tuesdays.' Nor is it always the best tennis players who become the best coaches. It is happening already today in those organizations whose *only* assets are their talented people – in advertising, in consultancy, in design – the energy roles are increasingly going to people in their thirties and forties, with the wisdom roles 'confined to Tuesdays'.

For the core people, the full portfolio of work only begins to expand after the job ends. The most difficult transition for them is in fact from a one-item portfolio to a multi-item one, not to an empty one. The transition is always a very personal bit of discontinuous change and one to which people could with advantage apply a bit of upside-down thinking. Alas, however, too many of the core seek to perpetuate the only concept of work which they have known, the full-time job in an organization, wage work at its best.

William came to see me one day. He was 48 and a senior account director and board member of a big advertising agency. The Chairman had just told him that they felt he should 'move on', leave them at the end of the year, along with one year's extra salary, the gift of his car and so on. It was a generous leaving present.

'I need another job,' said William. 'Have you any ideas?'

'What are you good at?' I asked him.

'I don't know, really. Running an account group in advertising, I suppose.'

'Why don't you try this,' I said. 'Ask twenty people who know you well, at work or outside work, to tell you just *one* thing which they think you do well. That's all. Not a critique of your personality just one thing you do well, in their experience of you.'

'O.K. I'll try it,' he said.

He found it difficult. He was a reticent Englishman, after all. But he came back in a fortnight looking puzzled but happy. 'I've got a list of twenty things,' he said. 'Quite surprising, some of them. Funny thing, though,' he added, 'none of them mentioned running an account group.' 'Maybe that's why it's time to move on!' I said. He didn't smile. We looked at his list in some detail. We discussed lots of ways, little ways, in which he could put his talents to use. There were ideas there for little business ventures, for voluntary activities, for some teaching, for personal learning, for some writing. None of them, however, added up on their own to a full-time proper job. He still did not smile.

He went back to advertising in the end, not as an account director, but as director in charge of administration in another and smaller agency. It was a proper job, but in a couple of years' time he will be around again, I suspect. Perhaps by then he will be able to accept that one full-time job in advertising is not the only nor even the best way to deploy his many and considerable talents. We are all, however, the children of our times, or, more accurately, the children of yesterday's times. Discontinuity in careers was not part of those times, nor were portfolios of different sorts of work.

For those now in the core, however, such discontinuity looks increasingly likely in their mid-fifties. For their children it will more likely be in their early fifties if not before. Nor are there going to be many alternative core jobs available. Like it or not, the ex-core employee will be forced into a portfolio life, and life without *some* work, as any of the long-term unemployed will confirm, is life without meaning. Portfolios stuffed only with memories soon gather dust.

Already the fashion is changing. 'Early retirement' used to be words spoken in a hush. The end of the job meant the end of life to many. Now you will hear many a person boast of how they have 'managed to arrange early retirement'. It has become a technical term signifying release or a key to new possibilities. Ask those people what they will do next and they do not talk of wage work but of ways of keeping their hand in (some small free work), of time for old enthusiasms, or new causes and hobbies (gift work), of helping out more with household chores or parenting (homework) or of taking up a new interest (study work). They don't call it work, but they should. They are building up a new portfolio and in so doing re-defining their lives and themselves. Early retirement is not the right word for them.

For others, the portfolios will have a different balance. It is not everybody's wish to work 45 hours a week or even more for someone else – although a Government minister spoke recently of her 100 hour-a-week job – and, statistically, half of all those in paid work won't be able to anyway.

For them the portfolio will be more varied. Sometimes there will be two or more part-time jobs (nearly 1 million Britons officially declare two jobs), sometimes they will save money rather than make money by increasing their self-sufficiency at home. Homework can often be a form of self-paid fee work. For many, small bits of proper fee work, or part-time self-employment, becomes an integral part of their way of life. They think of it as 'extra', money for the kids' presents, or for holidays – pocket-money. The authorities call it moonlighting and illegal. It is both, of course; understandable *and* illegal.

For many women, paid work has to give way to free work when they start to raise a family. As any woman will tell you a family is work, however much you love them. Understandably, many women want proper recognition for it, money to put it bluntly, but that is to play along with the conceit that only paid work counts. As more men re-balance their portfolios it should be increasingly possible for more women to put serious bits of paid work into their portfolios. Indeed, as I have argued earlier, organizations will increasingly need them and their skills, while the new technology and the new kinds of organizations will make it all much easier for them to fit bits of fee work into their lives.

Portfolios of work are not new. Small businesses have portfolios of products or of clients. Large businesses have portfolios of smaller businesses. As more and more people move their paid work outside organizations, or are moved, they are pushed or lured into becoming small independent businesses. They are paid in fees, not wages, and have to develop their own portfolios of customers and of activities.

From portfolios of customers, or products, it is an easy step to move to seeing some customers as free, some products or activities as non-financial, to include free work in the plans for the week or for the year. The free worker is by temperament a portfolio worker as is the working mother who has always had to juggle the demands of her time, and who knows that the responsibilities are no less just because the money is less. Free work is as serious as paid work.

Professionals, who charge fees, know about portfolios. So do craftsmen, particularly those who work for themselves by themselves. The plumber, the electrician, the weaver and the potter have to juggle the demands on their time like any mother. Too many customers leaves no room for anything else, even for the paperwork. Too few customers, of course, leaves no money for the bread.

Portfolios accumulate by chance. They should accumulate by choice. We can manage our time. We can say no. We can give less priority, or more, to homework or to paid work. Money is essential but more money is not always essential. Enough can be enough. Without deliberate choice portfolios can become too full. The irony of modern life is how busy people can be in what is meant to be a time for more leisure.

It is no bad discipline to calculate the days (or hours) spent each year (or week) on the different parts of the portfolios. My own portfolio, as a professional man in his Third Age, is as follows: 150 days fee work (at varying rates and including provision for administration, paperwork and abortive meetings with clients); 50 days gift work (for various associations, societies and groups); 75 days study (essential to keep up-to-date in my work); 90 days homework and leisure (it is hard to distinguish between the two).

Ninety days of domestic work and leisure looks a lot. It is salutary to remember that most people take 137 days (52 weekends plus 5 weeks holiday plus 8 public holidays). The danger of a portfolio life can, ironically, be that there is too much work since there is no one to say 'this is not a working day'.

Where will the money come from?
That is always the central issue in planning a portfolio. The

answer, once again, is from a portfolio of things. Portfolio people think portfolio money not salary money. They learn that money comes in fits and starts from different sources. There may be a bit of a pension, some part-time work, some fees to charge or things to sell. They lead cash-flow lives not salary lives, planning always to have enough in-flows to cover out-flows when both can be, to some extent, varied. Invoices sent and paid promptly with bills paid late has helped to keep many a small business financed, and portfolio people too.

'What sort of money do you earn?' I asked my friend Percy as we motored in his Jaguar from his shipbroking office to his house in the country. I was genuinely curious to know what it needed to live in his style.

'I've no idea,' he said.

'Come on,' I said. 'To the nearest two thousand, you must know.'

'Honestly, I don't,' he protested, and then, as I looked disbelieving, he asked, 'Look here, how much sugar do you use in your house in a year?'

'I've no idea.'

'Of course not, but I bet there's always sugar there. So it is with money, I don't add up the totals but I make sure there's enough coming in to pay the bills when they come in. If Paul McCartney can go out to work to earn a swimming pool I can do something when I have to pay the parking fines.'

It sounded very grand but I gradually discovered that that is how all small businessmen quite properly think, although it is not always that easy to find that something to do to pay the extra bills when we need to.

Portfolio money is a way of thinking. Portfolio people think in terms of barter. They exchange houses for holidays, babysit for each other, lend garden tools in return for produce, give free lodging in return for secretarial help in the evenings. Portfolio people know that most skills are saleable, if you want to sell them. If you love designing houses, design someone else's; if you like photographing dogs, photograph other people's dogs; if you like driving, drive other people's errands – and charge a fee if you need money. The fee can be as small, or as big, as you think fit; small for the first-time seller, big if you feel confident or if you do not really care whether you do it or you don't. Hobbies can be mini-businesses for portfolio people, their cooking can be their skill, their plants their merchandise.

Saleable skills and mini-businesses are the wherewithals of portfolio people. If they do not have them they need to acquire them, preferably before they start. This is the almost legal informal economy, only illegal when not declared to the tax man. It is growing rapidly, probably accounting for quite a lot of the gap in every country's national accounts, the gap between what they know we spend and what we say we earned. In the USA that gap is nearly $10 billion of missing money. We are seeing the consequence of taking work outside the organization, of taking work outside the formal job.

Portfolio Marriages

Everyone will live a portfolio life one day for part of their lives. Most people will match that with a portfolio marriage. A portfolio marriage is not a recipe for polygamy, a different partner for each day or night, nor is it an invitation to serial monogamy, a sequence of husbands or wives. Rather it is a way of adjusting a marriage to the differing demands of a changing portfolio in life.

Marriages have always needed to adjust to the stages of life, through child-rearing, to adolescence, to the empty nest and retirement. The new requirements of the workplace, the move towards more portfolio lives, more paid work for qualified women, more work from home and more telecommuting, the increase in earlier retirement, second careers and Third Age re-thinks, these all have their impact on the marriage. If the relationship does not flex in some way it will break. Too often, serial monogamy or a change in partner is the way many people match their need for a marriage with the need for change.

Portfolio thinking is one way of changing the marriage without changing the partners. It becomes increasingly important as an accompaniment to portfolio work lives. The idea originated in a piece of research which I did some years ago with Pam Berger at the London Business School. The research set out to explore how some successful managers in mid-career combined their busy executive lives with their family lives.

Some background is essential. The managers, all male in those days, had all been participants in a long executive development programme at the London Business School. They were in their mid-thirties with good jobs in large organizations. Twenty-three of them agreed to participate in the study. It was therefore a rather special sample, small, successful, well-educated and happily married (or they would not have agreed to participate). We cannot therefore say that everything which this group of people told us applies to all couples or even to all executive couples, nevertheless the marriage patterns which emerged do seem to make sense to a lot of people to whom I subsequently presented the study.

I knew all the men personally. Pam Berger did not. She therefore did all the interviews and the questionnaires, arranging always to meet the man first at his office, to travel home with him, to meet his wife and children, to meet with the wife alone and then with them both together. They filled in some standard questionnaires, responded to interview schedules and generally talked about the pressures on their lives and how they responded to them. We were looking for practical clues to managing marriages and work. We found none that were common to all. Instead we found a set of marriage patterns.

In their responses to one questionnaire (the Edwards Personal Preference Schedule) which draws out an individual's priorities and preferences, this group and their wives had unusually extreme scores on four dimensions: Achievement (ACH) or the need to succeed in something; and Dominance (DOM) or the need to have power and influence, which were highly correlated with each other; and Succourance (SUC) or the desire to help and support, which was highly correlated with nurturance (NUR), the work to take care of someone. Both of these, interestingly, corresponded closely with low scores on Autonomy (AUT), the desire to do your own thing. We were therefore able to put these scores together on a chart (see below) and to put an X for the position of each of the forty-six individuals in the twenty-three marriages.

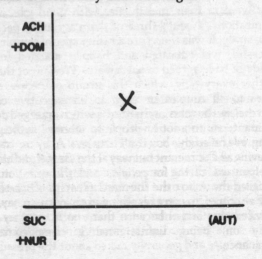

We then divided the chart into four quarters and gave them letters.

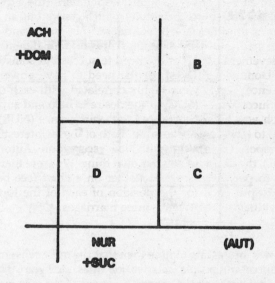

To make it more interesting we gave names to the four quarters. B was the archetypal western man, achieving, dominant, autonomous with little interest in helping or caring. We called this box the **Thrusters**. A, by contrast, was achieving and dominant but was at the same time interested in helping and caring for people, scoring low on autonomy. We called the A box the **Involved**. C we called the **Loners**, for they scored low on everything except Autonomy, and D we called the **Carers** because that was what they scored highly on, being uninterested in Achievement or Dominance.

The box now looked like this:

```
ACH
+DOM |
     |
     |        A            |            B
     |     INVOLVED        |        THRUSTERS
     |                     |
     |_____|_____
     |                     |
     |                     |
     |        D            |            C
     |     CARERS          |         LONERS
     |                     |
     |_____|_____
              NUR                    (AUT)
             +SUC
```

It was interesting to note then that the most conventionally successful people (salaries, job titles, etc.) were Thrusters, that over half the women and none of the men were in box D, Carers, that the Industrial Chaplain and the Civil Servants were in box A, the Involved, and that only one of the women, a full-time working wife was in Box B, a Thruster.

The distribution of the sexes would not be the same today, when at least a quarter of the executives on that programme are now women. This was, after all, in 1974. The world has changed, but probably not the marriage patterns which then emerged from this analysis.

With forty-six individual crosses on our chart, the marriage patterns emerged when we joined the crosses up to see which was married to which. There are sixteen different possible combinations of the four boxes, but only four of those combinations were relevant to this group. They were:

— The B-D marriage, a Thrusting man married to a Caring woman (this was by far the most common of the patterns).
— The A-A marriage, of two 'Involved' people, (the second most common pattern).
— The C-C marriage, of two Loners (there were two of those).
— The B-B marriage of two Thrusters (of which there was only one in this sample, but probably more common today).

Each of these patterns was quite different, reflecting the different combinations of the partners' preoccupations at that stage in their lives, a stage when most of them had been married for five to ten years, had between one and three children and a home of their own.

The patterns start to come alive when the way these couples lived is described. The B-D pattern was a marriage in which the roles of everyone and everything were clear and separate. It was the husband's job to earn the living, the wife's to run the home and look after the children. He looked after the drink in the house, she the food, he tended the vegetables, she the flowers. He had his friends, she hers. There were no overlapping friends except for family.

Even the rooms had separate roles – there were sitting-rooms and dining-rooms, studies and bedrooms. The children knew their place and their manners and went to bed when told. Conversation at meals was about things or events ('When is your mother coming to stay?' 'What is wrong with the hoover?') rather than ideas. We asked them what they did when they felt under stress. They moved away from each other, he to dig in the garden or hit a golf ball, she to suffer in silence in the bedroom – separate again. Interestingly, they usually came from the same part of the country but he was two or three years older and had three years more education than her (i.e. had been to university whereas she had not).

These seemed to be very secure marriages at the time. Everyone knew their role and everything went according to a schedule. Where his work led she followed, managing the home base for his career.

The A-A marriages were quite different. Here the partners were of the same age and had the same sort of education, in fact in this sample they had usually met at college. In these marriages the roles were overlapping, as were their homes. Both partners worked, although for her it was usually a part-time job. However, both took turns at child-minding and whoever felt hungry did the cooking. The rooms had no clearly defined roles, kitchen, living, dining, study were all one, bedrooms doubled as work-rooms, meals were haphazard and casual, the children precocious, advanced or ill-manne.ed, depending on your viewpoint.

The lives of both partners were intertwined. All friends were joint friends, all activities joint activities. Mealtime conversations were about ideas, were full of argument and discussion. When they had stress problems they shared them, drinking copious cups of coffee or cheap red wine late into the night then going off to be concerned but achieving workers the next day. Life was intense, interesting and, yes, involved.

The B-B marriage was different again. It was a very competitive partnership. There were no children and the wife earned as much as her husband in the same line of business. They were, therefore, a full dual career couple with what might be called, at that time, a low-slung lifestyle, low-slung cars, low-slung furniture, low-slung clothes, all quite expensive because they were the dinkies of their time

(Dual Income No Kids Yet). They argued a lot, discussed business more than ideas, and took their stress out on each other. The competition however was tempered by mutual affection; they were friendly rivals, so much so that she applied to follow her husband on the executive programme in order not to be left behind.

Lastly there were the C-C marriages. These were the partnerships of two people very similar in age and disposition and background who each wanted, above all else, to be able to do their own thing. Neither was hungry for success or for other people. They were very self-sufficient and encouraged the same in their children. In one home it was carried to extremes; there was no communal sitting room, no chairs to sit on except in the individual bedrooms. There was a kitchen but each member of the family got their own food. They lived their own lives, timing things precisely in the case of one couple, so that he would arrive home just in time for her to leave to go out to her work with one of them at home with the children. They were content, they said, and happy – two trees together in the wood, together but not touching, or even talking very much.

One conclusion from all this was just that it takes all sorts to make the world. As we discussed the findings with more people, however, we heard the same comments again and again:

— 'It is a snapshot of relationships at a particular stage. It would be interesting to know how they change over time.'
— 'My marriage started off as an A-A marriage. We shared everything. But the children came, my job hotted up, we moved to the country and, yes, we are now a B-D couple.'
— 'My firm assumes, I think, a B-D marriage because we ask an awful lot from our people and they need a secure base at home with no worries.'
— 'I gave up my career when I had the children – I had to because John was terribly stretched at work and could not

help – but I hope to get back to work and to an A-A pattern one of these days.'

— 'Your chart describes my life, an A-A start, moved to B-D when we had the kids, C-C when they left, and last month we divorced – nothing to say to each other any more, each with our own lives to lead now.'

— 'We try to live an A-A life but it has meant turning down two promotions because we would have had to move and I'm not sure that we can continue like this.'

— 'We think we try all the patterns in one year. A lot of the time it is a B-D marriage with one stuck at home with the kids, but at weekends it is definitely A-A because we do everything together while we always have separate holidays in the summer –C-C.'

The chart, I now believe, is a good although crude description of the options open to a relationship. The strong relationship is one that is flexible enough to move from one pattern to another when the need demands. It is a portfolio of possibilities. Most relationships these days start in an A-A mode, a partnership of equals sharing most things. The pressures of a job on one or other of the partners, together with children, lead to a B-D relationship – for a time. In our sample even the competitive B-B marriage moved to B-D when the children arrived, apparently to the satisfaction of the wife.

Not many women, however, are content today with the D or caring role for too long. They have tasted the excitement of paid work, domesticity is dull and lonely, they would like to mingle some fee work or study work with homework. Ideally, they would like to work back to A-A but this requires the husband to give up some of his priorities for autonomy and independence and move from B to A at the same time.

If a return to A-A is impossible then B-B is an option, the full dual career. It requires a lot of energy, organization and money to keep two successful careers going and a home. It can easily slip down to C-C with thoughts of achievement and power abandoned in favour of continued independence. It is hard, it seems, to go anywhere from a C-C position except out of the chart altogether.

More interesting, still, is the possibility in a dual portfolio life of mixing the patterns monthly, or weekly, or even daily. A truly flexible relationship can have B-D days, A-A weekends, C-C holidays and D-B spells (with the man doing the home-making and the caring), or some other combination.

The research made it clear that there is no optimal pattern for a marriage. All patterns are possible. It seems essential to have a joint understanding of what the pattern is, how and when it might change, what the consequences are of living in a certain pattern and what are the costs and benefits. People clearly *can* change their pattern if both parties want to. Separation and divorce often seem to occur because one partner wants to change the pattern and the other does not.

Bill and Frances had been married 26 years. Their children had all by now left home. Bill was 53 and at the height of his career as a marketing executive in a multinational company. Frances had minded the home and supported his career, moving home and country three times. Now she would, she felt, at last have the opportunity to develop her own career, at the age of 49. She enrolled in art college, with Bill's enthusiastic support, she met new friends, developed new skills and new interests. She went on trips with them, not as a spouse to Bill's conferences, she had them home to meals instead of Bill's business associates. They no longer planned their weeks together as they used to do but kept to their own schedules. Both were busy. Their old friends seldom saw them. Suddenly, one Sunday morning, Bill left home. 'I was a stranger there,' he said, 'Frances has gone into another world where I can't follow her. She has left the marriage so I might as well leave the house where I no longer belong and find another home.'

The irony is, of course, that Bill's career job will finish in a year or two. He will need new interests. A C-C pattern might in their case have been a necessary interlude after long years of a B-D pattern before returning to more of the A-A relationship they had when they first met. Two portfolio lives would then need a portfolio marriage, moving between the patterns. If they do not realize, however, that is only the *patterns* which are changing then it is the *relationship* which breaks. Portfolio thinking *and* talking are both essential.

In Praise Of Portfolios

Bits and pieces of work sound a poor second best to a proper job and a proper career. They often are, but they do have great compensations. In 1988 the Henley Forecasting Centre in Britain surveyed the attitudes to work of 2,000 people. They asked them to give a percentage ranking to what they found the most important aspect of their work. The list came out like this:

1. Having control over what to do. 50%.
2. Using knowledge and experience to make decisions. 50%.
3. Having a variety of things to do. 39%.
4. Amount you earn. 35%.
5. Being with and making friends. 21%.
6. Doing a job that you know people respect. 19%.

(The AB socio-economic group put money even lower at 25% and variety higher at 62%.)

A portfolio life sits rather well with those attitudes and

better than most full-time jobs. The things it lacks – a job title to swank about and lots of congenial company – do not seem to be of much interest. Nor is the money. That's all very fine, one might think, for those who have the money and the job title. For those without them a portfolio life will seem distinctly insecure. That is true. A portfolio existence comes easiest in the Third Age when, for many, a house is largely paid for and the children are self-supporting when, perhaps, some savings have accumulated or a part-pension is coming nearer, and when there is at least a job title in the past to reminisce about.

On the other hand, most households now are portfolio homes, with more than one income coming in. Arguably, a tolerable lifestyle is not possible for many households without multiple incomes. Collections of portfolios are themselves a kind of security for not everything goes wrong at once, whereas the one income family is perilously dependent on that one income. Should that one income go, as many studies have shown, there is nothing to fall back on, no other tradition of work or of money-making, no idea of self-sufficiency or of entrepreneuring, no sharing of roles, nothing except an abundance of time and a lack of cash. Employment can be riskier than self-employment, even for the whizz-kids of the money world where they can be fired at ten minutes notice, not allowed even to return to their desks. A high salary or a good wage guarantee neither security nor freedom.

Ray Pahl ends his fine compendium of papers *On Work* with a powerful image of a woman ironing. She might, he points out, be a homeworker for a laundry working in piecework for a miserly rate but as an essential part of the family's income; she might, on the other hand, be making pin money for herself by a spot of occasional extra work; she might be ironing a blouse for her evening out or a shirt for her lover, as a token of her affection; or it might be part of Monday's daily grind; she might even be doing it for a sick neighbour or to prepare a costume for the local dramatic society. Should it not, indeed, be a person ironing rather than a woman? Pahl observes, however, that if he had used the word 'person' most people would still instinctively have interpreted it as 'woman'. Will they still do so in ten years' time, I wonder.

Pahl's point is that it is all work and always will be. It is social attitudes and social constructions of work which change. If ironing for a wage disappears we shall perhaps do more ironing for love. My point would be that there have, indeed, always been all sorts of ironing, some done with a scowl on the face, some with a smile. It is and always has been a portfolio of ironing; but the portfolio can change, as the times change, as our circumstances change, as our relationships change and as our tastes and priorities change. That is good news. All work is becoming like ironing; a portfolio of choice and necessity. That could be even better news. After all, as Noel Coward said, 'Work is much more fun than fun.' It is, but only if it is work of our choice under our control, if we are all Noel Cowards of a sort.

Leisure, if we think about it, is only truly leisure when it is part of a portfolio, not the whole of it. The idea of a 'leisure society' with whole blocks of people with nothing to do except enjoy themselves, is to me a vision of hell not of heaven. The best form of leisure is nearly always active leisure, or work of a sort. The point is that the activity is of our choice, in our time and under our control. When we have had enough of it we can stop.

This chapter has largely been addressed to the career executive of the big organization because it is his or her way of life which will change most radically in an Age of Unreason and because it is they and their families who will find the idea of portfolio lives most strange. The chapter would, however, be no news at all to all those who have always lived their lives outside organizations – small farmers, craftsmen and skilled artisans, such as plumbers and carpenters, small shopkeepers and publicans, lorry drivers and taxi-drivers, artists and furniture restorers, gardeners and plant-hire people. The world of East Anglia, where I live, is full of such people, so are Italy and Southern Ireland where I visit. So is the USA where I was told 'In this country, everyone is first a business person and then something else.' Those people, the independent ones, well understand the necessity of a portfolio life. It may not be as rich or as varied a portfolio as they would like, or as much fun, but they know instinctively that life has to be a mixture, that work does not fit neatly into five days of eight hours, that money comes from many quarters and in different ways, that no one person or organization owns you – and most of them would have it no other way.

8 Re-inventing Education

If changing is really learning, if effective organizations need more and more intelligent people, if careers are shorter and more changeable, above all, if more people need to be more self-sufficient for more of their lives then education has to become the single most important investment that any person can make in their own destiny. It will not, however, be education as most of us have known it, the old-fashioned learning derided in Chapter 3 or the old British notion of education as something to be got rid of as soon as one decently could.

Education needs to be re-invented. Our schools first need to be re-designed for they are not immune to the principles of the shamrock or of federalism. But education will not finish with school, nor should it be confined to those who shine academically at 18. Learning, too, as we have seen, happens all through life unless we block it. Organizations therefore need, consciously, to become learning organizations, places where change is an opportunity, where people grow while they work.

These things will not happen automatically. The changes needed require some upside-down thinking, initiatives by government and determination by organizations. It is no exaggeration to say that we need to re-invent education if we are going to avoid the worst scenarios in this book and to profit from the best.

The Shamrock School

The ideas of the shamrock and federalism could turn schools upside-down. At present schools are bedevilled by the need to offer choice to a wide variety of students without running foul of the bureaucracy and anonymity that is inevitable in a large organization.

I stood one day and watched twenty double-decker buses disgorge hundreds upon hundreds of teenage girls into a cathedral to celebrate a school's silver jubilee. It was the first time that anyone had even seen the whole school gathered together in those twenty-five years. To me, watching, 1,500 girls was an awe-inspiring and a rather intimidating spectacle. Why, I wondered would anyone want a school so big that it could only meet in a cathedral? The answer is simple. Comprehensive education requires comprehensive institutions. If sixteen subjects are to be offered in the top class to a minimum of ten pupils per class, you will need, working backwards 1,400 pupils in an 11–18 age-range school. More choice at the top would mean proportionately more people lower down to provide the numbers needed in each class. Small schools may be nice in theory, they told me then, but they restrict choice.

One answer is to hive off the top, creating specialist colleges for the seventeen and eighteen year olds and leaving smaller schools behind for the younger ones. I suppose that principle could be carried even further with schools for the 11–13, 14–15, 16–18 age groups, but being so specialized in age they would not be very satisfactory communities for teachers to work in, or for students to study in, and they would inevitably cost more.

The alternative is to think upside-down and turn the school into a shamrock with a core activity and everything else contracted out or done part-time by a flexible labour force. The core activity would be primarily one of educational manager, devising an appropriate educational programme for each child and arranging for its delivery. A core curriculum would continue to be taught directly by the school but anything outside the core would be contracted out to independent suppliers, new mini-schools. There might then be a range of independent art schools, language schools, computing schools, design schools and others. These independent suppliers would be paid, by the core school, on a per capita basis, probably with an agreed minimum.

The job of the school proper would be to set and monitor the standards of these mini-school outsiders, to ensure an adequate variety, to help students and their families decide on an educational programme from all that was available and to manage a core curriculum itself in order to maintain some sense of group cohesion at the centre.

In this way the school as a whole could be quite big because for most of the time the students would be in smaller mini-schools. The parents would choose, not so much between schools as within schools, between the variety that was on offer. In big schools there could be a number of competing outside institutions offering courses in one particular area, such as art or languages.

The point, as always with the shamrock, would be flexibility. You do not make your suppliers redundant, you simply do not renew the contract. In a way it happens already. Work experience is now becoming part of the normal curriculum for 14–16 year-olds. Since work experience cannot, by definition, happen anywhere except in real work organizations, this part of the curriculum has, in effect, to be contracted out, although not for a fee.

Schools will say that it will be more difficult to organize. The shamrock always is more difficult; but it does provide more flexibility, too. The school need not now be run totally on an age-graded basis. The student who is gifted at language school could progress faster, irrespective of age, even though the core groups in the school proper would still be year groups. Everybody progresses at different rates in different subject areas – the shamrock design makes it feasible to recognize this. Of course the school day would have to change. The variety could not be programmed into the 35-minute slots beloved of school bureaucrats. The core curriculum could be taught on four mornings a week leaving the fifth day and every afternoon, and evening, for the mini-schools. There is, after all, no reason why every student has to finish school at the same time or could not learn to have a free afternoon followed by an early evening session in his or her design school. It is, come to think of it, more like the world of work they will be entering.

The shamrock federal school could go even further. It could give each student their own inverted do'nut in the form of an individual contract. In this contract there would be a core which the school would undertake to deliver and the individual to study. There would then be an area of discretion, out of which the student could pick a range of options. There would be a clear definition of goals and measures of success for the do'nut as a whole, including the demonstration of capacities, such as interpersonal skills, practical competences and organizing abilities which cannot be fully taught in classroom subjects. There would be planned opportunities to review and, if necessary, to revise the contract, on both sides.

This idea of an individual contract with each student, currently under study in Britain by the National Association of Head Teachers, becomes much more plausible when the school has the flexibility of the shamrock and is really a federation of mini-schools. It would change the relationship between student and school making it more one of partnership under contract and less one of teacher and child or warden and prisoner. School would be seen by more young people as a personal opportunity not a chore, they would be more like customers for some of the time, carrying a per capita income with them to the mini-schools they choose.

Everybody might begin to take themselves and everybody else more seriously.

Some of it is happening already. I telephoned a large community school, where adults study as well as teenagers and where activities go on until late into the evening. I asked to speak to the Head. 'Which Head?' said the receptionist, 'there are several heads of several schools here.' It was the outward sign of a federal shamrock.

Upside-Down Schools

Some years ago I was commissioned to study the organization of some of Britain's schools. I went to visit some typical big city centre comprehensive secondary schools. I remember that my first 'getting to know you' question on those cold November mornings was always 'How many people work here?' I always got the same sort of numbers, between seventy and ninety people. When I mentioned this, in some surprise to a Chief Education Officer, he exclaimed, 'Oh dear, they left out the cleaners.' 'No,' I replied, 'they left out the children.'

This was odd because at an earlier briefing session with the head teachers I had asked them what they saw as the role of the children in their schools, in comparison with other organizations. They are the workers, they said unanimously, while we teachers are the managers and the instructors. The early morning instinctive response was the right one, however, because who would expose workers to an organization which required them to work for ten different bosses in one week, in three or four different work groups, to have no work station or desk of their own but to be always on the move? What sensible organization would forbid its workers to ask their colleagues for help, would expect them to carry all relevant facts in their heads, would require them to work in 35-minute spells and then move to a different site, would work them in groups of thirty or over and prohibit any social interaction except at official break times.

The typical secondary school, I had to conclude, does not really think of its students as workers. Nor are they the customers, for they have no real choice, no consumer power, no right to complain or to be asked for their preference. Schools do not do much market research among their students. Instinctively, I felt, schools see their students as their products.

Organizationally, that made sense. Products start off as raw material. The material is processed, in batches usually, at different work stations. It is graded and inspected, so are students. The fact that some 40 per cent are below par is regarded mainly as a sign that standards are high. Unfortunately, the inferior batch is not sent back for further processing but is turned out to fend for itself in the world of work.

That world of work, however, is quite different. In that world people work on tasks in mixed ability groups. Mixed ability in the world of work means a group of people with different abilities of the same level. In schools mixed ability means people with the same ability but different levels. In schools collaborating is cheating, in work it is essential. In work 75 per cent quality is not good enough, in schools it is excellent. In work people see the result of their labours weekly, sometimes even hourly – success and achievement are obvious, and most people feel some success and some achievement each week. In schools success is rationed and you have to wait the best part of a term for it in many places. At work, your output is useful to someone somewhere, at school it is only useful to yourself. Work, most of the time, is interesting and even fun. School, for a lot of people, is not either very interesting or much fun.

The upside-down school would make study more like work, based on real problems to be solved or real tasks to be done, in groups of mixed ages and different types of ability, all of them useful. Not only would people learn more in such a school, because they would see the point and purpose of what they were doing, but it would give them a better idea of the world they would be entering. Most people's only experience of an organization and of work before the age of 16 is that of a school. If my investigation is anything to go by today's students will leave with a rather strange impression of both an organization and of work.

Other Types Of Intelligence

Society today sieves people in their late teens. The clever ones go on to further studies and qualifications, the rest are left to fend for themselves. We only use one sieve, that of intellectual achievement as measured by examinations. People are interviewed, it is true, by some universities and colleges but you only get to be interviewed if you have passed through that first intellectual sieve.

Upside-down thinking regards this as nonsense. We need more talents than the intellect, important though that is. Talent, we know, has many faces. So does intelligence. Howard Gardner, a professor at the Harvard School of Education took the trouble to classify seven different types of intelligence which, he claims, we can actually measure. Based on his analysis, but stretching it a little, we can in a commonsense way recognize some distinct sorts of intelligence or talent in people, even at a young age.

1. *Analytical intelligence* – the sort we measure in I.Q. tests and in most examinations.
2. *Pattern intelligence* – the ability to see patterns in things and to create patterns. Mathematicians, artists, computer programmers often have this intelligence to a high degree. (It is important to realize that the talents are not connected or

correlated. It is possible to be very intelligent in a pattern sense and to fail all conventional exams.)

3. *Musical intelligence* – some musicians, pop stars, for example, are analytically clever but many are not. Musically intelligent they undoubtedly are.

4. *Physical intelligence* – swimmers, footballers, sports stars of all sorts have this talent in abundance – it is no guarantee of the other talents.

5. *Practical intelligence* – the sort of intelligence that can take a television to bits, put it together again without instructions, but might not be able to spell the names of the parts.

6. *Intra-personal intelligence* – the person, often the quiet one, who is in tune with feelings, their own and others, the poets and the counsellors.

7. *Inter-personal intelligence* – the ability to get on with other people, to get things done with and through others. It is the skill that managers have to have, in addition to one or other of the first two types.

All these intelligences, or talents, we can recognize as having their place in life. If we look around in middle age at the people who are happy and successful we see it is because they have found what they are good at and are doing it. By that stage the first of the intelligences is by no means the most important.

Ironically, all these intelligences are also recognized in British schools but, apart from the first, analytical intelligence, they are collectively grouped under the heading 'out of school activities', and in too many schools there are now no out of school activities.

All the seven intelligences, and there may be more, will be needed even more in the portfolio world towards which we are inching our way. It is crazy, therefore, to use only the first of the intelligences as the criterion for further investment in any individual by society.

The system of universal educational credits would avoid

this blinkered approach. The upside-down school with study as work would also find that it needed to recognize the other intelligences *inside* school hours. Indeed, the upside-down school might usefully make it a point of principle that *every* student should leave school demonstratably successful, in at least one of the intelligences.

There are some signs of change in every country. Learning is increasingly accepted as meaning something more than acquiring knowledge. Capability, competence and social skills are rewarded and recorded in many schools. In Britain many schools use individual Records of Achievements to recognize different forms of success and different types of intelligence. In America, in similar vein, young people are encouraged to see their schooldays as an opportunity to start compiling their 'bios', their lists of accomplishments both inside and outside the classroom. In France they intend that 75 per cent of young people should get their baccalaureat but there will be different *baccalauréats* for different talents.

Education needs, however, to move further and faster if it is going to catch up the future. A system which has in the past allowed more than a third of its members to leave without even one acceptable mark of achievement has to be more de-skilling, particularly for a portfolio world. In that world, self-confidence, a saleable skill or talent and an ability to cope with life and to communicate are critical. Success, of some sort, needs to be part of everyone's early experience. That is why a wider and more formal acceptance of the other types of intelligence is so crucial.

Educational Credits

Education has to be a huge priority for everyone in the world of work that is emerging. It will not be enough to turn a few schools into shamrocks. We have got to do some more fundamental re-framing.

Upside-down thinking suggests that society should think of funding the individual rather than the institution wherever possible, as a way of releasing the motivation to learn in more people and to get the wheel of learning moving universally. If potential undergraduates, for instance, were each given an educational credit voucher to be cashed in at any university or college that would accept them, the institutions would be free to set their own fees, expand or contract as they pleased without reference to university funding councils or whoever. New institutions might be created to cash in on the new markets, whereas before only government could add to the supply. This way the state funds the customer and the supply creates itself.

Upside-down thinking goes on to wonder why it is that everyone has to rush off to college at 18 when so much of what one needs to learn only becomes apparent at a much later age. Furthermore, what logic is it which says that 18 is the age at which to decide that more formal education is appropriate? Indeed, if the numbers in Chapter 2 are even approximately correct we shall need to educate twice as many of each age group up to degree standard, but not necessarily all at once.

One answer would be to give everyone three years' worth of educational credits, to be cashed in at any time in their lives, as long as they could find a licensed college to accept them. The credits would cover the fees, not the grants, so not everyone would be able or want to cash them in, but more would study part-time later in life, more would be supported by firms or by their own savings, more institutions would arise to take advantage of the bigger market. It would be a cheap way for government to increase the supply of graduates, tapping into the ones that were missed in the bulge years of the early 1980s. All they would have to do to maintain quality would be to monitor the standards of institutions through a licensing system, which is already in existence in Britain.

Educational credits have long been a suggestion put forward by the European Community office in Brussels. They need now to be taken more seriously by individual governments. One way to reduce the cost would be to make a one year credit part of any redundancy notice, thus getting organizations to fund some of the scheme.

Upside-down thinking goes on to suggest that three or four consecutive years in one institution is not the only or even the best way to spend a precious three years' worth of credits. It should be possible to spread them out over a longer period or even over different institutions. Transferable course credits, as they have in West Germany, need to become part of our educational tradition if people are going to be able to build up a portfolio of learning, spread over time and over subjects. The Open University in Britain, with its open entry requirements, its credit accumulation scheme and its modular appeal is halfway there. When its approach is followed more widely and its course credits are more widely accepted in other institutions we shall be getting closer to the flexi-education we need for our flexi-lives.

The credit transfer does not have to be confined to formal colleges or universities. The great bulk of study is now taking place inside organizations. Provided this education is up to standard there is no good reason why it should not earn credits for its participants. We may soon expect to see business organizations seeking validation for their executive courses from business schools. The so-called 'consortium MBAs' recently pioneered in Britain, where a group of companies collaborated with a business school to mount a degree programme for their executives, is a move in this direction. It is another way for the upside-down state to get its further education done properly for nothing. Organizations in Britain like the BBC and Hewlett-Packard are taking clever arts graduates and training them, in one year, to be electronics experts. They do it because they have to, but in one sense, why should they *not* have to? Why should we not expect the world of work to educate its own people? The older professions have always done this, others will surely follow.

The Learning Organization

'The Learning Organization' is a term currently in vogue. It is, however, less than obvious what it means, except that clearly it is a good thing to strive to be. The model of learning on which this chapter is based gives us some clues.

The learning organization can mean two things, it can mean an organization which learns and/or an organization which encourages learning in its people. It should mean both. As an organization which learns, and which wants its people to learn, it needs to follow the precepts of the theory explained in Chapter 3 of the wheel and its necessary lubricants. In particular:

Asking questions and testing theories
A learning organization needs to have a formal way of asking questions, seeking out theories, testing them and reflecting upon them. Too many organizations are like Action Men or Pragmatists, reacting to events and adapting creatively and opportunistically.

The incoming Director of the Tate Gallery in London in 1988 deliberately set up a series of one-day think-ins with his new staff to answer a whole series of questions ranging from the role of the gallery to how do we fund it and staff it. He used his opportunity as a newcomer to lift the questions, and the possible answers, out of the everyday and to give them a special attention. Other organizations formally review their competitor's work and progress and use the review as a way to start the questions in some off-site top-level gathering. The Japanese are particularly fond of sending senior executives on study visits to competitors in other countries, raising questions and gathering ideas.

More typically, an organization does it in a corporate classroom, inviting a faculty from the world outside to raise issues and pose solutions. This can be an excuse to get stuck in the second stage of the wheel, listening to great theories in response to questions which nobody feels the organization has. These sort of seminars can too easily become corporate comfort pills, 'Thank God, we don't have to take any notice of that stuff since we don't have the illness it is intended for.' More accurately, someone on the staff has the questions and wants to use the experts to sell some answers, but unless all those present have the same questions and the same need to deal with them, nothing at all will happen.

Nor is it any use, of course, delegating the questions and the theories to some groups of scenario planners, corporate planners or even outside consultants. If the key executives feel no ownership of the questions and the theories they will not want to take the risk of testing them. The wheel will have got stuck. The top executives themselves have to be the ones who ask the questions, seek out the ideas, and test the best of them and then, deliberately, take time out to reflect on the results. It is no accident that the most successful corporate leaders give so much time to looking *outside* the organization, or that a leader's job requires so much time spent in *other* people's worlds if he or she is to avoid the dangers of 'group-think', the group that does not ask the uncomfortable questions or look at the uncomfortable ideas.

The wheel of learning cannot be left to chance or to the Chairman thinking in the bathtub. It has to be organized if the organization is to learn. John Harvey-Jones describes, in his book *Making it Happen*, how much time and attention he gave to creating the space for his top people to question, think and learn in his first years as Chairman of ICI.

A proper selfishness

The learning organization is properly selfish, it is clear about its role, its future, has goals and is determined to reach them. That sounds trite and obvious, but it is not that easy in practice. 'To make profits' or 'the bottom line' is not, by itself, a useful way of describing the purpose behind an organization. It does not begin to tell you what to do or what to be. It is akin to an individual saying that he or she wants to be happy. Of course, happiness and profitability is a state devoutly to be wished for but it is not a purpose. If anything, profits are a means and not an end. Without them, purposes are difficult to achieve.

Effective organizations know this now. Japanese corporations have always known it, which has been part of their strength. Their sources of finance know it, too, which sadly is not always the case in Britain and the USA. As in the case of an individual, the questions behind a proper selfishness in an organization are clear:

What are the organization's strengths and talents?
Its weaknesses?
What sort of organization does it want to be?
What does it want to be known for?
How will its success be measured, by whom and when?
How does it plan to achieve it?

The answers, for most organizations, must start with the customer or the client – who are they, what do they need, what do they want, how can we know? Without customers, after all, no organization has the right to exist. The story of the hospital administrator, congratulated on his efficient hospital, who replied, 'Thank you, but you should have seen it before we let the patients in, it was really beautiful then', may be apocryphal but it is all too reminiscent of organizations who seem to exist only for themselves. '*Involutus per se*', to be 'turned in on oneself' said St Augustine, was the worst of sins – *improper* selfishness.

A way of re-framing

The learning organization is constantly re-framing the world and its part in it. Leaders, I have argued earlier, need good conceptual skills. Even when these come with the genes they still need development and exercise. Every organization as it moves towards federalism and large do'nuts needs more leaders everywhere, more re-framing everywhere, not just at the top. Good do'nut definition is all about re-framing, just as the 'what business are we in this year' is also re-framing.

The quality circles in manufacturing organizations are, at their best, examples of re-framing at the shop-floor or office-floor level. They are, actually, the wheel of learning in action, with problems to be raised, ideas suggested, tested and reviewed. They will always work best, however, when the problem can be re-framed.

Quality circles are one example of how some organizations have incorporated re-framing and the learning cycle into their formal organization. Others create temporary think-tanks for their leaders in seminars in resort hotels, others hire consultants (with the attendant dangers of loss of ownership of the result). Once again, it cannot be left to chance.

Re-framing often needs some outside stimulus. Re-framers need to walk in other people's worlds from time to time. It is here that outside conferences, courses and seminars really have their uses, but those attending them should not look for neat answers but only for a stimulus to re-framing. The other worlds of books, of theatre and art and travel, are also good aids to re-framing. They need to be cultivated by a learning organization, not frowned upon as indulgences.

One of the problems of life in the high-pressure core of the shamrock organization is that there is too little time now for walking in other people's worlds. Even holidays can be interrupted, work can be done at home as easily or better than in the office, breakfast and dinners used as an opportunity for meetings, even visits to the opera turned into organization business. The learning organization must therefore make it an *organizational* responsibility to push people into those other worlds lest it be afflicted with a severe case of endemic group-think.

Negative capability

The learning organization must cultivate its negative capability. Disappointment and mistakes are part of change and essential to learning. 'How big a mistake can you now make without them stopping you first?' I asked a young friend who was boasting of his new promotion. I was suggesting that real responsibility entailed the risk of big mistakes. Learning organizations start by giving space, large do'nuts in my language. Large do'nuts mean discretionary space, space which will sometimes be misused. A learning organization will try to turn those mistakes into learning opportunities, not by using them as sticks to beat with but as case-studies for discussion.

Incidental Learning, Alan Mumford calls it, the learning that can be built around incidents in everyone's life and career. To be done without blame, however, and with implied forgiveness, the learning needs to be facilitated not by a boss or supervisor but by a neutral mentor or coach from inside, or, often, from outside the organization. Incidental Learning, properly done, uses the incident to raise the questions which start the wheel of learning. The mentor role will become increasingly important as do'nuts get larger. Properly selfish individuals will, if they are wise, look for their own mentors. Organizations could make this easier by maintaining a list of approved, and paid for, mentors, inside and outside. They will not always be people in great authority, those mentors, and will seldom be one's immediate superior. Mentoring is a skill on its own. Quiet people have it more than loud people; for mentors are able to live vicariously, getting pleasure from the success of others; they are interpreters not theorists, nor action men, best perhaps in the reflective stage of learning, people who are attracted by influence not power.

A list of mentors is one outward symbol of an organization's negative capability and of its endorsement of learning. More of these outward symbols are necessary if learning is going to be seen to be respectable, where time for reflection should be legitimate time. People could have individual educational budgets (in time or money) for their own discretionary self-development. Formal appraisal schemes could be re-formulated as self-development contracts, the language being the important symbol here because 'appraisal' sounds like judgement not help, looking backwards not forwards, smacking of authority not partnership.

The caring organization

Learning organizations want everyone to learn always, and bend over backwards to make that obvious. Large do'nuts, self-development contracts, recognized mentors, outside visits and seminars, incidental learning and corporate forgiveness are part of that. So are more formal arrangements such as tuition reimbursement schemes, as found in most American companies, more opportunities to listen in on higher-level debates as in Japan, projects beyond the immediate job, the public encouragement of questions at all levels, quality circles or their equivalent in study teams everywhere, brainstorming parties around new problems, horizontal careers to open up new possibilities, the encouragement of precocity and initiative even if it may offend, rewards tied to output not to status, to performance not age, constant celebrations of achievement and, above all else, a genuine feeling everywhere of 'unconditional positive regard' for the individual or, in more sensible language, of *care* for the individual.

Care is not a word to be found in many organizational

textbooks, or in books on learning theory, but it should be. Forgiveness is not easy without that unconditional positive regard of the sort we feel for our children, no matter how much we disapprove of their behaviour. People do not take risks with those they do not trust or genuinely care for. Subsidiarity comes from more of that trust and more of that positive regard. Loose, dispersed organizations depend on people liking and trusting each other. A culture of excitement, of question and experiment, of exploration and adventure cannot survive under a reign of fear. That kind of culture cannot be imposed, it can only be encouraged by demonstrations of warmth for all that is good, by celebration, by investment in individuals beyond the bounds of prudence. That kind of encouragement is only possible if one genuinely cares for the people being encouraged.

It is an attitude of mind and it shows in simple ways. Jim, the Manager of Indoor Recreation in a Metropolitan council in the north of Britain, has written a short description of his work for a Local Authority Competition on management. He called it 'My Love affair with Change'. He described one incident out of many,

'I should have known we were onto a winner with the staff there. They always made people welcome – even management. All they needed was attention, encouragement and freedom. But it became apparent after a meeting of supervisors of all pools.

'I hadn't been in the Swimming Session for too long and we had begun to meet regularly to talk and listen to each other (that's the best way I could think of putting it).

'The supervisors complained that they never had any money to spend ... so I gave them £500 for each pool. The two supervisors at this pool could decide how this money was spent.

'Some bought audio equipment, another bought an external sign and had information leaflets printed. The supervisors at one pool didn't spend their money. At the end of the year they wrote to me saying the interest was worth £50 and it was to go towards their cutbacks for the year.'

Little things and an attitude of mind – attention, encouragement, and genuine care and freedom – add up to a culture of learning, in a learning organization in love with change. It will, however, be more difficult to maintain, this culture of learning, in organizations when many people will be rather temporary inhabitants, passing through in the pursuit of their own careers. It is hard to give as much genuine care to your tenant as to your child who is yours for life. Japanese corporations, with their tradition of life-time employment at least for their core workers, made it easier to create the kind of culture and care for the individual's growth which learning thrives on. We cannot, however, afford to go the Japanese way nor do our Western individuals want that sense of permanent commitment or bondage, and even in Japan the system is beginning to erode.

The fact, however, that it will be more difficult in the shamrock, federal organization only means that it will not happen naturally. The learning organization has to be worked for, consciously. Most sensibly, and practically, it can start by getting rid of the *blocks* to change.

These blocks can be quite effective. Organizations know them well, and use them. Rosabeth Moss Kanter studied a range of large American corporations and reported the news about change in her book *The Change Masters*. She came up with ten rules for stifling initiative:

1. Regard any new idea from below with suspicion – because it is new and because it is from below.
2. Insist that people who need your approval to act first go through several other levels of management to get their signatures.
3. Ask departments or individuals to challenge and criticize each other's proposals.
4. Express your criticisms freely and withhold your praise.

(That keeps people on their toes.) Let them know they can be fired at any time.

5. Treat problems as a sign of failure.

6. Control everything carefully. Count anything that can be counted, frequently.

7. Make decisions to reorganize or change policies in secret and spring them on people unexpectedly (that also keeps people on their toes).

8. Make sure that any request for information is fully justified and that it isn't distributed too freely (you don't want data to fall into the wrong hands).

9. Assign to lower-level managers, in the name of delegation and participation, responsibility for figuring out how to cut back, lay off or move people around.

10. Above all, never forget that you, the higher-ups, already know everything important about this business.

The learning organization needs to break every one of these commandments, frequently.

9 An Upside-Down Society

The Upside-Down State

When Eisenhower was President of Columbia University in New York, before he became President of the USA, he received a deputation from the faculty. Could he, they asked, please use his authority to stop the students walking over the grass in the main quadrangle.

'Why do they walk on the grass?' he asked.

'Because it is the easiest way to get from the main entrance to the central hall.'

'If that's the way they are going to go,' he said, 'then cut a pathway there.' Problem solved.

There is, sometimes, little point in trying to stand in the way of what is happening. It is often better to recognize the inevitable and make it work for you. The changing pattern of work is one of those tides in the affairs of men and women which needs to be channelled, for it will not, cannot, be blocked or dammed. This book is not about politics, but if work is changing so much of our life so radically then it is bound also to have its impact on government and on the rules of society. Government, too, needs to recognize that the changes do make a difference, that more than a marginal adjustment is required, that discontinuity demands some re-thinking and re-framing.

The Henley Centre in Britain, in its 1988 report on Teleworking suggests, for instance, that gasoline stations will lose business along with the railways as commuting declines, that second cars will become unnecessary, road congestion will ease and that the greater availability of time for working (without travelling) might lower the rate of inflation by 0.7 per cent. House prices might even out as people have more freedom to choose where they live and a lot of office cleaners would lose their jobs.

All that however is only the tip of the iceberg. The implications go much deeper than the possible effects of telecommuting. For the past 100 years and more the work organization has been of great use to governments of every political persuasion. The organization has been the way in which wealth has been distributed to the population, in their wage packets or salary cheques. The organization has been, therefore, the natural and convenient way to collect taxes and to implement economic policy and to plan resources. If everyone has a job in an organization then the world is easier to control. At the very least we know where most of them are, and where most of them will have to live.

Similarly, organizations have been the easiest route for spending government money. It is easier to pay hospitals to help sick people than to pay the sick to find the hospitals, easier to pay schools or universities en bloc than to pay individuals to go to the schools, easier to run your own railways, coal mines or postal services than to leave it to others. Of course, there are ideological reasons for keeping vital services in government control but it cannot be completely accidental that the enthusiasm for governments to own and control so much coincided with the same fashion in organizations everywhere. 'If you want to control it, own it' was the message in every business in the 1960s and 1970s. Integration was the smart word – horizontal integration, vertical integration or both together. Buy your suppliers, buy your customers, buy your competitors if you can. That way your world is more yours. It was only natural that governments should hear the same message.

It was, as we have seen, an expensive message. Organizations now think differently. Shamrocks and federations are more economic even if they are more difficult to control.

The new fashion will not leave governments unscathed. They, too, will find that it makes sense to work out their core tasks, to do those well with the best people, and to contract out the rest for others to do. To call this privatisation is to miss a large part of the point. It is not all, or perhaps even mostly about ideology, it is about the most effective and efficient way to run organizations. The shamrocks of the state may be expected to spread for quite a while, nor will it be easy to reverse the trend.

More fundamental, however, is the way work is moving outside the organization. More fee work, more telecommuting, more self-employment makes it more difficult for the government to collect prices, influence earnings or manage welfare. Self-employed people cannot by law or logic be unemployed, only broke. Nor do the self-employed ever really retire, they only slow down. Unemployment and retirement begin to be technical terms only, not ones that usefully describe the human condition. So it is that a government can proudly announce a fall in unemployment while the opposition may simultaneously claim that the real number of people wanting work is rising. They are talking about different things. Inevitably, now, government will have increasingly to deal direct with individuals rather than with organizations, will have to re-think the categories it puts people into, and find some new ways to organize the collection and distribution of wealth if the organization cannot do it for them. The time of discontinuous change needs some upside-down thinking.

The shamrocks and federations of the state
The British Civil Service is devolving a large part of itself into agencies. Railways may become Track Authorities, with private companies running competing train services along those tracks, rather like an Airport Authority. The BBC may be whittled down to a centrally funded news service with all other programmes contracted out to small

documentary and film companies. The mail service in each country may be confined to the main track routes between big cities with franchisees bidding for the right to deliver the mail to our doorsteps, or more likely, to our private box numbers.

It could go farther still. In the USA prisons are put out on private contract, rather like security for the plant. Maybe parts of the defence contract could also be subcontracted. Schools, as we shall see, could become brokers in education, the intermediaries between leavers and a whole range of potential suppliers. Motorways and inner city streets could all become toll roads with automatic charging from strips in the road to meters in every car, allowing individual businesses to bid for building and running roads and motorways.

These are the signs of the principles of subsidiarity and the inverted do'nut creeping into government. Governments are doing what organizations are doing – re-thinking their core function. It should be no surprise that they often conclude that it is the job of the core to set and to maintain standards, to establish a framework and to choose the contractors but *not* to try to do the job themselves. If business organizations increasingly find that what they can most usefully do is to identify the essential core of the do'nut (the standards), to define the outer rim of discretion (the framework), to select the people, and to leave the rest to their individual initiatives, then governments will in time follow the fashion and start to do likewise. They already are.

They will not, of course, pay tribute to organizational thinking when they start to reform their ways. That would be unnatural. They will claim it always as a victory for their particular brand of politics for it is not difficult to make organizational effectiveness an essential plank in the political philosophies of either left and/or right. What today is called 'privatisation' to emphasize the diminished role of government as operator, could equally well be called 'democratization' to emphasize the return of choice to the client or consumer. No doubt in time it will be called just that. In the meantime I shall continue to believe that the laws of organizations are ultimately inexorable.

A National Income Scheme

Education is critical if we are going to give more, if not all, of our citizens the ability to work and live in this new world. But education on its own will not be enough. We have to find other ways of 'empowering' people as individuals. A national income scheme is one possibility.

The national income is conventionally the income of the nation as calculated by the statistical service. Upside-down thinking suggests that it ought instead to be defined as the income which every citizen should receive from the state. The idea has been around for a long time and has been given various names – a social wage, a national dividend, a citizen's salary, a basic income, but it has never been thought practical or, indeed, necessary as long as most people were guaranteed their income through their job.

Things are different now. People lose their job through no fault of their own. Ten per cent of the working population with no paid work at all is a lot of people. Others do not get included in the ten per cent but are still impoverished, like many of the self-employed. In order to get financial support from the state you have to classify yourself as old, unable to get work or poor. It is demeaning, people feel, in a free society.

A free society, and a rich society in comparative terms, ought to be able to guarantee its people enough money to pay for food, clothes and heating, as well as the free education and free health care which it already gives them. Upside-down thinking suggests that instead of paying cash to the needy few we should pay it to everyone and then claw it back progressively for those that *don't* need it.

Put more idealistically the argument is that as citizens we

are both entitled to an income from our collective property, our society, as well as obligated to pay a portion of our individual earnings for the maintenance of that society. *All* of us have the entitlement and the obligation.

It would work like this, at its most simple. Everyone would receive a weekly or a monthly income from the state. It could be smaller at 16 and 76 than at 36 or 46, to match the changing curve of spending. That income is never taken away from you, you do not lose it when you start earning – the penalty under the present system which discourages so many unemployed from re-entering the labour market. Instead you start to repay it when you start to earn. That repayment tax might start at 60 per cent and would then *fall*, not rise, as you earned more, giving even more incentive to keep on working. The repayment scheme would be in addition to income tax which would not, however, normally start to bite until the repayment tax was very small.

The results might be interesting:

— Because everyone would receive the national income there would be no need for people to classify themselves as unemployed or retired in order to get money. Those words would simply disappear, and with them the categories of people. More people would just be living off their dividends as the people of property have always done. Now anyone could do it, in a small way.

— Because the national income, although very basic, would cover essentials, it would make sense to do some extra work quite cheaply because one would keep about half of it. The marginal cost of labour would therefore tend to fall, more jobs would be worth doing, we should start to price some work back into existence, particularly at the low-skilled manual end where it is most needed.

— Because there would be more money circulating at the bottom end of the income scale there would be more consumers; therefore, in the end, more work making and doing the things those consumers want; (if we don't import them all of course).

There are problems, of course. Giving money to people does not necessarily mean that they will spend it sensibly. Some will waste it on booze, drugs or horses and *still* come to the state for support. Hopefully, they would be a small minority but they would be there and something would have to be done for them by someone. Would we consider that they had any further call on society, or would we leave it to charitable organizations to help any who cannot help themselves?

It would be hard to get started. This excuse is often made but I am not convinced. It is, after all, only the same amount of money being circulated in a different way. It would help if it were done in conjunction with the next piece of upside-down thinking.

Zero income tax

Upside-down thinking goes beyond a truly national income. Why have any income tax at all? It only raises the cost of labour and therefore the cost of the product and so ultimately helps to price more work/jobs out of existence.

Income tax has been, of course, the easy way to collect taxes, even though it was originally introduced as a temporary measure. It won't be easy for much longer when only half the working population and less than 20 per cent of the total population will be on the permanent payroll. Self-employment tax is much more difficult to assess and to collect and will get more so as more people become self-employed.

Income tax, however, produces half of the country's revenue with expenditure or indirect taxation (sales tax, customs duties, car tax etc) producing the other half. We would therefore have to double our expenditure taxes, or tax more things like food and books if income tax were abolished. This, it is argued, would be too regressive, i.e.

bear down too heavily on the poorest. However, if the national income scheme were in operation this argument would not be so crucial. The poorest would still pay proportionately more of their income but would be recompensed through their national income cheques.

A doubling of expenditure taxes might, however, be very inflationary since the prices of everything on the retail price index would automatically increase. It would only be seriously inflationary, however, if it were done at a stroke, as Britain did in the first year of Mrs Thatcher's government. A gradual progressive move towards a zero rate of income tax and doubled expenditure taxes might avoid the inflationary repercussions.

The implications would, again, be interesting:

— Any tax reliefs on, for instance, housing loans or pensions would progressively be reduced to zero, reducing the price of houses and directing more savings elsewhere, perhaps into more productive investments.

— As there would be no further point in people trying to conceal or reduce their apparent income, the workload of accountants and revenue officials would fall dramatically.

— Expenditure taxes as the only form of taxation would mean that you only pay tax when you spend money. Savings would therefore be automatically tax exempt, tempting people to save more.

— All forms of 'perks' would lose their rationale as tax-effective ways of paying people, making 'clean cash' contracts more sensible.

The switch from income to expenditure taxes will never happen overnight, but it could and should happen gradually. It needs to, because income tax will become progressively harder to collect, with the likely result that, the rate will rise rather than decrease, putting up the cost of salaries in the core and putting even more pressure on organizations to reduce the numbers of core employees. It is a spiral without end. We should deliberately try to go the other way, even if at first it seems perverse.

Part-time professionals

As the world gets more complicated we inevitably acquire more experts, in every field. We have already noted that sixty per cent of new jobs will be professional or managerial. Who will fill them? Technology will not make their jobs any easier but it could make them better. Computer diagnosis in every doctor's surgery will not remove the doctor but will enable him or her to be a *better* doctor. It will be the same for lawyers, architects, consultant engineers – for all our experts.

Professionals will be in short supply; professionals will be better equipped, professionals will, quite clearly, be very busy. One suspects that they will be the one group of people who will greatly exceed the 50,000 hour norm for the job. They will need help, particularly with the ancillary areas of counselling, of follow-up, of semi-skilled assistance. Upside-down thinking suggests that we should treat this as an opportunity not as a problem.

Can we not devise more ways to use the intelligence and the experience of people in their Third Age to help in these ancillary areas? As a part of their portfolio it would be of interest to many people in their fifties to have a part-time relationship with a doctor's practice, with a school, with a solicitor or in a parish. Some of this already happens: there are counsellors in some surgeries, teaching assistants in some primary schools. We will need more of them as the full-time professionals get busier, and they need to be given a more formal status and the necessary training.

It would not necessarily be expensive. Many would do it for free, for the chance of the training and the opportunity to contribute. Others would expect only part-time pay for part-time work. A lot of the time would be spent in adding a human touch to the gadgetry and technology that will increasingly become part of all professional services, and in listening and in explaining – things for which the expert often has neither the time nor the inclination.

Upside-down thinking would like these roles to be properly certificated and licensed, with required training procedures, rather than regarded as ad hoc voluntary help. In this way the public would feel reassured and the helper would feel properly recognized and qualified. It would enrich the portfolio of many a middle-aged person and enrich our society.

There are, to take one example, hundreds if not thousands of churches in communities which can no longer justify a full-time priest. They are now served by one man, or just occasionally now one woman, driving frantically from church to church with not much time for anything else, a visiting religious impresario, not at all the role for which he was trained. There must be many who would be eager, with proper training, to serve as part-time priest to their small community, licensed to that community only, and drawing on the expertise of the full-time priest, in the neighbouring town when it is needed. The concept exists, it is called the non-stipendiary ministry, meaning unpaid, but it is still seen as the assistant ministry. Upside-down thinking would argue that it should be the main ministry, a truly local ministry, served and advised by a small full-time core located in regional centres – the shamrock again.

It is, however, the professional caring services which are going to be overstretched in the new society as people live longer and more on their own. We will need more and better homes for old people, delivery services for them, information and home counselling services, dial-a-meal and dial-a-ride services, perhaps even dial-a-nurse. There will not be enough full-time professionals to man these services.

Part-time professionals in their Third Age could be a great help.

Time pay not money pay

If people are plentiful but money is scarce why not pay some people in time rather than money?

It was Stephen Bragg's idea originally, when he was Chairman of a Health Authority in Britain. Money was short in the health service. Consultants as they get older get progressively more expensive, therefore his Authority could afford fewer of them, getting older, while younger would-be consultants queued up, champing at the bit. Why not, he argued, pay all consultants the same, but require less time from them as they got promoted? They could use that time to work outside the system for money, or inside for no money, or they could use it to go fishing. The Authority would be able to afford more consultants, working the younger ones harder, but retaining the wisdom and exper-tise of the older ones. It was real upside-down thinking and, predictably, was never taken seriously.

The idea, however, becomes relevant when organizations want to shift people in their core from an energy role to a wisdom role. Expressed conventionally it often feels like demotion. Expressed as time pay in place of money pay it has another ring to it.

It is also a way of making sense of one's portfolio. Some things are done for money, some for love or goodwill, some for the discretionary time they give you. I write books. They don't, unfortunately, make much money. I know that but still I do it, partly because that sort of work forces me to set aside large chunks of discretionary time, to pay myself in time not money. Others take care to keep three days a week free of formal commitments, to make sure that they have 'free time', paying themselves, deliberately, in time.

One can give people time in other ways - time for education, time for children and a family, time for self-development as well, of course, as time for holidays. People in the core may well value time more than money in their pay packets. It is the sort of upside-down thinking which more organizations will cultivate as they look for ways to keep the best people in their cores.

There is, it seems to me, a real possibility that more and more of the most talented people in society may choose to exchange an executive role for a portfolio life quite early in their careers, preferring more control over their time even if combined with a more perilous financial future, preferring, in other words, to balance money pay with time pay. If that occurred, then our organizations would be in danger of becoming the reservoirs of the second best – not a good omen for their effectiveness.

Paying people in time rather than money, particularly towards the end of their job-life, would do something to put the curve of lifetime earnings more in line with the lifetime spending curve. It has always seemed odd that people got most money when they needed it least, in their late fifties and sixties, having scraped and scrimped in earlier years to raise a family. In a sensible world earnings would peak in the forties and would then scale down not up, replaced by more of that discretionary time which was so scarce before.

The Upside-Down Game

Upside-down thinking is like brainstorming. It is easy to think of violent objections to every idea. It is easy but unwise. It is unwise because that will stop the idea in its tracks, before it has had a chance to stretch itself, to get nudged into shape and, perhaps, to speak other and better ideas. It is easy to listen to a new idea and say 'Why?' It is more exciting to listen and say 'Why not?'

The ideas in this chapter are not intended to be a carefully worded prospectus for action. They are here to provoke, to suggest that the world does not have to be run as it has traditionally been run. Looking at things upside-down, or back to front, or inside out, is a way of stimulating the imagination, of spurring our creativity in an Age of Unreason when things are not going to go on working as they have been working, whether we like it or not.

It is a game, in a way, but a game with a purpose. If life *is* changing as fundamentally as I think it is, then creativity in our social order will be of immense importance. The status quo cannot be the way forward, nor will the status quo, slightly amended, be the best way forward. Then the Mancur Olsen argument comes into play, that the social order only changes when war, calamity or revolution upsets the status quo.

The danger of doing nothing is that the underclass (that new alarming word), excluded from the world we are moving into, takes its own initiatives, substituting terrorism for politics and bombs for votes, as their way of turning the world upside-down.

I hope we can find another way. It has been the British and American way to change things by a process of case law, of case law made into the new fashion, and, ultimately, the new social order. It is in a way a form of gradualism. Change so gentle that you do not take alarm. That way the censorship of literature in books or on stage was watered down until it has almost disappeared, that way homosexuality ceased to be a crime, that way divorce became a part of the new society, that way, I hope, smoking will disappear from public places, drunkenness from our roads and violence from our screens.

Ideas become fashion as a way to change. It is slow, but, as I argued in the beginning, ideas can change the world. I would like to see the upside-down game become fashionable in those quarters which affect to control or influence our social order. I would encourage the think-tanks of right and left to think boldly rather than too practically, the parties of opposition to challenge fundamentals not details, academics and teachers to encourage more why's? and why nots? in their students, rather than what? and how?

A changing world needs new ideas. The more there are the more used we shall get to them. Thinking the unthinkable is a way of getting the wheel of learning moving, in society as much as in individuals. If the upside-down game caught on, we might be on the move. It is because I am convinced that mankind is essentially a *learning* creature that I am, at heart, an optimist. I see the problems ahead as the necessary triggers for learning, and therefore for changing. I worry only that we won't worry enough, that like the boiling frog in Chapter 1, we shall continue to adapt ourselves to the changing scene until we boil ourselves alive.

We need more 'unreasonable people' who want to change their world not adapt to it, and who want to challenge orthodoxy rather than rationalize away its inconvenient bits. In the end it's a question of belief. I believe that we are the inheritors of a most interesting creation (however it occurred). It is our responsibility to make it better, not just to survive. I believe that holds true for organizations, who have a duty to do more than survive, for governments and for every individual. We cannot leave it to 'them' whoever we think 'they' are. In an Age of Unreason leaving it to 'them' would be foolhardy.

If, however, it is gradual change rather than violent change which we want, change by case law and by new ideas made fashionable, then it is crucial that those who might be 'they' get involved in some of the re-framing and the upside-down thinking. If they do not see change as an opportunity for everyone they will only invite violent change by those excluded.

This book, for that reason, is not about *un*employment but about employment, for only those in work can in the end improve the world for those without work. This book, for that same reason, is not addressed to the underclass, whoever they are, or to the undereducated but to those in positions of responsibility and respectability because only they can change things for those outside, *if* they have a care to.

My concern is that a world where the individual is left even more to his or her own devices, as more of work and life moves outside the institutions of society, could be a world designed for selfishness, and a selfishness which might not always be 'proper' in the sense of Chapter 8. Kingman Brewster, once President of Yale, then US Ambassador to Britain, once memorably asked a gathering of the British great and good 'Who are the trustees of our future?' There was an embarrassed mumble but no clear response. The question still holds good and my answer is that it has to be all of us, at least all of us who are capable of reading a book like this, and who have a concern for the world our children and our grandchildren will grow up in.

We may not, individually, be able to make their world safer from nuclear war, or to preserve the rain forests better, or to keep the ozone layer intact, but, as I argued at the beginning, it is often the little things of life which matter most, the ways we work and love and play, the ways we relate to people and the manner in which we spend our days as well as our money. These things we can affect. We do not have to accept them as they are. The Age of Unreason is inevitably going to be something of an exploration, but exploring is at the heart of learning, and of changing and of growing. This is what I believe and this is what gives me hope.

Epilogue

The world that our parents knew is not the world we live in today; nor is our world any sure guide to the way our children will live and love and work. We live in an Age of Unreason when we can no longer assume that what worked well once will work well again, when most assumptions can legitimately be challenged.

One thing however is clear: institutions will be less important. More of us will spend more of our lives outside formal organizations. 'What,' I said to the Chairmen of some large financial institutions, 'will your executives and your brokers be doing between the ages of fifty and eighty when, assuredly, they will not be working for you or with you?' 'It's a good question,' they acknowledged, 'and one we ought to look at sometime.' By the time they do many of those 50-year-olds will have moved on and out.

'I have ever hated all nations, professions and communities, and all my love is towards people,' said the poet Pope, 'but principally I hate and detest that animal called man, although I heartily love John, Peter, Thomas and so forth.' He would have been pleased with the way things are going, even with the chance to add a feminine name or two to the catalogue, for this is an age when individual differences will be important, both inside and outside organizations. The successful organization will be built around John and Peter, Mary and Catherine, not around anonymous human resources, while in the world outside the organization there will be no collective lump to hide under. We shall have to stand each behind our own name tag.

It should suit countries like Britain rather well. Condemned for decades for the ineffectiveness of much of her industry, Britain has always been renowned and even celebrated for her journalism, for her television and her theatre, for skills of finance and consultancy, of architecture and civil engineering, for medicine and surgery, for design and photography and fashion. These are all by-line occupations, meaning that the individual is encouraged to put his or her name to the work. They are all occupations where the organizations are more like a network than a pyramid, where hierarchy is minimal and individual talent of great importance. As more of industry and more of commerce become by-line occupations they will fit more naturally into the individual ethos of Britain and, indeed, of most Americans. The mass organizations of 'hands' and 'resources' never worked too well in the old democracies of either nation. It will be interesting to see how long they continue to work effectively in the newer democracies of Asia.

A society of individual differences, however, has its problems as well as its undoubted opportunities. Liberty, or the right to be different, and equality have always been the two proud goals of democracy. Unfortunately it has always proved difficult to have both at the same time. If people are encouraged to be different they will not end up equal and if they are to be kept level they will have to have their liberty curtailed; nor is equality of opportunity, normally defined as the right to go to school and hospital, quite the same thing as a full equality. A society founded on individualism could fall apart without the glue of fraternity that the French revolutionists added to liberty and equality; fraternity, or the awareness that there are others who are as important as oneself.

The Paradox Of Choice

People who are free to choose may choose wrongly. This is

the age-old paradox. Sin is the other side of freedom's coin. A world without sin would be a world without choice.

All the forces described in this book seem designed to set the individual free to be more truly himself or herself. Choice is multiple for the fortunate ones. They can choose when to work, at home or in the office: what to eat, with irradiated foods coming fresh from all corners of the world; what to buy via electronic catalogues. They can choose to live richly or thinly in a material sense and even, perhaps, when to die. Within society we may expect the abundance of choice to lead to the erosion of any one dominant set of values. No longer will we see some seeking to set or change the rules while others, the majority, wait to keep the rules they set. 'Anything (or almost anything) goes' will be the message of the next decade. It will be increasingly acceptable to do your own thing provided that thing does not interfere with the choices of too many others. NIMBY (Not In My Backyard) has always become the plea or bleat of those who seek, at the same time, to promote individual liberty and to defend their own islands of privacy, words once again heralding a change of tune.

Achievement and contentment in this society will have many different facets. It could be called a tolerant society, but it could also be a very fragmented society as an individualism rooted in personal achievement and material success replaces the mixture of institutional paternalism and dependency which we grew up in – good news for the strong but not for the weak. Choice, in the end, is only good news for all if everyone has enough to choose from, enough information and enough inner resources. To put it more paradoxically, a society dedicated to the enrichment and enhancement of the self will only survive and certainly will only prosper if its dominant ethic is the support and encouragement of others. Proper selfishness is rooted in unselfishness.

There is a real possibility that the generation now in their thirties, the first generation to experience the full range of choice, may use it to opt out of leadership roles in business and society. For the talented ones a portfolio life on the edges of organizations can be personally fulfilling, free and life-enhancing, but this might condemn organizations to be comprised of the second best and who then will run society? On the other hand, if the leadership roles are going to the talented ones, but also ones who want those roles for their own satisfaction rather than for the good of others, life will become a collection of private courts and courtiers – great if you are in, dismal and bleak if you are outside.

Choice in relationships now means that the extended family is not a collection of aunts, uncles and cousins, but of step-parents and half brothers and sisters, or of step-brothers and sisters with no blood connection at all. The courts may take care of the custody of the very young but who will be responsible for an ageing step-grandmother, or for the lonely sibling fallen on hard times? There are some who hope that new communities, sharing their homes or their workplaces rather than their parentage, will replace the old networks of the family which were so often riven with secret jealousies and ancient feuds. My own fear is that in the end shared bricks are not so reliable as shared blood, that these communities of common interest thrive as long as the interests are common, but fall apart when the interests diverge. Choice can seem a hollow mockery when someone is old and cold and poor; individual freedom can easily mean freedom not to care.

Organizations, for their part, need to think about *their* responsibilities in the midst of the pressures to maintain their flexibility and their freedom of choice. Who, for instance, will train and re-train the contract workers if the organization chooses not to? Education and training definitely increase choice for those educated and thereby give them passports to move to greener pastures but is this really a valid reason for *not* training one's executives? In the past it has been, and in many industries today it is still the plaint of the bigger institutions that they lose their best people as soon as they have trained them and are therefore tempted to turn poachers like the rest. Who then will train the game they want to poach? If organizations continue to think that way then choice will become the enemy of progress. Too much emphasis on organizational choice, on flexibility, can look like a lack of commitment to one's people, inviting a lack of commitment in return. Selfishness breeds selfishness.

Governments, in the meantime, having discovered that the market, the mechanism of choice, liberates initiative and penalizes inefficiency, are tempted to leave all to self-regulating choice. That would be dangerous. Markets do not look much beyond tomorrow, or at least next year. Markets are inherently selfish, disinclined to make investments whose outcomes cannot be precisely predicted or whose benefits cannot be claimed in advance. Basic research, for instance, in new sciences and new technologies has to be an article of faith. Who could predict in advance that the Science Research Council's investment in tracking down the structure of DNA at Cambridge would result in the whole new industry of biotechnology? The education of the next generation, too, has to be an act of faith. Left to individual parents and competing schools it would soon become a vocational rat-race for the few rather than a platform for growth for the many. Japan's government sees it as its responsibility, on behalf of the nation, to put national resources behind an infrastructure of creativity, building a new technopolis in nineteen locations and giving priority, in funding basic research and development, to seven emerging industry sectors. These long-term investments cannot be left to the chance and the choice of individual firms.

When Kingman Brewster asked who were to be the trustees of our future, his point was that governments tend naturally to think short-term and that a national conscious-ness is needed which makes it permissible to spend our money today for the benefit of grandchildren yet unborn. It would be a reversal of the tradition that it makes good economic sense to borrow from those grandchildren to boost our standard of living today. Market forces will not produce the wherewithals or the political will to tackle the problems of the ozone layer and our possibly melting climate, yet if the Netherlands and East Anglia are not to be submerged in 50 years' time someone must start spending now. That decision requires choice to be exercised by a few on behalf of the many, with the consent of the many – leadership on a big scale.

The New Ethic

In a world of individualism the dominant ethic can so easily become 'What harms no one is OK', or 'What the others do and get away with has to be all right', or even 'If no one knows then you're fine.' At the height of the insider trading scandals of 1987 a leading London banker called insider trading 'a victimless crime', implying that it was more a legal nicety than a sin, rather like taking an extra bottle of whisky through the customs. What is wrong, some athletes say, with the odd drug to boost your stamina – it harms no one save yourself. What is wrong with drawing welfare and doing work on the side, the state can afford it. If that ethic were to prevail then any attempt by governments or organizations to spend money today for benefit in 30 years' time, or to spend more of our money on other people would be futile; voters and shareholders and employees would shout them down.

The new freedoms and the new choices will only survive if those who exercise them take time to look over their shoulders, if they genuinely have a care for others as well as for themselves, others beyond their families and their own institutions. Just as businesses today invest in their local communities out of a sense of enlightened self-interest (good communities mean, in the end, better recruits and better customers) so, too, it is in the long-term interest of us all to make sure that choices are not rationed in our society because any rationing of choice might cause it to self-destruct. It is, however, for companies and individuals a calculation that has to be built on faith instead of genuflecting to the spirit of the times, talking the language of proper selfishness.

We need a new religion to save us, or at least a new fashion. Fraternity, the care for others as much as for oneself, must be our guiding ethic. First learn to love yourself, then your neighbour, but don't forget the neighbour. Hubris, the Greeks called it, when overweening pride, or excessive enthusiasm for your own achievements, aroused the irritation, even envy of the gods. Nemesis, or downfall, would follow. It was a way of putting a moral embargo on improper selfishness. It can't be done by laws, or by institutions, or by taxes, for fraternity is one thing that cannot be contracted out or outsourced. It is a core value, and it is established by the example of the people at the core, by the new élites, the fortunate ones.

The signs are not all that encouraging, but I am hopeful. Conspicious consumption, German cars, the electronic gadgetry, houses that cost more than most people's lifetimes' earnings, those are often the outward and visible signs of greed made respectable. When a company chairman, better nameless, boosts his salary by 37 per cent while his company's profits declined by 7 per cent, and sees no reason for explanation or apology, it can seem that private exploitation of public responsibility has become the norm.

On the other hand there is:

— The Bob Geldof effect. More people, particularly young people, are prepared to give to good causes. More companies recognize that good causes have a legitimate claim on their budgets and give less grudgingly.

— The willing taxpayer. Nearly 80 per cent of Britons, in many surveys, would like to pay more taxes if these resulted in better education, health care and social welfare.

— The young crusaders. Many young people want to spend at least part of their youth working overseas or helping out in places of adversity. The knowledge that they themselves will probably never be destitute seems to give them a new sense of freedom.

— The Third Age. As more and more middle-aged people discover that there is life beyond retirement, with real work to do, their values often shift. Having proved themselves in their work they now want to improve the lot of others – by helping in education, in voluntary organizations, in sports and community associations. Helping others becomes a way of giving new meaning to themselves.

— Institutional tithing. More organizations are encouraging their employees to lend their talents and/or their time to charitable causes, often in the firms' own time, sometimes through secondment, sometimes by corporate support for individual initiatives.

More needs to happen.

True fulfilment is, I believe, vicarious. We get our deepest satisfaction from the fulfilment and growth and happiness of others. It takes time, often a lifetime, to realize this. Parents know it well, as do teachers, great managers and all who care for the downtrodden and unfortunate. We need to give more public expression of what is a deep human characteristic, so that we are not ashamed to be seen to care for others as well as for ourselves, for the future of all as much as for our own, for everyone's environment as well as our own.

My hope is that as more people have more time outside organizations they will discover that portfolios are always enriched by work done for others. I believe that the intensification and the rationing of paid work will, ironically perhaps, encourage more gift work or unpaid work as people realize that it is the 'contribution' element in work which they miss most, and that contribution can be found in a wide variety of work, most of it outside organizations.

My hope is that as more people can choose where to live they will live in places more like villages than cities, places where your neighbours have a name and a face, where their concerns gradually become part of your concerns. It is always more difficult to care for strangers, or for people in the abstract. In a society of smaller communities there should be fewer strangers and more time to stand and talk as well as stare.

My hope is that life is now the right way round. Our wants are arranged in a hierarchy, as Abraham Maslow pointed out long ago, or, to put it more simply, life is largely a matter of crossing things off the list until you get to the bits that are really quintessentially 'you'. Success, money and achievement should now, to many, come earlier, leaving them free to be different while there is still time and energy. In the past, there was neither the time nor the energy – too many died without discovering their full portfolio of possibilities.

My hope is that a society of differences will produce many models for success. Achievement will not be measured simply in terms of money and possessions, but by creativity in the arts, by social invention, by lives of dedication to the care of others, by political leadership in small places as well as great, by writing and acting and music of quality. We need to make sure that the whole variety is honoured, by press and politicians alike.

My hope is that our various religions and faiths will be more outward-looking than inward-looking, realizing that to strive towards a heaven, or something like it, in this world, is the best guarantee of one in the next world, wherever and whatever that may be. Britain's countryside is dotted with ancient churches. They are important symbols, but they should be symbols not of spiritual escapism but of God's and man's involvement in the world around them.

My hope, finally, is in the nature of man himself, and particularly of woman. I believe that a lot of our striving after the symbols and levers of success is due to a basic insecurity, a need to prove ourselves. That done, grown up at last, we are free to stop pretending. I am conscious that we each have our quota of original sin but I also believe in original goodness. The people I admire most have grown up soonest and become their own people. That seems to happen more easily outside the constricting roles of institutions. The world I see emerging with its looser organizations, has many threats and many dangers but it should allow more people to stop pretending much earlier in their lives. If that is so, then the Age of Unreason may become an Age of Greatness.

For Reading and Reference

I have mentioned several authors and books in the text. These books and articles have influenced me and are all worth reading if you want to take any of the subjects a little farther. I list them here with a brief description.

Chapter One:

Olsen, M. *The Rise and Decline of Nations.* Yale University Press 1982.
   A penetrating study of how and why societies freeze up or change.
The Cookham Group. *Headlines 2000.* Hay Management Consultants 1988.
   A look at the world ahead by a group of young executives, sponsored by the Hay Group. Readable and thought-provoking.
Jones, B. *Sleepers Wake!* Wheatsheaf Books 1982.
   A warning directed at Australia to re-think her ways of work and life. Very pertinent to Britain.

Chapter Three:

Kinsman, F. *The Telecommuters.* John Wiley and Sons 1987.
   A glance at one part of the world of the future, built around case studies of organizations who have tried it. Readable and eye-opening.
Hakim, C. 'Homeworking in Britain', and Baran, B., 'Office Automation and Women's Work', both in *Pahl, R.E. (ed) On Work.* Blackwell 1988.
   Pahl's book of readings is a bit academic but provides a broad canvas of thought and research on the way work has changed over the centuries. A lot of the articles are by women. An interesting backcloth to this book.

Chapter Four:

Naisbitt, J. *Reinventing the Corporation.* Warner Books 1985.
   An anecdotal but upside-down view of corporate changes in America. A follow-up to the same author's best-selling *Megatrends* of 1982.

Chapter Five:

Deming, W.E. *Out of the Crisis.* Cambridge University Press 1986.
   The latest book by the greatest of the quality gurus. Important reading for managers.
Zuboff S. *In the Age of the Smart Machine.* Heinemann Professional Publishing 1988.
   An interesting but rather academic examination of the way the computer changes the notions of work and power in organizations.

Bennis, W. & Nanis, B. *Leaders*. Harper & Row 1986.
> Best read for its revealing description of interviews with a range of American leaders in all types of organizations followed up by Bennis' *On Becoming a Leader*, Business Books 1989.

Mant, A. *Leaders We Deserve*. Martin Robertson 1983.
> A wonderfully idiosyncratic book by an Australian with a psychological bent and a perceptive view of British ways.

Cooper, C. & Hingley, P. *The Change Makers*. Harper & Row 1985.
> Some good interviews with leading British men and women on what shaped their lives and their thinking.

Peters, T. *Thriving on Chaos*. Harper & Row 1987.
> Good for upside-down thinking. Another enjoyable and challenging book by one of the authors of *In Search of Excellence*.

Chapter Six:
Duffy, M. *Gor-Saga*. Methuen 1981.
> A fictional view of the world ahead. Worrying.

Chapter Seven:
Kolb, D. *Experimental Learning*. Prentice Hall 1984.
> The best exposition of how adults learn that I know of.

Argyris, C. & Schon, D. *Organizational Learning: A Theory in Action Perspective*. Addison Wesley 1978.
> A bit academic in tone but an important book for anyone who wants to move beyond training to learning in an organization.

Revans, R.W. *The Origins and Growth of Action Learning*. Chartwell Bratt 1982.
> The great prophet of action learning explains its history and its rationale.

Dewey, J. *Democracy & Educating*. Free Press 1916.
> A classic book for all liberal-minded educationalists.

Illich, I. *Deschooling Society*. Penguin 1971.
> A radical attack on educational tradition.

Harvey-Jones, J. *Making It Happen. Reflections on Leadership*. Collins 1988.
> A splendid and readable account of how one man, in my view anyway, changed a corporate culture, that of ICI in Britain.

Kanter, R.M. *The Change Masters: Corporate Entrepreneurs at Work*. Allen & Unwin 1981.
> An account of how and why companies change or do not change. Very authoritative. Also, her latest book *When Giants Learn to Dance*, Simon & Schuster 1989.

Mumford, A.L. et al. *Developing Directors: The Learning Process*. Manpower Services Commission 1987.
> A short account of how Britain's top managers learnt or did not learn as they progressed.

Gardner, H. *Frames of Mind*. Heinemann 1983.
> One of those important books which are difficult to read at times, but can change your whole way of thinking, in this case on intelligence and on education.

Index

THE EMPTY RAINCOAT
Making Sense of the Future

CHARLES HANDY

ARROW
BUSINESS BOOKS

This edition published by
Arrow Books Limited 1995

9 10 8

Copyright © Charles Handy 1994

First published in Great Britain in 1994 by
Hutchinson Reprinted 1994 (seven times).

The right of Charles Handy to be identified as
the author of this work has been asserted by
him in accordance with the Copyright, Designs
and Patents Act 1988.

Random House Australia (Pty) Limited
20, Alfred Street, Milsons Point, Sydney
New South Wales 2061, Australia

Random House New Zealand Limited
18 Poland Road, Glenfield,
Auckland 10, New Zealand

Random House South Africa (Pty) Limited
PO Box 337, Bergvlei, South Africa

Typeset by SX Composing Ltd, Rayleigh, Essex

Printed and bound in Great Britain by
Mackays of Chatham PLC, Chatham, Kent

British Library Cataloguing Publication Data

A catalogue record for this book is available
from the British Library

ISBN 0 09 930125 3

Contents

Acknowledgements

There is an invisible corps of people behind this book. They are the individuals who are out there living the lives and driving the organisations which I try to describe. Some of their problems and achievements, their hopes and frustrations, I hear from their own lips in seminars, conferences and private sessions. Some I glean from the writings of others, in journals, newspapers and books. These people must remain anonymous, unless they have chosen to write publicly about their world, but I owe them a debt of gratitude because it is through their stories that I glimpse reality.

I have learnt a lot from the writings of others, be they management theorists, old philosophers or modern thinkers. All those whom I have cited in the text have their relevant works listed in the bibliography at the end. That bibliography also contains some authors not specifically mentioned in the text but whose writings have been particularly influential as I worried about the theme of the book. It is a small recognition of my gratitude to them.

I have had the pleasure of working with two publishers simultaneously, in London and Boston. No one can serve two masters, it was said, but I have found it enormously helpful to be exposed to two sets of views and comments, particularly when they come from such insightful people as Gail Rebuck and Paul Sidey in London and Carol Franco and Natalie Greenberg in Boston. They, and every member of their teams, have been perfect midwives to this book during its rather prolonged birth pangs. I am for ever grateful for their interest in the book, their patience and their encouragement.

My family know all too well the problems of living with a writer. They have been wonderfully tolerant of my moods, have allowed me to parade parts of their lives in the book, and have been tactful critics of the work in progress. My wife's consistent belief in me and in what I am trying to do has been a particular source of strength, seeing me through the valleys of self-doubt, because writing is a lonely business most of the time. To Liz, Kate and Scott go my love and thanks.

Diss, Norfolk, England
September 1993

The Story Behind the Book

Four years ago, my earlier book, *The Age of Unreason*, was published. In that book I presented a view of the way work was being reshaped and the effect which the reshaping might have on all our lives. It was, on the whole, an optimistic view. Since then, the world of work has changed very much along the lines which were described in the book. This should be comforting to an author, but I have not found it so. Too many people and institutions have been unsettled by the changes. Capitalism has not proved as flexible as it was supposed to be. Governments have not been all-wise or far-seeing. Life is a struggle for many and a puzzle for most.

What is happening in our mature societies is much more fundamental, confusing and distressing than I had expected. It is that confusion which I am addressing in this book. Part of the confusion stems from our pursuit of efficiency and economic growth, in the conviction that these are the necessary ingredients of progress. In the pursuit of these goals we can be tempted to forget that it is we, we individual men and women, who should be the measure of all things, not made to measure for something else. It is easy to lose ourselves in efficiency, to treat that efficiency as an end in itself and not a means to other ends.

I cannot forget a sculpture which I saw in the open-air sculpture garden in Minneapolis. It is called 'Without Words' by Judith Shea. There are three shapes. One of them, the dominant one, is a bronze raincoat, standing upright, but empty, with no one inside it. To me, that empty raincoat is the symbol of our most pressing paradox. We were not destined to be empty raincoats, nameless numbers on a payroll, role occupants, the raw material of economics or sociology, statistics in some government report. If that is to be its price, then economic progress is an empty promise. There must be more to life than to be a cog in someone else's great machine, hurtling God knows where. The challenge must be to prove that the paradox can be managed and that we, each one of us, can fill that empty raincoat.

So many things, just now, seem to contain their own contradictions, so many good intentions to have unintended consequences, and so many formulae for success to carry a sting in their tail. Paradox has almost become the cliché of our times. The word crops up again and again as journalists and other writers look for a way to describe the dilemmas facing governments, businesses and, increasingly, individuals. Sometimes it seems that the more we know, the more confused we get; that the more we increase our technical capacity the more powerless we become. With all our sophisticated armaments we can only watch impotently while parts of the world kill each other. We grow more food than we need but cannot feed the starving. We can unravel the mysteries of the galaxies but not of our own families. To call it paradox, however, is only to label it, not to deal with it. We have to find ways to make sense of the paradoxes, to use them to shape a better destiny.

I know precisely when paradox became the key concept in my search for a way to make sense of the confusions. It was in Sausalito, California, when John O'Neil gave me the first chapter of his new book to look at. John is president of the California School of Professional Psychology, a wise and shrewd observer, and counsellor, of leaders and organisations. His new book was called *The Paradox of Success* and was subtitled 'When Winning at Work Means Losing at Life'. The book is about the personal dilemmas of leadership, but the important message for me was that there are never any simple or right answers in any part of life. I used to think that there were, or could be. I now see paradoxes everywhere I look. Every coin, I now realise, has at least two sides, but there are pathways through the paradoxes, if we can understand what is happening and are prepared to be different.

The ideas of *The Age of Unreason* are still relevant, therefore; organisations will become both smaller and bigger at the same time; they will be flatter, more flexible and more dispersed; our working lives will, likewise, have to be flatter and more flexible. Life will be unreasonable, in the sense that it won't go on as it used to; we shall have to make things happen for us rather than wait for them to happen. What I had not anticipated, however, in that first book, was the confusion which this would cause; that the opportunities for personal fulfilment which I so confidently predicted would be complicated by the pressures of efficiency, that the new freedoms would often mean less equality and more misery, and that success might carry a disproportionate price.

One criticism of *The Age of Unreason*, that 'it was all very easy for people like you', did hit home. I am more chary, now, of offering general solutions to our individual predicaments. We must each find our own way. The map, however, will be much the same for all of us, even if we choose to follow different paths. There are pointers to the future in this book, challenges which I think will face all organisations and all individuals, and some frameworks for thinking about them, but, this time, no sure-fire recipes for success.

The important question is whether we shall all be heading in the same general direction. Is there a point to it all, and if so, what is it? Vaclav Havel, the playwright turned president, could hardly be more immersed in worldly things and structures these days, but he has argued that we will only avoid 'mega-suicide' in our time if we rediscover a respect for something otherworldly, something beyond ourselves. It is a paradox, he says, but, without that respect for a superpersonal moral order, we will not be able to create the social structures in which a person can truly be a person. We cannot be the measure of all things, perhaps, unless we have something against which to measure ourselves. I come back to this issue in the last part of the book, but the question of the point of it all is lurking behind every page. The study of philosophy, I was once told, is the study of life, but don't expect it to tell you how to live. A bit like this book, I suspect.

Part One:
In the Dark Wood
Confused by Paradox

1 We Are Not Where We Hoped To Be

It Doesn't Make Sense

There will be no one to pick the olives in parts of Italy this year. The old people are too old and the young will not do it for the money on offer. In Tuscany they did not bother to replace many of the olive groves destroyed in the harsh winter of 1985. It was not worth it. Olive-farming now has to be a serious business, offering serious jobs for serious prices.

Changing, too, are those small family restaurants where the daughter helped her mother in the kitchen and the same waiter was there at lunch-time and in the evening, every day, every week. In most countries the law no longer allows jobs with hours like that, but the result is that eating out is more expensive, like the olives, and many small restaurants are now uneconomic. 'I'm really working for the government now,' said the owner of one, 'collecting their taxes and keeping unemployment down. There is nothing for me at the end of the day.'

We have priced many jobs out of existence all over the industrialised world. People need good salaries or wages to live in these countries. Governments need taxes. Not all products or services can carry these costs. Window-cleaning does not merit a craftsman's wage, nor is a bottle of milk delivered to a British front door each morning really worth more than the price of a bottle of wine. Remove the subsidy and the delivery will end.

Proper jobs are now expensive jobs, providing high-priced goods and services for those who can afford such things. For the rest, it is do-it-yourself, pick your own olives, clean your own windows or collect your own milk. Fair enough. Yet, across a narrow strip of sea from those unpicked Italian olive trees live the Albanians, a people in desperate poverty who would be happy to pick olives or clean windows for a pittance. Every rich country has its neighbouring Albanians. If we let them in to do the work which no one else will do, then someone else will have to pay for their lodgings, their health care and, ultimately, their old age. So we keep them out, mostly, if we can.

Many of them are here already, however. They are our own citizens, but not qualified enough, not perhaps diligent enough, to be able to add more value than the salary or the wage they need to earn in an expensive society. They are, literally, not worth employing in a proper job. Yet they are our citizens, with a right to a life, and, arguably, a right not only to a livelihood but to the sort of work that makes life worth living. They are also the customers for those who are in work. Keep them poor, as potential cheap labour when needed, and you bleed the market of demand. That, at present, seems to be the best that we can do, offering bits and pieces of pocket-money work. America, in the years from 1973 to 1989, managed to create 32 million net new jobs compared with only 5 million in the whole of Western Europe, but it was mostly hamburger work for hamburger pay.

It is one of the dilemmas of a rich society. There are more. Those proper jobs are not unalloyed bliss for all. Much is demanded and expected of those who have them. I asked a young friend, proud of his new job in a London bank, to come for a drink one evening. 'I cannot get away until 9 p.m.,' he said. 'Not ever?' I asked. 'Not really,' he said. 'My group expects me to be there until late, and on most Saturdays too. I can't let them down.' It was exhilarating work, for the most part, he said, and very well paid, but it was totally consuming. His neglected partner said, 'It's a crazy system. It doesn't make sense. Why don't they employ twice as many people at half the salary and work them half as hard? That way they could all lead a normal life.'

But they don't, and they won't and they can't, not if they want to remain competitive. A chairman of a large pharmaceutical company had summed up his policy very neatly once, but it was the other way round – '½ × 2 × 3 = P,' he said: half as many people in the core of his business in five years' time, paid twice as well and producing three times as much, that is what equals Productivity and Profit. Other businesses may not formulate it so crisply but that is the way they are all going: good jobs, expensive jobs, productive jobs, but much fewer of them. It makes good *corporate* sense.

Those jobs are not for everyone. They are not for those who want more space in their lives for other things. For families, for instance. Those kind of jobs are difficult for women if they want to raise a family, or for men, for that matter, who might want to do likewise. Child-rearing can be delegated, of course, but it is not what everyone wants. 'I insist that the company pays for me to read a bedtime story to my children over the international telephone lines when I'm away on business,' said one account-executive mother, but there is more to parenthood than telephoned bedtime stories.

Nor do they last for ever, these jobs. We rightly deplore age discrimination in our societies but 70 hour weeks do wear people out. At some stage, energy must yield place to wisdom, or sometimes just to exhaustion. 'Burn-out' would not have become a popular jargon word if there were nothing for it to describe. We seem, in many of these very full jobs, to be cramming the 100,000 hours of a traditional lifetime's work into 30 years instead of the traditional 47 years, as in days gone by. But then, do we really owe a job to a person who cannot do it any more? Concealed behind those high salaries and big wages is the risk that you may, one day, not be worth it. Sometimes it seems that there is nothing so insecure as a secure job.

A 30-year job leaves 20 years or more 'beyond the job' for nearly everyone, for, if we have not died by the age of 50, we are unlikely to die before 75 unless we do something silly. Those 25 years cannot properly be called 'retirement'. They offer the possibility of another life for all of us. Jung believed that the first half of life is the preparation for the second half. Now that most of us will have the opportunity of that second half in full measure, we are strangely unprepared for it. Many of us waste it. 'All I want is more of the same,' said a friend. Unfortunately, that is seldom on offer.

The dilemmas, and the paradoxes, continue. Akio Morita, the chairman of Sony, has commented that the Japanese worked an average of 2,159 hours each in 1989. That compared with 1,546 hours of the average German. Other countries fell in between. The young Japanese, suggested Morita, will not long tolerate such a divergence, particularly the young well-educated young women who are now joining Japanese corporations. The difference is equivalent, after all, to fifteen 40-hour weeks more than the Germans every year. No wonder, one might think, that the birth-rate in Tokyo is now only 1.1 babies per female, half of what is needed to sustain the population. There is, literally, no time for babies and work. How, and when, these traditions of work will change in such a country of tradition is anybody's guess, but if they do not change, Japan will have an increasingly resentful, ageing and diminishing workforce. Morita's remarks raised the eyebrows of Japan's elders, but, in a 1993 opinion poll, 87 per cent of respondents agreed that they wanted the change.

For Germany, on the other hand, the challenge is to continue to make every hour a German works as effective as one hour and 20 minutes done by a worker in Japan. The

Germans will need to do that in order to maintain their competitive position. It is a demanding standard, even if the Japanese begin to relax. It is a high standard particularly for the now united Germany; where two different traditions of work can still clash.

'Work,' said a friend in Dresden, in the old East Germany, 'used to be a place one went to, not something one did. We could not always work very productively because the parts or the tools we needed were not there. Anyway the customers were used to waiting and we got paid the same whether we did anything or not.' I must have looked appalled because he went on, 'I don't mean that it was right, or even sustainable as a system, but it did mean that there was a lot of time and energy for family and friends, for festivals and fun. Now,' he smiled ruefully, 'it seems to be all about profit and performance, pay and productivity. Sometimes I think that I preferred the four "f"s to the four "p"s! What is it all about?'

We all share, in some degree, the dilemmas of both Japan and Germany. When we worked to ensure our own survival, it was hard but it was understandable. Many are now fortunate enough to be beyond survival. But 'beyond survival' carries with it the question 'What now?' or 'What next?' and a whole variety of answers. They are answers which are increasingly demanded of our political leaders, of our businesses, of our schools and hospitals and prisons and, of course and most pressingly, of ourselves. One way out is to redefine survival. We can define it as keeping up with our neighbours, as individuals, as businesses and as nations. But that has a never-ending, no-win, nightmarish touch to it if we take it seriously. Only one firm can be the industry leader, only one country top economically, there are always richer or more successful neighbours to compare ourselves with. Competition is healthy, maybe even essential, but there has to be more to life than winning or we should nearly all be losers.

Maybe that is already happening. In 1992 the Congressional Budget Office of the United States, a scrupulously non-partisan body, revealed that personal income in the US increased by $740 billion between 1977 and 1989 after adjustment for inflation. Of this total, almost two-thirds went to just 660,000 families, the wealthiest one per cent. For that fortunate group, average income rose from $315,000 to $560,000, or by 77 per cent. The middle classes gained a miserly four per cent over this period while 40 per cent of all families actually ended up worse off in real terms at the end of this decade of affluence. The incentives, which may have been the fertilisers to grow more wealth, ended up consuming all the wealth which they created.

While there are some arguments about the precise interpretation of those figures, it is clear that wealth did not trickle down too well in America during that decade, the Reagan years. Nor did it elsewhere. The figures for Britain are no different. A government report in 1993 revealed that over the period 1979–90, the bottom 10 per cent saw their income in real terms *fall* by 14 per cent, while the average household income *increased* by 36 per cent. The wealth has been slightly less skewed in the other mature economies, but the trend has been the same. As ever, the rich got richer and the poor got, relatively, poorer the world over, and sometimes poorer in absolute terms. What held it all together was only the hope among the poor that, maybe, in a world of constant growth there would be room for some of them, too, amid the rich. It is beginning to seem a rather forlorn hope.

Al Gore, before he became the vice-president of the United States, wrote:

We have constructed in our civilization a false world of plastic flowers and Astro-Turf, air-conditioning and fluorescent lights, windows that don't open and background music that never stops, days when we don't know whether it has rained, nights when the sky never stops glowing, Walkman and Watchman, entertainment cocoons, frozen food for the microwave oven, sleepy hearts jump-started by caffeine, alcohol, drugs and illusions.

He could have made it sound much worse, had he described the wastelands of many inner cities. In these wastelands there are mindless murders of tiny children, rapes of old ladies, burglaries and thefts every 30 seconds in some places, a total disregard for human life and property, senseless anonymous violence.

Al Gore was writing out of concern for the environment. He could as well have been writing out of concern for the human spirit. That we have a spirit, most of us feel sure. We are not incidental curiosities, mutations in the evolutionary process. It would be a waste of all our progress if we sacrificed that human spirit in the pursuit of some imagined efficiency.

Even if we ignore, for a moment, the turbulent conflicts in the old Russian Empire, the endless dilemmas of the Middle East, the pitiless wars and famines of Africa and our continued inability to save what is left of the global environment for our grandchildren, there are enough problems in what we thought were the triumphant capitalist nations to make us wonder if we have missed the road to the future which we thought that we had won.

Some Unintended Consequences of Good Intentions

The millennium is only a statistical accident, but the ending of a thousand years of history does concentrate the mind wonderfully, particularly when it seems to be coinciding with the ending of some things we have taken for granted for the past few generations, such as the employment organisation.

Last Christmas, the family game was to list all the things which had got better in the last decade. The intention was to bring a note of cheer into the proceedings. We all agreed on New Zealand wine and hospices, but got bogged down after that. Some championed CD Walkmans and some the personal phone but these hardly seemed to classify as advancing civilisation. The game soon became too depressing to be fun.

Nevertheless, some things have got better over time. Because of what we have done in the last 50 years, everyone in our industrialised societies now has more things, more equipment, better health and better housing. That must be good news. But these things have their unintended costs and, when we look back, dispassionately, over the last half-century, the news is still mixed. These were the years of my generation, the generation now moving slowly into their Third Age, the age beyond the organisation and full-time responsibilities. It was this generation which set out to build a new world order after the Second World War, which saw capitalism triumph over communism and which kept muzzled the ogre of nuclear war. Some things, however, we did not foresee.

It was this generation which used technology to make a dramatic improvement in productivity, but thought too little about all those who would no longer be required to do the old, essential tasks. What work there will be in future will, for many, be non-essential work, selling goods and services which we could happily do without, building yellow-page economies of glitz and extras, hardly the stuff of real life.

The reward of productivity was increased consumption. To be a customer was seen as the new enlightenment. Even Britain's much-vaunted Citizen's Charter turned out, on inspection, to be a customer's charter. It was not realised soon enough that too much consumption has its costs, that the freedom to drive a car, for instance, ends up too often in the freedom to sit in a traffic jam, or that the delights of tourism dwindle when everyone you meet is also a tourist. We made consumption a measure of achievement, unwittingly creating a society of envy, in which to be poor meant to have less than the average even if the average was quite high.

We misinterpreted Adam Smith's ideas to mean that if we each looked after own own interests, some 'invisible hand' would mysteriously arrange things so that it all worked out for the best for all. We therefore promulgated the rights of the individual and freedom of choice for all. But without the accompanying requirements of self-restraint; without thought for one's neighbour, and one's grandchildren, such freedom becomes licence and then mere selfishness. Adam Smith, who was a professor of moral philosophy not of economics, built his theories on the basis of a moral community. Before he wrote *A Theory of the Wealth of Nations* he had written his definitive work – *A Theory of Moral Sentiments* – arguing that a stable society was based on 'sympathy', a moral duty to have regard for your fellow human beings. The market is a mechanism for sorting the efficient from the inefficient, it is not a substitute for responsibility.

As a result of all the 'progress' of the last 50 years, many have done well, but many not so well, even in the rich societies. In the world at large, the rich still get richer and the poor get poorer in spite of our best intentions. The road we have been on, throughout this century, has been the road of management, planning and control. Those who stood on top of society's mountains could most clearly see the way ahead; they could and should plan the route for the rest and make sure that they follow it. In many ways the bigger the mountain, we thought, the better and clearer the view. We applied this approach to our organisations. We thought this way in government. Even when we said that government should get off the backs of the people we did not really mean it, because the people would then not be managed to their best advantage. We have tried to plan and control world trade and world finance and to make a greener world. There should be a rational response to everything, we thought; it should be possible to make a better world.

It hasn't worked. Management and control are breaking down everywhere. The new world order looks very likely to end in disorder. We can't make things happen the way we want them to at home, at work, or in government, certainly not in the world as a whole. There are, it is now clear, limits to management. We thought that capitalism was the answer, but some of the hungry and homeless are not so sure.

Scientists call this sort of time the edge of chaos, the time of turbulence and creativity out of which a new order may jell. The first living cell emerged, some four million years ago, from a primordial soup of simple molecules and amino acids. Nobody knows why or how. Ever since then the universe has had an inexorable tendency to run down, to degenerate into disorder and decay. Yet it has also managed to produce from that disorder an incredible array of living creatures, plants and bacteria, as well as stars and planets. New life is forever springing from the decay and disorder of the old.

At the Santa Fe Institute, where a group of scientists are studying these phenomena, they call it 'complexity theory'. They believe that their ideas have as much relevance to oil prices, race relations and the stock market as they do to particle physics. In his book about their work, *Complexity*, Mitchell Waldrop describes the edge of chaos as the one place where a complex system can be spontaneous, adaptive, and alive. It is also uncomfortable if you are in the middle of it, as so many of our social institutions are right now.

The Inevitability of Paradox

We need a new way of thinking about our problems and our futures. If the contradictions and surprises of paradox are going to be part of those futures, we should not be dismayed. The acceptance of paradox as a feature of our life is the first step towards living with it and managing it.

I used to think that paradoxes were the visible signs of an imperfect world, a world which would, one day, be better understood by us and better organised. There had to be one proven right way to bring up children, I thought. There should be no reason for some to starve while others gorge. Freedom need not mean licence, violence or even war. Riches for some should not necessarily imply poverty for others. We lacked only the knowledge and the will to resolve the paradoxes. We did not yet know enough about how things worked, but eventually there would be what the scientists call a Theory of Everything and we would, as Stephen Hawking, the Cambridge physicist, put it, perhaps ironically, know the mind of God. In my own sphere, I wrote books which implied that there had to be a right way to run our organisations and our lives, even if we could not yet be completely sure of what it was. I was in the grip of the myth of science, the idea that everything, in theory, could be understood, predicted and, therefore, managed.

I no longer believe in a Theory of Everything, or in the possibility of perfection. Paradox I now see to be inevitable, endemic and perpetual. The more turbulent the times, the more complex the world, the more the paradoxes. The Theory of Complexity has been added to the Theory of Chaos. The turbulence, the theory goes, is a necessary prelude to creativity and some new order. We can, therefore, and should, reduce the starkness of some of the contradictions, minimise the inconsistencies, understand the puzzles in the paradoxes, but we cannot make them disappear, nor solve them completely, nor escape from them, until that new order becomes established. Paradoxes are like the weather, something to be lived with, not solved, the worst aspects mitigated, the best enjoyed and used as clues to the way forward. Paradox has to be *accepted*, coped with and made sense of, in life, in work, in community and among the nations.

There was, I now recall, a small framed printed motto which hung in my boyhood bedroom: 'Life goes, you see, to golf's own ditty: Without the rough there'ld be no pretty.' I have no idea why it was there. My family did not go in for such things and my mother had probably picked it up at some charity bazaar. Accidental or not, it was my first subliminal introduction to the necessity of paradox in human affairs. As I grew older, I realised that what I was told had been God's great gift to mankind – choice – was itself a paradox, because the freedom to choose implies the freedom to choose wrongly, to sin. You cannot have the one without the other. Original sin is the price we pay for our humanity. There was paradox at the centre of religion. Quite right, too, I came to realise, because paradox is what makes life interesting. If everything was an unmixed blessing, life would soon begin to cloy. There would be no need for change or movement. Offer me a heaven without paradox and I will opt for hell. Perfection, then, is neither possible nor, perhaps, desirable.

That conclusion was, for me, a revelation. Life will never be easy, nor perfectible, nor completely predictable. It will be best understood backwards, but we have to live it forwards. To make it liveable, at all levels, we have to learn to use the paradoxes, to balance the contradictions and the inconsistencies and to use them as an invitation to find a better way. Scott Fitzgerald once said that the test of a first-class mind was the ability to hold two opposing ideas in the head at the same time and still retain the ability to function. If he was right, then we are in for a time of paralysis, because there are not that many first-class minds around.

Schumacher also put it well: '[Some people] always tend to clamour for a final solution, as if in life there could ever be a final solution other than death. For constructive work, the principal task is always the restoration of some kind of balance.'

Living with paradox is not comfortable nor easy. It can be like walking in a dark wood on a moonless night. It is an eerie and, at times, a frightening experience. All sense of direction is lost; trees and bushes crowd in; wherever you step you bump into another obstacle; every noise and rustle is magnified; there is a whiff of danger around; it seems safer to stand still than to try to move. Come the dawn, however, the path is clear before you; the noises are now the songs of birds and the rustle in the undergrowth is only scuttling rabbits; the trees define the path instead of blocking it. It is a different place.

Prophets and Kings

'There are kings and prophets, I was always told,' said Tony Benn, the British socialist politician. 'The kings have the power and the prophets have the principles.' I am on the side of the kings, the people who make things happen, but every king needs his prophet, to help him, and increasingly her, keep a clear head amidst the confusions. No one, however, would want the prophet to run the show.

Prophets, in spite of their name, do not foretell the future. No one can do that, and no one should claim to do that. What prophets can do is to tell the truth as they see it. They can point to the emperor's lack of clothes, that things are not what people like to think they are. They can warn of dangers ahead if the course is not changed. They can, and often did, point their fingers at what they thought to be wrong, unjust or prejudiced. Most of all, they can offer a way of thinking about things, a way to clarify the dilemmas and concentrate the mind.

What the prophet cannot, and should not, do is to tell the doers what to do. That would be to take the power without the responsibility, the prerogative of the harlot, they used to say, not the prophet. It would be to steal other people's decisions. The prophet can provide a chart but cannot dictate where or how the vessel should sail.

It is my hope that this book will make it easier for people to see their way through the confusions of our times. Some of those people will be the leaders and executives of our institutions, because, in what I see as the ending of the age of the organisation, those institutions will have to find for themselves very different futures. Yet, in their new forms, they will be more essential than ever.

Some of the people reading this book will be individuals, trying to make some sense of their lives. Young people, in particular, face a world very different from the one their parents grew up in, a world where there are not many models from the past for them to draw on, where they really do have to reinvent their lives, their purposes, their standards and their priorities.

Lastly, I would like to think that the ideas and thoughts in the book might be useful to those responsible for the governance of our society, at all levels. They have the awesome responsibility of finding a structure for a society where most of the ground rules have changed but where the need for justice between groups, and between the present and the future, is greater than ever.

There is a need for a new perspective on life, on its purpose and its responsibilities. There are few great causes or crusades any more. Maybe it is the end of history. Some people are cocooned in comfort, others in poverty; but, for either group, their own survival seems to be the only point of life. If that is so, we shall all lose in the end. If anything is to happen, however, it has to start with us, individually, in

our own place and time. To wait for a leader to guide us
into the future is to be forever disillusioned.

2 The Paradoxes of Our Times

If we are to cope with the turbulence of life today, we must start by finding a way to organise it in our minds. Until we do that we will feel impotent, victims of events beyond our control or even our capacity to understand.

Framing the confusion is the first step to doing something about it. Analysts and therapists know this, of course, but so do the teachers of managers and of doctors. The management students at my business school are regularly confronted with 30-page case-studies, descriptions of the state of play in a business or an industry. This is not a facile attempt to give them an illusion of reality, but a way of teaching them that the first thing to do when confronted with a load of data, impressions and confused signals is to put them into some sort of framework, rather as the doctor learns to turn symptoms into a diagnosis. Only then can treatment begin.

I have identified nine principal paradoxes, nine ways of explaining what is going on in our societies and why some confusion is inevitable. 'Shall life succeed in that it seems to fail,' wrote Browning, '[is] a paradox which comforts while it mocks.' Simultaneous opposites are the other feature of paradox, as when we find that we can, at times, dislike those whom we love the most, but go on both loving and disliking. Paradox does not have to be resolved – only managed.

It is far from being an exhaustive list, but if we can manage the following nine paradoxes, if we can make sense of them, if we can combine their unexpected twists and their contradictions to forge a better world, we shall have done well. They are the paradoxes of the mature economies. Not all of them are yet to be found, for instance, in South-East Asia, still less in Africa. But their time will come, for these paradoxes seem to be the companions of economic progress everywhere.

1 The Paradox of Intelligence

In January 1992, Microsoft's market value, for a time, passed that of General Motors. The *New York Times* commented that Microsoft's only factory asset was the imagination of its workers. Tom Peters proclaimed the symbolic end of the Industrial Revolution. Peter Drucker heralded the post-capitalist society. This may, of course, be a bit premature – imagination is fragile, and Microsoft, it is already clear, should not be complacent. But organisations and individuals everywhere are waking up to the fact that their ultimate security lies more in their brains than in their land or their buildings. Even in the beleaguered world of American auto-making, brains are replacing brawn. In Ford's new Atlanta plant, each car needs only 17 hours of direct labour. Clever workers with clever machines have put an end to the mass organisation.

For a long time now, corporate chairmen have been saying that their real assets were their people, but few really meant it and none went so far as to put those assets on their balance sheet. That may change. Peter Drucker points out that the 'means of production', the traditional basis of capitalism, are now literally owned by the workers because those means are in their heads and at their fingertips. What Marx once dreamt of has become a reality, but in a way which he could never have imagined.

Focused intelligence, the ability to acquire and apply knowledge and know-how, is the new source of wealth.

Singapore, which calls itself the Intelligent Island, recognises in its latest plan that the traditional sources of wealth and comparative advantage – land, raw materials, money, technology – can all be bought in when and if needed, *provided* one has the people with the intelligence and the know-how to apply them. Singapore, along with Hong Kong, has exported all its manufacturing activities to cheaper places like Sumatra, the Philippines or Guandong in China, but retains the managerial control, the design and the distribution – the intelligence quotient.

What is true for Singapore is true everywhere. The new source of wealth in our societies is the intelligence quotient. Intelligence is the new form of property. Unfortunately, it does not behave like any other form of property, and therein lies the paradox. It is, for instance, impossible to give people intelligence by decree, to redistribute it. It is not even possible to leave it your children when you die. You can only hope that there is some of it in their genes. Of course, there is education – which becomes the crucial key to future wealth – but it is a key which takes a long time to shape and a long time to turn. The situation gets odder. Even if I do manage to share my intelligence or know-how with you, I still keep it all. It is not possible to take this new form of property away from anyone. Intelligence is sticky.

Nor is it possible to own someone else's intelligence. Peter Drucker is right – the means of production can, in practice, no longer be owned by the people who think they own the business. It is hard to prevent the brains walking out of the door if they want to. Buying shares in Microsoft is a bet that the imagination of its workers continues to be exercised on Microsoft's behalf and that the imagination never flags. It makes an insecure basis for the stock-market. Intelligence is a leaky form of property.

An added complication is that intelligence is extraordinarily difficult to measure, which is why intellectual property seldom appears on balance sheets. But this also makes it difficult to tax, unlike any other form of property, which makes any form of wealth or property taxation ineffective. Intelligence is tricky, as well as sticky and leaky.

The better news in all of this is that while it is impossible to redistribute intelligence by administrative fiat, it is also impossible to stop people getting it. Anyone can, in theory, be intelligent in some way or can get intelligent, and thereby have the access to power and wealth. There is little to stop any small firm muscling in on Microsoft's territory just as Microsoft did to IBM. Where the key property is intelligence you do not have to be big or rich to get in on the act. It is a low-cost entry market-place. It should make for a more open society.

Unfortunately, intelligence tends to go where intelligence is. Well-educated people give their families good education, which gives them access to power and wealth which, in turn, gives them advantage in the educational market-place for their children. The most likely outcome of the new form of property, therefore, is an increasingly divided society unless we can transform the whole of society into a permanent learning culture where everyone pursues a higher intelligence quotient as avidly as they now look for homes of their own. A property-owning democracy is an exciting thought with this new definition of property.

As a small indicator of the changing perception of property, we may observe that the richer we are the less need we seem to feel to own our own homes. In Bangladesh over 90 per cent of houses are owner-occupied, in Ireland 82 per cent. Go to rich Germany, the Western part, and the figure falls to 45 per cent. In richer Switzerland it is only 33 per cent. Where brains prevail, security lies not in the physical property but in the intelligence quotient. There are, then, better uses for one's cash than buying houses.

2 The Paradox of Work

We all need something to do. Activity is natural. It is hard
to see why there should be any shortage of it, yet enforced
idleness seems to be the price we are paying for improved
efficiency. Why should we worry? To be pleasurably idle
was the dream of the ancients, their concept of civilisation.
'If work were so great,' quipped Mark Twain, 'the rich
would have hogged it long ago.' They have, Mr Twain,
they have. The result is that some have work and money
but too little time, while others have all the time but no
work and no money. Those with the privilege of idleness
see it as a curse because they tend to be at the bottom, not
the top, of the heap. We seem to have made work into a
god and then made it difficult for many to worship.

Why has work become so lumpy? Part of the problem is
money. Work is society's chosen way of distributing income. We will do even boring work for the money it brings.
Therefore it would be convenient if everyone had some
work to do, even if it was boring work, as a way of getting
the money to them. This was part of the communist philosophy. Unfortunately, we also use money as the measure
of efficiency. Our organisations, therefore, want the most
work for the least money while individuals typically want
the most money for the least work. In a competitive world
where everything is traded, it is not hard to see that the
organisation is going to win.

Organisations are responding to the challenge of efficiency by exporting unproductive work, and people, as fast
as they can. Instead of keeping a pool of slightly surplus
labour and skills inside the organisation as a sort of cushion
for emergencies and comfort, they are pushing those skills
outside and pulling them in when necessary. If you
approve of this you call it 'getting rid of slack', if you disapprove of it you talk of 'exporting their flexibility on to the
peripheral labour market'. Put many of the full-time

workers outside and it is they, not the organisation, who will stand the costs of their unused time. Slack always costs money. It is only a question of who pays for it.

The irony is that these unused workers still have to have some money if they are to live and to enjoy some of the rights and pleasures of citizenship. The money has, ulti- mately, to come in some way from the organisations they left, usually in the form of higher taxes. In the end, much the same work gets done, for total output in the economy has not risen that much, and much the same money gets paid out, but in different ways. In theory it need not hap- pen like that. In theory, those spare workers with their spare time will invent new work to keep themselves busy and in cash. Unfortunately, they are usually the people least capable of creating new work for themselves, because they lack the kinds of intelligence and inclinations which would allow them to be independent. Conditioned to life as employees, we now expect them to be entrepreneurs.

To herald the New Year of 1993, Burton, the British chain of clothing shops, announced that they would be cutting 2,000 full-time jobs but creating 3,000 part-time ones. It was, they said, a strategic response to the stretched day and the stretched week of modern retailing. They were typical of a trend. It is no wonder, then, that only 55 per cent of Britain's workforce is now in full-time employment. There is a lot of spare capacity in the economy these days, but it is in individuals not organisations. It is not clear how we unlock it, except by giving these outsiders a share in the new property – the intelligence quotient. Until we do, re- lumping the work, so that some have too much and some too little, will only divide society.

In fact, Britain and the US have the most open labour markets and, therefore, the highest number of people in work – but their workers are the least protected and often the worst paid. Some 70 per cent of working-age Americans and Britons are in paid work. That compares with 60 per cent in France and only 50 per cent in Spain. Over the last 20 years the numbers of people in paid work have grown by 30 million in America but only by 10 million in the European Community. But the Americans and British have to work longer and odder hours, accept more part-time work and self-employment and enjoy less protection. Fifteen per cent of British workers put in more than 48 hours a week and 20 per cent regularly work on Sundays. The Continentals think this mad. Britain and America add on less than 30 per cent to the wage or salary to take care of social security and pensions. Italy, France and Germany add 50 per cent. Should you have fewer, better-paid, better-educated and better-protected workers, or more but cheaper ones? The argument rages, with the continental Europeans arguing that only good, and therefore expensive, labour is tolerable and worthwhile in this modern age, and that no work is better than bad work. The British and Americans believe that any work is better than no work, even if the result is a progressively downskilled workforce. One consequence of that is a more divided society. In America the top 10 per cent of earners are paid six times as much as the bottom 10 per cent. In Germany the ratio is just over two.

Work is more than a job. There are more forms of activity than paid work. Indeed, if work is priced at zero there is unlimited scope for it. 'I know that only too well,' my housewife friends respond. 'If we were paid for what we do, much of what we do would not be worth doing. We could not afford the price of a clean house or an evening meal if that price had to include our reasonable wages.' If, therefore, people want work for reasons other than money – for self-respect or identity, to make a contribution or to feel part of something – the answer is to price more work at zero. In a society where a lot of the work is not priced everyone is busy. Go to China or any developing country if you want to see bustling activity. Ironically, the more you price work, the less paid work gets done, because so much of it is not now worth the cost. Any work which is worth its price is quickly turned into a business, where few are paid well rather than many paid badly, because that way efficiency lies. Perhaps we should only have work which is priced expensively and work which is priced at zero, rather than fiddling around in between. That, however, leads to the paradox of productivity.

3   The Paradox of Productivity

Productivity means ever more and ever better work from ever fewer people. That is good for the customer and good for the organisation, be it a business or any public service. No one has ever been against efficiency. It has generally, in the end, been good also for the workers, even those who are not included in the 'fewer'. The ones who stayed got better jobs, and better-paid ones. Those who left found work in other growing organisations. Over time they moved into the new growth sectors in the economy. Thus it was that the agricultural workers 200 years ago began to find new work in the new factories, and their descendants (when the factories started slimming and closing) moved to the offices and shops of the service sector. Growth and work went on. As long as the overall growth rate was at least equal to the rate of improvement in efficiency, plus the rate of growth of the population, there would always be jobs somewhere for everyone.

This time, however, the new growth sector for work is the do-it-yourself economy. Some of that do-it-yourself economy is paid for and counted, being the self-employment sector which is growing everywhere; some of it is paid for but not counted – the black economy; some is the purely destructive do-it-yourself of drugs and theft and violence. Much of this do-it-yourself economy is, however, neither paid for nor counted nor illegal, as when we look after our old and sick, do our own repairs, grow our own food. As more and more people get pushed out or leave organisations, it makes good economic sense for them to do for themselves what they used to pay others to do for them. They should, logically, go in for a little personal import substitution, something which every government advocates as desirable on a national basis, but would rather that we did not do individually and domestically. Why pay other people to do or make what you can do or make yourself if, now, you have more time than money on your hands? Because this new growth sector is invisible, productivity does not seem to be producing the output increases, nor the conventional jobs, which we would have expected.

This is not a temporary paradox, governments and the unemployed please note. Society, and individuals, will have to get more used to the do-it-yourself economy as the new growth sector. More of us are going to be in it, whether we like it or not. Better technology means that more and more of us can run businesses or services by ourselves. More of us will be outside the organisation and the formal economy. The OECD calculated that, in 1992, only 33 per cent of the British aged over 55 were in paid work. Before you write that off as a British peculiarity you should know that the figure for France was 27 per cent and for Italy 11 per cent. The rest were not all doing nothing, but what they were doing was not counted, statistically or, more crucially, socially.

Economies have traditionally grown, in measured economic terms, by turning unpriced work into priced work, because then that work can be counted. The irony is that you may then actually reduce the work that is done, although the economy appears to grow. By pricing the work, we turn 'activity' into 'jobs' and so create employment, but some work then gets too expensive for the customers to afford and so on longer gets done. In many cases, it can't be done by ourselves for free because we have forgotten how to do it. The activity disappears. By pricing work we can destroy work, but we will never notice it because it never got counted in the first place.

My friend used to grow all his own vegetables; it was a source of pride to him that he ate for free, even producing his own seeds. The visible economy was the poorer for it, because nothing was bought or sold. As he grew older and richer, however, he calculated that this was a poor use of his time. He would be better off spending more time on his own work and buying the vegetables in the supermarket. The visible economy grew a notch or two thereby. But my friend lost his job and could no longer afford to buy any but the cheapest vegetables. Unfortunately, by this time he had disposed of his vegetable plot and all his tools. He had no energy to start all that again. He was bored, poor and hungry. The economy had slipped back a notch again, but now less vegetables in total were being consumed in that house, there was more idleness and more dissatisfaction. By pricing his work my friend had ultimately destroyed his work.

His story was a parable of the rich societies, who by pricing work have increasingly drawn more types of work into the formal economy. By so doing they have encouraged specialisation and efficiency but have then, as a result, priced some of that new work out of existence, deskilled many of its citizens and created a class of people who have nothing to do if they have no job. It is all an unintended consequence of good intentions, a fall-out from progress, but it is one of the more uncomfortable paradoxes of modern times.

4   The Paradox of Time

In this turbulent world we never seem to have enough time, yet there has never been so much time available to us.

We live longer, we use less time to make and do things as we get more efficient, and should therefore have more time to spare. Yet we have made this strange commodity into a competitive weapon, paying over the odds for speed. If we were wise would we not take the price-tag off time, and give ourselves time to stand and stare?

There was a time when we knew what time was. Patricia Hewitt of Britain's Institute of Public Policy Research has put it neatly – the time that men spent on paid employment determined how much time they had for their families; the time women spent caring for their families determined how much time they had for work. Most men spent most of their time in or around organisations. Most women spent most of their time working in the home. Organisations, you might say, were organised for male convenience, but, as a result, time was more or less fixed. We all knew who was where and when.

I have been using the past tense. Only one-third of British workers now work the 'normal' nine-to-five day, give or take an hour or two at each end. The normal is now the minority. Time is coming unfixed. Organisations want more flexibility. We have to rethink time and the words that we have come to attach to time. I can see a situation coming in society when it will no longer be possible to draw a hard distinction between full- and part-time work, when 'retirement' will become a purely technical term, indicating an entitlement to financial benefits, and when 'overtime' as a concept will seem as outmoded as 'servant' does today. At present, however, time is more unbalanced than balanced for many, which means that their life is also out of balance. Some have more time than they know what to do with, while others have too little time to do all they want to.

Organisations are now rethinking time for their own advantage. It is as if they had finally realised that there are actually 168 hours in the week, not 40. Sleeping assets make no money, so why keep them shut down for 128 hours a week when half of the world is still awake, when customers like to shop at the end of days and the end of weeks, and when some people like to work when others sleep? Most factories are now like processing plants, working the 24-hour day. There are night shifts in financial offices, stores in London stay open until 9 p.m. or 10 p.m. and on Sundays. Schools in Wandsworth in South London have abandoned the long summer holiday, originally designed to allow pupils to help with the harvest, in favour of five 8-week terms. No time demarcations are sacrosanct any more.

There is now a long list of the ways in which organisations are re-chunking time. There is flexitime, which has been with us for a while now, but if we moved to a 35-hour week, flexitime could mean an hour off each working day, or Friday afternoons off, or a nine-day fortnight. Then there is part-time working for new parents, part-time before retirement, job-sharing, term-time jobs, weekend jobs, four 10-hour days a week or eight-day fortnights, annual-hours contracts, zero-hour contracts (being available as and when required), parental leave, career breaks, sabbaticals, time-banking (accumulating holiday entitlements over several years), and individual-hour contracts where individuals and their bosses agree on a timetable of hours each week or each month.

On the face of it, there is enough flexibility available for everyone. Why, then, does Juliet Schor need to write a book called *The Overworked American* which sells so well that it must have struck a chord with many? The average American, she finds, now works 164 more hours per year than 20 years ago – the equivalent of an extra month. The typical American now works 47 hours per week and, if current trends continue, in 20 years the average person would be on the job 60 hours a week, for an annual total of 3,000 hours. That compares with 1,856 in Britain in 1989. Why do they do it? Schor says that two things come together:

organisations want fewer people working longer because it saves them overheads; while individuals want the money. This 'Faustian bargain of time for money', says Schor, has created an insidious cycle of work and spend, as people increasingly look to consumption to give satisfaction and even meaning to their lives.

The paradox is that they seem to know that it is stupid. In a US Department of Labor survey in 1978, 84 per cent said that they would choose to trade off some future increases in income against more time, with almost half opting to trade all the increases. In Britain, Andre Gorz recorded the overtime-loving workers at a shoe factory. When hard times hit, the factory went into work-sharing, and the employees who had chased all the extra hours they could get – including Sundays and holidays – now found themselves with time on their hands. One worker reported:

> Bit by bit, there was an unbelievable phenomenon of physical recuperation. The idea of money really lost its intensity. It's quite true that we lost a good deal of money [25 per cent of previous income] but, quite soon, only one or two of the blokes minded. It was about now that . . . friendships began: we were now able to go beyond political conversation, and we managed to talk about love, impotence, jealousy, family life . . . it was also at this time that we realized the full horror of working in the factory on Saturday afternoon or evenings . . . we were once again learning the meaning of living.

Schor says that we seem to have decided to take the benefits of the improved productivity of the last 50 years in money rather than time. Work and spend has become a habit. She is the first to recognise, of course, that for some people there is no choice. Nearly one-third of American workers earn wages which, on a full-time basis, would not lift them out of poverty. The same is true of Britain.

Millions of households can only make ends meet through overtime, moonlighting or multi-earning households. They would willingly give more time to make more money, just to live, just to make ends meet.

The trouble started when we turned time into a commodity, when we bought people's time in our organisations rather than buying their produce. The more time you sell, under these conditions, the more money you make. There is, then, an inevitable trade-off between time and money. Organisations, for their part, get choosy. They want less time from the people they pay by the hour but more from the people they pay by the year, because, in the latter case, every extra hour during the year is for free.

Time turns out to be a confusing commodity. Some will spend money to save their time, others will spend their time to save money. Others, again, will trade money for time at certain periods of their life, preferring to work less long for less money. This makes time a contradictory sort of commodity but one which will become more and more important in our societies.

Busy people will, if they can afford it, spend money to save time, buying time-saving equipment for their homes, pre-cooked meals and help with their chores; they will prefer taxis to buses, child-minders to child-minding, gardeners to gardening, if it helps them to spend their time on what they really want to do. Their needs create an important market opportunity. The unbusy, on the other hand, spend money to buy time – time to travel, time to learn, time to play and time to keep fit – or they spend their time doing themselves what they used to pay others to do, in the do-it-yourself economy. Time, therefore, creates the new growth area. Personal services for the busy, to save time; health, education, travel and recreation for the affluent unbusy, to spend time; equipment and materials for those who want to spend time to save money. It is, perhaps, no accident that these new growth areas will not be best served by large corporations but by small independents providing a personal and local delivery, linked maybe by franchising or other networks into bigger combinations.

5 The Paradox of Riches

Economic growth depends, ultimately, on more and more people wanting more and more of more and more things. Looking at the world as a whole, then, there should be no shortage of growth potential. If, however, we look only at the rich societies, we see them producing fewer babies every year and living longer. Fewer babies mean fewer customers, eventually, while longer lives mean, usually, poorer and more choosy customers. Older people, even when they have the money, are in a slimming-down, passing-on stage, not a stocking-up one. We could be running out of customers at home.

But not abroad; not, anyway, in the multiplying needy areas of the developing world. They, however, cannot afford to buy most of the things we have to sell. What they want is the know-how and the capital to make things to sell to us, before they can start to buy from us. Ultimately, therefore, we will have to invest in our potential competitors in order to fuel our own growth. No government has been able to persuade its people to accept that paradox, although the multinational businesses are beginning to see the sense, for their shareholders, of making things where they are cheaper, wherever that is, and exporting their know-how to make that possible. In the short term, however, exporting factories, and know-how not products, is nothing but bad news for those who used to work in the factories back home. It is their children who will benefit from a richer world outside, not them. Will they be prepared to make the sacrifice?

Back home, the traditional answer has been to create

even more demand among those who do have the money. Growth has to be fuelled by what the American economist, Thorstein Veblen, first called 'conspicuous consumption' 100 years ago, the need to be up with the neighbours or better than them. Growth, then, which is necessary for society, is increasingly dependent on a climate of envy in that society, increasing its divisions. Paradox again. There are, however, some signs that the 'Gucci factor', the high-fashion luxury trade which is based on envy, may have peaked in the Eighties, along with the firm of that name. It is, said the *Financial Times*, 'the demise of de luxe'. Couture houses in Paris are worried that no one will want to pay the prices for their creations. Consumers have become more discerning, less interested in conspicuous consumption, asking more often 'Will it work well?' or Will it last?' We have, paradoxically, to wonder whether this is good news or bad. It is bad for growth, good for common sense.

We shall miss one customer, the artificial customer of the defence industries of the West. Politically legitimate, the defence industry created a demand for advanced technology which spread knowledge and work throughout the economies of America, Britain and most Western countries. In yet another paradox, one must hope that this customer will never again be needed to the same extent. For the good of our economies, however, an alternative, and politically legitimate, artificial customer would be very beneficial. We could, for instance, define the environment as the new target for defence expenditure, fending off our own deterioration. Sadly, turning swords into plough-shares has never proved easy. Peace dividends quickly disappear into the national loan account.

6 The Paradox of Organisations

We used to think that we knew how to run organisations. Now we know better. More than ever they need to be global and local at the same time, to be small in some ways but big in others, to be centralised some of the time and decentralised most of it. They expect their workers to be both more autonomous and more of a team, their managers to be more delegating and more controlling. The paradox is neatly summed up in Charles Savage's story, in his book *Fifth Generation Management*, of the manager saying to the new recruit, 'The good news is that you have 120,000 people working for you, the bad news is that they don't know it.'

John Stopford and Charles Baden-Fuller, in their study of rejuvenating businesses, report that the successful ones live with paradox, or what they call dilemmas. They have to be planned and yet be flexible, be differentiated and integrated at the same time, be mass-marketers while catering for many niches; they must introduce new technology but allow their workers to be the masters of their own destiny; they must find ways to get variety and quality and fashion, and all at low-cost; they have, in short, to find a way to reconcile what used to be opposites, instead of choosing between them.

Charles Hampden-Turner, in his book on corporate culture, also focuses on the inevitable dilemmas of organisations, arguing that managers have to be 'masters of paradox', turning the horns of the various inevitable dilemmas into virtuous not vicious circles. He quotes, as an example, the Berkeley consultants, Meridian, who use the mythical Greek image of Scylla, the rock, and Charybdis, the whirlpool, which Odysseus and his sailors had to steer between, to characterise the hard and soft features of organisations, the structured, controlled, masculine side and the flexible, responsive, feminine side, both of which are needed for success.

These authors speak as if we would know an organisation when we see it, full of paradox though it may be. The organisations of the future may not be readily recognisable as such. When intelligence is the primary asset the organisation becomes more like a collection of project groups, some fairly permanent, some temporary, some in alliance with other parties. Instead of an organisation being a castle, a home for life for its defenders, it will be more like a condominium, an association of temporary residents gathered together for their mutual convenience. The condominium may, in fact, not have any physical existence, because the project groups or clusters do not have to be all in the same place. This has caused some to talk of the 'virtual corporation', something that can be discerned more easily on the computer screen than in the physical world. The challenge for tomorrow's leaders is to manage an organisation that is not there in any sense which we are used to.

It is, however, a challenge that must be won, because these minimalist, partly unseen, organisations are the linchpins of our world. We may, most of us, not belong to them, but we shall be selling our services into them; the wealth of our societies will depend upon them; they will, ultimately, be the source of our well-being. The age of the organisation may be coming to an end in one sense, when to be a full-time employee is a minority occupation, and when even for this minority the time in the organisation represents less than half one's adult life, but in another sense the organisation, or what is left of it, will be the critical component of society. Organisations will organise, but to do so they will no longer need to employ. An organising organisation will look and feel very different from an employment organisation. Because it will be less visible as an organisation we should not think it is less important.

7 The Paradox of Age

We all age, but each generation ages differently. This is technically called the cohort factor. Each cohort or generation is affected by its own history. It is, therefore, very unlikely than my children will have the same sort of life-cycle as I have had, or that mine would be like my parents'. My parents' generation saw a world war, in some cases two world wars. They went through a long and deep recession in the Thirties. They valued security above all else and they expected to, and did, work until almost the end of their lives.

Society expected that it would be the same for their children. It wasn't. Work inside organisations has petered out for many in their fifties, creating the kind of mid-life crisis for many which their parents had never known. Change speeded up. The world got smaller. Children did not die and were not killed in wars with the result that we planned for smaller families, one child, sometimes, in place of three. Divorce replaced death as the end of many a marriage, creating the kind of spreadeagled families which to our parents were a rarity. The problems which we encountered were new. The crises were different. Society, however, was still geared to the ageing patterns of the generation before. Pension schemes, divorce laws, social expectations were all inappropriate and took time to change.

It will happen again. My children, unlike previous cohorts, will find conventional jobs and careers harder to get. Their work lives will start later and end earlier, creating a gap between adolescence and adulthood which their parents never knew, a gap which, therefore, they, and we, do not really know how to fill. Their relationships will be different again from ours. Because they have grown up without wars they will be more carefree with their plans and their lives. Their education will have to be more pro-longed, if not indefinite. Women will all do paid work for most of their lives but both sexes may want and need to find intervals of child-rearing and learning. Children are now a decision not an accident. The roles of the sexes will change, and bring with that change different values and priorities.

The paradox of ageing is that every generation perceives itself as justifiably different from its predecessor, but plans as if its successor generation will be the same as them. This time it needs to be different.

8 The Paradox of the Individual

Society speaks with two voices. One voice urges us to discover our 'authentic self', to be ourselves, to plan our own path through life and, whilst respecting the rights of others, to hold fast to the right to be true to ourselves. Individualism acquired a bad name in the years of Reagan and Thatcher when it was used to justify the uninhibited pursuit of private gain, masquerading as 'enterprise'. There was once, however, a more honourable British tradition, drawing on Darwin's idea of self-reliance and a rich tradition of eccentrics and opinion-leaders. It was then, and is now again, respectable and desirable to be yourself.

The other voice is that of the receptionist or the conference-organiser. 'Who do you represent?' 'To whom are you affiliated?' 'What organisation are you from?' Recounting his problem with receptionists and switchboards, the British writer, Anthony Sampson, who works on his own from home, says, 'I'm tempted to reply that I represent the human race . . . the inalienable right to life, liberty and the pursuit of happiness, but it won't get me through the switchboard. I have to reply that I represent no one or that "I'm just a friend". I feel even more freakish at conferences where everyone else seems to represent some company, organisation or group.' It was, he points out, John D. Rockefeller, the creator of Standard Oil, the first modern corporation, who remarked, 'The day of combination is here to stay. Individualism has gone, never to return.' He was only partly right. An MIT study comparing American and Japanese working methods, did conclude that the individualism of American workers had to be balanced by the combination of a good team if they were to match the productivity of the Japanese. The Japanese, however, are looking for some of that individualism and creativity to balance the conforming force of their combinations.

It is a paradox, one best captured by Jung, who said, years ago, that we need others to be truly ourselves. 'I' needs 'We' to be fully 'I'. Looking up, however, at the office-blocks in every city, those little boxes piled on top of each other up into the sky, one has to wonder how much room there is for 'I' amid the filing cabinets and the terminals. It was A. E. Housman, Sampson reminds us, who wrote in one of his poems, 'I, a stranger and afraid in a world I never made.' Who, we must wonder, will be the 'We' to whom we would want to belong? Is it the minimalist, virtual organisation? Or our current 'edge city' in suburbia? Or the disappearing family? Can a personal network substitute for these?

9 The Paradox of Justice

Justice is the bond of society. We are happy to belong to a society which treats us fairly, which gives us our due and which is impartial. The problem is that 'giving each their due' can mean a variety of contradictory things. It can, for instance, mean giving us what we deserve, be that a reward for achievement or a punishment for offences. On the other hand it can mean giving us what we need. Political parties will champion one or the other definition and claim to be the party of justice. Both will be right.

Michael Young, writing 30 years ago, summed up the dilemmas of distributive justice very nicely:

One could say that it was wrong to pay one man more than another because there should be distribution according to needs.

One could say that it was wrong to pay the lazy scientist more than the diligent dustman because there should be distribution according to effort. One could say that it was wrong to pay the intelligent more than the stupid because society should compensate for genetic injustice. One could say that it was wrong to pay the stupid more than the intelligent because society should compensate for the unhappiness which is the usual lot of the intelligent. (No one can do much about the brilliant, they will be miserable anyway.) One could say that it was wrong to pay the man who lived a long and serene life in Upper Slaughter as much as a scientist who wore himself out in the service of knowledge. One could say that it was wrong to pay people who liked their work as much as those who didn't. One could – and did – say anything, and whatever one said it was always with the support of . . . justice.

Thirty years on, the dilemmas remain. Justice, argue some, needs to treat everyone fairly, that is equally – unless there are very good arguments for unequal treatment. That is fair to the underdog but is less fair to those who, perhaps, 'deserve' more, because they contribute more. What is clear is that a society which is perceived to be unjust will earn no loyalty or commitment from its citizens; there will be no good reason for anything other than selfishness. Such a society is doomed, in the end, to destroy itself.

Capitalism thrives on the first definition of distributive justice – those who achieve most should get most. But it will not long be credible or tolerated if it ignores its opposite, that those who need most should have their needs met. To put it another way, capitalism depends on the fundamental principle of inequality – some may do better than others – but will only be acceptable in the long term in a democracy if most people have an equal chance to aspire to that inequality. It is a paradox which we cannot afford to ignore.

Part Two:
Finding the Balance
Pathways Through Paradox

Paradox confuses because things don't behave in the way we instinctively expect them to behave. What worked so well last time around is not guaranteed to work as well next time. Governments seem surprised when each recovery soaks up fewer of the unemployed. They have not taken account of the paradox of organisation, and the fact that organisations belatedly have realised that it is possible to grow without growing the labour force. Governments have been used to thinking of organisations as the delivery vehicles for social policy, not noticing that they now employ only 55 per cent of the workforce on a full-time basis, which is, in turn, only 38 per cent of all adults of working age. The organising organisation is very different from the employment organisation. Governments need to reframe their view of the world.

Paradox also confuses because we are asked to live with contradictions and with simultaneous opposites. Work will be priced highly or at zero. It looks neat to say that we should price it all in the middle, so that everyone has the same, but it would be wrong, it would not work. We have to learn to live with opposites.

To live with simultaneous opposites is, at first glance, a recipe for indecision at best, schizophrenia at worst. It need not be. My mother-in-law was generous to a fault *and* tight-fisted – she would have called it thrifty. We all knew her ways and understood. We ourselves can, in the same hour, make plans to move house next year and decide on the menu for tonight's dinner. Parents are simultaneously tough and strict on their children *and* tender and relaxed. If they do it right, the kids understand. Organisations, similarly, are tight *and* loose; concerned only about the longer term in some areas but passionate about detail in others. We all encounter and handle paradox in our daily lives. When we are used to it, and understand it, paradox is no bother. The nine paradoxes may be new, or newly important, but paradox itself has been with us forever.

It is, however, the understanding which is the key. Balancing the opposites, or switching between them, must not be a random or haphazard act. Without a clear rationale for what is happening, the balancing and the switching can be bewildering to those on the receiving end and frustrating for anyone doing the balancing. Without understanding, things do not work out as they should. Living with paradox is like riding a see-saw. If you know how the process works, and if the person at the other end also knows, then the ride can be exhilarating. If, however, your opposite number does not understand, or wilfully upsets the pattern, you can receive a very uncomfortable and unexpected shock. Children know the game well, and can take a malicious delight in upsetting the mutual understanding.

As it is with see-saws, so it is with life. If we know how and why things work, we can live with the ups and the downs, knowing that the opposites are necessary to each other. We can even come to recognise that for the see-saw to work effectively, others must get as good as we get. What follows, in this part of the book, are three general principles for living with simultaneous opposites. You could call them rules for riding see-saws. They are followed, in Part Three, by examples of the principles at work, in our organisations and in society.

3 The Sigmoid Curve

The Road to Davy's Bar

The Wicklow Mountains lie just outside Dublin in Ireland. It is an area of wild beauty, a place to which, as an Irishman born near there, I return as often as I may. It is still a bare and lonely place, with unmarked roads, and I still get lost. Once, I stopped and asked the way. 'Sure, it's easy,' the local replied. 'Just keep going the way you are, straight ahead, and after a while you'll cross a small bridge with Davy's Bar on the far side, you can't miss it!' 'Yes, I've got that,' I said, 'straight on to Davy's Bar.' 'That's right. Well, half a mile before you get there, turn to your right up the hill.'

It seemed so logical that I thanked him and drove off. By the time I realised that the logic made no sense he had disappeared. As I made my way down to Davy's Bar wondering which of the roads to the right to take, I reflected that he had just given me a vivid example of paradox, perhaps even the paradox of our times: by the time you know where you ought to go, it's too late to go there; or, more dramatically, if you keep on going the way you are, you will miss the road to the future.

Because, like my Irishman, it is easy to explain things looking backwards, we think we can then predict them forwards. It doesn't work, as many economists know to their cost. The world keeps changing. It is one of the paradoxes of success that the things and the ways which got you where you are, are seldom the things to keep you there. If you think that they are, and that you know the way to the future because it is a continuation of where you've come from, you may well end up in Davy's Bar, with nothing left but a chance to drown your sorrows and reminisce about times past.

Although he knew it not, my Irish friend had also introduced me to the Sigmoid Curve, the curve which explains so many of our present discontents and confusions. It is this curve, and what follows from it, which is the first of the Pathways through Paradox, the first of the three devices for finding a balance between the contradictions.

The Sigmoid Curve

The Sigmoid Curve is the S-shaped curve which has intrigued people since time began.

The Sigmoid Curve sums up the story of life itself. We start slowly, experimentally and falteringly, we wax and then we wane. It is the story of the British Empire – and of the Russian Empire and of all empires always. It is the story of a product's life-cycle and of many a corporation's rise and fall. It even describes the course of love and of relationships. If that were all, it would be a depressing image, with nothing to discuss except to decide where precisely on the curve one is now, and what units of time should go on the scale at the bottom. Those units of time are also getting depressingly small. They used to be decades, perhaps even generations. Now they are years, sometimes months. The accelerating pace of change shrinks every Sigmoid Curve.

Luckily, there is life beyond the curve. The secret of constant growth is to start a new Sigmoid Curve before the first one peters out. The right place to start that second curve is at point **A**, where there is the time, as well as the resources and the energy, to get the new curve through its initial explorations and flounderings before the first curve begins to dip downwards.

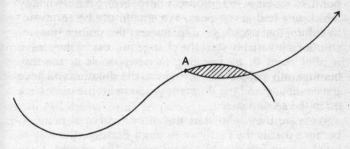

That would seem obvious; were it not for the fact that at point **A** all the messages coming through to the individual or the institution are that everything is going fine, that it would be folly to change when the current recipes are working so well. All that we know of change, be it personal change or change in organisations, tells us that the real energy for change only comes when you are looking disaster in the face, at point **B** on the first curve.

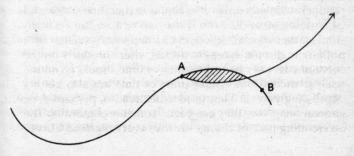

At this point, however, it is going to require a mighty effort to drag oneself up to where, by now, one should be on the second curve. To make it worse, the current leaders are now discredited because they are seen to have led the organisation down the hill, resources are depleted and energies are low. For an individual, an event like redundancy typically takes place at point **B**. It is hard, at that point, to mobilise the resources or to restore the credibility which one had at the peak. We should not be surprised, therefore, that people get depressed at this point or that institutions invariably start the change process, if they leave it until point **B**, by bringing in new people at the top, because only people who are new to the situation will have the credibility and the different vision to lift the place back on to the second curve.

Wise are they who start the second curve at point **A**, because that is the Pathway through Paradox, the way to build a new future while maintaining the present. Even then, however, the problems do not end. The second curve, be it a new product, a new way of operating, a new strategy or a new culture, is going to be noticeably different from the old. It has to be. The people also have to be different. Those who lead the second curve are not going to be the people who led the first curve. For one thing, the continuing responsibility of those original leaders is to keep that first curve going long enough to support the early stages of the second curve. For another, they will find it temperamentally difficult to abandon their first curve while it is doing so well, even if they recognise, intellectually, that a new curve is needed. For a time, therefore, new ideas and new people have to coexist with the old until the second curve is established and the first begins to wane.

The hatched area beneath the peak is, therefore, a time of great confusion. Two groups of people, or more, and two sets of ideas are competing for the future. No matter how wise and benevolent they be, the leaders of the first curve must worry about their own futures when their curve begins to die. It requires great foresight, and even greater magnanimity, to foster others and plan one's own departure or demise. Those who can do it, however, will ensure the renewal and the continued growth of their organisation.

I cannot pretend that is easy even with that foresight. I have sat and watched the chairman of a great company speak to his assembled barons. 'I have two messages for you today,' he said. 'First, I want to remind you that we are a very successful business, perhaps more successful today than we have ever been. Secondly, I must tell you that if we want to continue to be successful we shall have to change, fundamentally, the way we are working now.' He went on to explain why the different futures he foresaw would require different responses, but no one was listening. The first message had drowned out the second. If they were so successful, they felt, it would be folly to change. He was right; he was standing at point **A** and looking over the hill, but he could not get his changes implemented. Three years later, by now at point **B**, the company knew it had to change but the first person they turned on, and removed, was the chairman. He was no longer credible, nor had his conviction that he was right endeared him to his colleagues.

What is true of organisations is as true of individuals and their relationships. A good life is probably a succession of second curves, started before the first curve fades. Lives and priorities change as one grows up and older. Every relationship will sometime need its second curve. Too often, couples cling on to their old habits and contracts for too long. By the time they realise their need of that second curve they are already at point **B**. It is too late to do it together. They find other partners. On the other hand, I sometimes like to say, teasingly, that I am on my second marriage – but with the same partner, which makes it less expensive. Because we managed, in time, to find that very different second curve – together. I would not deny, however, that the hatched period beneath the peak was difficult, as we struggled to keep what was best in our past while we experimented with the new.

Capitalism, newly triumphant, probably has to reinvent itself. Things which we took for granted, like nation states and large organisations, seem to be impediments to progress not its helpers. When both monarchy and the judiciary, in Britain, are seen to be wanting, few institutions in that country can be sure that they are still on the upward curve. We ask our politicians for a lead, by which we mean a sight of the second curve, but we want them, all the same, to do nothing to disturb the first curve. In our own lives we sense that there is often another hill to climb now that life is longer and, in many ways, larger, but we have no sense of where to find it. We are, so many of us, living in that hatched area, worrying that the first curve will turn down before we find the second.

The second curve is the road up the hill to the right. We stand today at the crossroads, asking the way to our future. Words like hierarchy, loyalty and duty, no longer carry the weight they once did. Other words like freedom, choice and rights turn out to be more complicated than they seemed. What was once obvious, like the necessity of economic growth, is now hedged around with qualifications. We thought we knew how to run organisations, but the organisations of today bear no resemblance to the ones we knew, and so we have to think again, to find the second curve of management before it is too late. Meanwhile, we have to keep the first curve going. As long as we can do that, we will keep the balance between the present and the future; we can manage to live with paradox because we understand what is happening.

The Discipline of the Second Curve

The concept of the Sigmoid Curve has, I find, helped many people and many institutions to understand their current confusions. The question which they always ask, however, is 'How do we know where we are on the first curve?' One way of answering that is to ask them to make their own private and personal assessment of their position, or that of their organisation, to draw the first curve as they see it, and to mark an X on it to show where they are now. Almost invariably, when they reveal their perceptions of the curve, there is a consensus that they are farther along the curve that any of them would previously have admitted. They are nearer to point **B** than to point **A**.

Like the story of the road to Davy's Bar, you will only know for sure where you are on the curve when you look back. It is easier, too, to see where others are on their curves than to see yourself. We must therefore proceed by guess and assumption. There is no science for this sort of thing.

The discipline of the second curve requires that you always assume that you are near the peak of the first curve, at point **A**, and should therefore be starting to prepare a second curve. Organisations should assume that their present strategies will need to be replaced within two or three years and that their product life-cycles are shorter than they were. Richard Foster of McKinsey studied 208 companies over 18 years in order to discover those who were consistently successful. There were only three who lasted the course for the whole 18 years. Fifty-three per cent could not maintain their record for more than two years. Individuals should also work on the assumption that life will not continue as it has for ever and that a new direction will be needed in two or three years.

It may well be that the assumption turns out to be wrong, that the present trends can be prolonged much longer, and that the first curve was really only in its infancy. Nothing has been lost. Only the exploratory phase of the second curve has been done. No major commitments will have been undertaken until the second curve overtakes the first, which will never happen as long as the first curve is still on the rise. Keeping the two curves going will become a habit.

The discipline of devising that second curve will, however, have had its effect. It will have forced one to challenge the assumptions underlying the first curve and to devise some possible alternatives. It is tempting to think that the world has always been arranged the way it is and to delude ourselves that nothing will ever change. The discipline of the second curve keeps one sceptical, curious and inventive – attitudes essential in a time of change, and the best way of coping with the contradictions which accompany such a time.

The discipline of the second curve follows the traditional four-stage cycle of discovery. Questions start it off. The questions spark off ideas, possibilities, hypotheses. The best of these must then be tested out, tentatively and experimentally. Finally, the results of the experiments are reviewed. The first two stages cost nothing except the time for imagination. They can be very stimulating, particularly if they start from the greenfield hypothesis – 'If we did not exist would we reinvent ourselves and, if so, what would we look like?' Or, in a more personal example of second-curve thinking, 'If we did not live here, or do what we are doing, what would we be doing, where and how would we be living if we had the chance to start again?' The discipline of the second curve requires that you do not reinvent the same life, because that would merely perpetuate the first curve. The second curve is always different, although it builds on the first and grows out of it.

In *The Paradox of Success*, his book on the personal renewal of leaders, John O'Neil uses the model of the second curve to describe how leaders do, or do not, move on in life.

He points out that one essential is to let go of your past. If one is too emotionally attached to what has gone before, it is difficult to be different in any way. One can then cling on until it is too late. He quotes Odysseus as an example of a young warrior chief who was so committed to roaming and raiding, at which he once excelled, that he spent 20 years coming back from the war in Troy to his kingdom of Ithaca, reluctant to assume the responsibilities of government. By the time he did get home he was a failed commander, in rags, with his kingdom in a mess. It is the story of the man who did not want to grow up.

If success comes early, it can be particularly hard to turn one's back on it when one's star begins to wane. It was sad to watch Bjorn Borg return to the tennis courts in an attempt to recapture past glories, long after his talents had faded. It is often easier to move on from disasters than from successes. I have always, therefore, been impressed by people like Leonard Cheshire, the distinguished and heroic British fighter pilot who, after the war was over, left all that behind and set out to create a network of homes for the elderly and disabled. I am impressed by the family business in France which, at just the right time, turned its back on the textile industry in which it had made its name, and launched a chain of supermarkets. 'Where did you find the courage to do something so completely different?' I asked. 'It would have required more courage to do nothing,' the head of the family replied. 'We had the responsibility to provide a future for the family, and the past, distinguished though it was, could not have been that future.'

Curvilinear Logic

Moving on requires a belief in what Schumacher used to call curvilinear logic, the conviction that the world and everything in it really is a Sigmoid Curve, that everything has its ups and then its downs, and that nothing lasts for ever or was there for ever. Just-In-Time Manufacturing was developed in Japan, and later copied everywhere. The idea of a constant stream of deliveries to your factory door, as and when you needed them, was blindingly obvious when you thought about it. Cut out the warehouse and all those storage costs. Let the suppliers carry the inventory costs instead, or rather, eliminate them completely, provided always that you can guarantee that the lorries with the bits will arrive 'just-in-time'. Unfortunately, the idea became too popular. They tell me that the delivery vehicles now jam all the freeways around Tokyo, meaning that just-in-time often gives way to just-too-late. The costs of the traffic jams are beginning to outweigh the costs of the original warehouses, to say nothing of all the environmental damage caused by those idling exhausts. You can have too much of a good thing, or, curvilinear logic strikes again.

Curvilinear logic is not intuitively obvious if you are still ascending the first curve. Business history is littered with the stories of founding fathers who thought that their way was the only way. The French textile business mentioned above is a notable rarity among family businesses. The paradox of success, that what got you where you are won't keep you where you are, is a hard lesson to learn. Curvilinear logic means starting life over again, something which gets harder as one gets older. It is better, therefore, in organisations, to entrust the curvilinear thinking to the next generation. They can see more clearly where the first curve is heading and what the next curve might look like. It is the job of their elders to give them permission to be different, and then, when the next curve is established, to get out of the way. For that to happen, there has to be a new curve for them, outside.

'My father brought me back from America to run the business here in Treviso,' his daughter said. 'But he still comes into the office every day, even Sundays. He wants me to run the business as if I was him, and I'm not. And the business has to change, if he would only let it. It's very frustrating.' Her story was not unusual. The father had nothing else he wanted to do. The business had been his life, and now he had no other. 'Wet leaves, we call them in Japan,' said the Japanese lady, describing the reaction of Japan's women to their retired executive husbands. 'You know how it is with wet leaves, they just stick around!' For curvilinear logic to work in the organisation there has to be a life beyond the organisation for the heroes of the first curve.

The Coca-Cola Company is, on the face of it, the great exception to the concept of the second curve. For 104 years they have sold the same product in the same packaging with much the same advertising. The only time they changed the formula they were forced by their customers to reverse the decision. Their secret may lie, however, in the motto which is inscribed in their central offices and in the minds of all its officers – 'The world belongs to the discontented'. It was the favourite saying of their early and long-time chairman, Robert Woodruff. He was warning against complacency and advocating a perpetual curiosity – the itch of the second curve. Coca-Cola's Japanese company, I was told, test-markets a new soft-drink variety or other product every month. Even if most of them fail most of the time, it keeps the questing spirit alive. When and if Coca-Cola's 104-year curve turns down, they hope that they will be prepared.

The Japanese, of course, have their own word for it – *kaizen*, or continuous improvement. The assumption behind *kaizen* is the assumption behind this book – that there is no perfect answer in a changing world. We must therefore be forever searching. Anita Roddick, of the Body Shop, puts it more succinctly: 'What is so wonderful about the Body Shop is that we still don't know the rules.' As long as they think that way, so long will they thrive. Complacency is the enemy of curiosity.

The Royal Dutch Shell Group has yet another approach. They call it scenario planning. It has been well explained by Peter Schwartz, one of the early members of the planning group, in his book about it, *The Art of the Long View*. A group of executives, aided by some outsiders, spends a year or more drawing up alternative scenarios for the oil business and the countries and cultures in which it operates. These are not plans but possibilities, deliberately set at the opposite ends of a spectrum. The planning group then uses these scenarios educationally, exposing their managers around the world to the alternatives and asking them to consider how they would respond if either happened. Shell want no surprises, and were not surprised by the oil crisis of the early 1970s nor by the collapse of the Russian Empire. Their second-curve thinking was ready. It was not so, says Schwartz, in the case of the American military. They made every sort of contingency plan for the Cold War but they never asked the scenario question 'What if we won?' When they did win, they knew not what to do.

Peter Senge, in his classic book on the learning organisation, reminds us that our mental models, or private scenarios, are crucial to the learning process. We all carry mental maps around with us – that hierarchy is natural, for instance, that women can't manage or that men don't care; that careers last until 65 or that every next job has to be a promotion. We need to check that these assumptions are still valid because they lock us into our existing curve. They inhibit second-curve thinking. My first book on organisations was written 20 years ago. Quite unconsciously, I used the male pronoun exclusively throughout the book. It became a standard textbook, used by those training to work in schools, hospitals and social services as well as business. My book caused a great deal of offence to the many women who had to study it because it appeared to imply that I, the supposed authority, thought that there was no place for them in management. My unconscious mental map of 20 years ago only mirrored what many men felt then, and some still do. That map locked them into their first curve; it made it difficult for them to envisage another kind of world and another way of doing things. My book was not only offensive, it was harmful.

Many of the ideas in this book stem from second-curve thinking – the discipline which says that the past might not be the best guide to the future, that there can be another way, and that some 'myths of the future', as Schwartz calls them, will help. We must, however, beware that we do not abandon the first curve too early. The second curve needs the resources and the time which only the first curve can provide. It has to grow out of the first. 'Dreams give wings to fools,' my young daughter used to tell me when she heard me fantasising about other lives which we might live. She was expressing her instinct that the future needs to be rooted in the past if it is to be real. The secret of balance in a time of paradox is to allow the past and the future to coexist in the present.

Fertilising the Second Curve

Second-curve thinking will come most naturally from the second generation, those who will inherit the future of the institution or the society. They will, however, need both permission and encouragement. They must realise that what they might privately think of as revolution, or even sedition, is possibly the way ahead in due course. New ideas can coexist with old.

One organisation openly entrusted its second-curve thinking to a group of executives in their early thirties. It happened, however, almost by accident. They wanted to celebrate the twenty-fifth anniversary of their organisation. Their first thought was to commission a history of those first 25 years. That seemed, on reflection, to be too self-indulgent and uninteresting. They therefore decided to commission an outside look at the next 25 years for their industry. They were persuaded that the most fruitful way to do that would be to entrust that forward look to the brightest and best of their own people, people who might be leading their organisation when those years arrived. The look at the future should, therefore, include some thoughts and recommendations on how the organisation should adapt to the changes they might foresee for their industry and the world around them. They were giving these young people the responsibility for their inheritance.

I was asked to act as mentor to the study. I agreed, provided that the board of the organisation agreed to publish the non-confidential part of the exercise as a booklet, without censoring it in any way. The board agreed, but went further. They offered to invite all their customers to a reception to celebrate the anniversary, to listen to a presentation of the findings of the group, whatever they might be, and to receive a free copy of the uncensored booklet. The effect of this advance commitment was impressive. The group saw that this was not some ingenious educational exercise but a genuine attempt to build some new thinking into the existing fabric of the organisation. They were begin publicly trusted by their seniors to develop some new thinking. Their seniors were not only impressed by the results of the study, they took them to heart. Their advance commitment had ensured that they would not feel it necessary to defend the status quo, the first curve, and squash the beginnings of the second.

It is important that the seniors give permission and encouragement. It is also important that the next generation accepts their responsibility for second-curve thinking. Preoccupied with the immediacy of their own careers, it is tempting to think that second-curve thinking can be left until later, that the present is their proper priority, the future the priority of those in charge. In actual fact, it should be the other way round.

I helped, once, to organise what came to be called the Windsor Meetings. They took place at St George's House, a small study centre in the middle of Windsor Castle, often used for weekend gatherings of influential individuals to discuss, privately and informally, social and ethical issues. They were, inevitably, discussions about the present, because the people who came were in charge of the present. We decided, with the help and support of some businesses, to bring together representatives of the next generation of influential people, individuals from all sectors of society who were identified for us as likely future leaders in their spheres.

Thus it was that a young colonel, tipped as a future general, found himself beside a rising trades-union official, a talented young headmistress, a banker, some civil servants, three of the younger and more thoughtful politicians from the different parties, a campaigner for human rights, the new editor of one of the quality newspapers, a television newscaster, a doctor and a lawyer, five business executives – all people successful in their thirties, but preoccupied with their own careers, too busy, at this stage, to look outside or to know anyone not involved in their line of work. They were all at the lower end of their personal curves, and rising fast. Invited to Windsor Castle, as guests, for a week, they were asked to debate and discuss the shape of the society which they would inherit, as people likely to reach the higher level of their spheres of influence.

Few of them had thought about such broad issues. None of them had met such a wide range of other interests. Their discussions were always stimulating and their reports insightful, but the ultimate benefit was the realisation that they had a responsibility to help shape the society which they were likely to inherit. It was a consciously élitist exercise, because if those soon to be in power are not conscious of their responsibility to shape a second curve, who is?

Many of those groups still meet, because, in spite of their very different preoccupations, they found that they also shared a concern for the future of their society, that it should be civilised as well as rich, humane as well as adventurous. There is strength in companionship when it comes to shaping the second curve. We have to hope that, when and if they reach positions of eminence, they will not forget their commitment to that second curve.

Both of these examples used insiders. Some organisations prefer outsiders, feeling that they may have a more objective view and a clearer perspective. Consultants thrive on contracts for what are, effectively, second-curve thinking. The thinking, however, is only part of it. There needs to be the commitment to carry it through, to endure the early dip before the curve climbs upwards, to live with the first curve while the second one develops. These things cannot be done by outsiders. To manage paradox, you need to live with it as well as analyse it.

4 The Doughnut Principle

The Inside-Out Doughnut

The doughnut in question is an American doughnut, the
kind with a hole in the middle, rather than the British version, which has jam instead of a hole. The doughnut
principle, however, requires an inside-out doughnut, one
with the hole on the outside and the dough in the middle. It
can only, therefore, be an imaginary doughnut, a conceptual doughnut, one for thinking with, not eating.

A doughnut may seem to be an unlikely Pathway through
Paradox, but the concept of balancing a core and a bounded
space is crucial to a proper understanding of most of life, as
I shall hope to show. It is a way to find the balance between
what we have to do and what we could do or could be. It is
a way of getting around the problem of the empty raincoat,
of being an instrument of society but also a free individual.

We might look, for instance, at our job, whether that is
our paid job or our unpaid role in life, as parent, wife,
husband or carer, student or friend. The heart of the
doughnut, the core, contains all the things which have to
be done in that job or role if you are not to fail. In any formal

job, these things will be listed and will be called your duties. Even where they are not listed, these duties are often well understood. The core, however, is not the whole of the doughnut. If it were, life would be all chore as well as core. There is, thankfully, the space beyond. This space is our opportunity to make a difference, to go beyond the bounds of duty, to live up to our full potential. That remains our ultimate responsibility in life, a responsibility which is always larger than our duty, just as the doughnut is larger than its core.

The doughnut image is a conceptual way of relating duty to a fuller responsibility in every institution or group in society. Doughnuts stimulate our thinking about the proper equation between commitments and flexibility, in all the structures of our work as well as in our personal life. We can draw a doughnut to represent a relationship, or an organisation, or a work group, just as we can use it to reveal the balance in our own life between work and family or between necessity and choice. It is a visual tool for balancing what often seem to be contradictions.

Much of life now looks like that doughnut. Organisations as well as individuals have come to realise that they have their essential core, a core of necessary jobs and necessary people, a core which is surrounded by an open flexible space which they fill with flexible workers and flexible supply contracts. The strategic issue for organisations, nowadays, is to decide what activities and which people to put in which space. It is not always obvious. Businesses have their core obligations or duty to their shareholders, but their responsibilities go much farther. Finding the right balance between this duty and a wider responsibility is a dilemma at the heart of capitalism.

Schools, in most countries, now have their required core curriculum, with discretionary space around it. The argument, again, is about balance. What, and how much, should go in which space? Too much core and there is no room for individual student difference or for local school in-itiatives. Too much space and there is too much variety in the standards of delivery.

We can apply the doughnut principle to processes as well as to structures. Reward systems tend to lay down the minimum remuneration with space for options, bonuses and performance money beyond. Our implied contracts within our personal relationships contain a core of obliga-tions, with space for individual difference around the core. In your marriage, wrote Khalil Gibran in his poem, *The Prophet*, which gets read at countless weddings and is then, too often, forgotten, you should stand together, but 'let there be space in your togetherness'. What every couple needs to define, however, is what should go into that space and what the boundaries are to be. A marriage without boundaries is, I suspect, an unreal doughnut, and doomed to fail. Every couple could, with advantage, draw their own doughnut.

The doughnut principle starts early. I remember my own schooldays. I had passed the big examination and was studying the certificate when I was confronted by my dis-appointed teacher, obviously quite distressed by my results. 'What's wrong?' I said, 'I passed, didn't I? Isn't that enough?' 'Enough is never enough,' he replied, 'until you have exhausted your potential. To pass was easy. You could have done better, much better.' Enough is never enough. I recalled John Donne's lines, 'When you have done, you have not done, for there is more.' To pass was the essential core. To fill the doughnut I had to do more. Life, my teacher was trying to tell me, should not be a half-filled doughnut. I have spent most of the rest of my life wondering how I ought to fill it.

That principle now applies to much of our work. That ugly word 'empowerment' could better be interpreted as the doughnut principle at work. In the past, jobs used to be all core, certainly at the lower levels, because too much dis-cretion meant too much unpredictability. One of my early jobs had the fine-sounding title of Regional Co-ordinator Marketing (Oil) Mediterranean Region. My friends were impressed, but they did not know the reality. The reality was a three-page job description outlining my duties, but the hard truth was contained in the final paragraph: 'Authority to initiate expenditure up to a maximum of £10'. My doughnut was all core and no space. That way the organisation got no surprises, or so it hoped. All was predictable, planned and controlled. It was also dull and frustrating, with no space for self-expression, no space to make a difference, no empowerment. My memoranda went from my role – MK/32 – not from me. I was merely a 'temporary role occupant' and I felt like an empty raincoat.

There are some, on the other hand, whose jobs are nearly all space, with little core and no boundary. Ministers of religion have a visible core to their work – the church services, some sick visits, committees and finances – but there is no limit to their responsibilities for the souls of their congregation or for their evangelising work. Some of the most stressed people that I have known have been people with jobs like these, because there is no end, no way in which you can look back and say 'It was a great year', because it could always have been greater. Empowerment, in a sense, has gone too far. Without a boundary it is easy to be oppressed by guilt, for enough is never enough. Entrepreneurs revel in the space for discretion, but the successful ones are careful to give themselves targets and limits. Even then, the record of early entrepreneurship is one of long days and no holidays, of unremitting effort to fill the space beyond the core. A sensible job is a balanced doughnut.

Type 2 Accountability

More space, in fact, is not always welcomed, even in a conventional job. More space means more choice but also, paradoxically, more room for error, or, more precisely, another type of error. In statistics, as I recall, there are two types of error. There is a Type 1 error which, in simple terms, means getting it wrong, and a Type 2 error which, in effect, means not getting it right, or as right as it could have been. There is an important difference. A Type 2 error means that the full possibilities of the situation have not been exploited or developed; enough was not enough. In the old tightly planned world in which everything was contained in the inner circle, you only had to look out for the Type 1 errors. As long as you avoided those you could call yourself successful.

Management was easier, too, since the priority was to check for Type 1 errors. Avoid those and the system was designed to deliver. For many people, life was keeping one's nose clean, compiling, as the years went by, a fault-free curriculum vitae, lived by the book, with retirement as the promised rest at the end, just as the life-insurance advertisements would have it. 'He walked in many corridors of power,' someone said of a politician, 'and left no footprint in any of them.' It was a life free of Type 1 errors.

It was also a life devoid of the Type 2 errors. These are the errors of omission not commission, the things one did not do which one could have, the failure to fill the space between the circles. The old prayer book of the Anglican Church puts it nicely, I discovered, as I mumbled my way through the familiar words one day: 'We have left undone those things which we ought to have done [Type 2]; and we have done those things which we ought not to have done [Type 1].' I used to think that what was meant by the first bit were those chores I had neglected, the difficult meetings I had put off, the letters I had not written, but those, I realised, are all Type 1 errors. The important sins of omission are the things I did not do, which could have made a difference. Enough is not enough.

We hanker after the freedom of more space in our lives

and our work. Leaner, flatter organisations provide that space; but now it is up to us to fill the space. We used to be held accountable only for Type 1 errors. Now we have a new accountability, for the things we could have done but didn't. The two accountabilities are a new fact of life. With space goes responsibility. Only when that is generally accepted will we be able to have a truly free society, one in which the freedom to be what you want to be is accompanied by the responsibility to do no harm to others (Type 1) and to use the freedom to some purpose (Type 2).

One day, too, our public bodies will recognise that it is not enough to make no mistakes, Type 1 accountability, it is also important to have done the work as well as it could have been done, to have been better than expected. Public accountability needs to be redefined to include the recognition of Type 2 responsibilities. John Major's idea of the Citizen's Charter in Britain is a small step towards this recognition, and will be a bigger step when it recognises that there are rewards for excellence in service, as well as penalties for lapses.

Personal Doughnuts

Some people make their work the whole of their life. That necessary core of the job fills the whole doughnut, leaving little or no space for anything else. Are they right or wise? There is an argument that capitalist businesses do not exist as, theoretically at least, communist structures did, to liberate and develop people's humanity and allow them to become moral and fulfilled human beings. Existential development, says Britain's Elizabeth Vallance, is not the primary aim of business but of churches or educational or artistic institutions. Businesses will look to the self-development of their people only to enhance the business's ability to make profits. If she is right, then those who seek their fulfilment in demanding business jobs are likely to be disappointed. It would probably be no better if they worked full-time for her churches or educational or artistic establishments. In all the organisations of a capitalist society, the individual is, in strict theory, the instrument not the purpose.

Against that, there is the view that all work should be a calling or vocation; that the wealth creation of business is as worth doing and as valuable as the health creation of a hospital. We can and should, that argument goes, get our fulfilment out of our work. There can be no single answer. The doughnut principle would suggest that if you cannot get your existential development from your current job you should either change the job or make sure that the empty spaces in your personal doughnut are filled somewhere else. One job does not have to fill all needs.

I used to think that it should. I looked for a job which would provide me with interesting and exciting work; work, too, that I would be proud of doing. I also wanted enough money and the chance to make more of it, if I needed to, good companions and a pleasing location with the chance of travel. Needless to say, I never found the perfect job. There was, however, a doughnut solution. If I adopted a 'portfolio' approach to life, meaning that I saw my life as a collection of different groups and activities, of bits and pieces of work, like a share portfolio, I could get different things from different bits. A part of that portfolio would be 'core', providing the essential wherewithal for life, but it would be balanced by work done purely for interest or for a cause, or because it would stretch me personally, or simply because it was fascinating or fun.

It was easier, I found, to make money, if that was all that you were bothered about, than if you tried to combine money-making with all the other attributes. Similarly, it was easier to find work that was involving and worthwhile if you weren't too concerned about the pay. It meant, however, turning down the offer of one of the 70-hour-a-week jobs which would have left no time for anything else, and putting together a package of different kinds of work, a work portfolio. My life, now is doughnut-shaped. I can even specify the amount of days which I am prepared to allocate to core activities and the amount left over for personal space. As I get older, the core begins to shrink, leaving me with the interesting but difficult problem of how best to fill the space beyond the core, to live up to my responsibility for my life.

Increasingly, it should be possible to arrange a portfolio of different sorts of work within the same organisation, by joining a number of their different doughnuts. Wise organisations recognise the advantages of these internal portfolios. Different tasks and different groups bring out different talents in the individual; they confront him or her with different experiences. Some businesses now actively encourage their staff to take on some voluntary activities in the community, allowing them time from work if necessary. Other organisations are happy to see their executives sitting on public bodies, teaching a course at a local college, serving on a school board or standing for political office. It is, they say, an excellent form of development. It is also a way of building a work portfolio with the company's blessing.

There are fewer, smaller cores in the job doughnuts these days, in all spheres and levels of work. If we wait around for someone to tell us what to do, we shall wait for a long time. If we look for a standard route through life, a sure way, guaranteed to get us through to the end, we shall be disappointed. We have to fill our own spaces.

Societies which overemphasise the core can be too regimented. A place for everyone and everyone in their place was Plato's version of a just society, but it meant that everyone's role in life was predetermined, all core and very little space for individuality. It was an idea that lingered on in Britain when I first came to live and work in that country, even though the core was more socially determined than official. There were strong norms on dress and behaviour. 'Wear brown on Sundays,' I was told, 'and never telephone anyone after 10 o'clock at night.' I envy the freedom of my children and their friends who respect neither of those conventions nor many others, but they can suffer from the burden of too much space. There is too much choice of career, too many varieties of life styles from which to choose. It is no longer mandatory to be married in order to be a parent, let alone to share a home. It is hard for them to see what the core of life can be apart from earning the bare necessities, and even those will, if need be, come from the state.

They have the freedom to design their own doughnuts. They would be wise to give themselves both core and boundaries, a base-line for the kind of life they want to live and some areas they will not touch, some things they will not do, some rules of conduct which they will keep. A society which emphasises rights but neglects obligations can leave too much space for its citizens. The problem for the unemployed is not so much that they are hungry but that they have no core to their lives. Empty doughnuts are not easy to live with, any more than doughnuts which are all core.

Doughnut Organisations

Work, itself, is no longer organised as it used to be. Organisations are not now drawn as pyramids of boxes. British Steel is said once to have had an organisation chart which, when unfolded, stretched across a room. Those charts now have circles and amoeba-like blobs where the boxes used to be. It isn't even clear where the organisation begins and ends, with customers, suppliers and allied organisations linked into a varying 'network organisation'. Work no longer means, for everyone, having a 'job' with an employer. As organisations disperse and contract, more and more of us will be working for ourselves, often by ourselves.

The new shape of work will centre around small organisations, most of them in the service sector, with a small core of key people and a collection of stringers or portfolio workers in the space around the core. David Birch, an economist with the research organisation Cognetics, studied the job market in the USA from 1987–91. He found that the big firms laid off a net 2.4 million workers in that period, while firms with fewer than 20 employees added 4.4 million new jobs, with slightly larger firms adding another 1.4 million. Nor were all these jobs, any longer, hamburger jobs. Software, telecommunications, environmental engineering, health products and services, and specialised education are increasingly the province of the tiny partnership. They are all well suited to the portfolio worker, who costs much less if the firm does not have to house him or her. Their work, and that of their larger brothers, increasingly fits the doughnut pattern.

We can see the doughnut pattern most obviously when we look at the new-style organisations. The $\frac{1}{2} \times 2 \times 3$ formula, which all organisations have to work towards in this competitive age, means that every organisation these days has its smaller core and its surrounding partnerships. Some of these partners are their traditional suppliers, some are independent professionals, some are the part-time peripheral workforce and some are the allied businesses, partners in joint ventures of one sort or another.

The British government, in an attempt to reduce costs, is 'market-testing' many of its traditional core activities. Functions which have traditionally been done by the core Civil Service are now required to be tested for cost and performance against outside tenders. If they compare unfavourably, the activity moves into the space of the doughnut. The collection of Britain's National Insurance contributions, a form of wages' tax worth nearly £40 billion a year, is one activity proposed for such market-testing. There are, however, some reasonable concerns that it would be too risky to contract out such a vital source of national revenue. It should, some feel, be designated a core activity, impervious to market-testing. The Home Office is contemplating putting activities as diverse as the Criminal Injuries Compensation Board, the customs control at ports and airports and even the Research and Planning Unit out to tender. The BBC's contentious policy of 'producer choice', under which all decisions have to be market-tested, means that the doughnut balance of the Corporation is being decided piecemeal, by individual producers, on a short-term cost basis. Many fear that this process is not guaranteed to be the best way to arrive at a long-term strategic balance, at the optimum doughnut for the BBC.

Businesses routinely put their materials-suppliers in the space of their corporate doughnuts. The vertically integrated organisation, one which wanted to own and run the whole of its doughnut, is a thing of the past. Some, however, also contract out crucial service functions. Eastman Kodak sees sense in contracting out their whole information system. Others give their strategy formulation to consultants. There is not limit to what you can, if you wish, put in the space of the doughnut. It is the balance which is crucial. The British Civil Service is worried about the effects on morale if too many of the key elements of their work are given to outsiders. Short-term savings may result in long-term damage if a demoralised service fails to recruit new talent as a result. There is no neat general answer. It is always a question of finding the appropriate balance.

There can be worries that the new partners may effectively become part of the core if they are bonded too tight. The flexibility, which was the point of the doughnut structure, disappears if the supplier becomes dependent on one customer for most of its business, or the firm on one supplier. Contracts should be flexible, experience suggests, and not more than 30 per cent of capacity or requirements should be tied to any one outfit.

Ricardo Semler, president of Semco in Brazil, deliberately designs his whole company as a doughnut, or what he would call a double circle, with a group of counsellors in the middle and all the other workers, the partners and associates, as he terms them, in the outer space. They are then held together in smaller doughnuts, or circles, by co-ordinators. Managing doughnuts is the new organisational challenge. It is a challenge because one is managing the doughnut, and its different spaces, rather than the person. Managing other people's spaces is not easy. It is no longer the manager and the managed, but the designer of the doughnut and the occupant; a different relationship, one built more on trust and mutual respect than on control.

Organisations everywhere are being 'reinvented' or 're-engineered'. They are breaking down, or rather, blowing up their functions and their old ways of working and are regrouping people, equipment and systems around a particular task. They are creating work doughnuts, groups with complete responsibility for discharging the task, with specified rules and duties – the core – and a lot of discretionary space to do it in the way that they think best. The results can be startling. The most famous is Ford's accounts-payable department which thought that they had done well when they reduced their staff by 20 per cent to 400 until they found that Mazda did the job with only five! Ford thought again and got their numbers down to 100, the $\frac{1}{2} \times 2 \times 3$ formula beaten twice over. The term 'Business Re-Engineering' has been patented by a consulting firm, but the concept at its heart is as old as the doughnut.

The doughnut organisation is even laid out, physically, as a doughnut. The centre no longer dominates from a headquarters tower block. It is smaller and more club-like, with outlying or satellite offices around the country. Frank Becker, who is leading an American project called Work-scape 21 at Cornell University, believes that more and more workers will split time between a central office, a computer-equipped home office and a satellite office in a suburban business park. The central office itself will be doughnut-shaped, built around 'common rooms' which will increasingly resemble hotel lobbies, or the rooms of a clubhouse.

I was meeting with the senior executive group of one of the country's leading manufacturers of office furniture. The subject for discussion was the executive suite of the future – what sort of furniture would it require. We decided to start by quizzing Anita, the Human Resources director, on how she spent a typical working week, in order to get some feel of how she would use her office. In the last month, it turned out, Anita had worked out of hotel rooms, airplanes and airport lounges, in the premises of the subsidiary businesses, and in her home in the evenings and early mornings. She had spent two Friday afternoons in her office, collecting the non-urgent mail which had not caught up with her on her travels, and checking schedules with her secretary. The only classy furniture she really needed was a bag to hold her bits and pieces of electronic equipment. For her, the office was a club which she checked into occasionally.

Doughnut Thinking

This has, for me, been the year of funerals. I have listened to many a eulogy on the life of old friends or relatives. Those eulogies always relate the facts and the distinctions of the life now ended, but they go on to the important and most interesting bit – a description of the person as they were to those who knew and loved them. By the time we die, I realised again and again, our doughnuts have to be complete. The real 'us' is, ironically, not in the core but in the whole, if we think of the core as the necessities of life, that curriculum vitae which most of us so assiduously compile in our early years. It is up to us, and only us, to fill the space before we die.

I seldom know, in any detail, what it is that my friends really do in their work, because when we meet we talk of other things. Ironically, I think, I like them better when they are not succeeding, and they me likewise, because there is then more space and time for friends and fun. To put it crudely, they, and I, are less boring when less successful. There is, then, more space in our doughnuts.

We overdo the core. In our personal lives we often exaggerate the necessities. Few need as much as they think that they do, or as much security as they hanker after. Organisations build bigger cores than they need, and impose bigger cores on their internal doughnuts than are necessary. Schools, everywhere, impose timetables on their students, filling all their hours with things they are required to do. In a world which seems crammed with rules and duties, responsibility goes unregarded. Even the rules and duties become devalued, as we instinctively reject the idea that so much of us can be prescribed. No one wants an empty doughnut, one with no obligations and no commitments, but one with too large a core breeds a sense of impotence.

We find it a paradox that people clamour for rights but ignore their responsibility, that people want democracy but expect others to sort out all the problems for them, that they complain when others take the initiative but take no initiative themselves. We find it odd that there is so little time to enjoy the fruits of our labours, but later find that we don't know how to enjoy the fruits when we do have time. We are unused to all that space in our lives. We have been so burdened with duties that we have never learnt the delights of responsibility, of making a difference to someone or something.

By overemphasising the duties and the rules of the core, organisations unintentionally breed distrust. A £10 discretionary authority hardly indicates any confidence in one's judgement or integrity. Obsessed by the need to control, organisations create self-fulfilling prophecies when their people find that the only way to be independent is to break the rules. My children learnt to smoke because the schools they went to made non-smoking a rule. They justified the rule with all the lessons about the dangers of nicotine, but the implicit message was, 'We don't believe that you will heed these warnings so we will make it a core obligation.' Such a deliberate denial of responsibility made it legitimate, in the eyes of the students, to ignore the rule. Smoking became a symbol of free choice, a personal space in their doughnut.

If we do not allow people space, we cannot expect responsible behaviour. There are risks, of course. Not everyone can handle the same amounts of space and responsibility. Doughnuts have to be adjusted to the capacity of the individual or the group. As parents we allow more space as the children grow, but always within boundaries. The risks of not doing it, the Type 2 error of restricting space, are, however, much more serious. Too much space can cause an error or an accident. Too little can impoverish a life. We were not meant to be an empty raincoat.

5 The Chinese Contract

I remember my first exposure to the 'Chinese contract'. I was the manager in South Malaysia for an oil company, responsible amongst other things for negotiating agency agreements with our Chinese dealers. I was young, enthusiastic and, I suppose, naïve. After the conclusion of one such negotiation, the dealer and I shook hands, drank the ritual cups of tea, and were, I felt, the best of friends. I took the official company agency agreement out of my case and started to fill in the figures, preparatory to signing it. 'Why are you doing that?' asked the dealer in some alarm. 'If you think that I am going to sign that you are much mistaken.' 'But I am only writing in the figures which we agreed.' 'If we agreed them, why do you want a legal document? It makes me suspect that you have got more out of this agreement than I have, and are going to use the weight of the law to enforce your terms. In my culture,' he went on, 'a good agreement is self-enforcing because both parties go away smiling and are happy to see that each of us is smiling. If one smiles and the other scowls, the agreement will not stick, lawyers or no lawyers.'

I think that I persuaded him that it was just a piece of company ritual and of no significance, but the episode sent me away thinking. I had grown up in a culture which believed that a good negotiation was one in which only one of us, myself, came away smiling, but concealed that smile lest the other guess that one had got the better of him or her. Negotiation was about winning at the expense of the other party. You then had to enforce your side of the deal, using the law or the threat of the law. I had met a culture where negotiation was about finding the best way forward for both parties. No wonder we needed so many more lawyers in our culture.

The Chinese contract, I later realised, embodied a principle which went far beyond the making of lasting commercial deals. It was about the importance of compromise as a prerequisite of progress. Both sides have to concede for both to win. It was about the need for trust and a belief in the future. Writ large, it was about sacrifice, the willingness to forego some present good to ward off future evil, or, more positively, it was about investment – spending now in order to gain later.

We have no chance of managing the paradoxes if we are not prepared to give up something, if we are not willing to bet on the future and if we cannot find it in ourselves to take a risk with people. These are our Pathways through the Paradoxes, if we have the will. The pursuit of our own short-term advantage, and the desire to win everything we can, will only perpetuate animosities, destroy alliances and partnerships, frustrate progress, and breed lawyers and the bureaucracy of enforcement.

The Chinese contract, as I discovered to my chagrin, involves a major rethink of our cultural habits, even in China, where they may not appreciate my magnification of their trading habits into a principle of life. The pursuit of self-interest has to be balanced, as Adam Smith's two books remind us, by 'sympathy', a fellow feeling for others which is, he argues, the real basis of moral behaviour. Only if we are conditioned by this 'sympathy' will we want to take any risks with our fellow men and women, will we trust them farther than we can count them, or want to make life better for those we never meet. As Arthur Okun put it: the 'invisible hand' needs to be accompanied by an 'invisible handshake'. Self-interest, unbalanced, can only lead to a jungle in which any victory will mean destroying those on whom our own survival will ultimately depend. That would be the paradox to end all paradoxes. The tragedy of the commons, it was labelled, when the individual farmers maximised their own short-term use of the common land only to find that, when everyone did the same, the land deteriorated until all the grazing failed.

There are those who think that 'sympathy' will remain a very weak force, always yielding to self-interest. The evidence, however, is against them. Jean Piaget studied young children playing, and observed an inherent sense of fairness, particularly in older children who had longer time horizons. 'It makes her happy' or 'I don't want to see him cry' were the common explanations for gifts of generosity, and there was more generosity than there was hoarding. The Chinese will be relieved. Their policy of one child per family means that all young children spend their early years without siblings. The Chinese have, therefore, started courses in 'sharing' in the primary schools – to help them learn the principle of the Chinese contract! Adults don't always lose the habit. Most people don't put up the price of candles in a power strike or shovels in a snow-storm. There is sympathy in humankind as well as greed and cruelty.

The Morality of Compromise

The 'morality of compromise' sounds contradictory. Compromise is usually a sign of weakness, or an admission of defeat. Strong men don't compromise, it is said, and principles should never be compromised. I shall argue that strong men, conversely, know when to compromise and that all principles can be compromised to serve a greater principle. I have said 'strong men' because I am assured that strong women have always known the value of compromise in the interests of progress.

Most of the dilemmas which we face in this time of confusion are not the straightforward ones of choosing between right and wrong, where compromise would, indeed, be weakness, but the much more complicated dilemmas of right and right. I want to spend more time on my work, *and* with my family; we want to be good corporate citizens *and* return a decent profit; we want to trust our subordinates *but* we need to know what they are doing. At other times, the interests of different parties are in conflict. Without compromise by both, there will be no movement. Stalled by a refusal to make concessions, things stagnate. Progress is sacrificed to pride.

I once listened to Lord Owen, then Dr David Owen. He had just finished his stint as the Foreign Secretary in Britain's Labour government of the Seventies and was not yet the leader of the Social Democrats. He was addressing a group of bishops on a topic of his own choosing – the morality of compromise. He had, he said, one August, while on his own in the Foreign Office, when most of the staff were on holiday, received a request to provide riot and control equipment to the Shah of Iran, whose regime was fast falling apart. The Shah, he said, and his regime were deeply repugnant to him; they offended all the principles of democracy and social justice in which he and his party believed. Nevertheless, as he weighed the alternatives, with no one around to give advice, he had concluded that to meet the request was preferable to the only alternative, a shoot-out by the Shah's army with bodies dead in the street. He gave support to a regime he abhorred because the alternative was worse. One principle was sacrificed to a greater principle.

If you stick too fast to your position, he told the bishops, you may have the comfort of feeling that you are in the right, but you may also have committed the greater wrong of stalling any movement in what is generally the right direction. It is ironic that, some years later, it was David

Owen's too-rigid adherence to his own position which helped precipitate the demise of the party he led. Years later again, he found himself trying to persuade Serbians, Bosnians and Croatians to compromise in order to move forward, towards peace in the old Yugoslavia.

Peter and Pam Richards grow fruit and vegetables on their farm in the Channel Islands. The market is very competitive, they say, and life is not easy. They are also signed-up members of the Friends of the Earth, and ecological enthusiasts. 'But,' says Peter, 'if we did not cover our new potatoes with polythene they would be ruined in two weeks.' 'We have had to learn to balance our idealism with pragmatism,' said Pam, 'to compromise. I suppose,' she added, 'that it's part of growing up!'

There is, however, a seductive power in certainty. If you have no doubt, then you never see the need to compromise. Unprincipled people are not, in fact, unprincipled. They have, instead, one overriding principle, which may be self-interest, or the good of the business or the nation as they see it, or even what they might call 'the will of God'. These principles they will not compromise. There will be no way forward with them, except on their chosen road and in their chosen vehicle. For them, compromise is a weasel word, signifying capitulation. Their certainty gives them power, but at a cost. There is no room for anyone else in their camp, except for converts. Such people never see the need for a second curve, and, in time, their curve turns down. The certainty and self-assurance of a good leader must be tempered with the spirit of compromise if others are not to feel excluded. Margaret Thatcher was one who never felt the need to compromise. Her certainty gave her strength, and was much admired, even by those who disapproved of what she did with it. But in the end, the refusal to compromise brought her down. Compromise is essential to democracy. It is also essential to leaders who want willing and able followers, not sycophants.

On the other hand, excessive compromise can give away too much. It can be seen as weakness, not as consensus-building. The wrong compromise can block progress not promote it. Like many people, I hate conflict. I shrink from confrontation. To avoid it, I am prone to give anything away. To escape the inevitable conflict I have refrained from removing people who were, by their incompetence, I knew, harming the organisation. I have been tempted to let a bullying neighbour have his way rather than confront him. That is bad compromise, compromise for the wrong reason. I was compromising the truth for the sake of a quiet life, a minor principle for a greater one. It should be the other way round, as I always knew.

Arriving at one management programme, the executives found on their desks an English translation of Sophocles' Greek tragedy, *Antigone*. This was their first homework of the course, to be discussed in class the next week. They thought at first that they had been mixed up with a liberal-arts course but they realised the point of it when they started to talk about it as a group. Antigone's brother had been defeated and killed by their uncle, Creon, in a battle for the control of Thebes. He had been left outside the city walls to be picked at by the vultures. Antigone's faith required her to see that her brother was properly buried, lest he be pursued for ever by the Furies. Creon forbade it, on pain of her death. Do you obey authority, or do you do what you think is right, come what may? Or do you find some compromise? It has been the dilemma of conquered peoples down the ages. It is a conflict not unknown in businesses, or even in families. Antigone stuck to her principles, and died for them. There *are* some principles worth dying for. The question is – was this one of them? It is because that question is forever topical that the play is still performed 2,500 years later.

Only when the compromise is in pursuit of a greater purpose, or a greater principle, is it right to compromise a principle. As well as conflict, I abhor war and violence. But there are bullies, and there are bully states, who respect only those who are stronger than them and who are prepared to show it. I will, therefore, condone limited wars and the controlled use of force in pursuit of peace and order, if all else fails. I will even fight myself, if the cause is just. To stick too tightly to my principles would be to give a licence to all bullies and all criminals. The greater principle of a just order legitimises the abandonment of a lesser principle.

Most compromise in life, however, is not about our principles but about our interests. No compromises on these can ultimately mean no allies, and no progress. The philosophy of Chinese contracts can then prove more fruitful if less glorious.

Contracts with the Future

Time also demands its compromises, as we try to balance the demands of the present and the future. Short-termism is an ugly word for a tough dilemma. Businesses are accused of it, governments are plagued by it, none of us can escape it in our own lives. We all live in the knowledge that those things which we most want, and which are best for us – health, affection, long life – all require us to give up immediate delights or to do things which we would rather not do. Personal short-termism damages our health. We know, in other words, that this sort of personal compromise is one way of dealing with the paradox that most of the things we enjoy are bad for us.

The dilemma is this – to what extent should you shortchange or compromise the present in order to benefit the future? All ·investment involves taking something from today to improve tomorrow. It only makes sense to do that if you believe in, or want, what tomorrow may bring. It is always another compromise. To what extent are we prepared to curb our bad environmental habits to ensure a cleaner, safer world for our grandchildren, a world which we may not live long enough to enjoy? To what extent will we curb our own behaviour if others do not do likewise? Will the tragedy of the commons be played out on a global scale or will we compromise, adjust, our short-term behaviour for a greater common cause, to make life better for people we shall never meet? We will only do it, I believe, if we can look beyond the grave, if we can accept that there are some things that are more important than ourselves, and longer-lasting.

At a more personal level, young dual-career couples struggle with this issue of common cause and compromise, as they try to decide whether or when to start a family. The sacrifices in the present will be considerable: a loss of income, a change of life style, an altered relationship. The commitment of both of them to a new future is critical, if they are to make the compromises which will be necessary to the start of another family. It is, however, an impossible decision to make, if they want to preserve all that is in their present, while growing that future. They have to start by understanding that compromise is essential to most progress, but that voluntary compromise is only possible if there is a common cause, a cause greater than oneself, and a trust in the other. When compromise goes out of fashion among the young, so do babies.

In a business, to increase a dividend is also to reduce the sums available for new capital spending. If the shareholders are not interested in the future of the company because they can sell their shares tomorrow, they will want to see dividends, not retained profits, in the account. The managers, on the other hand, with their own futures linked to the future of the business, will want to invest as much as they can in that future. There can often be a conflict of priorities.

If there is no common cause, no agreement on the longer-term goal, the more pressing priority, or the most powerful party, will win out. If we think that we need shareholders more than managers, as we seem to, then the shareholders will win. Compromise will be enforced, not voluntary – a British contract rather than a Chinese one. Only if the shareholders are also locked in to the future of the business, as shareholders more often are in Japan and Germany, will they have common cause with the managers and be prepared to forego some present gains for future profits. As long, that is, as that common cause seems a worthwhile one. In the end, for the long-term to prevail over the short-term, we must want what the long-term promises. Where there is no vision, there you find short-termism, for there is, then, no reason for compromise today for an unknown tomorrow.

The concept of stock options, common in Britain and America, is an attempt to make common cause between senior managers and the shareholders. The thinking is that this will tie the managers' compensation more closely to the longer-term performance of the company. It does, but because they can only make use of those options after a period of years or if the share price goes higher than the price of the options. If all shareholders were treated this way they would look at the company a little differently. It would significantly alter the balance between the present and the future and so make compromise easier.

The Third Angle

If we want self-reinforcing relationships, those Chinese contracts, we need to find a common cause, one which jus-tifies some personal sacrifice by both parties for a greater common good. Without that sense of common cause, everyone will fight their own corner, trust between individuals or groups will be rare and compromise will be something imposed on the weaker by the stronger, a sign of defeat not progress. In a democratic culture, if it is not to degenerate into a battle between interest groups, it is particularly crucial that we find that common cause.

Where there is a third corner, we can often agree to combine our individual corners against the common enemy. The calculation is that we have more to gain by combining than by standing alone. The value of the compromise seems self-evident. Common enemies, however, must, by their very nature, result in temporary combinations because the compromise was made on the assumption that the enemy would be defeated. When the defeat occurs, the alliance evaporates. If, on the other hand, the enemy continues to resist defeat, the compromises made for the alliance begin to be questioned when there is no pay-off. When businesses define their purpose as being bigger or better than one of their competitors in the hope that this will unite their workforce, they are playing short-term games. When the British government sets its sights on outperforming Germany or France, they are playing games too long to be real.

A common enemy is seldom a good basis for a lasting compromise or for long-term sacrifice, except in times of real, not economic, war; times which, we must hope, will seldom come. In many a situation there is, however, a third angle, a way of finding that balance between opposites which is a necessary Pathway through Paradox.

1793 was the bicentenary of one of the most influential graffiti of all time. On 30 June of that year, the Club des Cordeliers of Paris passed a resolution that all houseowners should be invited to paint on the façades of their houses, in big letters, these words, 'Unité, indivisibilité de la République, Liberté, Egalité, Fraternité ou la Mort'. It was the first recorded example of what was to be the motto of the French Revolution – Liberty, Equality and Fraternity. It was also the best-known example of trinitarian thinking, the 'third term' which reconciles opposites. Liberty, notoriously, cancels out equality, and vice versa. The two can only survive in any sort of harmony if there is fraternity. If we care for each other I will not press my demands for individual liberty so far that it intrudes on your equal right to be free, nor will your pressure for equality be pushed so far that it denies me my liberty.

Most of life is made up of opposites – male and female, work and leisure, life and death. In the British tradition it is always assumed that a conflict between opposites is the best recipe for fairness. The system of justice is based on this assumption, as is the British parliament. In the view of many it is neither fair nor always just.

Trinitarian, or third-angle, thinking is always looking for solutions which can reconcile or illuminate the opposites. A third party may yet be the answer to the see-saw of British politics, a see-saw that periodically gets jammed so that one party stays in power too long for fairness. An independent assessor in the judicial process may yet emerge as a solution to the battle of the courtrooms where victory for one side or the other is not always the same as justice. A common humanity is the concept which makes sense of the conflict between male and female. If we knew better what we meant by eternity we might not see life and death as such polar opposites. Learning might be a way of linking work and leisure so that they blend into each other. Love quenches rows and turns differences into stimulants; and sympathy, Adam Smith would remind us, makes the market moral.

Trinitarian thinking urges us always to be on the look-out for another approach, a third angle. Trinitarian thinking says that if money is so divisive, why not de-monetarise society? If more of the good or necessary things in life were free to all, like education, housing, health care, travel and essential foods, there would be more equality around. It would be less easy to distinguish between rich and poor, and there would be less reason to pile up one's riches. Trinitarian thinking suggests that if the struggle between 'owners' and 'workers' is endemic, we could get round it by thinking, instead, of 'members'.

I remember only too well the arguments with my two children over the telephone. We tried budgets, time-limits, locks and total prohibition as ways to curb their insatiable appetite for telephoning their friends as teenagers. It only resulted in evasion, lies and rows. Trinitarian thinking suggested another route, a third angle. I paid for them each to have their own telephone and paid the standing charge provided that they then paid the bills for all their calls. If the bills were not paid they got cut off. My phone would not then, or ever, be available. They saw this as freedom, but I noticed that, from then on, it was their friends, no doubt using their parents' phones, who telephoned them. My hugely reduced bills more than compensated for the extra standing charges, and, besides, I now had unrestricted access to my own telephone! It was a compromise which worked without any sacrifice of principle.

In one condominium, the problems of parking were the hardest problem to solve. It was seen as a basic right to be able to park your car, and that of your visitors, outside your apartment. On the other hand, no one wanted to have their view interrupted by other people's cars. Endless arrangements and architectural devices were explored but no one was satisfied. Trinitarian thinking suggested that the fairest solution would be to provide a communal parking site away from all the apartments, to declare the main area a car-free site and to landscape it appropriately. Some shared inconvenience became a small price to pay for enhanced beauty and peace. Another compromise which worked, because we found the third angle. Shrewd negotiators know all about such unblocking trinitarian devices.

This book will contain many examples of trinitarian thinking. It is often a path to acceptable compromise, a third angle which reconciles the opposites. However we get there, we need more Chinese contracts in our lives, in our businesses and in our societies. The Japanese are famed for the slowness of their decision-making but also for the strength and reliability of those decisions once made. The reason, as we know, is the length of time it takes to reach a consensus. You could say that the Chinese contract is a Japanese habit! The rest of us could learn it with advantage, but it will mean changing some of our cultural traditions: the idea, for instance, that winning necessarily means that someone loses, instead of the possibility that all can win a little less; that compromise is a sign of weakness not of strength; that a good lawyer is better than a good agreement; and that if you look after the present the future will take care of itself. These things are culturally determined, they are not engrained in human nature. We can change the way we think.

The starting premise of this book was that there is no perfect solution to anything, and that no one can predict the ultimate effect of any action. Only when you look back can you see the truth. Even science knows no perfect answers, nor believes that there can be any. Given this premise, one would have to be very arrogant, very stupid or very insensitive to claim to know the complete truth of anything in advance. Karl Popper once said, 'We all differ in what we know, but in our infinite ignorance we are all equal.' Even popes can be wrong, which won't stop them or many others from seeking to impose their wishes on the world.

We all have the right to think that we are right, because the good news from that starting premise is that there is room for each one of us to make a difference. Fluttering our wings, we too, like the butterfly in chaos theory, may cause an upset in the weather. Where no one knows the future with any certainty, we have the right to dream. But for anyone's wishes, or their dreams, to be accepted without enforcement, some form of Chinese contract will be necessary, one in which the interests of all parties, both now and in the future, are heard and heeded.

In turbulent times we look for certainty and sure authority. We want to be followers, not leaders, even in a small way. We want 'them' to solve our dilemmas, and give us back a quiet life. It is hard enough to look after oneself, without taking other people into account. I am arguing that these things cannot and will not be. The paradoxes are too complicated. We have to get involved if there is to be any point to our existence. In the last Part of the book I shall argue that there is a point, that we are not just incidental accidents in the evolutionary chain. In the meantime we have to put these principles into practice, in our work and in our lives. That is the concern of the next Part of the book.

Part Three:
Practising the Preaching
Managing Paradox

The Federalist Idea

The symbol of the empty raincoat challenges us to find a place for our individual wishes and decisions in the greater scheme of things. Different cultures give a different prominence to the idea of the individual, but one can sense a growing sense of impotence, everywhere, in the face of institutions and government and transnational bodies. Democracy used to mean that the people had the power, but that now translates into 'the people have the vote', which is not the same thing. The vote is an expression of last resort, a useful reminder to our rulers of the source of their bread and butter, but hardly a way for an individual to influence what is going on around them. Moreover, in the institutions of everyday life, particularly those of business, the only people with the vote are those outside, the financiers or the governors. Those who work in them are effectively disenfranchised. Democracy has its limits. A vote is not enough to fill a raincoat.

If we want to reconcile our humanity with our economics, we have to find a way to give more influence to what is personal and local, so that we can each feel that we have a chance to make a difference, that we matter, along with those around us. We have no hope of charting a way through those paradoxes unless we feel able to take some personal responsibility for events. A formal democracy will not be enough. We have to find another way, by changing the structure of our institutions to give more power to the small and to the local. We have to do that, with all the untidiness which it entails, while still looking for efficiency, and the benefits of co-ordination and control. More is needed, therefore, than good intentions to 'empower' the individual to do what we want him or her to do. The structures and the systems have to change, to reflect a new balance of power. That means federalism.

Federalism is an old idea, but its time may have come again, because it has been designed to create a balance of power within an institution. It matches paradox with paradox. Federalism seeks to be both big in some things and small in others, to be centralised in some respects and decentralised in others. It aims to be local in its appeal and in many of its decisions, but national or even global in its scope. It endeavours to maximise independence, provided always that there is a necessary interdependence; to encourage difference, but within limits; it needs to maintain a strong centre, but one devoted to the service of the parts; it can and should be led from that centre but has to be managed by the parts. There is room in federalism for the small to influence the mighty, and for the individuals to flex their muscles.

We think of federalism as something which applies to countries – the United States of America, Germany, Switzerland, Australia, Canada. Her politicians might not admit it, but the United Kingdom is really a federation of its separate regions, as is Spain and, increasingly, even France, as its regions gain more autonomy. The concept, however, goes beyond countries. Every organisation of any size at all can be thought of in federal terms. Hospitals, schools, local government and most charities are, if we look at them with federal spectacles, made for federalism – local and separate activities bonded in one whole, served by a common centre. All businesses of any size have federal propensities, and a need to be all the things which federalism offers.

We might then wonder why such a good idea is not so obviously popular. Few businesses are consciously federal, nor does history have many, if any, examples of a monarch or a central power voluntarily moving to a federalist structure. The hard truth is that we are always reluctant to give up power unless we have to, and federalism is an exercise in the balancing of power. The federal idea is an example of the second curve, but one which too few institutions or societies develop until they are forced to. It is a very different and a very uncomfortable way of thinking about organisations. It is messy, untidy and always a little out of control. Its only justification is that there is no real alternative in a complicated world. No one person, or group, or executive, is so all-wise and so all-sensitive that they can balance the paradoxes on their own, or run the place from the centre, even if people were prepared to allow them to. We have to allow space for the small and the local.

Federalism relies on a set of Chinese contracts between its various parts and operates through doughnuts of varying size and shape, doughnuts which leave, of necessity and of right, considerable space for local decisions. The goals of the parts have to adjust to the requirements of the whole, and vice versa. No one in a federal organisation can have everything exactly as they would want it. It is, therefore, an excellent example of putting the preaching of this book into practice, with all the difficulties as well as the opportunities.

Federalism is not, let us be clear, the easiest of concepts to make work, or to understand. Yugoslavia is hardly an advertisement for the concept, nor is Canada. California is creaking under an excess of federalism from within and without. IBM proclaims its conversion to the idea, but may not be its most successful exponent in the years ahead. A federal Europe frightens many, not just in Britain. Nevertheless, we have to persevere with it, because it is the best way of returning some sense of meaning to our larger institutions, a way of connecting their purposes with their people.

Much of the confusion and difficulty arises from a misunderstanding of what federalism is. A confederation, for example, is not the same thing as a federation. A confederation is an alliance of interested parties who agree to do some things together. It is, therefore, a mechanism for mutual advantage. There is no reason for sacrifice or trade-offs or compromise, unless it is very obviously in one's own interest. A confederation is not an organisation that is going anywhere, because there is no mechanism nor will to decide what that anywhere might be. The Confederation of Independent States, which replaced the Soviet Union, will never be an effective body. The British Commonwealth, another confederation, is a thing of sentiment and language, not a real organisation. These are not the stuff of federalism.

Confederations adapt when they have to, usually too late. They do not lead, nor do they build. They are organisations of expediency not of common purpose. The British would like Europe to remain an economic confederation, a common market. Many in the rest of Europe want a more federal state, one with a greater common purpose, within which sacrifices and compromises become acceptable, one in which the rich are readier to help the poorer, one with common standards and common aspirations.

What is true of Europe is also true of organisations. Alliances, joint ventures and networks are the tools of confederations, arrangements of mutual convenience, inevitably fragile as the conveniences change. Organisations with a clear purpose will want to be federal not confederal. The distinction is important.

The key concepts in federalism are **twin citizenship** and **subsidiarity**. They are explained in the two chapters which follow. They are old ideas, reinvented for today's world.

6   Twin Citizenship

The Texan, when I visited him, was very obviously a Texan, and proud of it. On his front lawn, however, there was a tall white flagpole flying the Stars and Stripes. 'Why not?' he said, in response to my query. 'I'm an American, aren't I?' He was American *and* he was Texan. So, too, the lady from Munich, a Bavarian first, she said, but also a German.

Big but Small

Twin citizenship is a critical component of federalism: you belong to your own state and to the larger federal union of states. Each of us will probably have a number of twin-citizenship situations in our lives, if we think about them in that way. It is important that we do. Even in personal life one ends up with twin loyalties more often than not. When I married, I thought that I was joining two lives together, mine and that of the girl I loved. It was only when we started to arrange the wedding that I realised that I was also becoming the affiliated member of a new tribe, her large and extended family. I now had my own tribe and hers, twin citizenships and twin loyalties to be reconciled and balanced. Organisations, for their part, are going federal, just as countries have, because they want to give a measure of independence to local units or to specialised groups. At the same time, they want to retain the benefits of scale. Being big and small makes sense, but managing it makes problems.

Small units are faster, more focused, more flexible, more friendly and more fun – to borrow Rosabeth Moss Kanter's five 'f's. Small units can get closer to the customer and the citizen, to the patient or to the student. They can be less bureaucratic and more personal. Most of us fish prefer a smaller pond. In smaller groups there is more chance to be yourself, less likelihood of being an anonymous empty raincoat.

On the other hand, there are always economies of scale to be had in any organisation. They are most easily found in finance, distribution and purchasing; less often, these days, in manufacturing. Research, if it is any good, is increasingly expensive; it needs large cash flows to support it. Pharmaceutical companies have to be large, as do oil companies and aeroplane-makers. Large organisations offer better hopes of security to their people, more variety and more scope. They can afford to invest in the kind of fundamental training which takes years to pay off. 'Now that you've been with us for ten years,' my oil company told me, 'you may be worth your keep!' Many worry that if the BBC in Britain were to turn itself into a host of mini-independents, there would be no one with the interest in paying for the professional training which grooms all the directors and technicians of the future.

Federalism is an age-old device for keeping the proper balance between big and small. Big in some things, small in others. It is never easy, because it means allowing the small to be independent while still being part of the larger whole, to be different but part of the same. Federalism is, therefore, fraught with difficulty because it is trying to combine those two opposites, to manage the paradox. Twin citizenship makes it possible. If there is the sense of belonging to something bigger as well as to our own smaller unit, we can see the sense in accepting some restrictions on our local independence, if it helps the larger whole. Sovereignty is not ceded but shared. The larger unit is not 'them' but also 'us'.

To many Britons, Europe has always been a place one went to, not a place one belonged to. Until they instinctively realise that they are in it, geographically as well as politically, Europe and the European Community will remain 'them' not 'us'. There will be no sense of twin citizenship and therefore no gut feeling for federalism, which will remain a dirty word, a synonym for a loss of independence without any compensating new belonging.

The local citizenship is the easy part. We can all identify with our immediate neighbours, particularly when we are also working with them. Our futures then depend on them. We share a history, we know their faces, often too well; we know where we belong. In the words of an old Chinese proverb, those who do not know the village they have come from will never find the village they are looking for. Richard Rogers, the architect who designed the Pompidou Centre in Paris and the Lloyd's building in London, has commented that Europe is becoming increasingly defined by its cities. Barcelona's Olympics were about Barcelona not Spain. Dresden is intent on being, once again, a centre of culture, art and education, a place for Europe not just Germany. We can relate to our cities more easily than we can to the idea of Europe, or America.

It is that larger citizenship which is harder to establish, yet it needs equal prominence if there is to be a proper balance. In a business, it may make good logical sense to combine functions, to group some regions together, to manage cash or purchasing centrally, but these actions all steal power and decisions from the independent units. Those units will resent this, not understanding the paradox that in order to get the most value out of their independence, it often pays to sacrifice some of that independence to a central function. That kind of compromise is only done willingly if there is some confidence in the central function, some sense of belonging to a larger whole of which it, too, is part. We need that second citizenship.

The £5 Auction

To prove this obvious point I used to play a simple game with executives on training exercises. It was a variety of what logicians call the Prisoners' Dilemma, except that in this game I offered to auction three £5 notes between two participants. I would place two volunteers in chairs facing away from each other so that they could not see the other's face. I asked them to bid in turn for the first note. Invariably the first person bid £1, the second upped it, and so it went on, by alternative bids, sometimes going up by £1, sometimes jumping by £2, sometimes by parts of a pound, until one of them reached £5 at which point the other normally, but not always, stopped bidding. In one case, someone actually bid £23 for the first £5 note! The auction for the second note gave first bid to the other side but the outcome was the same – £5 or more bid for my £5 note. So it was for the third note, although there was often overbidding for this note, too, so that one side could claim a sort of Pyrrhic victory – more notes won, and to hell with the cost!

The rest of the group would be watching, amazed by the apparent idiocy of the bidding. There would be a rush of volunteers for the next round, eager to try their theory of pre-emptive bidding or whatever. The result would be the same, as long as I was careful to pick them from different sides of the room. Finally, I would choose a couple who had been sitting and whispering together and who volunteered in unison. When they started the bidding, the first person would bid 10 pence and the second would say 'no bid'. The note had been sold for 10p. The same happened the other way round with the second note. The third note was more tense. Usually their agreement held. The first person bid the now-standard 10p and the other passed. At the end, they took the three £5 notes, paid me 30p and shared the proceeds. Occasionally, however, competition flared up again for this final note and the second bidder

would come in with a pre-emptive £5 bid. They would then
have to make do with a £4.90p profit and live with a sense
of betrayal.

What was going on? I would ask the group. Logical, sensible, mature individuals were competing to the point of
lunacy because I had kept them apart. By not allowing
them to communicate, I had also prevented them from
establishing an alliance, an agreed objective and a means of
proceeding. Only when I picked people who had had a
chance to talk together were they able to achieve a common
goal which benefited them both, although even that broke
down on occasion. A common cause, the willingness to
deny oneself in the interests of that common cause, and the
trust that the other party will do the same – these are the
essentials of sensible organisation behaviour. Much of the
time this sensible behaviour does not happen because
people do not talk, do not trust and have no common
cause. To put it more crisply, there is no sense of a second
citizenship, and therefore no possibility of sensible compromise, of a proper balance between the whole and the
parts.

The depressing thing was that the experiment never
failed. It always worked the way I knew it would. We instinctively work for our own immediate advantage unless
there is an obvious common cause with people whom we
can trust so that an initial sacrifice turns out in the end to be
to our mutual advantage. We can, today, see the £5-auction
game being played for real around the world.

The Queen's Great Matter

The second citizenship is critical. Interestingly, politicians
and managers both use the same sort of devices to reinforce
that larger loyalty. They make sure that there is a federal
flag, or company logo, which is displayed wherever and
whenever possible. They have their national anthems, or

vision and value statements in organisations, things more symbolic than real but important none the less because they give expression to the ideal which holds the whole together, the sense of common cause to which we are, they hope, committed.

Modern organisations spend a lot of time working on that common cause, establishing what it is, communicating it, reinforcing it. It can look like waffle, and it sometimes is. Properly done, it is not waffle but the glue of the enterprise. More respectfully, Richard Pascale and Anthony Athos call it the 'spiritual fabric' of the corporation. They are describing companies in present-day Japan. The tradition is older still. In Elizabethan England they called it the Queen's Great Matter, the common cause that bonded her merchant venturers and built an empire. In America, every president goes out of his way, in his inaugural address, to emphasise that he will now govern for all his fellow citizens, not just the ones who voted for him. He points out that they can only help themselves if they also help each other. He reminds his audience that there is this place, this tradition called America which they need to rediscover. 'We must prove that we deserve our heritage.' This is not empty rhetoric but the necessary forging of a common purpose. Sadly, the rhetoric too easily gets lost in the day-to-day reality. Living up to the rhetoric of the larger citizenship is one of the toughest parts of leadership.

Presidents, leaders, to be effective have to represent the whole to the parts and to the world outside. They may live in the centre but they must not be the centre. To reinforce the common cause they must be a constant teacher, ever travelling, ever talking, ever listening, the chief missionary of the common cause. This role sits ill with that of chief executive, which is why many organisations are now separating out the two roles. The missionary task is a role which cannot easily be fulfilled by committee or by memorandum because logic makes few hearts beat faster and no one has ever followed a committee into battle. The life of the federal president in a large organisation tends to be one long teach-in. Successful presidents and prime ministers know that their main task is to carry the people with them. Roosevelt with his fireside radio talks, Clinton with his town meetings, Churchill and his wartime broadcasts, were all, in effect, running popular teach-ins.

Twin citizenship, however, needs more than flags, national anthems and articulate, visible presidents. It is lubricated by cross-fertilisation, by moving people between the parts, and between the parts and the centre. In that way more people are exposed to more of the bigger reality; they not only grow themselves, but their vision and their understanding of the total organisation grows with them. Shell, one of the oldest of the corporate federations, knows that its corps of 5,000 expatriates is the bond which holds it all together, far more than any shareholdings or formal authorities. On a different scale, the Club Méditerranée, another federal organisation with its independent holiday centres, insists that the site managers change locations every two or three years, creating an international family of shared habits and values.

The Law and the Currency

A common legal framework and a common currency are the other essentials. They both remind everyone, constantly, that they are part of something bigger. That is their symbolic role; they also have a practical one, to allow the parts to work together.

A common legal framework translates, in organisations, into a basic set of guidelines – 'how we do things around here'. They call it the 'bible' in some places, but they would be wise not to make it as bulky or as subject to devious interpretation as the Bible proper. Too much law only breeds lawyers, who come expensive. A common currency translates into a common information system, so that inputs and outputs can be measured and compared across the parts. That sounds like common sense were it not so uncommon. Too often the sales section talks of sales but knows not what contribution they make to added value, while purchasing talks costs but knows not what difference they make to sales. In the past, in Britain, when doctors prescribed drugs or referred their patients to specialists, they neither knew nor thought it right to know the cost. To know would, they felt, have influenced their medical judgement. They then complained that the money to cure their sick was never adequate. In the National Health Service at that time there was no common currency and, therefore, no sense of involvement in, or responsibility for, the financial aspects of the organisation. Paradoxically, by breaking down the health-care system into more self-accountable units, the sense of common cause has become stronger because the parts now have to talk to each other and have the means to do it. As they say, an organisation that talks together stays together.

We must, however, take care that the laws and the currency are not so pervasive that they swamp the local citizenship. The centre may yearn for uniformity, for an identikit organisation in which every bit is the same as every other bit, but the customer or client wants it to be his or her preference at the point of delivery and the local unit wants to be able to be appropriately different. Uniformity, like equality, is the enemy of liberty, but too much liberty can destroy efficiency. There has to be a balance.

Our new local superstore does not stock risotto rice. Risotto rice might be thought exotic in an out-of-the-way corner of England but I delight in the infinite variety that is possible with this simplest of ingredients. We asked for it to be stocked. I spoke with the store manager. He was regretful, but the shelf lay-out and the stock-list were laid down from the centre and he had no discretion. How, I wondered, could the centre be so all-wise as to know the rich randomness of tastes in our neck of the woods, or did they not trust him? What, if any, discretion was allowed to him in other areas or was he but a walking automaton, there to give standard non-responses to people like me? There was little sense of local citizenship there. An identi-kit, facsimile organisation imposes uniformity on its world, thinks that the centre knows best, that discretion is dangerous and that local differences are unnecessary. All those assumptions, I suggest, are dangerous because they deny the paradoxes, they bury them instead of balancing them.

Money Talks

We would be wise, too, to remember another lesson from that auction game which I played with my students. Money talks. Money may not be the most important thing in the world but it provides the counters. Twin citizenship is much easier to believe in if there is some financial involvement in both citizenships. Without the tokens the game may not seem to be real. Our pay is beginning to reflect this. Profit-sharing schemes are not as rare as they once were. They may go farther still. The time will come when an individual will find that the annual pay packet comes in four lumps. The largest lump will be the pay for the job, reflecting one's standing in the organisation, one's level of experience, expertise and previous record as well as the level or grade of job. That is nothing new. What would be new, except in Japan, is that this lump might be only 50 per cent of the total take-home pay in a good year. The other lumps would be a share in the overall surplus of the group or corporation, a share in the value added by one's work unit, the first citizenship, and, finally, a personal bonus reflecting one's individual contribution. The two shares might normally be expected to amount to 20 per cent of the total packet leaving 10 per cent for the individual contribution.

At first sight these numbers seem huge. Remember, however, that they start with a base salary or wage which is set at 50 per cent of normal take-home pay. That sum will not vary but the other numbers will, in line with actual performance. When times are good, the money will be good and there will be that much more to distribute because the basic costs are only half of what they could be. When times are hard, however, or performance slips, then total pay declines, but no one need be dismissed to reduce the labour costs; they reduce automatically. In that way the obligations of citizenship are met – you keep your job – and the rewards are shared when there are rewards to share. It is this kind of payment system which has helped Japanese companies to maintain their system of lifetime employment for their key workers.

The percentages need to be big to be interesting. A total bonus element of 5–8 per cent, the kind that some organisations play around with, does little more than pay for the Christmas or the New Year break. It is a gesture not a bond. The percentages must also be seen to be fair and objective. They must be based on real numbers, not on percentages or judgements. The exception may be the percentage allowed for individual contribution. This can seldom be totally objective unless one is a salesperson on commission. Opinions have to count. The sense of local citizenship will be reinforced if the opinions are those of the group itself, which is given a total sum of money to distribute amongst its members. A good, open group will not flinch from the task of allocating the money, accepting that they will have to give their reasons for giving anyone less or more than the mean. On the other hand, one's work group is not the only arbiter of one's contribution; superiors and colleagues outside the group have relevant opinions, while many a group will duck the issue and will share the money out equally. Balance is best. Opinions from both inside and outside the group also increase the opportunity of feedback. Critically, however, this individual element in the bonus should be less than the two group elements if the sense of twin citizenship is to be reinforced.

Obviously, such a dramatic rearrangement of the reward system in an organisation could only be instituted in one step on a greenfield site. Established organisations will have to get there more gradually, taking full advantage of good years to move forward faster, never forgetting the ultimate goal and being careful to explain, at all times, the why and what of it all. It has to be seen as a way of sharing in the rewards of citizenship as well as in its risks.

The Disappearing Middle

Twin citizenship implies that we are citizens of only two states. It should in theory be many more. I am a citizen of my town, then of my region, then of my country. Above and beyond that comes the trading bloc or the larger federal state and beyond that, why not, the world. Theory, however, does not always sit easily with psychological reality. Most of us seem to be capable of only two levels of loyalty in any one area of our lives. The ends of the chain, therefore, often get dropped and the centre levels get squeezed out. 'I am a Scotsman first,' my friend said, 'and then a European. I don't feel British at all.' Only those countries which are, like my Ireland, small enough to be tribes, do not get squeezed between the tribe and the federal union. Businesses which try to put another layer of loyalty, often a geographical one, between the operating company and the corporate centre, can end up confusing and weakening the sense of citizenship.

Governments, in their turn, have to decide which layer

to omit in dispensing health, education or welfare to their citizens. If they insist on retaining the central control while delegating delivery to local units, the intermediary levels will only get in the way and will atrophy. Either the national government has to shed its power to the intermediary level, retaining only the roles of service- and advice-provider, with money allocated according to formula, or it turns the intermediary levels into optional resource centres for the units to draw on if they wish. Federalism has then become a mechanism for centralisation.

A more interesting example of the disappearing middle in government is suggested by David Osborne and Ted Gaebler in their book *Re-inventing Government*. They want to see more of the ownership and control of public-service institutions passed out of the hands of bureaucrats and government professionals into communities and individuals. Citizen groups, neighbourhoods, volunteer organisations would be authorised, and, where necessary, be centrally funded, to carry out many of the local activities of government. If that were to happen, whole layers of administration would be unnecessary.

The new executive agencies in Britain are a step along this route. These are autonomous entities charged with the delivery of government services, ranging from the Benefit Agency to the Central Office of Information. When they are truly autonomous, the federalism of government services will be well established. At present, the British Treasury is still reluctant to let go all the strings. The pay and the grading and the numbers of staff, for instance, are centrally controlled. There cannot be a true feeling of local citizenship when you cannot determine your own staffing levels. Nor is the monitoring of technical details a substitute for the second and bigger loyalty which will be essential if the old traditions of the Civil Service are not to get lost in the new proliferation of independent bodies. Federalism is not easy.

There can, however, be too many definitions of local citizenship. The State of California is fast becoming bogged down in too many layers of government. It is hard to know where real responsibility lies, what with school and hospital boards, local communities, the state and the federal levels, and the continuing experiment with direct democracy whereby the voters can vote to make specific propositions into law. Too many layers of citizenship end up as a bureaucratic nightmare, be it in a corporation or a country. More of the middle needs to disappear.

National parliaments in Europe's larger countries, which are themselves federations of tribal regions, know that they are likely to be squeezed out if and when Europe becomes a fuller federation. Understandably, they do not relish the thought. It is not nice to be a disappearing middle, even if a greater loyalty requires it. It is not only national parliaments which face this dilemma of the disappearing middle; layers in organisations have been collapsing for a decade at least, not least because those organisations are reorganising federally, even if they do not always call it that or recognise it as such. In the federal structure, hierarchies are limited and local; you relate to people in the wider organisation because their role is relevant to your needs, not because their status in the organisation requires it. Forget the hierarchy, use the network.

I listened to the chairman of a large French supermarket and hotel chain explaining his federal, devolved organisation to a sceptical Spanish audience who were still hooked on hierarchy. 'Please explain to us,' one of them eventually asked in some frustration, 'to whom does the manager of the store in Lyons report?' The chairman clearly did not understand the question: 'Well,' he said, 'if it's a question of distribution he will go to the expert who is, I think, in Marseilles, but if it is a purchasing problem the right person is in Paris.' 'Yes, but who is his immediate boss?' 'There isn't any one person whom he would call "boss".' You could see the mystification on the faces of the Spaniards who live in a partially federal country but do not, yet, run their organisations federally. Twin citizenship needs no middles.

The Loss of Loyalty

Twin citizenship is key to one set of paradoxes, in our societies and in our organisations, be they businesses, hospitals, government agencies, charities or whatever. Deny the local smaller loyalty and we kill all liberty, incentive and initiative and rely on the centre to be right, as IBM did, to its great cost, in the early 1990s. Deny the bigger loyalty, and inefficiencies, duplications and misunderstandings will proliferate. We need both loyalties.

In 1993 the Social Affairs Unit of the British Home Office produced a book of essays entitled *The Loss of Virtue* which argued that words like 'Duty', 'Loyalty' and 'Obligation' had disappeared from common usage. They blamed it on the growth of an amoral culture. Some attributed it to the failure of religion to cultivate a sense of right and wrong. Tony Blair, the Labour Party spokesman, then, on Home Affairs, pointed out that the words had no meaning unless one felt that one belonged to something, something which one could draw from as well as give to, something bigger than one's gang or club. He was, in my words, saying that, without a sense of a second and a bigger citizenship, selfishness is inevitable. If we cannot create that feeling of a bigger citizenship in our people, there will be no balance in society and our language will, indeed, begin to change.

Federalism, properly understood, can restore that sense of a local belonging and a broader, bigger citizenship, both in our organisation and in society.

7   Subsidiarity

Subsidiarity is an ugly word. But once you have learnt how to spell it and get your tongue around it, you will be unlikely to forget it. Subsidiarity is the idea at the centre of federalism; it is the key element in learning; change, if it is to be effective, depends upon it; the work of teams requires it, as does any attempt to make individuals take more responsibility for themselves. It is, however, a confusing word, because it has nothing to do with subsidiaries.

Reverse Delegation

Jacques Delors once offered a prize for a good definition of this ugly word. He need not have bothered, as various people were quick to remind him. Politically, the tenth amendment to the US Constitution, laying down the principle of States' rights, does it, without using the actual word. Much earlier, the Roman Catholic Church, borrowing the idea from political theory, coined the word and turned it into a moral principle. It was last restated in a papal encyclical, Quadragesimo Anno, in 1941: 'It is an injustice, a grave evil and a disturbance of right order for a large and higher organisation to arrogate to itself functions which can be performed efficiently by smaller and lower bodies . . . ' Strong words. I translate them more simply – stealing people's responsibilities is wrong. You could also define subsidiarity as 'reverse delegation' – the delegation by the parts to the centre.

Not so long ago my young daughter started her own

business with a partner. They had a good product, but they had never run a business before. As I watched them making what I was sure were dangerous and foolhardy decisions, the temptation to intervene and give them the benefit of my experience was overwhelming. I loved my daughter and I badly wanted this venture to succeed. I wanted to help. I was bluntly told to mind my own business not theirs. I realised, belatedly, that I was stealing her decisions, taking away their choices and their chance either to claim success as theirs or to learn from their failure. I apologised. Next time I would wait for them to ask – reverse delegation. I understood, then, why subsidiarity was a moral principle.

Federal organisations take subsidiarity seriously. They have to because they work on the principle of reverse delegation. The individual parts, or states, cede some of their powers to the centre because they believe that the centre can do some things better on a collective basis than they can on their own. They therefore retain as much independence as they think that they can handle. These 'reserve powers' of the centre are negotiated jointly and are then recorded in a formal constitution. All federal organisations have written constitutions. It may be that Britain's aversion to a written constitution has something to do with her intuitive distrust of federalism and its formality. There should be nothing vague or woolly about federalism or the place gets cluttered up with overlapping responsibilities and misunderstandings.

As more and more organisations collect alliances around their cores, they are forced to negotiate what should be done by whom and the pressure will be to allow as much discretion to the parts as is sensible and possible. What you do not own you cannot dictate to; negotiation is inevitable, so is subsidiarity – leaving power as close to the action as possible.

The New Centre

Homa Bahrami, describing the new hi-tech organisations of Silicon Valley, calls them multi-polar, saying that they:

> are more akin to a federation or constellation of business units that are typically interdependent, relying on one another for critical expertise and know-how. They have a peer relationship with the centre. The centre's role is to orchestrate the broad strategic vision, develop the shared administrative and organisational infrastructure, and create the cultural glue which can create synergies.

One company employs 100 professionals in roles which are classified as 'corporate'. These include finance and administration, infrastructure support (which includes purchasing), legal services, human resources and corporate communications. All these roles, we should note, are service roles rather than decision-imposing roles.

The 'horizontal organisation' is also in fashion. As described by McKinsey consultants Ostroff and Smith, these organisations have ten key principles, including: 'organise work around processes not functions and select key performance objectives, flatten hierarchy by minimizing non-added-value activities, make teams not individuals the principal building blocks of organisations'. What they are saying is that the trick is to find the optimum level of subsidiarity and then collapse as much into that as possible so that the group or team or individual have the means at their direct disposal to do what they are responsible for. In their view it is the team which is closest to the action that is the appropriate level of subsidiarity. That done, it is the job of the centre to set standards but not necessarily to specify how they should be delivered. The unit is then judged, after the event, by its performance against those objective standards. Some call all this 'process re-engineering', but that is only to give a modern name to an ancient principle, a principle which needs to be rediscovered, if we are going to have any chance of coping with the turbulence of the times. No longer do people believe that the centre or the top necessarily knows best; no longer can the leaders do all the thinking for the rest; no longer do people want them to.

Following this principle, organisations, everywhere, have been collapsing and dispersing their centres. The 100 professionals of Silicon Valley seem to be about standard. ABB, the Swedish–Swiss engineering giant, oversees 225,000 people with about that number in an undistinguished office building in Zurich. British Petroleum, in London, has twice that number but would like to make it less. Richard Branson's Virgin empire makes do with five! One way that they do it is by dispersing the centre. There is no need to have all the people with responsibilities across the organisation sitting in the same central place. Those who are responsible for co-ordinating a particular product range may sensibly be located in the place which does most of the work on that product. The research co-ordination can go to the biggest laboratory, a geographical watching brief to a country or state in that area. It spreads power around and down. That gives those who are nearer to the action a sense of involvement, of ownership, in the policies of the whole. It is subsidiarity in practice, as it is when they locate the European Bank for Reconstruction and Development in London or the European University in Florence, or the European Parliament in Strasbourg. To put everything in Brussels would be to take too much power into the centre. It would be stealing responsibility.

Small the centre should be, and partially dispersed, but it must be strong and well informed. The centre, after all, carries the ultimate responsibility for the whole. Its reserve powers typically include 'new money', i.e. the choice of strategic investments; 'new people', i.e. the right to make the key personnel decisions in the group; the design and management of the information system, which is the artery of the organisation; and, most controversially, the 'right of invasion' when things go wrong. Only those in the centre can have a view of the whole. They cannot run it, and should be too few in number to be tempted, but they can nudge, influence and, if they have to, interfere. The centre's principle task is to be the trustee of the future, but it needs to be sure that the present does not run out before the future arrives.

Federalism, insists Mike Bett of Britain's BT, cannot work without a strong centre. In the past, this meant that the strong centre was also a big centre. In order to co-ordinate plans and monitor activities, a lot of people had to be around. Power was then concentrated in one place. Federalism existed in name only. The information revolution which has overtaken us means that the centre can now be well informed but small, it can be strong but dispersed. Power can be more balanced. The nerve centre of the organisation can be in the chief executive's laptop computer – and in several others simultaneously. The 'Virtual Organisation' – the image of the organisation on your screen – is almost here, in our briefcases. The information age has made federalism possible.

This new, dispersed, centre has still, however, got to talk to itself as well as contemplate its screens. Video-conferences, voice mail and other technological devices help, but there is no real substitute for looking someone in the eye while you talk or they talk. Dispersed centres mean a lot of travel and red-eyes. The physical centres of these new dispersed organisations increasingly begin to resemble clubhouses, places where people meet, eat and greet but do not do their daily work. Like a club, there is a resident staff, those corporate services listed above, for instance, but the key players in the organisation live and work elsewhere and use the club for their necessary meetings. It is not even essential that the chairman or chief executive works out of the central club. For a large part of their time the officers will be, anyway, out and about, with the troops, where the different decision centres are, teaching, coaching, looking, listening. When they do go to the 'club', they can even have their own up-market 'puppy' or 'cart', a mobile desk with all its electronic paraphernalia, which is wheeled out and plugged in whenever the owner checks in.

Italian Style

One begins to wonder, then, what will happen to the cathedrals of corporate power, the tower blocks which shape our skylines. Centres of 100 professionals and corporate clubhouses do not need rows of little boxes piled high into the sky. It has often seemed strangely appropriate that the executive suite should be so high that it is, on occasion, above the clouds, but now that it is recognised that those in the centre are not all-seeing we may find them coming, physically and metaphorically, closer to the ground. Will their old suites become apartments for rich geriatrics or will the whole edifice be pulled down? A changing skyline will be the outward sign of real subsidiarity.

The skylines of most Italian towns have not changed for centuries. It would, of course, be a cultural crime to tamper with the roofscapes of Siena or Florence, Rome or Bologna; but I suspect that the organisation of Italian society has something to do with it. In Italy, much to the frustration of its central government, real power still resides in the family and the local community. Subsidiarity has always bypassed the formal institutions of government. After I went to live, for part of the year, in Tuscany, I soon realised that there was no way that I could conform to the myriad Italian laws regulating the buildings you could build, the cars you could buy, the permits you should have, the taxes you ought to pay, the people you could employ and the people you might allow to rent your home. Not only do the regulations change rather frequently, but the bureaucracy cannot cope with anyone, such as a law-abiding Anglo-Saxon, who wants to do it all by the book.

Nobody, I began to understand, expects you to abide by the letter of every small regulation, but should you fall out with the local community they have an array of laws to throw at you. The community where we live is a network of families. Everybody knows everybody, and knows what everybody is up to. You disregard the locals at your peril, with the law as a weapon only of last resort. Outsiders are welcomed but will never be insiders. Government can pontificate, legislate and regulate but much of it has no effect. It is a very effective but informal system of local control.

Many would argue that, in Italy, subsidiarity has gone too far. The country is broke, and may, conceivably, be split into two or even three, while the locals seem to thrive. The Mafia, the biggest of the families, still rules in parts. Government is impotent, and has proved to be corrupt. The power has to be rebalanced if the country is to be a viable entity. This will only happen, however, if there is a general recognition that some powers have to be ceded to the centre for the good of all, because federalism depends upon reverse delegation. This recognition is slowly dawning; the old politicians who let subsidiarity run riot, often to their own advantage, are on the way out. The balance will, I hope, soon be restored.

Italy is a land of families, of small units linked by networks, in business as well as life. What the Italians do instinctively, we must do deliberately.

Subsidiarity means small units, small units with real responsibilities. Richard Branson likes units of 50 or 60, Anthony Jay, in *Corporation Man*, favoured 400 or 500 and provided evidence from schools, Paris suburbs and Australia. Bill Gates of Microsoft likes 200 as a maximum. Tom

Peters has documented many cases of organisations like Union Pacific Railroad breaking themselves up into smaller units, in that case of 600 people each, but comes down in favour of 150 as the natural size. He cites the findings in the *New Scientist* magazine that 'in most modern armies the smallest independent unit normally numbers 130–150 men', that 'there is a critical threshold in the region of 150–200, with larger companies suffering a disproportionate amount of absenteeism and sickness', that 'once an academic discipline becomes larger than [200 researchers] it breaks into two sub-disciplines', that 'neolithic villages from the Middle East around 6000 BC typically seemed to have contained 120–150 people' and 'the Hutterites, contemporary North American fundamentalists, regard 150 as the maximum size for their communities'.

Forget the precise size. The point is that we need the unit to be big enough to be competent to do what it has to do and small enough so that we can know everyone in it and they can know us. The Bishop of Occam would have understood. According to the principle of Occam's Razor, the unit should be as small as it can be and as large as it has to be, a paradox in balance.

Signatures and Rowing Eights

Subsidiarity, however, depends on a mutual confidence. Those in the centre have to have confidence in the unit, while the unit has to have confidence in the centre and the members of the unit have to have confidence in each other. When the mutual confidence exists, there is no need for the books of procedures, the manuals, inspectors, performance numbers and counter-signatures which clutter up large organisations. These are all the signs of distrust, the atmosphere of fear which makes so many organisations seem like prisons for the human soul. They should not, need not, be like that. Our work can be our pride. Put it this way: we want to be able to sign our own work. A lot of people already figuratively do sign their work. Every member of the team that makes a television programme puts their name on the end of it. As you watch the credits roll you wonder why anyone needs to know all those names. You don't need to know, but they need to tell you; they want the acknowledgement and the credit.

A friend was appointed manager of a small art-printing works. Shortly after his arrival he called the whole workforce together and told them that he was ashamed of the quality of much of the work that had been going out of the place. 'In future,' he told them, 'I want everyone who has worked on an order to sign their names to a slip that will go out with the order saying, "We are responsible for this work. We hope that you are pleased with it." I expected a revolt,' he said, 'but instead they cheered.' 'We, too, have been ashamed of much of the work. But we thought that that was what you wanted – the lowest acceptable quality at the lowest cost. We are happy to sign our names provided you supply us with the machines to allow us to do work to our standards.' Subsidiarity depends on a mutual confidence, but putting your name to it is the best guarantee of quality that I know. It is the reason why professionals always sign their work. The signature acknowledges their responsibility. We know who to blame if things go wrong – and who to thank if they go right.

Such mutual confidence, however, takes time to build up. It has to be earned by all concerned. I once described a typical British work team as being like a rowing eight – eight people going backwards as fast as they can, without talking to each other, commanded by the one person who can't row. I thought that it was witty. I was quietly rebuked, afterwards, by a member of the audience who happened to be an oarsman. 'You couldn't be more wrong,'.

he said, 'to make fun of it. We couldn't go backwards without talking, or be content to be commanded by a non-rower, if we did not know each other very well and have complete confidence in each other's ability to do the job we are supposed to do. That's why we practise together so much, eat together and even live together for long periods.'

I remembered, then, that Japanese groups are renowned for the time they spend together off the job, and I notice how actors not only rehearse together but socialise together. You have to know each other well, it seems, both on and off the job, to know whether you can have confidence, or more, trust, in someone. My son went through a typical British education, one designed to bring him out as an individual and to emphasise his personal qualities and skills. He stood out in a crowd. Then he went to drama school, where they select a group of 27 young people to work together, learning to perform plays, for three years. He quickly realised that he stood or fell according to the quality of the group as a whole. It is no use being a star in a mediocre team. He became a devoted groupie, teaching others what he knew and they didn't, and learning, in turn, new skills from them. Competition was out, co-operation was all. He had no time, he said, to see his other friends during the terms. The group came first. 'We all depend upon each other.' I accused him of going Japanese. 'That would be a compliment,' he replied, 'because they understand what is needed in a group.'

Tough Trust

Subsidiarity in a group sounds warm and reassuring. It is, in practice, tough, and has important consequences for those in charge. For one thing, the group has to be small enough and be together long enough for the mutual confidence to grow. Confidence and trust cannot be ordered up from the store. A person must remain in a post long enough for others to judge the consequences of their actions and decisions. One-year assignments will seldom cover the feedback loop. More important even than that is the necessity to be ruthless if the confidence turns out to be unjustified. If you cannot have confidence in a member of the team, that member must go. If the whole team does not merit confidence, the team must go. Without mutual confidence the principle of subsidiarity cannot work. Checks and checkers have to be installed. Suspicion and evasion become rife, morale declines, the work deteriorates and any remaining confidence evaporates. Mistakes can and should be tolerated, provided one learns from them, but too many mistakes erode confidence, particularly if they are what one company, W. L. Gore, calls below-the-water-line mistakes, mistakes which imperil the organisation. Those are not easily forgiven. It is better, then, to be tough than sorry.

Tom Peters tells a nice story of Mike Walsh taking on the job of turning around Teneco. Four months into the job he heard that local managers at the Louisiana site had called the employees together for a 'safety meeting'. When the workers arrived they were told to lie on the ground and were searched for drugs. This, felt Walsh, was not going to help the kind of organisation he was trying to create. He flew to the site, apologised for the search, and used the occasion for another general meeting. During the meeting some employees started to complain about a safety problem in some of the bunk cars where the employees lived when on the site. Local managers started to explain away the problem by detailing how much the company spent on bunk-car maintenance. Walsh interrupted. 'Why not just visit the cars?' 'But it's raining outside,' some of the managers said. 'It's OK,' Walsh told them, 'managers won't melt.' He visited the bunk cars, decided that they were indeed unsafe, and saw to it that they were fixed.

That action may not have seemed very important in the great scheme of things at Teneco, but stories spread, and that kind of action helped greatly to establish the kind of two-way confidence which is essential to subsidiarity. Confidence depends on knowing who the other person is, what they stand for, how far they will go – on basic human qualities like authenticity, integrity, character. These are a far cry from the spreadsheets and committees which permeate organisational life. Tom Peters devotes a whole chapter in his book to 'The Missing X-Factor: Trust', but has no easy solutions to offer. 'Read more novels and fewer business books,' he says. 'Relationships really are all there is.'

Subsidiarity sounds like another ugly word – empowerment. There is a significant difference. Empowerment implies that someone on high is giving away power. Subsidiarity, on the other hand, implies that the power properly belongs, in the first place, lower down or farther out. You take it away as a last resort. Those in the centre are the servants of the parts. The task of the centre, and of any leader, is to help the individual or the group to live up to their responsibilities, to enable them to deserve their subsidiarity. In this way it is possible to handle one of the paradoxes of individualism, that we want to belong but we don't want to be bossed around, or to be 'empowered' if the hidden message is 'I empower you to do this, but I can disempower you if I don't like the way you do it'. Subsidiarity, therefore, is a tough deal. One has to understand one's responsibilities and then deliver. It means, too, that we have to be able to face up to disagreements. If we are going to take responsibility we need to be clear about what the criteria for our success are to be, what is acceptable and what is not. Only if there is a mutual confidence can disagreement, argument and conflict be handled positively. Organisations based on subsidiarity are full of ambiguity and argument and conflict, but if it is argument among trusted friends, united by a common purpose, then it is useful argument. Truth, said the Scottish philosopher David Hume, springs from arguments among friends.

It is, as a result, extremely demanding to run an organisation on the basis of reverse delegation and confidence. It also feels quite lonely at the centre. As one director of ABB commented, 'All we can do is to watch the herd and observe, with some relief, that in general it is heading in a westerly direction!' Why, then, are so many organisations trying to make reverse delegation work? It is partly in response to the paradox of individualism, the recognition that the well-educated knowledge-worker increasingly wants both freedom and structure. To attract and keep the best of these knowledge-workers, to be a so-called 'preferred organisation', subsidiarity has to be guaranteed.

Most of us are little different from the knowledge-worker. We want to own our work, but we like to work within a structure. We need to know what is expected of us but then to have the discretion to do it our way. Subsidiarity is also, and more urgently, a response to the need in our institutions to be flexible but coherent, to be all things to all people but still recognisably the same to all. Deep down, however, subsidiarity is a moral imperative. Power belongs to the people. It is the manager's, or teacher's, or parent's challenge to help them to exercise it responsibly.

Subsidiarity, with its emphasis on our individual rights and duties, is the basis of any concept of citizenship and critical to any concept of society. If we want our personal freedoms, and if we want them underwritten with guarantees of health care and welfare, we must accept our responsibilities to our fellows and earn the confidence which will allow the freedoms. That is the kind of thing one learns from parents as much as from teachers, but, then, the messages implicit in subsidiarity are a good guide to parenthood. Give a child as much responsibility as she or he can handle and then help them to live up to it. Subsidiarity is an old word, packed with meaning. It may sound out-of-date but it carries a modern punch. We would be foolish to discard it.

The Meaning of Business

A book which starts with the symbol of an empty raincoat and the challenge to find our human selves again, amid all the pressures for progress and economic success, has to examine the place and meaning of business in our societies. Even those who lead lives far removed from the factories and shops of manufacturing and commerce need to have a view on business, who it is for and what it is for. Directly or indirectly, their economic well-being depends on it. A recession brings home to everyone the importance of a healthy trading sector in the economy. When business goes down, everything goes down – jobs, tax receipts, house prices, government spending. Does this mean, however, that business is purely a wealth-creating instrument, best left alone to do what it has to do, or does it mean that, precisely because of its social impact, it has to recognise a wider accountability than making its owners seriously rich?

More directly, the business ethos has invaded our life. Everything is now thought of as a business of a sort. We are all 'in business' these days, be we doctor or priest, professor or charity-worker. *Every* organisation is, in practice, a business, because it is judged by its effectiveness in turning inputs into outputs for its customers or clients, and is judged in competition against its peers. The only difference is that the 'social businesses' do not distribute their surpluses. Americans, I was once assured, have always known this, but the hard reality of it had escaped most Europeans until lately.

Britain, however, has recently turned its schools, hospitals and medical practices, and even the service-delivery.

parts of the government, into independent businesses, funded still by the state but judged by their effective use of resources and required to compete for customers. When the full implications sink in of what it means to be 'businesslike', we shall realise what a revolution it will be to our way of life. One of the implications is, however, that all these organisations, in which one-third of our people work, will all have to answer the same difficult questions – what is this business for, and to whom does it belong? Are we who work in these businesses, be they social or commercial, their instruments or something more than that? What are our rights, and what, conversely, our responsibilities?

We have managed to evade most of these questions while we were preoccupied with our common enemy in communism. Anything, we assumed, must be better than such a centrally controlled system. This conveniently ignored the fact that many of our largest organisations were run in a similar totalitarian way. Now that communism has been discredited, capitalism must be its own sternest critic. Anglo-Saxon capitalism, when we see it exported in all its nakedness to the old socialist countries of Eastern Europe, is revealed to be good for some but not obviously for the many. It is, also, increasingly clear that there is more than one variant of capitalism. Michel Albert has spelt out the differences between the Anglo-Saxon version and the continental European version in his book *Capitalism Against Capitalism*. But there is also the capitalism of Asia, what might be called Confucian capitalism and, in particular, its Japanese variant.

The Anglo-Saxons have much to learn from the other varieties. Some hoped that the businesses of Britain and America would start to emulate the way in which the Japanese and the continental Europeans had a form of Chinese contract with their six different stakeholders – their financiers, employees and suppliers most obviously, but also their customers, their environment and society as a whole. Such a six-sided or hexagon contract inevitably changes the priorities of the business, leaving more room for the concerns of the other parties. A business, then, is no longer just an economic instrument. Ironically, the pressures of competing in a global world are pulling the others towards the Anglo-American model as fast as they, on their part, move towards them.

The question, 'What is a business for?' is addressed in the chapter on **The Corporate Contract**, in which I argue that the different systems of capitalism do indeed need to move together, borrowing the best of each other's traditions, in order to forge a new image of capitalism, one more obviously in the service of its society, but one still flexible and efficient.

The other question, 'To whom does a business belong?' is equally tendentious. I question whether the idea of a company as a piece of property which can be owned by anyone with enough money to pay for it, or bits of it, a property which can be bought and sold over the heads of all those who work and live there, is still a valid concept in an age when people not things are the real assets. Property is certainly not a valid concept when we think of the new 'social businesses'. So what sort of institutions are they? Instead of arguing who the rightful owners ought to be, I suggest a third angle – that ownership is not a valid or relevant concept, any more than property is. We ought instead to think of 'membership'.

The consequences of this line of thought are explored in the chapter on **The Membership Business**. Membership gives meaning, and responsibility, to those who work in the business. They cease to be instruments or employees and become enfranchised. Ironically, if we return to the old meaning of the 'company' we realise that a company was a group of companions, members one of another. That original meaning of a company still lingers on in the occasional theatrical 'company', or in some of the old livery companies in London, now charities not businesses. Perhaps we should rediscover the original meaning of the word.

The concept of a 'company' in this sense already exists in the way many volunteer groups and not-for-profit organisations think of themselves. Just as these organisations are becoming more 'businesslike', so we may see businesses looking to the non-profit arena for new models for themselves. The non-profit world understands all too well the combination of core funding and optional space, the doughnut principle, and is familiar with the necessity of Chinese contracts in a good cause. These organisations may, unexpectedly, hold the clues to the second curve of capitalism.

There are more clues in places as far apart as Michigan and Brazil. We need many more if capitalism is to prove that it has a human face.

8   The Corporate Contract

Capitalism has, supposedly, triumphed. Some claim there is no better way to run our societies than a mix of liberal democracy and free-market enterprise. Business gives wealth and opportunity to us all. Consultants and economists from the West swarm into the new market economies of central Europe, with their overnight cases, to show them how to do it our way in 24 hours flat.

Capitalism Triumphant?

The first results of the new capitalism are, however, far from reassuring. Industrial output in Poland fell by 35 per cent between 1989 and 1991; inflation reached 260 per cent. In Hungary, arguably the best-prepared of the new economies for the transition, food and basic expenses absorbed 45 per cent of the average household's expenses in 1989 but 70 per cent in 1991. In the Czech Republic they hoped, at best, to keep the fall in real wages to 12 per cent in 1991 and 10 per cent in 1992. Russia is a catastrophe, where the figures do not even make sense.

The full sad saga is forcefully described by William Keegan in his book *The Spectre of Capitalism*, where he comments:

> The terrible thing about the *sudden* adoption of capitalism is that the two necessary conditions preached by the reformers are in conflict. 'Price Liberalisation', needed to make the markets work . . . almost inevitably involves a disturbing

acceleration in inflation as people rush to protect themselves from higher prices. 'Stabilisation' is, then, an uphill task in the face of 'liberalisation'.

The paradox is hard to balance. It was a director of West Germany's Audi who said, 'There are lots of books on how to move from capitalism to socialism, but none on how to do it the other way round.' He added, ruefully, 'We seem to be doing the research for that new book!'

Western capitalism in countries like Russia has come to mean 'trading'. The black market and mafias abound. 'Yellow Page' services proliferate. Street bazaars and back-yard markets are everywhere. Keegan reports that people can buy cars in Poland and, 48 hours later, sell them in Moscow for profits equivalent to 10 years of a professor's salary. Visitors happily spend the annual salary of a Russian on a piece of fashion or a call-girl. Such 'Wild East' capitalism, he says, is never going to be the foundation of a proper market economy. Nor does it, at present, seem to promise the sort of freedom to shape our lives that many hoped for.

The big manufacturing enterprises are lacking, but a country as large as Russia cannot survive on services and trades alone, nor will it be content to be the cheap labour shop for Europe after its past as a world power. 'We used to build rockets to circumnavigate the moon in this plant,' said one Russian colonel. 'Are we to turn round and make pots and pans to compete with central Asia?' Even in Hungary, only 10 per cent of the larger enterprises have been privatised. Most of the rest are probably not viable on their own.

Keegan was writing about Eastern Europe. My fear is that he could have been describing a possible scenario for Britain and America in a few years' time. The version of capitalism so triumphantly carried to those countries is the Anglo-American version. There are other versions, notably those of Japan and continental Europe, which have had a better record of combining liberalism and stability. They have made a better job of balancing economic freedom with relative equality, of giving more chances to more people.

The different versions of capitalism share certain fundamentals – free markets, the private ownership of assets, private direction of investment. They also share the idea of the hexagon contract. In each version the company operates in a space bounded by six interest groups – the shareholders or financiers, the employees, the customers, the suppliers, society and, lastly, the surrounding community and environment community. Where they differ is in the emphasis which they give to each of the interest groups. The difference is highlighted by the answer each version would give to the question 'What is a business for?'

What IS a Business for?

In my American business school in the Sixties the answer was clear. It was inscribed above the blackboard in every class so that we could not ignore it – 'maximize the medium-term earnings per share'. Medium-term, mark you, not short-term, and 'maximize' not optimise. Twenty-five years later things had not changed. Just before announcing his resignation as chief executive of IBM, John Akers complained that, 'The average IBM'er has lost sight of the reasons for his company's existence. IBM exists to provide a return on invested capital to the stockholders.'

From this basic premise all else flowed, given, of course, a perfect market and an intelligent one, managers who were clever, energetic and wise, and an educational system which provided an intelligent and rational workforce. Looking back, it is amazing that none of us challenged either the premise or the assumptions. Yet my own life up to then should have given it the lie. I had been the lowly regional manager in a distant outpost of a great oil company. I suppose that I must have seen the published results of the company but its earnings per share, its profitability, did not keep me awake at night, nor get me leaping out of bed in the morning. I was not a fool. I knew that any new project, rationally, needed to earn a rate of return above a certain figure, and my proposed projects were always expected to do just that, although neither I nor, as far as I know, anyone else ever checked whether those projects in fact lived up to their estimates.

If I'm honest, it was not the shareholders but my own self-respect which drove me. Sitting in that far-off country, the idea of maximum earnings per share was very remote, very intellectual, very unreal. I had, I was sure, a much more serious social function, as I told a maiden great-aunt back in Ireland who had complained that I was the first of the family to go into 'trade'. I was there to help produce things for people which were badly needed, in good condition, at a fair price, on time, without mucking up the local scenery or upsetting the local councillors or villagers among whom we lived and worked. It was a form of social contract, but, of course, it needed profits to make it work and go on working.

My business school in America was wrong, I am now convinced. The principal purpose of a company is not to make a profit, full stop. It is to make a profit in order to continue to do things or make things, and to do so ever better and more abundantly. To say that profit is a means to other ends and not an end in itself is not a semantic quibble, it is a serious moral point. A requirement is not a purpose. In everyday life those who make the means into ends are usually called neurotic or obsessive. We have to eat to live, but if we live to eat we become distorted in more senses than one. In ethics, to mistake the means for the ends is to be turned in on oneself, one of the worst of sins, said Saint Augustine.

'Profits are the principal yardstick,' stated the Watkinson Report on the responsibilities of the British public company 20 years ago, but a yardstick for what? And how can a yardstick be a purpose? It's like saying that you play cricket to get a good batting average. It's the wrong way round. You need a good average to keep on playing and to get into the first team. We need to clean up our logic.

Different Cultures, Different Dreams

Lester Thurow, in his book *Head to Head*, argues that Anglo-Saxon economics stem from the Anglo-Saxon emphasis on the individual and, in particular, on the individual as consumer. The individual is not so much interested in the work itself as in the results which that work will produce for himself or herself. Personal wealth is the result which the Anglo-Saxon wants, because that wealth will make possible the life style for which he dreams. The work is a means to an end, not an end in itself.

Take, for instance, William Caxton, who brought the printing press to England in 1477, an early example of technological pioneering: 'Caxton was an early and prominent example of a well-known modern type,' says Anthony Glyn, 'the individualistic Englishman following out his own hobbies . . . As a successful merchant he made enough money during thirty years to devote his later life to the literary pursuits he loved.' British businessmen, when pressed for their real purpose in life, nearly always say that they want to make their pile and then do something 'which really interests' them. Business is only a means to an end.

The British businessman tends not to be interested in sustained continuity. Private businesses, for instance, seldom turn into third- or fourth-generation family businesses. They are sold or go public long before then.

Many a British entrepreneur would feel that to ask children of the next generation to take on the business would be to constrain their freedom. The Victorian entrepreneurs who built Britain's industrial fortunes wanted their children to have nothing to do with business, but to be country gentlemen.

It is different in Japan. Thurow describes the Japanese business leaders as empire-builders and social builders, gaining their satisfaction from being part of a great and growing empire. To such people the use and ownership of production goods may be more important than consumption goods; they would, in fact, be happy to trade personal consumption for the success of 'their' empire. Imperial Rome, he points out, had many more grand public buildings than fancy private homes. In America it is, often, the other way round.

Japanese workers join a firm in much the same way as volunteers join an army, not for personal wealth or glory, but to be part of some great endeavour. Today it is the business enterprise which offers the best chance for empire-building. Given those attitudes it is hardly surprising that the Japanese put long-term growth above short- or even medium-term profits, indeed that profitability calculations hardly figure in some of their strategic decisions. To keep IBM at bay, Fujitsu won the computer contract for the water-distribution system of Hiroshima City with a bid of just one yen. The required rate of return for a 10-year R & D project averages 8.7 per cent in Japan compared with 20.3 per cent in the US and 23.7 per cent in the UK. As a result, there is more investment in the future in Japan than in the other countries. In 1992 Japan invested the equivalent of 34.2 per cent of its GDP in fixed assets. The figure was 16 per cent in the UK and 14.8 per cent in the US.

Germany is different again. Germany thinks of itself as having a 'social market' economy and not just a 'market' economy. Business is seen as serving all the people, not just its shareholders or even its employees. Heinrich Henzler, the chairman of McKinsey's German offices, has written that: 'Laws on co-determination, combined with a tradition of patriarchal concern, have made European C.E.O.s deeply committed to their employees, treating them more like partners in a long-term enterprise than anonymous "factors of production".' When he says European he means continental Europe, not Britain. He goes on to argue that this is a source of great competitive advantage.

Every employer in Germany of any size regards it as part of their duty to take part in the 'dual system' of workplace training, even though they may not employ the trainees at the end. They see that training as their investment in the continuity of German business, of which they will be a continuing part. The *Mittelstand*, the family businesses which are the backbone of the German economy, rarely sell out to others but are seen as a trust to be carried on by the family.

One reason for the small size of the German stock-market (only 665 stocks are quoted compared with 2,300 in the smaller economy of the UK) is that the pension provisions of these smaller firms are unfunded. The pension money is held in the company. The assumption is that the firms will always be around and be able to pay the pensions of their ex-workers. It also assumes that those workers would naturally want to work for the same company all their lives. Continuity is built into the system along with an acceptance of expensive social welfare policies, designed to take good care of those who are temporarily outside the system. German business exists for the good of all.

It helps, of course, that the firms are allowed tax relief on the reserves which they build up to pay those pensions, but they have the choice as to how they use those reserves in the meantime, unlike the separately funded pension schemes of British and American firms, where the moneys are managed by outsiders, charged with considering only the interests of the pensioners. Not unnaturally, the German firms often use those reserve funds to reinforce their links with key suppliers or agents by investing some of the reserves in their businesses, just as the Japanese do with *their* unfunded pension reserves. It is another force for continuity.

The role of the banks reinforces the sense of continuity. The banks are not short-term financial helpers, concerned mainly to make sure that their money is secure so that they can call it back to lend to others who are a better or more profitable risk. In Germany the banks are there for the long haul, with a stake in the business. In 1987 the *Economist* calculated that the large banks owned 10–25 per cent of the shares in 48 of the 100 largest firms, 25–50 per cent of the shares in 43 others and over 50 per cent of nine. In other words, every major firm was locked into the big-bank network and vice versa. No wonder that contested takeovers are almost unknown in Germany. They would not succeed.

The New Blend

Our versions of capitalism are the products of our histories. As a German Foreign Minister once said, 'The British were very generous after the war, they insisted on federalism, co-determination and single plant unions for us but took none of these for themselves!' Thurow and Keegan are not alone in seeing problems with the Anglo-American version, with its hint of selfishness, and favouring the German model, accepting that the Japanese version is probably unique to their culture. The Chinese, for instance, with their history of family enterprises are closer to the Italians and the Germans than their Japanese neighbours.

Paradoxically, however, although the German and Japanese models have been clearly the most successful in building rich and relatively equal societies, there are signs that as the world becomes one market-place, the versatility of the Western-style capital markets and the freedom of the individual in the Anglo-Saxon cultures become seductive. The third generation of the *Mittelstand* families are not as keen as their forebears on the idea of a family trust, if it locks them into one firm and one town for life. Pensions will soon be funded and that money will boost the German stock-market – to thrice its size in 10 years, some think. Meantime, as both the Germans and the Japanese acquire foreign shareholders in their pursuit of global empires, they are meeting with investors who cannot be expected to share the Japanese quest for economic supremacy, but want shorter-term rewards.

As a result, the balance of forces among the six interest groups is changing in all the countries. In Anglo-Saxon capitalism the shareholders have, traditionally, come first, with the other parties seen as a constraint, legitimate maybe, but still a constraint on the primary purpose. It is now accepted that all the so-called 'stakeholders' matter. The principle of the hexagon contract is now written into most corporate statements of purpose, even if the shareholder is still the first, because the most essential. The shareholder has to be the core of the corporate doughnut, but it is widely agreed that the business is not fully developed unless the interests of the other stakeholders fill the empty space in the doughnut.

In Japan the usual view is that the employees come top of the list, but Akio Morita of Sony maintains that it is really the customer who heads the others, not from any idealistic notion of wanting to please the man or woman in the street, but because the customer represents the empire they are seeking to build. Morita is now sounding cautious, because he senses a backlash from competitor countries who resent the competitive advantage which Japanese companies obtain by starving the other stakeholders in order to keep prices low for the customer. A readjustment is needed, partly for the sake of global harmony but partly, also, to placate the other stakeholders who would like bigger pickings.

In Germany there has always been a very conscious effort to balance the interests of the six stakeholders. Henzler calls it 'a social balancing act', arguing that business in his country has always accepted that homelessness, illiteracy and other social ills are not only morally unacceptable but are also economically harmful. Business has therefore been willing to bear the considerable social overhead because of its long-term benefits. Some rebalancing is now starting.

In the past, German firms refused to trade their stock on the New York Stock Exchange, arguing that the requirement to publish quarterly reports distorted the priorities of the business and distracted its management from its proper longer-term concerns. Recently, the need for funds to finance its restructuring and expansion has forced Daimler Benz to change its mind. Others will follow. Foreign stockholders will not share the preoccupation with Germany's social balancing act, any more than they want to encourage Japan's economic empire-building. German investors, too, want more than they have been getting. A recent survey of 11 stock-markets over the past 20 years ranked Germany number nine in terms of returns to investors. These investors are now growing restive. One group is even suing Deutsche Bank.

Even without this outside pressure, German business is worried lest the cost of the social balancing act may have grown too high. Jobs are draining out of Germany. BMW sites its new factory in the USA, Volkswagen is looking to Spain for its mega-plant. Hungary and the Czech Republic are close neighbours with skilled labour at a quarter the cost of German labour, even in the east of the country. The social costs of that eastern part are also stretching consensus to a breaking-point. One young German executive put it dramatically: 'If they had to buy some underdeveloped country,' she said bitterly, 'why couldn't they have chosen a smaller cheaper one?' The new generation of Germans may not be as prepared to pay the price for social cohesion as their parents were.

The Existential Company

As the cultures blend, the purposes of a business become less clear. Germany's social balancing act, Japan's economic imperialism, America's and Britain's priority on the returns to the owners, these all become more muted as the other forces in the hexagon contract become more powerful. What then is a company for in this new, more blended, world? The only real answer, I suggest, is 'for itself'. We might call it the existential company.

The existential company operates with the hexagon contract, but within the bounds of that contract is primarily concerned to grow and develop. Its continued existence, its immortality, is its purpose. It may, of course, turn out not to deserve immortality – the life-cycle of the average public company is only 40 years – but it is a worthy aim because, unless all the six interest groups are satisfied, the company will be unlikely to live that long. I liked the family business head who said, looking down at the roofs of the little Belgian town which was dominated, and employed, by his firm, 'We had to sit out two world wars, but they counted on us. In a family business you have to think beyond the grave.'

No one can lay claim to immortality. They have to deserve it. A company will only be allowed to survive as long as it is doing something useful, at a cost which people can afford, and it must generate enough funds for their continued growth and development. Existentialism in business is not, therefore, a form of selfishness. There has to be what James O'Toole, in America, has called stake-holder symmetry, and most of those stockholders are likely to have a vested interest in immortality. Employees, customers, suppliers and the community would all prefer that a business continued, as long as it was good. Even shareholders, now that so many of the institutions are locked into their stakes because they are too large to switch around, will settle for 'continuity provided it is justified by the results'.

'Stakeholder symmetry', however, doesn't get the blood beating any faster than 'shareholder value' which is why I prefer to settle for immortality.

Better not Bigger

What then, would be the purpose of such an existential company? The answer will be different for every business. Satisfying its financiers is a necessary condition, the core of the business doughnut, as is satisfying customers and stakeholders, but a necessary condition is not a purpose. That purpose may be, as in Japan, to conquer the world, but it can be less grandiose. You can grow without wanting to be the biggest or even big.

After one sun-drenched day in the wine country of Northern California I asked the owner of the winery about the future. He was passionate about his winery, he said; he was putting back every cent he could into its growth. 'Where can you grow?' I asked, looking around at the val-ley where every inch of land was by now fully planted with other people's vines. 'Oh, I don't want to expand,' he said, 'I want to grow better not bigger.'

Better not bigger. It is one definition of a purpose, one way to grow, one recipe for immortality. What we *are* can be as important an aspect of purpose as what we *do*. The existential hexagon company would, however, require some changes in the law, at least in Britain and America, because the rights of the shareholders would be severely curtailed. Perhaps not. The law in both countries already recognises the company as an entity in its own right. Lord Justice Evershed, summing up in 1947, said, 'Shareholders are not, in the eyes of the law, part owners of the undertaking. The undertaking is something different from the totality of its shareholdings.'

The judge was describing an existential company, one that exists in its own right, something which has a life and a future of its own. He was suggesting that all companies are, in law, existential. We have to take that judgement seriously, and give it meaning. We have to assume that every company has a life of its own which needs purpose and direction. It is an end in itself, not an instrument owned by others. If we don't, if there is no shared sense of identity to which all parties subscribe, there will be little chance of finding a compromise between the different interest groups. Each will then quite understandably fight their corner and the toughest requirement will become the dominant purpose.

To Find a Purpose

The Anglo-Saxon countries do not start with the cultural beliefs which still pervade the businesses of Japan and Germany. The leaders of business will have to create that purpose which commands assent. Essential though profitability is for the continued existence and growth of a business it begs the questions 'for whom?' and 'for what?'; it is not, in itself, enough. At present, to many people the answer to those questions seems to be 'the shareholders' and 'their enrichment'. The managers, with a proportion of their rewards linked to the share price, are seen as being allied to the shareholders rather than to the workers, unlike in the other countries. The workers and the other stake-holders in the hexagon are then seen by the managers as costs, and costs are things which, instinctively, we seek to reduce. There is seldom a shared sense of belonging.

In one week in the recession-afflicted Britain of 1993, four large public companies reported huge drops in profits, turning them into loss-makers in two instances, but they did not change their dividend. As the president of Britain's Board of Trade commented at the time, 'Presumably the implication is that shareholders can make more money by withdrawing their funds from the business than by allowing the business to invest in itself.' It does not say much for the hope of immortality in those companies.

Again, the figures speak for themselves: since 1975, British companies have retained, on average, 45 per cent of their profits for reinvestment, American firms 54 per cent, Japanese firms 63 per cent and German firms 67 per cent. In such a situation it made perfect sense, as it still does, for British shareholders to take their money out of generous British firms and invest it overseas where the companies clearly believe in their own long-term future.

Not all Anglo-Saxon companies think that way. Johnson and Johnson's credo is famous in America. Formulated four decades ago by President Robert Wood Johnson, it lists the corporate priorities:

– service to its customers comes first
– service to its employees and management comes second
– service to the community comes third
– service to its stockholders comes last

The credo was put to the test during the Tylenol affair when some bottles of its best-selling pain-relief tablets were tampered with, and several people died. J. and J. famously responded by pulling all 30 million capsules off the shelves.

In the long term they gained, because their reputation soared.

Johnson and Johnson might not be so renowned for their credo in America if it wasn't so unusual. It is no different from the batting order in any Japanese company. In a study by Fons Trompenaars, managers from different countries were asked whether they agreed that 'the bottom line' should not be the only real goal of a business, but that the other stakeholders should be taken into account. Ninety-six per cent of Japanese managers agreed with the statement, as did 86 per cent of the Germans, but only 53 per cent of the Americans. The British were in-between at 78 per cent in favour of the stakeholder balance.

If we don't change our ways more quickly, we may see capitalism in our lands deteriorate into the kind of Wild East now to be seen in central Europe, although at a higher level of consumption and corruption, no doubt. To think in terms of an existential company, striving for growth and immortality within the hexagon, is one handle on the problem. Another is to rethink what we mean by a 'company'.

9 The Membership Business

A business is owned by its shareholders. It is a strange type of ownership. To begin with, those owners normally have limited liability, something that goes with no other form of ownership that I can think of. Secondly, the 'thing' which they own mostly consists of people. Owning people, no matter how well you treat them, is considered wrong in every other part of life. There was once a time, in parts of Europe, where a man, in law, owned his wife. No one now, however anti-feminist, would think that right.

The reasons are to be found in history, but history, I have argued before, is not necessarily the best guide to the future. Limited liability was a most ingenious invention which allowed private businesses to take the risks which expansion required. It was a privilege given, then, a century and a half ago, to people who really did own their businesses, ran them and stood or fell by their success. They were locked into the fortunes of their enterprises. The 'property' they owned was physically there to see, bricks and mortar, machines, raw materials. The people were 'hands', employed to work the property, just as they used to be employed to work the land. It made sense, if they were to expand as fast as they might, that they should not have to put all their personal wealth at stake. Hence the privilege, granted to the people of a certain time and of a certain tradition. With the privilege came some implied responsibilities, for the welfare of the workers and the quality of the work. These responsibilities were not always honoured, but the privilege of ownership and limited liability endured. Without it the railways of Britain, for instance, would never have been built, nor would the industrial revolution have happened on the scale it did. Whether what was right then is right now must, however, be another question.

Owners or Punters?

Ownership may no longer be the appropriate concept, but if it is, then it is the proprietors of the private businesses who have the best claim to be the inheritors of that tradition, with its mixture of privilege and responsibility. Their futures are tied to the futures of the business. For the publicly owned businesses the situation is different. The 'owners' of these companies are, for the most part, institutions – investment funds, pension funds, insurance companies. They have no direct involvement with the business. They do not manage it or work in it. They do not know those who do. They are not locked in. The average shareholding by the big institutional investors in Britain is held for four years. Their responsibility is discardable. If things are not going well their best strategy is to walk away from the problem, to sell their shares. Fair enough. The rules allow it and their own shareholders or fundholders require it. The result is to turn the shareholders of public companies into what the *Economist* once called 'punters', equating them with the backers of racehorses at the track.

To expect the punters who backed the bay gelding to stay with that horse throughout its career, or to insist that the trainer took their advice, would not be reasonable. If they don't like its form they transfer their money to another nag. Punters or speculators they may be, owners in any real sense they cannot be. Devices to lock them in by tax incentives or legal requirements would be but 'sand in a free market' as these things were once described. Nevertheless these punters have an extraordinary privilege. They are, for the price of their bets, given a vote from time to time in the auction ring as to who should own their horse. This means that they have to be wooed, continually, for who knows when the auction bell may toll? Every public company, under these rules, is potentially up for sale every day.

It is argued that the constant possibility of the auction ring concentrates the mind of the trainer. It has been known to do that for the occasional bad corporation, but not always for its own good. I asked one supermarket chairman why he was expanding so energetically into France and Belgium, buying up competitors wherever possible. Was it, I said, to take advantage of the new enlarged European market? 'No,' he replied. 'We want to make ourselves so big and so complicated that no one will be tempted to swallow us up.' The best defence against being bought in that ring, apparently, is to buy. Yet all the evidence is that the bidder does worse, most times, than the loser at the end of the day. The cost is, presumably, judged to be reasonable if it gives one protection from the diversion of the auction ring, but it does nothing for the original business.

You do not even have to be under threat in the ring to feel the distraction. The chairman of one large German company was asked why he constantly refused to be listed on the New York Stock Exchange. 'Because,' he said, 'the requirement to report my results quarterly would distort the perspectives of my managers. The access to American funds is not worth that loss of perspective.' He may yet be forced to follow his compatriot companies into that auction ring, but he knows the risk. Managers and investors have different time perspectives, by the nature of their responsibilities. That is as it should be. What is needed is a compromise, not the dominance of pseudo-ownership.

Some say that making the managers, and perhaps also the workers, into the owners removes the pressure of that auction ring. But the history of management buy-outs in recent years suggests that owner-managers are just as susceptible to large offers as anyone else. I have known quite a few who profess a dedication to long-term stewardship in October only to be out to pasture, richer by several millions, in November.

Others look to create a consortium of institutions who will act as proper long-term owners – banks, pension funds, mutual funds and other companies – leaving other punters to flutter in the margin without affecting the long-term ownership. The pension funds, however, who own more than half of all British or American shares, are responsible for other people's money and have always shied away from locking themselves in. In America they are not allowed to sit on the boards of the companies in which they invest.

Some hope that the size of the funds involved will effectively lock the institutions into the index of stocks so that they will be content to stay where they are. There is little sign that those institutions, or, more precisely, their fund-managers, will be content to be so inactive as punters. And as for individual shareholders, one report predicted that the last individual shareholding in Wall Street would be sold in 2003. The idea that we could become a nation of small independent shareholders, which some dream of, is just that, a dream. Whether they would, in any case, behave any differently from their bigger brethren is open to doubt. Why should they?

There are a few signs that the punters are being pushed into behaving more like real owners. A batch of state legislation in the US has made hostile takeovers more difficult, forcing the shareholders to put pressure on the boards of corporations if they want change instead of waiting for someone else to buy them out. Several chairmen of major companies in the US and Britain have 'retired' rather more precipitately than they expected as a result of this pressure, but usually too late and leaving too much for their successor to do.

Property or Community?

Instead of fiddling with the rules, we ought to be asking whether we are still playing the same game as we once used to. Why is it sensible to think of an organised group of people as a piece of property, to be bought and sold according to its market price? Because that is what companies really are these days, organisations of people. A business does not have to be as rarefied as Microsoft to realise that its key assets are its 'human resources' and the kinds of intellectual advantage that they carry around with them – not just their creativity and their technical knowledge, but their network of contacts, their human skills and their experience. Everyone accepts that Japan's economic success has nothing to do with raw materials but is entirely based on the way they educate and manage their people. We have been slow to draw the obvious conclusion – that the same might have to be true for the rest of us; we must make our people our assets, and turn most of our property into the intellectual variety.

'Intellectual property' is a neat phrase, but it may delude us into thinking that the same traditions of ownership can continue. They can't. Intellectual property means people. Organisations are nothing if they are not communities of people, and a community is not a property. It does not make sense to say that a community is 'owned' by outsiders. A community is not a commodity to be bought or sold. A community has 'members' not 'employees' and it belongs to its members – only outsiders, not insiders, get to be 'employed' or hired by the community. If it needs money it raises loans or mortgages, secured, maybe, against part of the physical assets. It could, conceivably, sell a share in the future stream of net income – a form of equity – so that its financiers could share in its fortunes, but such a share would give no other rights. A community belongs to its members.

What would this mean in practice? Businesses would be self-governing communities. Limited liability would still apply, justified now once again because the business 'belongs' only to its members. Financiers would, in effect, hold mortgages but could only intervene managerially if the business reneged on its payments. Some mortgages would carry no repayment obligation but, instead, a share of the income stream for perpetuity. Mortgages could be traded, stock-markets would continue, but only as betting-rings not auction rings. Businesses would only merge or fold by decision of their members, who, doubtless, would normally take their financiers into their confidence. Outwardly, little would look different, but inside it would feel very different.

I spoke with the management of a smallish electronic company in East Anglia. They had had three different corporate owners in three years. It had not, they said, been very conducive to long-term planning or to morale. I could, at least, admire their British genius for understatement! They had become just part of the business portfolio of the big groups, to be bought, sold or exchanged as they re-arranged their corporate-asset profile, to present a more pleasing picture to their owners in their turn. It did not make a lot of sense.

A View from Abroad

In Japan and Germany, for slightly different reasons, the idea of the company as a community, and of financiers as mortgage-holders, has long existed. Michel Albert calls it the Rhine Model, because it prevails in those countries which line the Rhine, but versions of it are found in Sweden and, with a slightly different twist, in Japan. It is, says Albert, who has worked with both Rhine model of capitalism and the Anglo-Saxon variety, markedly different from the property concept of a company.

In Japan the shareholders are more like preference debenture-holders; their dividends are related to the par value of the shares and not to the market value. Many of them are suppliers or associates of the business and get their rewards from being in business with a sound and growing company. They are the bankers, leasing companies, insurers, part-suppliers, distributors and agents who, as Carl Kester points out in a recent study, see their shareholding as the entry fee to a mutually beneficial system.

Unlike the Anglo-Saxon tradition, the board and management, in Japan, are not seen as the representatives of the financiers, but of the workers. The senior managers are not rewarded by linking them into shareholder interests by share options, as in Britain and America. Instead, they are linked, through a bonus system, to the performance of their workforce, the members of the company. By law, any merger or takeover requires the agreement of a majority of the directors of the company, but the directors are almost all insiders, career managers, representing the people with whom they work. If the financial returns are satisfactory the shareholder in Japan has almost no power.

Japanese companies will borrow fiercely to finance growth, but once secure will do their best to finance future growth out of retained earnings. In the 1980s, Japanese companies, on average, carried four times as much debt as American companies. Toyota, on the other hand, had no debt at all and was known as the Bank of Toyota because of its self-contained financial strength. Toyota does not want its investors to be its controllers.

The much-discussed lifetime employment policies of

Japanese business also fit the community concept. Members of a community cannot be expelled. They are there for life. The Japanese company will, however, make sure that they have as few people in their 'organising core' as possible and that they are the best around. It is not always realised that the lifetime system applies only to men, only to large organisations and only to full-time employees. It is generally thought that these true community members amount to less than 30 per cent of the total workforce. No wonder there is such competition to join one of those business communities. No wonder, either, that the organisations spend so much of their time on the learning and development of their people. They have no other choice. They can't sell their people-assets and buy in others.

In Germany and some of the other continental European countries the same concepts apply but for different historical reasons. Unlike Japan, German business is not dominated by the big names. In 1989 *Business Week* listed the 1,000 biggest businesses in the world. There were 353 American firms, 345 Japanese and 30 from Germany. Those are the only firms actively traded on the Frankfurt Stock Exchange, which anyway only has 665 stocks compared with the 2,400 in London's Exchange. Germany's strength, as we have noted before, lies in its *Mittelstand*, its small- to medium-sized family businesses.

Tom Peters, who first revealed the *Mittelstand* phenomenon to America, says that there are maybe 300,000 of these firms with anything from 10 to 3,000 employees. Less well-known, but equally important, are the family businesses of Northern Italy making knitwear, textiles, bricks, tiles, furniture, hydraulics, farm machinery – all the middle-technology, design-conscious products which are the staple ingredient of Italy's exports. The big industrial combines in Italy are mostly state-owned.

These German and Italian businesses are families. They want global reach but not global size. They concentrate on what they know that they can do well and make sure that it is good enough to be among the best in the world. That way they can grow better without growing bigger and can remain a family. Their financiers are investors rather than owners or controllers. They are the banks and insurance companies who are effectively locked in for the long term. It would be difficult to get rid of their shares except to another friend of the business.

The point of these businesses is to be able to go on doing it, profitably and enjoyably, for as long as possible. It is a way of life, not a means to an end. Since immortality is the point, and since shareholders are locked in and cannot be too greedy, the family heads inevitably think long-term, invest hugely in innovation and keep their core group small but excellent. These businesses, however, are families, not communities which belong to the members. The head of the family is still the owner. The best of them, and not all of them are best or even good, think of themselves as responsible for not only their children's futures but the futures of their workers' children. That way it makes sense to trade off the short term for the longer opportunities. Tom Peters records that the *Mittelstand* chiefs he met talked in decades not quarters, when, that is, they bothered to put a timescale on it at all.

Family businesses, however, depend on the family for immortality, and that tends to be a fragile base. The Italians talk of the 'Third Generation' syndrome, when the family talent peters out or goes in search of other pastures; rags to riches and back again, as the British put it. Many of the *Mittelstand* businesses are now approaching that third generation. The Sigmoid Curve is beginning to turn down for some. They are losing their innovative thrust, the family is becoming lazy, or greedy, or both. Some are looking for ways to sell. Immortality for the *Mittelstand* would be better ensured if the family came to mean the family of workers, the members of the work community. In the bigger companies the German concept of co-determination, which puts equal numbers of shareholders and workers on the supervisory board, is an attempt to create that sense of one family even in a large enterprise.

I suggested, in discussing the corporate contract, that companies could only keep the interest groups in balance if they were 'existential' in the sense that they felt completely responsible for their own destiny. This is only possible if they are independent, not owned or in thrall to outsiders. To the Japanese the company is a community. To the continental Europeans the best companies are run like families. Neither concept appeals to the British or the Americans. They both sound weasely, undynamic. There is a word, however, an old Anglo-Saxon word with all the right history, until recently; it is a 'company', meaning a fellowship, a group of companions. Somewhere along the line it acquired its technical legal definition and lost its connotations. There was a time, maybe, when we had got the concept right.

The Reinvented 'Company'

The models of this old-style 'company' already exist in our societies in some unlikely places. We can borrow their ways but not, I think, their names. There is, for instance, the 'club'. A club is a place which belongs to its members and whose underlying purpose is its continued successful existence. It can best ensure that continuity by doing what it is best at doing. Its financiers are investors in its future, not owners or controllers, and its management works for the members not the financiers.

Perhaps, however, the most interesting models are to be found in the charitable and non-profit worlds. These organisations are owned by no one. They have constitutions, members, boards of trustees as well as boards of management, sources of finance rather than shareholders, and their purpose is their meaning. They are not properties, they cannot be bought or sold, although they can join forces, merge and make alliances. They have, in their doughnut, a core of professionals and, beyond it, a space full of helpers. These latter are often called 'associates', with limited rights of membership. The title which these organisations often carry is that of 'Society'. Thus there is, in Britain, for example, a host of Royal Societies for this and that, all prestigious, all communities. Society, or *société*, is the word in France for a business, and it might also serve in the Anglo-Saxon countries, but it would be preferable to reinvent the 'company' in its old meaning. The 'company' would have a core of 'companions' with 'associates' in the space around the core. It would be existential, responsible for its own destiny within the constraints of its hexagon, striving for immortality by doing better what it does best.

The Separation of Powers

A self-governing business, some will say, must be a licence for abuse. Self-determination has been a charter for scoundrels down the ages. Not all businesses deserve immortality. All this is true, but the market is a great corrective. Over time it sorts out the rotten apples in the system. That is not enough. Democracies, and federal democracies in particular, lay great store in the separation of powers. So it should be in the reinvented 'company'.

The legislative, or policy-making, function is separate from the executive, or management, and from the judicial, or monitoring roles. The roles overlap, in that the executive will propose most of the policies, while the laws which the judicial branch enforces are laid down by the legislature; but the functions are distinct and are usually performed by different people in different bodies. That practice is gradually being extended to organisations. It is seen most clearly in the charitable or non-profit bodies where the board or council is quite separate from the executive, and where, in Britain, there is an outside regulatory body, the Charity Commissioners, whose job it is to see that the charity is doing what it said it would. Continental European countries also favour two-tier boards for their corporations.

Britain and America are going the same way although they typically give the management board the title of 'executive committee'. The Cadbury Report in Britain in 1992, on the financial requirements of corporate governance, recommended that the roles of chairman and chief executive should normally be split and that there should be a substantial group of outside directors on the board. That is a small step in the same direction. More corporations are also putting their judicial function under a separate hat, with board committees to ensure compliance with their own rules and standards. There is even talk of a small trustee board of independent shareholders with limited powers of inspection and oversight, for the accounts and the appointment of board members.

After a fracas with Virgin Airlines in 1993, British Airways set up a new committee of its board on compliance. Some said it was a case of shutting the stable door after the horse had bolted, but it was, nevertheless, another step towards a proper balance in what is, in effect, a self-governing body. In Volkswagen in Germany and Phar Mor in America large-scale fraud was apparently conducted for years without the board being aware of it.

Effective and independent control systems are critical to the governance of self-governing bodies. The powers need to be even more visibly separated and separately staffed in an 'existential company'. It may be necessary to put the judicial or auditing powers outside the organisation, in the hands of an independent regulator. This already happens where the industry is dominated by a small number of companies who are, thereby, largely in control of their own destiny.

One existential community which, for many years, would have no truck with the separation of powers, believing instead that a concentration of the three functions of policy, execution and regulation would make it more effective, was Lloyd's of London, the insurance co-operative. They have changed things now, separating out the three roles into different bodies, but not before there had been a catalogue of frauds, mismanagement and bad policies, resulting in losses to its 'names', the members of this community, of some £5 billion over three years. There is a strong consensus that the concentration of powers led to a blindness to irregularities, to stupidity in strategy and laxity in management, rather than to any increased effectiveness.

The Membership Contract

In the end, however, a self-governing club in a competitive system should only survive as long as it deserves to survive. One threat to that survival will be a constantly changing membership. There will be no pressure to plan for the future of the children if even the fathers and mothers of those children are unlikely to be around in five years' time. The current tendency in Britain and America to use the organisation as a stepping-stone in a personal walk to glory and riches will make a nonsense of an immortal club. Loyalty has to be reciprocal. Temporary contracts will beget temporary time horizons.

We need to see more lifetime contracts again, remembering, however, that a corporate lifetime is going to be much shorter in future. I can see a period of apprenticeship, or articles, for new young employees, of perhaps five to seven years, followed by a fixed term 'tenure' contract of from 10 to 20 years, during which time they will be full 'members' of the 'company' or club. Professor Iwao has calculated that the average stay by core staff in one firm in Japan is 14 years. Lifetime in practice means only long-term. People might well serve their articles with one company and then join another as member, as accountants already do. After their membership period expires it could be renewed or they may well 'go portfolio', becoming independent advisers or suppliers to their old club. Membership will then be a privilege, akin to partnership but with limited liability, for a select minority – the core – requiring reciprocal obligations and loyalty.

In 1993 the Director-General of the BBC was discovered to have sold his services to the BBC through his own private company. This was a perfectly legal device which was common in the world of short-term contracts of commercial television from which he had come. It was not thought appropriate in the culture of the BBC where long-term loyalty was the norm, even though it is operating in the same industry. The feeling expressed by many was that this loyalty could hardly be demanded from others if the person at the head of the organisation appeared to see his own job as a temporary assignment.

It was a dispute symbolic of the times. More and more professionals think of themselves as on a temporary assignment with an organisation. Loyalty goes first to one's team or project, then to one's profession or discipline and only thirdly to the organisation where these skills are practised. In the City, whole teams of dealers and analysts move together from one organisation to another. Senior jobs in business are often on three-year contracts. Executives, like doctors, move from location to location as they advance their professional careers. 'Company' loyalty will be very short-term if this trend continues. The BBC was right to be alarmed.

My own belief, and hope, is that this trend too will be subject to the Sigmoid Curve, and that companies will want to hug their key 'members' to themselves for the duration of their, shorter, working lives. To do that they will need to give those key workers all the benefits of membership, including the effective rights of ownership. These rights will have to go beyond the current fashion for share options which gives the holder only a minority stake in the punters' bets, but will be something more akin to partnership, locking the key people into a self-governing membership group. Only then will we find the motivation to plan for immortality. Few would want to commit themselves to an organisation owned by punters.

Glimpses of the Future

If, however, the business as a self-governing, membership organisation is such a good idea, why don't we see more of them? The number, and the record, of co-operatives and their ilk is small and, with some notable exceptions, poor. Co-operatives often confuse ownership and management. Because ownership is in common they think that management also has to be shared. Democracy, however, does not require that all who vote should also have the right to manage, or even to demand a referendum on every decision. That way chaos lies. German and Japanese organisations do not make that mistake.

There are also, however, the ESOP companies, the employee share-ownership schemes which many companies have adopted as a way of giving their workers a stake in the organisation. The evidence on these is mixed. Some make a difference to motivation and commitment, most don't seem to matter much either way. A well researched study in America by Corey Rosen and others, found that the ones which did work had large employee contributions (8–10 per cent), a true philosophy of partner-ship and multiple ways of participating. The percentage of stock owned by employees made little difference, nor did the stock-market performance of the shares. In other words, it was membership not ownership that really mat-tered. If there was no sense of membership the ownership made no difference.

In Britain, the best-known membership business is the John Lewis Partnership, with its chain of retail stores. This business 'belongs' to its members, who receive dividends from its profits, elect their chairman but entrust the management to a conventional executive structure. They do not, however, own shares which they can sell. It is a true business community. It has had, however, few imitators.

This must be because we are hung up on ownership, on the idea of property. It is largely the fault of an outmoded legal system, in Britain at least. George Goyder, in his book *The Just Enterprise*, points to a prescient comment by Lord Eustace Percy in 1944:

> Here is the most urgent challenge to political invention ever offered to the jurist and the statesman. The human association which in fact produces and distributes wealth, the association of workmen, managers, technicians and directors, is not an association recognised by the law. The association which the law does recognise – the association of shareholders, creditors and directors – is incapable of production or distribution and is not expected by the law to perform these functions. We have to give law to the real association and to withdraw meaningless privilege from the imaginary one.

Our rules do not allow for a wealth-creating club which is not someone's piece of property. It does make it difficult to balance the contradictions inherent in a company owned by some and worked by others, but managed by the agents of the owners, because, whatever the rhetoric, it will be hard to find the elusive common purpose. Ultimately, we shall have to change the rules.

I take heart, however, from that research on share-ownership plans. Ownership makes little difference unless there is a sense of membership; therefore, presumably, the technical conditions of ownership make little difference if there is a real sense of membership. Laws tend to follow practice not lead it. If we can create that sense of member-ship in our organisations, by more subsidiarity, more twin citizenship, more sharing of the added value of closer teams and better boards, then, conceivably, the so-called owners would revert to their proper role, as financiers and owners only of last resort. The formal position would be irrelevant, as it is in Japan and, to a lesser extent, in Germany.

It is hard, nevertheless, to conceive of our giant multi-nationals and other mass organisations becoming membership 'companies'. We may well, however, see these organisations breaking down into alliances of much smaller ones. You no longer have to be big to be global in the information age. The *Economist* in London has 55 jour-nalists but covers the world, in scope and in readership. The *Economist*, too, is owned, in effect, by one proprietor who holds the bulk of the voting shares. Other financiers have stakes with smaller voting rights. There is a board of management, to oversee the business, and a board of trustees to protect editorial freedom. Given its current benevolent proprietor, the *Economist* is almost a member-ship 'company'. It feels like one when you visit it. Give the voting shares to the members and the model for the 'com-pany' would be complete.

Words and titles can help, even without the legal back-ing. When Ricardo Semler decided to make his Semco company more of a self-governing community he called the directors 'counsellors', the senior managers 'partners' and everyone else 'associates'. He then had to live up to the expectations the new words raised. He described the results in his book *Maverick*. If it worked as well as it did in the difficult conditions of the Brazilian economy, and without any change to the legal situation of ownership, it must be possible elsewhere. Ralph Sayer did the same at Johnsonville Foods, calling his workers 'members' and his managers 'co-ordinators' in order to symbolise the new order, one in which profit-sharing and autonomy went hand in hand. We need not wait for the law to change.

Redesigning Life

Changing the structures of our institutions, and changing the meaning of business, will help to clear a pathway through some of the paradoxes, but we can only find meaning and value in our lives by living those lives. A time of chaos is a time of opportunity. The old patterns are changing. We don't have to live as our parents lived. We can shape our own lives more easily than ever they did. The fragmentation of work looks scary but offers new freedoms at the same time. Time's paradoxes mean that the old blocks of time, the 40-hour week and the 50-year career, are probably gone for ever as a way of life. Women have more opportunities, as well as all the old responsibilities, responsibilities which can themselves be new opportunities for men, for the old divides are breaking down, slowly.

At the beginning of the century, 50 per cent of workers were independent. They were outside the formal organisation. By the end of it the percentage might be the same again, yet only 20 years ago 90 per cent of us worked inside the organisation. New thinking, aided by new information technology, is beginning to alter not only the way we work but where we work, when we work and how we charge for it. The result is a new way of thinking about the organisation of work and the way we use people to do it.

Governments are worried because work seems to be disappearing. It is. But it is also becoming individualised and informal, and therefore invisible and unregulated. Jobs are disappearing but not necessarily work, if we define work as useful activity. Pushing jobs back into organisations will be counter-productive. The more governments try to set proper terms and conditions of work, by, for instance, the Europeans' Social Chapter, the more they will encourage the spread of the minimalist organisation and further individualisation. Unfortunately, we are often our own worst employers, putting up with terms and conditions of work which no decent employers would contemplate inflicting on their people. We shall have to learn to live with this second curve of work. The first one will not return. However, this is our chance to make our working time more suited to our taste, to shape our own raincoat, if you will.

The demise of the traditional job, the re-chunking of time and the new areas of choice for would-be parents, combined with longer and healthier lifespans, mean that the traditional sequence of events in life – school, job, house, children, retirement – is no longer fixed. Flexilife is now the mode. Serial monogamy seems to be the new respectability. 'Has your wife got a daughter, too?' the woman asked, when I was telling her something about my daughter. The assumption was that at my stage in life I would be on my second marriage.

To add to the options, a whole new section of life has opened up beyond the time of full-time work or parenting. There will be some 25 years of healthy life for most of us beyond the job – a new compartment. But it will not be 're-tirement'. We won't want to retire and most will not be able to afford it. Work will still go on, but it will be, mostly, work at a different pace and work of a different kind, but work it has to be, because work provides the structure of our lives, the core of our individual doughnuts.

The new divisions of work, time and life will redraw our maps of society. The new maps offer the chance of greater individual choice, but also of individual calamity. It will be more confusion at first; it already is, with people hankering after that first curve they had grown to know. In time, we shall learn to balance the contradictions and enjoy the second curve. It will be a new way of living and working for all of us. As always with the second curve, it will be the new generation who will find the adjustment easiest. The opportunity lies in the chance to live several different lives in the space of one – spliced lives, I term it. For their elders, the Third Age offers another chance to live some of the life they wish that they had had. They would be foolish to turn it down.

10　Working Time

Work is not what it was, inside or outside the organisation.
The paradox of time combines with the changing nature of
work, to force us to rethink what we mean by the whole
idea of work and time – when we work, where we work,
how we work and why we work.

The Minimalist Organisation

I was meeting with a journalist in Atlanta. We talked at her
desk, cluttered as it was with papers, telephones, keyboard
and screen, in the middle of the vast newsroom, 200 people
chatting, typing, telephoning, smoking. There was no
chair for me. I perched on her desk. 'It's not going to be
easy,' I said, 'talking to you like this. Do you not work at
home, at least for some of the time?' She smiled ruefully.
'Never. Of course I could do much of my stuff there, and I
would do it much better with less hassle, less travel, less
noise and I could always come in here when I needed to,
but my work could all go down the telephone line – as it
does anyway,' she added, 'from this desk.' 'So why don't
you?' '*They* won't let me.' She pointed to the end of the
room where, behind two large glass windows, sat the two
deputy editors. 'They like to have me where they can see
me and shout at me.'

One day those people will realise that an office, even a
newsroom, does not have to be designed as a factory and
that the cost of all that space in the centre of Atlanta is not
worth the convenience of seeing and shouting. One day.

We all want our work clubs, places to go to, places to meet and greet and eat, but we no longer have to work there all the time. Unless, of course, you are there to serve the customers or the clients, in the store, in the reception, in the classroom, hospital or restaurant. These servers, however, do not have offices, private spaces of their own. Their work is where the client is. It is those offices with their private spaces which will gradually go, and with them a way of life. Many will lament their passing, but sentiment and nostalgia will not prevail in the new businesslike age.

We have to rethink the organisational contract, what we mean by an organisation, what we expect from it and what we are prepared to give to it. No longer can society rely on these new businesslike places, which are very unlike the businesses of old, to provide life and livelihood for everyone, even in times of economic boom, to collect their taxes from them or to pay their pensions. No longer will the office or the plant be the home-from-home for most men and many women. No longer will a career mean climbing the ladder of jobs in an organisation. For one thing, there will not be more than three or four rungs on the ladder. No longer can one expect to sell 100,000 hours of one's life to an organisation. No longer will your job title define you for life, or even for very much of it.

There has to be a major shift in the way we think about organisations. They are now living up to their name – they are *organisers* as much as or more than they are employers. They are minimalist. It shows up in the numbers – many fewer people inside the large organisations, more people in small ones, more people working on their own, more people, unfortunately, left without any work at all because they do not have the specialist skills needed both inside and outside the organisations. Boom or bust, it makes little difference. In Britain's boom years of 1985–90 manufacturing output went up by nearly 19 per cent, but the manufacturing labour force still fell by nearly 5 per cent. It simply falls faster in recession. Now it is the turn of the service sector, where productivity has hardly been tackled until recently. By 1993, in Britain, as we noted, only 55 per cent of all those in work or seeking work were in full-time jobs inside organisations. In the US it was 60 per cent. The figure in other countries is higher but coming down. More by accident than design, Britain leads the way. Before very long, having a proper job inside an organisation will be a minority occupation. Then the world really will have changed. What then will everyone do? How will they live? How, metaphorically, will they fill out those raincoats?

This is all happening at a time when the total workforce, those who are able and wanting to work, is growing. There may be some 25 per cent fewer teenagers now than there were 10 years ago, but we have to remember that this dip was preceded by a bulge, a bulge which is now in its thirties and will be around and looking for work for another 20 or more years. The workforce is getting older, certainly, but it is also growing, not least because the wives or ex-wives of many males in the bulge years now want to re-enter the workplace. The workforce in Britain will probably grow by one million during the Nineties and in the US by as much as 12 million. It is no longer, however, going to be, largely, an employee workforce. That simple fact is going to make all the difference. What was a way of life for most of us will have disappeared. Organisations will still be critically important in the world, but as organisers not employers.

From Diamonds to Mud

Inside the organisation it is also changing, as the principle of the doughnut begins to spread and organisations become redesigned and re-engineered. In times past, almost all the spaces in an organisation were predetermined. The prescribed core filled most of the jobs. In those days it was fashionable to make organisations as predict-able as possible. They were designed like railway timetables, in the hope that all one then had to do was to press the button and watch the trains run on their pre-planned routes. That way efficiency lay. Too much dis-cretion lower down disrupted things, set off unpredictable chain reactions. No one would want the train-driver to be creative and miss out a station or two in order to improve the running-time.

Those were the days before chaos theory or the newer complexity theory in science. The Newtonian classical view of science pervaded even the pragmatic world of organ-isations. There should be an explanation and a set of rules for everything, everything should be planned and pre-dicted in a properly ordered world. People were part of a well-ordered system. If only they did as they were sup-posed to do, everything would work fine. As people become more educated and more expensive, it does not make sense to treat them as automata, nor do those better-educated people enjoy having so little space for discretion in their jobs. The first, inner circle, of the doughnut has gradually become smaller, the outer one bigger. In-be-tween, the space expands.

Ian Gibson, chief executive of Nissan Motor Manufac-turing in Britain, told the graduating class of the London Business School that his first discipline was physics.

> I tend to think of things in a scientist's terms – in this case in terms of the difference between crystalline and amorphous structures. As an example, the most easy way to recognize a crystalline structure is in a diamond, and perhaps the most common, if unglamorous, amorphous material is mud. The typical western organization is crystalline; clearly defined, facets that have their own shape, with obvious joints between them. The features of our organizations are comparable – clear definitions of role and responsibilities; well-defined

boundaries within different parts of the organization; each part of the organization in a known and fixed relationship to the others.

In contrast, Japanese organizations are more like mud. They are far more blurred, separation between responsibilities and functions is ill-defined and in a constant state of flux. Reverting to the analogy, a diamond is clear, tough and precise. Mud is vague, it changes shape and form. It has, however, one over-riding benefit – it is easily shaped and changed and is flexible and responsive to external forces and circumstances. As organizations, we must become increasingly able to change quickly and easily. This means building on and around people's abilities rather than limiting them for the convenience of easily recognized roles.

For organisations the opportunity is now there to apply the doughnut principle to most of their work, devising a structure made up of muddy doughnuts, a system of interlocking double circles, in each of which the inner circle, the core, is tightly specified and controlled, as are the outer limits of authority, but where the space in the middle is to be developed. In a lax organisation, that can be a recipe for anarchy, if they cannot manage the inevitable contradictions. Individuals and groups may exploit their spaces to their own satisfaction, but not necessarily to the organisation's advantage. The centre cracks down, cores expand again, individuals resent the contraction of their discretionary space and mutual resentment saps morale. Large doughnuts work best when there is a clear consensus about the purpose of the work and the goals of the organisation.

More and more we shall see organisations divide their work into project teams, task-forces, small business units, clusters and work groups – smart words for doughnuts. These groups will change shape and membership as the needs of the organisation change. Individuals may well work for more than one group at the same time, for multiple membership is a feature of doughnut organisations, with one group having an operational responsibility, another an advisory role and a third having a temporary project assignment. It all helps to make life exciting, but much less predictable. Organisations, for example, are no longer guaranteeing to provide planned careers but are instead offering 'career opportunities'.

Look at an advertising agency for an approximate model of how we shall all be working tomorrow. An advertising agency arranges its people in clusters and task-groups, two sorts of doughnut. The clusters are clusters of expertise, the creatives or the planners or the people who book the space in the media. They are drawn from these clusters into a range of account groups where they work on the requirements of a particular client or product. They may work on several different account groups, and the membership of the groups will flex with the demands of the work. It is a fluid-matrix organisation. So is any consultancy firm. So is a hospital ward or a surgery team – they are all, conceptually, doughnuts, with their members drawn from other specialist doughnuts. They all have a tightly specified core but a space for initiative and improvement, often a great deal of space. The better the people, the bigger the space can be.

The old language of management no longer seems appropriate. It never was appropriate in some quarters. Professional organisations, doctors, architects, lawyers, academics have never used the word manager, except to apply it to the more routine service functions – office-manager, catering-manager. The reason was not just a perverse snobbery but an instinctive recognition that professionals have always worked on the principle of the doughnut. This was necessary because every assignment was slightly different; flexibility and discretion had to be built in. It was possible because the requirements of the profession, its rules and disciplines, meant that one could be reasonably sure that whatever one's colleagues (note the

word) did in the space between the circles would be acceptable. Doughnuts work well when everyone knows, not
only what the purpose is, but what the standards are.

The Portfolio World

Outside the organisation, things seem even more confused
for that 40 per cent or so of outsiders, most of them reluctant independents. They may be the way of the future
but few wanted to be the pathfinders. There are, however,
some trends and ideas beginning to emerge. As organisations restructure themselves into their minimalist
shapes, they are going back to buying produce not time.
That amounts to taking the price-tag off time. Instead of
employing their lawyer they now, in the minimalist organisation, buy his or her services, for a fee. Professionals and
craftspeople have always charged fees. The fee will include
a time element, but it will also charge for the quality of the
work, for reputation and reliability. When Ruskin sued the
artist Whistler for overcharging him for a portrait which,
Ruskin claimed, he had dashed off in a hurry, the judge
asked Whistler how long it had taken him to paint the portrait. 'Ten minutes,' Whistler replied, 'and a lifetime of
experience.' It is the quality of the produce one is paying
for, not the time spent on it.

More and more individuals are behaving as professionals
always have, charging fees not wages. They find that they
are 'going portfolio', or 'going plural'. 'Going portfolio', I
suggested earlier, means exchanging full-time employment for independence. The portfolio is a collection of
different bits and pieces of work for different clients. The
word 'job' now means a client. My wife, a portrait-photo-
grapher, has, at any one time, a number of 'jobs' on the go,
as does our builder when he tells us why he cannot fix the
roof this week. I told my children, when they were leaving

education, that they would be well advised to look for customers not bosses. If they could find people who were willing to pay them money for something they could make or do, that would be the best qualification for impressing a boss when they did finally want to join an organisation and sell their time to someone else. They have 'gone portfolio' out of choice, for a time. Others are forced into it, when they get pushed outside by their organisation. If they are lucky, their old organisation will be the first client in their new portfolio.

The important difference is that the price-tag now goes on their produce, not their time. I read, enviously, of the man who had met a man in a nightclub in London. They got talking. The second man was from the Middle East, looking for a solution to a big and tricky problem of irrigation in his part of the world. It just happened that the first man knew a woman who ran a business which turned out to have exactly what was needed. He received a £5 million commission for the introduction. It was not time that he was paid for but a crucial bit of knowledge, rather like Whistler. We can't all be so lucky, or so well connected, but in smaller ways the principle always applies; the price-tag is on the produce not the time.

It works the other way round, too. If I was paid by the hour at the average national wage for writing this book I would be counting my income in many tens of thousands of pounds. Sadly, the royalty advance takes no account of my time, but prices my produce at the level my publisher thinks it will fetch in the market-place. I therefore sell my time cheaply to myself, in the hope that it will be an investment worth the making. That way, I know, many authors starve! The reality, however, is that it is applied intelligence now, not time, which is the crucial element.

Professionals, the knowledge-workers of all types, are obvious candidates for portfolio lives. So are those who make or fix things, the traditional fixers and makers like plumbers, builders, carpenters and electricians, but now, also, the new fixers: the agents, brokers, conference-organisers, house-finders and sellers, travel agents and tour-arrangers. There are the new servant businesses, often one or two partners with a supporting cast of occasional stringers: the cooks, drivers, gardeners, health specialists, language-teachers, child- and house- and dog-minders, cleaners, even, I am told, people you can pay to change your light bulbs. There are, also, the old and the new crafts: the potters, weavers, bakers, painters, writers, computer software-designers and photographers.

Read the yellow pages in any city, anywhere, to find the portfolio world. These people charge for their produce not their time. It is not that they don't work as long or as hard as employees, because most of them work both harder and longer. The difference is that they have more freedom to chunk their time in different ways, if they so choose. What matters now is *how* we use our time, not *how much* of that time we use. When you can use time in this way it is a form of freedom. Those who charge by the hour can only make more money by working more hours. Those who charge for their produce can get richer by working smarter, not longer. This has always been true for some activities. It is now potentially true for almost everything. A wise jobbing gardener will quote you for keeping your garden in good trim, not for so many hours a week, and if you are wise you will accept this basis because the onus is now on him or her to use their time productively, not on you to make sure that they do.

Technology enables more and more people to go portfolio. Organisations are latching on to the possibilities, as we have seen. They are even extending the principle of product not time to their own internal operations. To a unit, a group or a person they say, increasingly, as the farmer or the businessman once said in times gone by, 'Do this by this date; how you do it is up to you, but get it done.

on time and up to standard.' This is subsidiarity in practice. What it means is that, even inside the organisation, people have more discretion as to how they chunk their time. If they want to chunk it in fewer bigger segments, they are, in theory, free to do so.

As this practice spreads, the difference between full- and part-time work will be mainly one, not of time, but of rights and entitlement. I have little doubt that we shall, increasingly, see both laws and best practice equalising the benefits, proportionately, between full- and part-timers. This will happen, politically and legally, because part-timers are no longer marginal extras in the workplace and will demand more social justice. We can see the Social Chapter in the Maastricht Treaty as one piece of evidence of this in Europe. It will happen, anyway, in the forward-thinking workplaces because they will want to bind their growing 'peripheral' workforce to themselves. Left neglected on the periphery the part-time workers will lack loyalty and will leave the business dangerously exposed.

Juliet Schor wants those organisations who still buy time rather than produce to specify how much time they are buying and to offer to repay extra time with time. Everyone would, then, in effect be on an annual-hours contract, or some variation of it. Some prized and special people might sign on for 3,000 hours, or 60 hours a week and two weeks' holiday, others for the more conventional 2,000 hours or less. People would have the right to claim repayment of the extra hours worked during the year by doing fewer hours the next year. Obviously the sums, and the repayments, could also be calculated on a monthly or six-monthly basis if so desired. Overtime would be repaid by undertime.

Patricia Hewitt describes the principle as time-banking. If you build up time credits in one part of the year, or over a number of years, you can draw on them later. You could do it, practically, by putting the money equivalent to a set number of hours per week into a pension fund, so that it would, under existing legislation, be tax-free. You then draw out that money when enough has accumulated, and use it as a substitute for your wages for a period. There is a proposal in Norway to allow people to do it the other way round, to exchange future earnings for present time, like running a loan account. If I wanted to take six months off to help with my family, I could pay it back later by putting in the normal number of hours but only drawing the pay for, perhaps, 80 per cent of them until the loan of time was repaid. My own preference would be to find a way to pay for time with time and to keep the money out of it but the practicalities are, I accept, difficult.

Women's Working Time

The concept of time-banking, whichever way it is implemented, would help to solve a growing dilemma for organisations and for many women. As organisations go minimalist they shrink their cores, pursuing that elusive formula of $\frac{1}{2} \times 2 \times 3$. Those in that core are, then, better-paid but harder-worked. The 3,000-hour year and the 60-hour week are not uncommon. Organisations are greedy places when they have bought you for a year or more. For these jobs the organisations want quality people, well educated, well skilled and adaptable. They also want people who can juggle with several tasks and assignments at one time, who are more interested in making things happen than in what title or office they hold, more concerned with power and influence than status. They want people who value instinct and intuition as well as analysis and rationality, who can be tough but also tender, focused but friendly, people who can cope with these necessary contradictions. They want, therefore, as many women as they can get.

They want them, or should want them, because not only do women make up at least half of all the well-educated people in our societies, but they are also more likely to exhibit the kind of qualities listed above. Men have these qualities, too, of course, but male conditioning over the generations, in both home and workplace, has emphasised singularity of purpose, one thing at a time, rank and formal authority, toughness rather than tenderness, rationality not intuition. Women, on the other hand, over the generations, have had to make things happen and get things done, with or without formal authority. They have had to handle endless variety in managing the home, taking decisions on inadequate information, backing hunch and judgement. They have had to be in turns disciplinarian and loving mother. Not all women do these things well, by any means, but few men have had that much practice.

Organisations need talented women in their core jobs, therefore, not only for reasons of social fairness, important though that is, but because many of those women will have the kinds of attitudes and attributes that the new flat flexible organisations need. If they screen out the women they will handicap their futures. Yet screening out is exactly what they are in danger of doing. It is difficult to combine those 60-hour jobs with raising a family. Many don't try. A 1992 survey by Britain's Institute of Management found that 86 per cent of the married men in their sample of executives had children, but only 49 per cent of the married women.

Every working woman, they say, needs a wife, particularly if she has children, and some are fortunate in having a partner who will be house-husband and full-time parent. Others delegate these roles to nannies, home-helps and crèches. Many very competent women do not want to do either, or cannot. For them, the portfolio life with its, now, expanding possibilities offers the flexibility and freedom to combine work with home. They would often, however, have preferred to stay in the core in some way, or at least to have the chance of going back when the children are a little older. Organisations can ill afford to lose them. Time-banking, and the organisation re-engineered to fit the process not the function, creates some of the flexibility which these women need. The chance to deliver the work in their own way without having to conform to rigid time-tables, combined with the right to bank or chunk time so that school holidays, for instance, can be mostly time away from the office, would allow more women to keep a role alive in the core while the kids are young.

Other things would help. Organisations could rearrange their time so that all normal meetings took place on fixed days of the week, Thursdays and Fridays, perhaps. This would allow people to be physically absent from the organisation for part of the week without missing the meetings which are still the warp and woof of organisational life. One day we shall have to learn how to manage our dispersed organisations without meetings, but until that distant day comes we should at least take pains not to marginalise any absent friends. We can always be in touch telephonically and electronically, of course, but those who work four days a week say how strange it is that the really important meetings always seem to take place on the fifth day! Only in real emergencies, after all, do organisations now have meetings on Sundays. If they can rearrange time to exclude Sundays they have already granted the principle; now they need to extend it.

As we have noted, organisations are changing parts of their offices into work clubs. The 'outworkers' will be free to use the clubhouse at any time and will have their own personal 'cart' or 'hot desk' or 'puppy' which they can pull out, plug in and key in, giving them immediate access to all the systems and an instant extension number when anyone calls. IBM and other electronically minded organisations already do this. So does any small television production company where office space is at a premium and where most people are out most of the time.

Regular meetings in these 'clubs' will be scheduled for the 'meeting-days' but the rest of the time there will be no way of knowing where anyone is or what they are doing without contacting them directly by phone, fax, E-mail or voice mail and asking them. When that is happening to the majority of executives – as it will – it will no longer make sense to think of people as full-time or part-time. They will be paid for the type and size of the job they are required to do, an internal fee. Their time is now theirs to manage more than ever before. They can use it wastefully or thriftily; either way their pay will be the same. We will have put the price on the produce not the time. Time will have its new and flexible compartments.

Rethinking working time does not do away with the diffi-culties. It makes those difficulties more manageable. It puts more responsibility on to the individual in return for more independence. To make the balance fair, organisations will need to be less greedy in their expectations of the people they buy by the year and less mean in dealing with those they buy by the hour. They will undoubtedly need the en-couragement of the law to do the latter, because employers like their labour cheap, although all the evidence is that you get more net added value in a knowledge economy from better dearer workers than cheaper worse ones, as long as you give them the chance to add more of that value.

11 Spliced Lives

'Live as if you will die tomorrow, but plan to live forever.' It is a useful maxim because perceptions change with age. We look as far ahead as we look back. I used to be frustrated because I could not bribe my tiny children with promises of treats the next weekend if they would only keep quiet that afternoon. They could not connect the two events. Slowly I realised that a week in the life of a small child is, maybe, 20 per cent of all that they can remember. It is like asking a 60-year-old to take account of something 15 years ahead when deciding what to do today. Young people live in the present. That is part of their delight. It is also part of their problem because, in this complex world, it seems harder and harder to find the kind of balance we want in any one bit of it. It need not be so. We can now flex the four traditional stages of work and four different types of work. We can, if we so want, put them in a variety of combinations, splicing a life together by twisting its strands in the way we want.

The New Flexibility

In the old Hindu scriptures, life had four stages: student, householder, retirement and sannyasin, that final stage when one neither hates nor loves anything. Nothing about work or jobs in those times! Shakespeare added infant, lover and soldier to give us his seven ages. Gail Sheehy, writing her best-selling *Passages* in the 1970s, settled for four, this time divided by decades: the Trying Twenties, the Catch Thirties, the Forlorn Forties and the Refreshed (or Resigned) Fifties. Not a happy-sounding list, nor a very long life! Daniel Levinson, who wrote *The Seasons of a Man's Life* at around the same time, also liked the idea of four stages, but with rather duller titles, and he also stopped at the fifties. A pity, too, that it was only men whom he interviewed, but this was the Seventies. Sheehy subtitled her book 'The Predictable Crises of Adult Life' and predictable the stages have always seemed, even if their details varied over the centuries.

Last month, however, I met, on separate days and by chance, a range of people who reminded me that there is more freedom to change the sequence than we might have thought. There was Peggy, a happy grandmother of 38, having had her first baby at 18, who then had her first baby at 19. 'I'm a daytime mother,' Peggy said, 'so that Katie [her daughter] can have the chances which I never had. She's studying design, you see, at the local college and Reg, her man, is off driving his lorry.'

Rebecca is two years older than Peggy and a lawyer. She is four months pregnant with her first baby, having decided that she could leave the start of a family no later than 40. She will find it hard, she said, to leave her stimulating job but she had decided that a baby should be a full-time job and she was looking forward to it. Robert, her husband, is none too sure about babies and the changes they will bring to their rather comfortable life style, but he does not intend to alter his pattern of life – he is an international banker, jetting round the world half the time. 'We shall see!' said Rebecca.

Joshua, another acquaintance, is different. He has 're-tired' at 37 in order to bring up his son, having been separated and then divorced from his wife. He is living in the West Country in a farm cottage, surviving on the rent of what used to be his London apartment. 'It is so much more fulfilling than all those meetings. I am really enjoying being a father and I suspect that I'm a much nicer person now than I used to be. I have taken up metal-working and will do it as a business once Harry is old enough to go to school.'

'Who said anything about retiring?' growled Lord King, aged 75, when he handed over his chairmanship of British Airways to become the part-time president. He might only come in two or three days a week but he would need the new space to give time to all his other activities.

Work's Variety

We could all add anecdotes of our own to this list. They are examples of the new flexibility which we have – to be a grandmother for the first time at 40, or a mother for the first time; to 'retire' at 39 or 75; to be a full-time parent or not. In fact, however, all that these people are doing is to define their work in different ways. Work is useful activity, and it comes in four varieties. There is, therefore, *paid work* in its various forms, be it for wages or for fees, depending on whether you sell your time or your produce, but there is also the *gift work* we do for free, for the community, for charities, sports clubs or political parties.

Then there is *home work*, not the preparation for school but the maintenance of the home and the care of the people in it, one's children, maybe, or ageing parents, or sometimes both. The Legal and General Insurance Company in Britain regularly estimates the replacement cost of a spouse as household-manager, for insurance purposes. In 1993 the figure was £18,000, well above average earnings that year in Britain. This, as women have always known, is real work. Fourthly, there is *study work*. In the knowledge age, the acquisition and development of intelligence, the new form of property, is an essential investment. It is also hard work. It should not be dismissed as a leisure activity or as something which is a tedious necessity at the start of life but unnecessary thereafter.

These extra categories of work are important. If, for instance, gift work and study work were accepted, officially, as 'work' in Britain, we would not have rules which prevent the unemployed studying full-time or working for more than 16 hours a week for a charity, on the theory that they are not then 'available for work'. They would *be* working. A balanced life is a blend of all these types of work. A full 'portfolio' has some of each most of the time. It will, however, be a changing mix as we move through life. We have more freedom than we think to change the mix.

Like the Hindu scriptures, I would settle for three active ages in life, with a fourth which is really the readiness to die, which we must not gloss over. The descriptions of student, householder and retirement are not, however, the right ones for the world we live in. Life is longer now, more things are possible. Women can bear children, safely, into their fifties. Fathers have it easier; they can and do start a new family in their sixties. We are likely to be as healthy and as fit at 70 as our parents were at 50. 'Retirement', therefore, can be a movable event if it literally means withdrawing from active work of any sort. Householding (and housekeeping) has still to be done but need not describe the whole of the middle of life for anyone. Over 80 per cent of women do some paid work these days, even though they still also bear the brunt of the home maintenance and almost all of the caring, the 'home work'.

The Four Ages are:

1 The First Age, the time of preparation for life and work, which includes schooling, further education and qualifications, guided work experience, and, I believe, the chance to explore the world beyond the home environment. The French word – *formation* – describes this period rightly. It is the age of 'forming' oneself, something which is more, much more, than formal education.

2   The Second Age, the time of main endeavour, either in
paid work or in parenting and other forms of home work.
3   The Third Age, the time for a second life, which could
be a continuation of the second but might, more interestingly, be something very different. To do nothing is no
longer a realistic option.
4   The Fourth Age, the age of dependency.

Each age will, very roughly, last for 25 years, although I
suspect that we shall see the Third Age stretching out to 30
years or more for many people. This age will only end
when the Fourth Age begins, when we enter that ante-
room to death. Naturally, the longer we can postpone the
Fourth Age the better.

The First Two Ages

The success of each age depends very much on what went
before. A successful First Age makes a Second Age much
more likely to be successful in its turn, and that, again,
helps to increase the options for the Third Age. It is crucial,
therefore, that we see life as a whole if we are to use the
opportunities of the three ages to build a cumulative
balance to our lives. Most of us, we must remember, will, if
we survive the dangers of the road and of drugs in our First
Age, live on into our seventies or even eighties. The most
difficult thing to do, however, is to think beyond our own
experience, to conceive that there is a good life after 50, or
sex after 40 when we are only 20.

The elders in society need to make it easier for younger
members to see life as a whole and to prevent them, as far
as possible, from mortgaging their futures too early. The 40
men whom Levinson interviewed for his book reckoned
that life got serious at around 28, with a novice, or apprenticeship phase for the four or five years before. We may

mature, physically, a bit younger now, but I doubt that many want to get serious about life and mortgages any earlier than they did.

For that reason we need to accept as a society that the First Age lasts for 25 years. It is already that length for the professional classes, for those symbolic analysts, the high-skilled knowledge-workers who make up 20 per cent of the population with 60 per cent of the income. They get their degrees and follow that with a professional qualification and/or a period of tutored apprenticeship. In Germany the process can continue until the age of 27, or until 31 if you want a doctorate. If we are going to spread the new bases of wealth, knowledge and intelligence more broadly, then everyone will need this extended 'formation' period. To shorten it for some would be to ration the new property.

It is odd, I often think, that we, the symbolic analysts, lament the 'idle scroungers' who are not actively seeking jobs at 18, but worry if we catch our own children wanting to dive into serious work at that age. 'But your degree!' we cry. 'And don't you want to see more of the world before you settle down?' If we want to see more of that potential intelligence wealth created we should start by applying the same standards to all and finding more ways to fill the First Age of preparation usefully for all. It would be a better in-vestment for society to spend money early on our young of all classes. They might, then, be better able to fend for themselves in the Second and Third Ages. As it is, we skimp on the First Age and, as a consequence, spend more supporting many of them in the longer and more expensive ages which follow.

The Second Age is the age of serious endeavour. For many that will mean a job, for others parenting, for most a mix of the two types of work. It is in this age that the re-thinking of time becomes so crucially important. It is easy to get trapped in other people's time cages, be it the employer, the school, the shopping-routine or the parents' roster. This, too, is the age which has been sharply reduced for many with the advent of the 'compressed career', making the cage even tighter.

No longer can the average employee, as we have seen, look forward to 45 or 50 years of continuous work, the 100,000 hours. For those in the core those 100,000 hours may be compressed into 30 years, if they are lucky and can stand the pace. Many will not want to, some will not be up to it, some will burn out. Even if the organisations rethink time creatively so as to give people more control of their time, some may still burn candles at both ends for the corporation because the pressures to perform will be high. 'There is no way that I could do this job,' said one senior woman, 'if I wasn't prepared to give it all my time.'

This Second Age is an uneven balance for most of us. There is too much home work for some, too much time given to paid work for others, too little study work or gift work, too little or too much time without work of any type. It is easy to say that we ought to stand back, and we should look at how we live and try to rebalance our time and our work. It is less easy to do it. We are caught in the cages. For some, the cage is the workplace, for others the home. Necessity doth make prisoners of us all. If we feel like that we have to remember that it is not a life sentence.

The Third Age

The big change in recent times has been the gradual emergence of the Third Age, which will for many be the longest phase in their life but, paradoxically, the one for which they are probably least prepared. Because it did not happen to the generations ahead of us we did not expect it to happen to us, although, as *The Paradox of Age* noted, we know that every generation has a different life course.

The Third Age is not a synonym for retirement. For one

thing it starts too early for that to make sense. Some will extend their Second Age until their sixties; some, like Lord King, until their seventies. They will be the exceptions. Some women will find that the empty nest never empties, as ageing parents move in to replace the children. Most will find that, with the new compressed careers, the main work of their Second Age comes to an end in their fifties, or even earlier. No one seems to know what happens to the boys and girls of the dealer rooms who peak in their twenties. It is not ageist thinking to note that swimmers are past their best at 20 and tennis-players (even Jimmy Connors) at 35. Nor is it ageist to note that soldiers are less good at storming beaches in their forties, creative directors often less creative as they near their mid-life and that journalists must turn columnist or leave in their forties. They should not despair. The Third Age, whenever it starts, is the opportunity to change their blend of work, not to stop activity altogether. Some women, for instance, may want to increase the proportion of paid work in their mix, while their partners want, or are forced to decrease it.

Some paid work will be essential for nearly everyone in this Third Age. Necessity will make portfolio workers of us all in the end. Neither society, nor organisations, nor individuals have prepared properly for the support of their people for the 25 years or more of this Third Age. To the extent that this Third Age existed in previous generations, it was much shorter, at least for men. The Geneva Association, a research foundation of the insurance industry, speaks of the four pillars which are necessary for a financially comfortable Third Age. These are a state pension, a personal or occupational pension, personal savings or inheritance and some paid work, the fourth pillar. The state pension is going to get less and later everywhere. In Britain it will be down to eight per cent of average earnings by 2030 if it continues to be indexed to prices not earnings. In any case, 31 per cent of men retiring in Britain in 1991 did not qualify for a full pension because they had not contributed regularly over 44 years. Very few will meet that requirement in future.

The idea that one contributes to one's state pension during one's working-life, contributions which are then salted away for us until we need them, is, anyway, a form of deceit, in Britain and elsewhere. Our pension contributions are just another tax which goes into the general pool. It makes sense when you think about it. There is little point in the government putting our savings into a government fund which would then be mainly invested in government bonds, i.e. lent back to the government again. The pension is, therefore, an undertaking by those behind us to pay for our old age, the generational contract. That was fair enough when there were six of us working to every one of them, when they did not live too long or get too expensively ill, and when we were demonstrably better off than they had been. Those conditions no longer apply. By the year 2020 in most countries there will be only three workers to pay for every person over 65, and only two people in the Second Age for every one in the Third. There is no way that successive generations are going to agree to pay huge taxes to keep their elders as comfortable as they have been.

Few have noticed what a number of recent studies have confirmed, that for the first time in history, the elderly in North America, Europe and Australasia are, on average, receiving more income, spending more and saving more than people in their twenties and thirties, when responsibilities for dependent children are taken into account. This has come about despite the rise in the number of young women in employment, despite earlier departure from the workforce and despite the fall in the number of dependent children. This disparity will only increase. The new Third Agers are not the old of the welfare generation; many of them carry with them substantial assets from their Second

Age. In New Zealand the signs are there already. The median single-income two-child family has seen a 20 per cent fall in real purchasing power in the past 20 years, whereas the elderly have experienced a 100 per cent rise.

Given these sort of statistics, there is little doubt that the generational contract will gradually be renegotiated. Pensionable ages will be raised, as is already happening in Italy, America and probably in Britain (for women). It will go farther. Society will concentrate its money on the old old, not the young old. Those in the Third Age will, increasingly, be expected to make more provision for themselves. The fourth pillar of paid work will, then, be a financial necessity unless they have taken great care to build up their savings or private pensions in the Second Age. Those in the Second Age should take careful note.

We should not find the prospect of *some* paid work too daunting. Most people in the Third Age would like at least half a week of paid work and the new flexibilities of the workplace make that very possible. At the professional technical skill level, age is an irrelevance when you are self-employed and outside the organisation. Do you need to know how old your lawyer or your electrician is provided he or she can deliver what you need? At the semi-skilled level, age is sometimes regarded as a positive advantage. Supermarkets regularly report that part-time older employees are more reliable, less disruptive or ambitious and more friendly to the customers than the youngsters whom they can hire at equivalent pay.

The Third Age is, however, one's best chance to experiment with a different blend of the four types of work. It can go either way. Some, particularly women, may want the chance to increase the amount of paid work in the blend, if they have been largely restricted to home work in the Second Age. This would probably mean expanding their existing portfolio because they may find it difficult to enter the core of an organisation at an age when others are leaving. On the other hand, as the baby boom of the 1960s works its way through life, organisations are going to be less youth-conscious and more talent-conscious. Provided that the stock of intelligence, which the new recruit brings with her, is up-to-date and relevant, age may be less important than the new intellectual property. Once again, the use one makes of the Third Age is very dependent on preparation in the Second.

I like the story which my one-time publisher, Robin Waterfield, tells of Gerard Groote who was a successful professional cleric back in the troublesome times of the fourteenth century in Europe. He became the founder of a religious movement, called the Brothers and Sisters of the Common Life, which was strongly opposed to the hierarchical Church of that time. What interested me, however, was the way he decided to change his comfortable life and make his small mark on history. A stranger approached him one day, out of the blue, and said, 'Why are you standing here, intent on empty things? You ought to be another man.' The Third Age is, I feel, our opportunity to be another person. Not everyone has, as yet, got that chance. With four pillars of finance the Third Age is more than comfortable. With only one pillar, and that the diminishing state pension, there is little scope to be anyone else. I shall argue, in another chapter, that social justice requires that we make that choice more readily available.

Life is long, for most of us. In each stage of that life there are difficult choices to make. In the Second Age, particularly, it is easy to lose oneself in busyness or in emptiness. I have met as many empty raincoats rushing hither and yon as I have seen huddled lonely in a corner. Properly used, the First Age of 'formation' should be a time to grow an identity before the consuming busyness. Properly balanced, the Second Age is the time of one's major contribution, to work or home or community. The Third Age is the opportunity to be someone different, if we want to be; or to go on doing what we used to, only slower. If it is true, and it is unverifiable, that by the time we die most of us have only discovered one-quarter of what we are capable of doing and being, this is the age to find the missing three-quarters.

Because their numbers will be so big – one-third of the population in most countries – and because they will be spending and saving more than those a generation behind them, and because they will bring with them all the expertise and contacts of their Second Age, the members of this Third Age will be a powerful influence in our societies. Their values, their money, and their votes will count. It is not a homogeneous group, nor is it or will it be organised, but if their spending is on time not things, time to travel, time to study, time to eat and time to watch, they will alter the pattern of work for the rest of us. It will be even more of a service and a knowledge society. If they also prove, in this stage of their lives, to be more concerned that things should be better not bigger, they will affect our priorities. The environment might get more practical attention, and more money; town-planning might be more people-friendly than car- or store-friendly; consensus might become preferred to confrontation. On the other hand, given their influence, and their votes, the Third Age population could pull down the shutters on change, huddled in their ghettoes of rich and poor, and let the world go hang.

The Fourth Age

The Fourth Age presents the biggest challenge to the idea of a balance in our lives. The questions are only beginning to be explored. When is a life not worth living, and by whom and how is that decided? The Dutch are the first to have licensed euthanasia under certain specified conditions. Others will follow. Some worry that we shall always get the balance wrong on that, but doing nothing may also get the balance wrong. Maybe the old Hindu tradition that one should go into the forest to die when one's life was over was a good one. I have always thought that I would like to attend my own memorial service. That way I could, before I left for the forest.

The more urgent question is the cost of one's final days, and sometimes years. More health-care money is spent on the last year of our lives, on average, than on all the rest of life. Can that be a sensible balance? If it is public money that is so used, then it is at the expense of better care for generations behind. The trade-off or compromise is hard to make, but, again, no decision is still a decision. It is, I suspect, impossible to find that compromise without a clearer consensus on the meaning and purpose of life, and death.

Splicing It Differently

Most people will progress through the stages in due order, using, if they can, the Third Age to fill out those parts of their lives which were left untouched in the first two, and postponing as long as possible the arrival of the Fourth Age. It could, however, be different. Many women would like to have the opportunity of a Second Age of paid work and a serious career in their late forties and after, the time when most men will, in future, be entering their Third Age. With the new flexibility of working time, there is more and more possibility of this happening. Others would like to postpone the Second Age more or less indefinitely. Attracted by the possibilities of the Third Age, they would like to bypass the Second Age and enter the Third as soon as they have finished their schooling. Provided that they do not expect society to, as it were, pay their pension in advance, but are able to support themselves on the fourth pillar, there is no reason why they should not do this. We do not all have to be successful careerists in our middle time.

The contradictions and paradoxes of life cannot be removed. We will seldom be able to get all that we want out of life at the same time, nor be able to give to it all that we might like, at one stage. The solution may be a Chinese contract, a trade-off between what you dream of and what is practical, but it may be a third angle, taking and giving different things to life at different stages.

One of the more moving moments of my life was watching a degree ceremony at Britain's Open University. It was held, appropriately I thought, in a cathedral, because each graduate was there because they had made an effort towards some form of personal renewal. What was moving was the huge variety of the graduating class. Grannies were there, and great-grandfathers, photographed by their progeny in their caps and gowns with their degree certificates, instead of the other way round. There were people in wheelchairs and others with guide dogs. Age was no barrier in that place, nor class, nor creed, nor colour, nor previous success in anything, for it is a truly 'open' university. It was, for me that day, a splendid example of the infinite possibilities of life. That First Age of formation and learning can come again at any age.

Changing stages is, however, a version of the second curve. There is always a downward beginning before the upward swing. I have, myself, changed careers three times, from oil executive to academic, from tenured academic to life on a priest's salary, and finally, or perhaps not finally, to working as an independent writer. In every case my finances took a dip. Each time I was again the new boy in an alien world and had to earn my credibility anew. Each time, however, the difficulties decreased with time and a whole new life emerged. Others have been even more courageous, forsaking the office for a circumnavigation of the globe, starting farming in mid-life, reversing roles in the family in mid-stream, moving from priest to advertising executive, from nursing to founding a software consulting business, or from chief executive of one such to a full-time artist.

Life is full of possibilities for a second curve. In searching for it, we will need some sort of core to our personal doughnuts, some basic wherewithal, but it can be smaller than we think. Some Chinese contracts with those around us will often make it possible for everyone involved to mix it differently. The first three ages of life can be lived in any sort of order, and the new chaotic state of our world makes it unusually possible to be different from the norm.

A State of Justice

The individualised working lives foreseen in the last chapters could fill out the raincoats for some but could also leave many of them emptier than before, bereft even of a place of work to go to, no matter how boring or anonymous, and lacking the means and the know-how to be an independent individual. The spectre of a divided society looms over us, no matter how federal we are or how well-meaning our businesses. We have to tackle the paradox of justice and, in particular, the paradox of intelligence. If we don't, we may well bring the whole edifice down about our ears, because it is ultimately not tolerable for the many poor to live beside the fewer rich. It would, anyway, be crazy, as well as immoral, not to want to create a full property-owning democracy when intelligence is the property, because of the happy paradox that more intelligence for some does not mean less for anyone else.

These chapters are not intended to be a discourse on the nature of justice. Justice is, however, the bond of society. Justice allows us to dwell together in unity, building a beneficial compromise between the rights of the individual and our responsibilities to our fellow human beings, enabling us to love both ourselves and our neighbours. If we want to avoid that spectre of a divided and embattled society, we should do our best to create a state of justice in our land.

At its simplest, justice means fairness. Fairness means, for instance, that society should not deal with people arbitrarily but with 'due process' – this is the legal side of justice, which need not concern us here. Fairness also means that not everyone should get the same, because not everyone needs or deserves the same. In practice, anyway, a strict equality does not work. As Abraham Lincoln said, you don't make the poor rich by making the rich poor. Fairness could mean, however, either that we gave the brightest of our young the best of our education because they would make the most of it, or, conversely, that we gave the least talented the best because they needed it most. Fairness is always a complicated question.

Fairness, when it descends from lofty principles to hard decisions, always means a compromise, a blend of two 'oughts'. In the case of education, for instance, fairness means that everyone should, as far as is practically possible, have the same chance to be different. We should not tilt the scales against anyone from the start. We should also give people the chance of more than one start if they are slow off the mark. On the other hand, we should also encourage with our help those who make the most use of that early start. No one should want to cut back the education of doctors to create more schools for delinquents, on the grounds that the latter need it more. Justice always seeks to balance the needs of the individual with the needs of the wider community.

In the context of the issues discussed in this book, fairness means giving everyone a decent chance of a life on the second curve. In Britain, the Commission for Social Justice put it this way in their first report in 1993: 'we cannot help but regard a commitment to the extension of opportunities as a radical doctrine, and one that lies at the heart of social justice'. In a democracy where wealth derives from property, fairness, therefore, means giving everyone a chance to get some of that property, which, in the new millennium, means intelligence of one sort or another. Fairness therefore requires an **investment in intelligence**, an investment in the education of all people throughout their lives, accepting that some people will make more of that investment than others. Chapter 12 investigates what that might mean – the different types of intelligence, the forms which education might take, and the help which people might need to develop their skills and aptitudes as they go through life. In a state of justice, everyone has a right to some property. What use they make of it, however, is up to them. We must each take responsibility for our own doughnuts in life.

Fairness also suggests that there should be more chances to win in life than to lose. A third angle on this problem is to propose that there should be more than one measure of success. Where there is only one scale, there will always be winners and losers, and usually more losers than winners. In a contented society, with more winners than losers, there need to be multiple scales, a variety of ways to feel good and to count yourself successful. Society will then have more givers than takers, and a greater variety of life.

Chapter 13 looks at some of the alternatives to money as the measure of all things, and proposes a **new scoreboard**. What is counted is what counts. It is not enough, therefore, to say that a good life is more than jewels, or that the environment is important to us all. We have to make some sort of stab at measuring such good intentions or that is all that they will remain.

More measures will mean more compromises between the numbers on the different scales, in personal life as well as in business and in society as a whole. The principle of the doughnut, that there are the necessary things of life, the core, and the other things, which are the ones which make the difference, provides one path to that compromise. There is, however, no one answer for all. Justice requires that we eliminate the worst inequalities where we can. Justice does not require that all should be the same. That, in fact, would be unjust, a denial of our right to be different within limits.

12 The Intelligence Investment

When Intelligence is Property

In a property-owning democracy which claims to be fair to all its citizens, it is only right that everyone should have a share in that property and the wealth which it brings. When property meant land, social and political revolutions redistributed that land, most recently in bits of ex-colonial Africa. When property meant stocks and shares and the ownership of enterprises, governments went out of their way to encourage more of their citizens to catch the share-holding habit. Alternatively, governments sought to persuade them that nationalisation was one way to give all citizens a stake in the property of the nation.

Now that intelligence has replaced land as the source of wealth we have to take seriously that opening sentence of *A Nation at Risk*, the 1983 report on American education: 'All, regardless of race or class or economic status, are entitled to a fair chance and to the tools for developing their individual powers of mind and spirit to the utmost.' If we don't make this new property more widely available, if we don't invest in the intelligence of all our citizens, we shall have a divided society.

You can already see that divide deepening. Robert Reich has divided the modern American workforce into three categories: there are the routine operators, who are still needed to pack the airline meals, operate the tills and put the data on to the discs. They make up maybe one-quarter of the labour force, a proportion which is declining as their jobs get automated or are exported to lands with cheaper labour. Secondly, there are the personal-service providers in restaurants, hospitals and security, 30 per cent and growing. Thirdly, there are those people whom Reich calls the symbolic analysts, those who deal with numbers and ideas, problems and words. They are the journalists, the financial analysts, the consultants, architects, lawyers, doctors, managers, all those whose intelligence is their source of power and influence. They now make up perhaps 20 per cent of all workers. Farmers, miners and government employees make up the rest. It is the symbolic analysts, the knowledge-workers, the professionals and the managers, who are the real beneficiaries of the information age because they own the new property.

Under present policies this 'fortunate fifth' is getting richer almost by the minute, while the others get poorer. Reich calculates that in 1989 this top fifth had a higher after-tax income than all the other four-fifths combined. In times gone by, the rich had a vested interest in supporting the poor – in the final analysis the poor were both their customers and their neighbours – but the new rich, the symbolic analysts, sell their stuff to each other, or to other firms, internationally. They do not venture downtown, use public transport, or send their children to the public schools. Why then, they say, should they pay more to support more of such things? They do not benefit themselves, even indirectly.

The conventional wisdom has been, both in the United States and Europe, that the private sector pays for the public sector. Help the private sector to get rich and the other sector will benefit. Selfishness makes sense. That was true when property was the old-fashioned sort – land, bricks and machinery. Wealth did trickle down. More of that sort of property needed more people to work it. Intelligence-as-property changes that beneficial sequence. The causal chain is reversed; a rich private sector no longer results in a richer public sector, it goes the other way round. Without investment in the public sector, in housing, in telecommunications and transport, and, most of all, in education, the number of those symbolic analysts cannot increase significantly; the stock of useful intelligence will remain confined to one-fifth of the population. The rest will be progressively cut off from the world of property in the new sense, increasingly poor and effectively disenfranchised.

The Nature of Intelligence

If intelligence is the new basis of property and wealth, it is odd that we don't always seem more eager to grab more of it for ourselves. In Britain nearly three out of 10 youngsters leave full-time school as soon as they can, at 16, without any qualification and often without any educational certificate in any subject. We know, by contrast, that in Germany, Japan, the Netherlands, France and America, 90 per cent stay in school or formal training until at least 18. In America, however, it may not do them all that much good. As the Education Committee of Congress discovered, fewer than four in 10 young adults can summarise in writing the main argument from a news column. Only 25 out of 100 young adults can use a bus schedule to work out how to get from here to there at a particular time. Only 10 per cent can select the least costly product from a list of grocery items on the basis of unit-pricing information. Something isn't working as it should. Either the young are short-sighted and stupid or, just possibly, they are right – they don't feel that they are learning what they should while they are at school, not in Britain or America, at any rate. It is not, they may instinctively feel, the right sort of intelligence in which to invest.

Consider, on the other hand, this question from an entrance paper at Tokyo University.

Given a regular pyramid V with a square base, there is a ball with its centre on the bottom of the pyramid and tangent to all edges. If each length of the pyramid base is of length a, find the following quantities: (1) the height of V; (2) the volume of the portion common to the ball and pyramid.

How many of our students applying to study maths at university, one wonders, would be happy to tackle this problem on their way in? The snag is – this was not a question in the maths entrance exam, it was in the paper for humanities students! The academic standards are high in Japan. None the less, when these sophisticated learners start work, they have to start learning all over again. The businesses of Japan see the universities as a recruiting-ground, not an education. As they used to say of Oxford, it only needs to run a recruitment office and a placement office; what happens in-between is irrelevant.

The Japanese themselves worry that their educational system is no longer preparing people adequately for a complex and shifting world. Other countries are also puzzled as to how best to deliver this new form of property. Intelligence may be the source of wealth, power and freedom, but, inconveniently, real intelligence is not a substance, it cannot be pre-packaged, sorted and delivered as if it were a consumer product. Some elements of it can, it is true; intelligence defined as information can be treated in just that way, it can be pre-packaged, disseminated, stored and retrieved; it can be mass-produced, made consumer-friendly, distributed in multi-media and tested for reception. It is very tempting to think that when that form of intelligence has been dispersed, the job has been done. But to know all is not to be able to do all.

I have long admired Howard Gardner's concept of multiple intelligences, as described in his book *Frames of Mind*. In that book he lists seven intelligences and describes how they can be measured. He arrived at his theory by watching brain-damaged patients. Some had a normal intelligence but could not remember their personal history, or recognise faces, even their own. Others could do everything except count. The important conclusion is that none of the intelligences is necessarily connected with any other. You can be as bright as a button in one and a dunce in another. You can shine in five or only in two. My own list has nine different forms of intelligence:

Factual intelligence: the sort of walking encyclopedia who wins the Mastermind competitions in Britain, who knows the answer to every question in Trivial Pursuit and can give an impromptu lecture on the state of the Romanian economy over dinner. We are envious but often bored.

Analytical intelligence: the person who loves intellectual problems, crosswords and puzzles. Such people delight in reducing complex data to more simple formulations. Strategic consultants, scientists and academics are strong in this type of intelligence. When this intelligence is combined with factual intelligence, examinations come easy. When we describe someone as an intellectual it is often this combination which we have in mind.

Linguistic intelligence: the one who speaks seven languages and can pick up another within a month. I envy such people, since I don't have this facility myself, but we have to remember that it is not necessarily connected with the first two intelligences.

Spatial intelligence: the intelligence which sees patterns in things. Artists have it, as do mathematicians and systems-designers. Entrepreneurs have it in dollops, but without necessarily having the other intelligences, which explains why many an entrepreneur failed at school and would never go near a business school.

Musical intelligence: the sort that gave Mozart his genius, but which also drives pop stars and their bands, many of whom would never have a chance of going to college, because their scores on the first two intelligences would have been too low.

Practical intelligence: the intelligence which allows young kids to take a motor-bike apart and put it together again, although they might not be able to explain how in words. Many 'intellectuals', intelligent in the first two sense of the word, are notoriously impractical and unworldly. 'Am in Crewe', Chesterton cabled his wife. 'Where should I be?'

Physical intelligence: the intelligence, or talent, which we can see in sport stars, which enables some to hit balls much better than others, to ski better, dance better and generally co-ordinate mind and muscle in ways that defeat me.

Intuitive intelligence: the gift which some have of seeing things which others can't, even if they cannot explain why or wherefore. It is said that women have this intelligence to a greater degree than men, which may be why men often disparage it.

Interpersonal intelligence: the wit and the ability to get things done with and through other people. Notoriously, this intelligence often does not go with analytical or information intelligence. 'Too clever by half' – the jibe aimed at the Conservative politician Iain Macleod in years gone by, to explain why he would never be the great leader he could have been, applies to others as well. Without this form of intelligence, great minds can be wasted.

My list is based on observation. There may be more types of intelligence than nine. The important point is that intelligence has many faces, all of them useful, all of them potential property in this new world of intelligence. We will not all be symbolic analysts in the future, but we will all have to create and manage our own work doughnuts. To do that we need to have a clear idea of our best intelligences, and have learnt to make the most of them. It may be more an article of faith than a researchable fact, but we should make the starting assumption, in a just society, that *everyone* is intelligent in at least one of the nine ways. It should, then, be the first duty of any school to discover one's intelligence(s) and develop them. 'Know Yourself', said Juvenal, were words given from the gods, and inscribed on the ancient temple of Delphi. An impossible precept, grumbled Carlyle, it should be replaced by the more nearly possible 'know what you can work at'.

The Three 'C's

Discovering your intelligences is one thing, applying them is another. We need to be able to recognise and identify problems and opportunities. We need to be able to organise ourselves and other people to do something about them, and we need to be able to sit back and reflect on what has happened in order that we can do it all better the next time round. It is the cycle of discovery at work.

The skills involved are conceptualising, co-ordinating and consolidating – the three 'c's. They are the 'verbs' of education as opposed to the 'nouns', the 'doing' words not the facts. We don't learn to use these verbs by sitting in rows in a classroom, but by practice. Without them we may be a potential Nobel prize-winner or a star athlete but no one, least of all ourselves, will ever find out. These three 'c's should be the core of any educational doughnut. Unfortunately, they seldom are; they are regarded instead as add-on extras, optional skills for what space is left in the doughnut. That is why the businesses in Japan have to re-educate their clever new recruits as soon as they arrive. That is why some kids may be right to leave school early – they will learn the three 'c's more quickly on the streets.

I asked a professor of English at Cambridge University what they did there to educate his students for the demanding and prestigious jobs which most of this talented group would surely move on to in life. That, he said, was no business of his. 'They come here to read English, and that is exactly what they do.' Tony Benn once listed his education in *Who's Who* as taking place 'in the intervals between terms at Westminster School and Oxford'. He may have been right. The children of the symbolic analysts learn the three 'c's as they grow up, mentored and coached by their elders as effectively as the new recruits are in the Japanese firms. Their parentage thus accentuates their advantages.

A just, and sensible, society will do something about that accumulating difference between the children of the successful and the others. Since 80 per cent of the young do not have symbolic analysts as parents we have no choice but to use their early schooling as a substitute. That means intensive care and attention in the years from four to 10, when the 'c' skills are beginning to be formed. At present, in Britain, there are 25 children to every teacher at this level, but only 10 students per teacher at the undergraduate level. We ought to reverse the ratios.

If they were properly educated at the start, students ought to be able to take responsibility for more of their own learning at the university level, something which they are unfairly expected to do at the primary stage. When it is argued that there is no evidence to show that class size at the primary level affects learning, I have to point out that what is being measured in that research is the retention of information or the acquisition of repetitive skills, the 'nouns'. The 'verbs', as we know from trying to develop them in adult life in organisations, need mentoring, small-group experience and real-life problem-solving. You have to live them to learn them.

With 10 small children to a teacher it is possible to approximate the kind of real-time, real-life learning that the children of the symbolic analysts pick up. With 10 children it is possible to move between the classroom and life outside in a way which is not logistically possible with 25. It can be any 10 children. There is a lot of piecemeal evidence to suggest that you do not have to be the child of a symbolic analyst to learn these things. Most people can do it if they start young enough.

In a famous programme in America Jaime Escalante got low-income Hispanic students through the Advanced Placement Examination in calculus, one of those conceptual subjects normally restricted to the so-called 'brightest' in the class. If he could do that with one of the toughest of noun skills there is no saying what he might have done with the verb skills. What small groups and close mentoring and learning from life can do, and that which large classes can rarely do, is to give a child self-confidence.

Portfolios at School

We could go further. Instead of requiring the student to reach certain standards before she or he gets their leaving certificate from school, we could require *the school* to ensure that the student has reached those standards before they let them go. School should be a place for compiling a portfolio of competences. Those competences need not, and should not, be age-linked, with levels or tests or examinations to be passed at particular ages, because people learn these verb skills at very different paces. Like music tests or driving-tests they should be taken when one is ready for them and likely to pass. If every 16-year-old takes the same examination at the same time, and if that examination is graded, half of the population will, inevitably and logically, do better than the other half. The net effect is to persuade half of the population that they are failures, however often you tell them that they have passed.

Wherever we need tests we must make a distinction between age and competence, and allow retakes of everything. In the end, almost everyone everywhere passes their driving-test. My daughter passed hers at 18, my son at 24, because he was not in such a hurry to learn to drive. Neither of them, now, a year later, thinks that they are a better or worse driver than the other. If everyone took the same driving test at 18, and only the top half were considered competent to drive, we should have fewer, better drivers and safer roads. We should also have a lot of very deprived and discontented people, including many who might well have developed into very competent drivers a few years later.

If the age-bonding of our schools went on throughout life, we should be very resentful. If only 25-year-olds could take the accountancy examinations or only 39-year-olds apply for full professorships, there would be an outcry. It can only be for reasons of administrative convenience that schools remain the most ageist of all our institutions. The effect is to make half of our young feel that they are failures.

Students should each be required to compile a bulging portfolio of certificates of competence or achievement. Apart from certificates of competence in the traditional subjects, I see no reason why driving, swimming, first-aid, word-processing, cooking, tax law, telephone and presentation skills, and any other practical life-skills should not be certificated and collected during this period of life. These are certificates of competence. They can be formally tested, as with music or driving, or they can be examined on the evidence of their work, as with artists' portfolios.

This form of portfolio collection should and does go on throughout life, but the habit needs to be acquired young. It will be an essential part of the portfolio life which we are all going to experience at one stage or another. Even inside the organisation, as I have argued, portfolios will be the way people develop their careers with the organisation encouraging them to add to their credentials at every level, sometimes by new accredited experience, sometimes by certificated tests or courses. The Records of Achievement which are becoming increasingly common in British schools are a step in the direction of portfolio collections. To be effective they need to become part of a nationally accepted scheme of educational portfolios, not the icing on the cake that they are today, the sop for those who cannot excel at the traditional examinations. When we make all examinations age-independent and when we happily include certificates relating to all the intelligences, we shall begin to see a proper balance in our education.

There is, however, no need for all this portfolio collection to take place *in* school although it should happen while *at* school. Nobody would seriously expect the school to teach driving or, perhaps, word-processing. The school can and should be the organising hub for all the extra-curricular activity. Come to that, there is no reason why subjects like languages or domestic science should not be taught by specialist agencies, under the general supervision of the school.

If the education service is unwilling to see its role so enlarged we should develop a separate Youth Service which took over where the formal schooling left off, handling all the sports, work experience and community activities as well as the more practical aspects of the portfolio. School proper might end, as on the Continent, at 2 p.m. when the Youth Service would take over, staffed by some full-time professionals but with the help of many part-timers, voluntary workers or parents, portfolio people themselves.

It could go further still. Technology, and the possibilities of multi-media, will make independent learners of us all. There is no reason why some may not choose to learn for themselves by themselves in some topics, presenting themselves for examination when they are ready, rather as one already does for a driving-test. The function of the school, or the Youth Service, would then be to act as a tracking-station to make sure that no one was falling through the net, or losing the benefits and lessons of the three 'c's. The school would then be the core of an educational doughnut organisation. Some teachers would be core staff, well paid for long hours and flexibility. Others would be specialists, working outside the core and selling their expertise to a range of schools or institutions, portfolio people themselves. Some would move between the two roles during their career.

The Double Bond

Portfolios and the doughnut school may not, however be enough. We learn about life from life and we learn about work through working, mixed with a judicious amount of coaching, teaching and reflection. The German model of a blend of workplace experience and formal instruction for all but the most academic at age 16, has been widely admired and is beginning to be imitated in many countries with subtle national variations. There is, however, always a danger that this is a recipe, in a changing world, for training people in jobs and skills which will soon be obsolete. Unfortunately, if you go along with curvilinear logic, all is ultimately obsolete.

This kind of learning must, therefore, be complemented by some of that 'verb' learning which might, in a sensible world, have been learnt earlier but probably won't have been. We should, therefore, present every young person on adulthood, at age 18, with a double bond. One part of that bond would guarantee to pay the fees, up to a defined level, with basic maintenance, for two years or the equivalent, of full-time study at any recognised learning institution. This part of the bond could be used at any stage of one's life. There would be no age barrier. It would be up to the individual to apply and up to the institution to accept or reject them. The state would guarantee payment but not admission. The assumption would be that sufficient institutions would create themselves to meet this demand once it was seen to be underwritten to this extent.

This part of the double bond would automatically be taken up by those who were going on to university from school. They would, therefore, get the first two years of their higher education free. If their course lasted longer than two years they would have to pay the cost of the extra time. At present, first-degree courses in Britain are three or four years long. If the proposal of a double bond were introduced there, we might expect to see the first degree compressed into two fuller years, to be followed by an optional two years of graduate study. These graduate years could be paid for by a graduate tax on further earnings. Those who earn less would then, automatically, have more years in which to pay it off. It is fair.

The other part of the double bond would be to guarantee to find a full-time job for any citizen who presented themselves, for two years in the local region, either in a voluntary organisation or in a government agency, at a level equivalent to the minimum wage, where such a thing exists. It would be a recognition that there are many things about life and work which you can only learn by working and living – the 'verb' skills in particular. The government would organise what would, in effect, be a brokerage or employment agency in each region. Since this would be labour in excess of the requirements of the labour market, the jobs would have to be located in the voluntary sector or in non-statutory government work where they did not substitute for longer-term jobs and workers. The two bonds could be used in conjunction, if the individual so wished and could so arrange.

This double bond would be a recognition of society's continued investment in every individual citizen when they reach adulthood, not just in those who see themselves on the academic track. In return, society would be entitled to refuse to support anyone until the two bonds had been used, accepting always that there will be exceptional circumstances in some individual cases. The double bond would be one way of providing the essential extra investment necessary to launch the individual into the 'intelligence society' with the skills, both intellectual and practical, which he or she will need to survive.

Although only a minority of people would, in fact, cash in their bonds, although the bonds would effectively replace many welfare payments, and although they would allow work to be done in the community which might not otherwise be affordable, the scheme would, potentially, cost a lot of money. It would have to be seen as an investment in the long-term future. Its pay-off would come in the reduced need to provide for these people in later life, if they were, as a result of the bonds, more able to look after themselves. It would come, indirectly, in the lower costs of policing and repairing a more contented and just society. If Singapore can think it right to invest 25 per cent of her GDP in education, training and development the rest of us should be able to do at least as well. It is naïve to think that learning for life can finish at 16 or even 18, yet that is the implicit message which we are giving today to many of our young.

Learning, like life, goes on for ever. It would be reasonable to expect that the workplace would see the good sense of investing in intelligence, at least for its core workforce. We would be often disappointed. Too many organisations do not think far enough ahead to wait for the pay-off from the investment. Others hope to cash in on other people's investment and entice their educated and trained staff to join them. Some rely on the individuals to invest in themselves. Some compromise is needed if learning is to become the fashion throughout life.

One way to encourage the fashion would be to set a legal benchmark for organisations, requiring them to spend a set percentage of their pay-roll on education and training, a figure to be reported in their audited accounts. Any organisation falling below the standard would forfeit the difference to a central training fund. The French require 1.2 per cent of the pay-roll to be spent in this way. Most firms exceed it. With the minimum of bureaucracy a minimum level is thus established, but to set the level at 0.5 per cent, as the British Labour Party recently proposed, is to underestimate the investment required in the age of intelligence. My university requires that an average of one day a week be spent on research, keeping ahead of my subject. That is 20 per cent of my time. One half of that – 10 per cent – might be a minimum standard for anyone in the years ahead. Five days a year, the norm for good employers, leaves a large gap to be filled.

Some of this money and time could be seen as the entitlement of the individuals, to invest in their own development as they thought fit. The organisation does not necessarily or always know what is best for one. If an individual is entitled to annual holidays, sick leave and maternity leave, it would seem only sensible to extend the entitlement to intelligence. The slogan of some American corporations – 'individual initiative and corporate support' – has the right ring to it, but is usually interpreted only to mean attendance at some selected courses. It needs wider application – a guaranteed sum of money per annum, accumulated for up to seven years if need be.

It is, however, the outsiders who are most likely to miss out on any continuing investment in their developing intelligence. Most organisations will leave it up to the individual, and most of those will be too poor, too busy or too short-sighted to do it for themselves. Here lies the biggest danger of the intelligence age, a diminishing competence at the bottom end of the labour market. Outsiders need help.

The New Agents

All independents need an agent. A good half of us will be independent at any one time in the future, and all of us will be independent at one stage or another. Independents are never unemployed, officially – they just have no work. Resting, they call it in the theatrical world. If the unemployment figures eventually decline in Europe it will be, in part, because many people will perforce have gone independent, have got a small portfolio and so taken themselves off the unemployment registers. To make the portfolio bigger and better they will need an agent. While some independents will have bulging portfolios and full diaries, many will be among the most vulnerable of our societies, unprotected, unwanted, deteriorating assets. That will be in no one's interest.

Actors and models have agents, writers have agents as do golfers, tennis-players and boxers. It is hard enough to market and price yourself when you are a star; it is impossible when no one knows you and when you are unsure of what you can offer. A good agent will not only find buyers for your talents and negotiate the deal, he or she will be a coach or mentor, helping you to review your experience and guiding you to appropriate educational opportunities. Good agents will prod your creativity by floating ideas in front you – 'Have you ever considered . . .?' or 'Would this sort of thing interest you . . . ?' They will suggest what you need to do or where you need to go to improve your skills or to enlarge your experience.

They will also, if they are any good, help to organise your life so that there is some order in the necessary chaos of the independent's schedule. This is not altruism. It is in their interest to increase the value of the asset they are managing. It is, for the independent, a great comfort to know that there is someone whose interests entirely coincide with theirs, because it can be a lonely world outside the organisation. There is a growing market for agents of portfolio workers. The executive-leasing agencies have been quick to move in to the upper end of that market. They offer to provide executives to organisations to cover short-term skill gaps or project-managers. They are, in effect, agents for portfolio executives.

The need is critical for those lower down the skill range. This would have been a natural opportunity for the old trades unions, whose membership and influence has inevitably waned as the minimalist organisation has waxed. The unions, however, have been noticeably reluctant to recognise this new market. We must therefore look to new intermediaries. It would be pleasing if the employment agencies were to be more than brokers, and were to live up to their name and act as agents, not of the hiring organisation, but of the individual. If they were far-sighted enough, it would pay them to spend money upgrading the skills and the knowledge of those on their books in order to increase the rates which they could then demand from the hiring organisation. Some are already beginning to offer training opportunities; more must follow suit.

Portfolio workers need more than agents, they need somewhere where they belong as of right. Learning is alienating if you do it all by yourself. Teleworking is fine in technological theory but lonely in reality. That asset which is yourself can atrophy in isolation. We independents need somewhere other than the home, somewhere where there are colleagues not clients, somewhere where we can find the companionship and gossip of the old office or factory but without the boss. Somewhere where we can exchange experience and contacts. We need a club. I have argued, earlier, that the hub of the minimalist organisation will be a clubhouse for the members of the dispersed core. It should also be available to key portfolio workers to use when they need it. One piece of everyone's portfolio should, if possible, include the use of a club facility as part of the fee. For the many who cannot negotiate that privilege, I would like to see the employment agencies begin to offer a similar facility in exchange for an exclusive right to sell your skills.

As the portfolio market becomes more competitive, we may see these new intermediaries actually employing a reserve labour force which they then sell on, keeping the risks and rewards for themselves. The portfolio worker would then be trading some freedom for more security, the guarantee of training and traditional employee benefits such as holiday pay and sick leave. Some organisations, Hewlett Packard in France for one, IBM in London for another, do something of the sort for their newly redundant or retired workers, putting them on a retainer or a guaranteed-fee basis for a certain proportion of their time. They have created clubs which pay you to belong to them, but to keep your membership you have to keep your skills up to date, you have to keep on growing your asset.

Some portfolio workers form their own clubs or networks. Networks are useful, but if they reside mainly in your address files they lack the spontaneity of a club. An address book is not quite the same as a bar and a reading-room. Every network needs a club at its hub to add the human face to the electronic impulse. Clubs for the unemployed offer the right facilities but can, too often, be places of shared misery rather than shared learning. Only if their members start to think portfolio does the club take on a new life, looking, now, not for jobs but for customers.

The independent workers of our societies are among the most vulnerable and the least protected. Europe's Social Chapter is an attempt to remedy that, but will, one suspects, be more often honoured in the breach than in the observance. Britain's refusal to sign it may only be the more honourable face of non-compliance. In a competitive world, with a surplus of labour sloshing around, independents will need all the help that they can get. It is in all our interests to give it to them.

13   The New Scorecard

Unfortunately, Macnamara was right. He said, in what has come to be known as the Macnamara Fallacy:

> The first step is to measure whatever can be easily measured. This is OK as far as it goes. The second step is to disregard that which can't be easily measured or to give it an arbitrary quantitative value. This is artificial and misleading. The third step is to presume that what can't be measured easily really isn't important. This is blindness. The fourth step is to say that what can't be easily measured really doesn't exist. This is suicide.

What does not get counted does not count. Money is easily counted. Therefore, all too soon, money becomes the measure of all things. A just society needs a new scorecard.

The Distortions of Money

It is not always realised that the idea of national income-accounting, on a regular standardised basis, the GDP and the GNP numbers which we all now assume is what we mean by 'national income', is quite a new idea. In Britain it started in 1940 when the government, helped and advised by Keynes, needed to work out how much money they could raise in order to fight the War. Before that time there had only been occasional and non-standardised estimates. My first job with my oil company was in Singapore, where, in default of anyone else, they appointed me, trained in classical history and philosophy, to be their first 'regional economist'. I was asked to prepare a series of forecasts relating oil consumption to national income, drawing on ratios established elsewhere in the world. Unfortunately there were no national-income statistics for Singapore. This was in 1956, when it was still a British colony. I may have been the first to make a very rough and inadequate estimate of Singapore's GDP, an estimate which, I recall, involved guessing at the earnings of Singapore's colony of prostitutes.

Things are different now. Singapore is proud to boast of her per-capita income. League tables of national income proliferate. It is assumed that these equate with standards of living, but the statistics measure only the visible transfers of money. So, for instance, and most notoriously, they don't measure the unpaid work in the home. If, however, the wife dies and her husband hires someone to do the work which she did for nothing, the apparent prosperity of the country would rise by the £18,000 which the Legal and General Insurance Company say it would cost in the 1990s. Voluntary and charitable work – gift work – is not included because no money changes hands, nor the caring of the elderly if it is done for love or compassion in one's own home. Put your parents in a home for the elderly, however, and society, by these accounts, is immediately the richer.

More insidiously, if the cars and the highways are so bad that accidents proliferate, then hospital, car-repair and insurance bills increase, and so does the supposed wealth of the country as these transactions find their way into the national accounts. You can spend money polluting the clean air of the countryside with a factory, muck up its rivers and destroy the peace and stillness of the place, and it will all be counted as an increase in wealth because nothing is deducted for the damage. If the firm were fined, or charged, for what they had done, it would, apparently, make us even richer. We are encouraged to be a disposable society by the way we count. The more you throw things away and buy new things instead of having them repaired, the richer the society appears.

The distortions go on. Leisure, the precious commodity, only gets counted if you spend money on it. I have sometimes, half jokingly, suggested that the reason that the Germans are richer than the British is because the Germans tend to live in apartments while the British like their homes to have gardens. If you live in an apartment, every time you go out you will, normally, either spend money or make money. Meanwhile the Briton goes into the garden and watches the cucumber growing, or weeds the flower-bed. No money, so no wealth. Love is for free, so buy diamonds instead – it will make the country richer. Don't cook her a meal, take her to a restaurant instead. Don't make music, buy music. Riding the bullet train from Tokyo to Osaka through hundreds of miles of desolate industrial landscape, I have to remind myself that the people who live there are richer than most Europeans. They don't always think so. In one survey the Japanese who were questioned reckoned that they had, in reality, a lower quality of life than every European country except for Portugal.

Adding up all the financial transactions by all the companies and institutions in a country, converting it to dollars and dividing it by the number of people in a society does not tell you how comfortable they are. Cold climates have to spend more money than warm ones. In Britain, if you want hot sun or cold snow it gets expensive. In Italy they have these things for nothing. Poor Italians! Income is not equally distributed between people or between organisations and people; Japan keeps more of its money inside its organisations than Britain does; ageing societies spend more than young societies and have fewer people. They therefore look richer, but can feel poorer.

When the IMF used Purchasing Power Parities (PPPs), instead of the normal market exchange rates, to compare the output of countries, they found that China, for instance, went from $370 per head to $2,460, and India from $275 to $1,255. A little money goes a long way in China and India. PPPs reflect that fact. The $370 was clearly unreal when 70 per cent of Chinese urban households have colour television and 80 per cent have washing-machines. When the IMF added up the output of all the countries of the developing world on this new basis, they discovered that the developing world's share of the world's output had jumped from 18 per cent to 34 per cent, and that of the industrial world had fallen from 73 per cent to 54 per cent. China, in fact, because of all the hundreds of millions of its people, is, on a PPP basis, the second-richest country in the world, after the USA and above Japan. The way you see things depends on the way you count them.

There have also been attempts to add some of the invisibles to the visible. Most countries make an estimate of their informal, 'black', economies; one or two add this estimate into their national income. In one year, 1987, Italy jumped over Britain in the international league table when she did this, adding 18 per cent to her GNP in one keystroke of a statistician's computer. No one has yet added home work or gift work to the money numbers but the time might not be far off. It would be a painless way to get rich quicker and would benefit Britain with her long tradition of voluntary work. We should, therefore, remember the principle that no one set of numbers can ever serve all purposes. What we need are two sets of national accounts, one which records the money transactions and one which lists all the other indicators of life.

Counting Invisibles

This second list would include health and death statistics, infant mortality, age of death, cause of death. It would include education numbers, employment numbers and statistics on other forms of work; there would be details of housing, of environmental indicators such as carbon-dioxide emissions, deforestation and energy use and of more subjective indicators such as people's feelings about their quality of life. All these numbers currently exist in most countries. In Britain, many of them are published annually in documents such as *Social Trends* which has its equivalent elsewhere. What we need is not a new system of national accounts so much as another companion set of national statistics which can be compared year by year and country by country. The UN's International Comparison Program, which attempts to do some of this, may yet turn out to be one of the more important of its initiatives.

The statistics collected, we need to give these numbers the same sort of public prominence as we give to the money figures. They should, for instance, be presented as an annual review to every parliament or congress, be debated and discussed in the media and contrasted, for celebration or lament, with the statistics of other countries. Over time they would provide a set of benchmarks for a civilised society, to run alongside the national-income figures. Both sets of figures are necessary, if what we count affects the way we behave, and if we want a more balanced and just society.

Practical Action

We could start the reforms by making the national-income accounts a little more honest. Governments run the country on a cash-flow basis, 'money in' versus 'money out' each year. The difference is the deficit, or what the British quaintly call the Public Sector Borrowing Requirement. This allows them to take no account of the difference between an investment and an expenditure – they are both outgoings, even though the investment may save money in the future whereas the expenditure is gone for good. Education, therefore, is always a cost and never an investment. The cash-flow convention allows them to sell assets and call it revenue, even though it will never be repeated. The same convention allows them to treat bonanzas, such as Britain's North Sea oil production in the 1980s, which was never going to last very long, as an addition to revenue rather than the equivalent of Aunt Agatha's legacy, a one-off bounty, something to be invested in one's future.

The result is to distort priorities. There is no incentive to think long-term. There is no way to trade an expenditure today against savings or benefits in the future. There is no need to take account of future liabilities piling up; the costs of not maintaining roads and railways, or of the pension liabilities that accrue for each worker in the unfunded state-pension scheme. If we behaved that way in our own lives we should never buy a house, we would run our cars until they fell apart, and we would spend the minimum on our children's education, because the long-term future would always come second to paying the bills. In our private lives we get round that problem by turning large lumps of investment, such as a house, into smaller streams of expenditure, by means of a loan or a mortgage. If we are wise, we borrow only to finance investment not to cover the monthly bills. Government muddles them up. No business would want to behave like that, nor would it be allowed to. Politicians have always and consistently resisted the pressure to do their accounts in a proper 'businesslike' way, arguing that it would tie their hands unnecessarily and that, one way or another, they have to finance both the running deficit and the capital expenditure by borrowing, so why separate them out artificially?

One country, however, has made an attempt to be businesslike and to present a proper balance. New Zealand produced a national balance sheet for the first time in 1991. It revealed that its assets, state companies, roads, lands and buildings, financial reserves and investments totalled NZ$14.4 billion less than its liabilities, by which it meant its borrowing at home and abroad and its pension liabilities. Technically, the country was bankrupt. Realistically, it means that future taxpayers will have to pay for the relative profligacy of their predecessors. New Zealand will continue to publish its old cash-flow accounts but the new 'business' accounts will help to show how well the present and the future are balanced. The *Economist* calculated that, using these sort of figures, the net worth of New Zealand Inc. had deteriorated by $12 billion dollars over the past 20 years. By not counting, you could say, the New Zealanders had mortgaged their future. The present system of government accounting in other countries allows expediency to flourish because no one knows the true costs. Better counting would allow a more informed debate about the longer-term balance of priorities and would bring the issue of national purpose and direction to the surface.

A Scorecard for Business

Companies may have better balance sheets than governments but they, too, have a long way to go. These things do not normally count or get communicated:

The intellectual assets of the company (including their brands, their patents, their skill base)
  Their expenditure on the enhancement of these assets, including R. & D., training and development
  The introduction of new products or services
  Employee morale and productivity
The customer
  Quality of goods and service
  Customer satisfaction

The environment
   Investment and expenditure on environmental control
      and improvement
   Expenditure on community work
   Investment in the community

These things are difficult to count and in themselves they mean nothing. It is only when you start to compare last year with this year, or your company with your competitors that the numbers get interesting. Comparison provides the benchmarks. Without any sort of numbers, however, the cash-flow numbers are the ones that count. It is hard, then, to know whether the business is in proper balance, whether the future is receiving the right resources and whether the stakeholders' requirements are in balance. If, as an investor or a customer, you are betting on the intellectual property of the concern you will need more than historical money numbers.

William Reilly, when administrator of America's Environmental Protection Agency, was asked what the Eastern Europeans should do first in the long haul to clean up the massive pollution in their countries. He replied:

> My answer is to begin with the disclosure of emissions. Require that the data be published in the local newspapers. Then support a healthy non-governmental, environmental movement. At that point a fascinating dynamic will begin to occur: the community will interact with plant managers, workers and government to reduce pollution levels. Such is the power of information.

Counting it makes it visible, and counting makes it count.

IBM now measures each of its 'Baby Blues' on seven parameters: four financial numbers (revenue growth, profit, return on assets and cash flow) and three new measures (customer satisfaction, quality and employee morale). In Britain, Dr David Budworth is exploring the concept of an 'innovation ratio', relating the amount spent on innovation (research and development, training, and the development of brands) to the value added by the company. Others are looking for ways to measure a company's 'knowledge bank'. Some already do it anyway, in their published accounts under the heading of 'intangible assets'. The trouble is that you have to read the very small print in the Notes to the Accounts to find out what this means, and it will mean different things to different firms, measured in different ways. To a publisher it can mean the publishing rights which they hold. To WPP, the communications firm, it meant the brands of their two big advertising-agencies, J. Walter Thompson and Ogilvie Benson Mather. They did not say how they had valued them, but it was, at least, a recognition that intellectual capital had a value.

Putting estimates of intellectual assets on the balance sheet may, however, only confuse matters. If we give them money numbers we shall be trying, once again, to use one set of numbers to count different sorts of things. Just as we use different measures for liquids and solids, so we should happily use different measures for each stakeholder. For the environment, for instance, the United Nations initiative suggests that each organisation should include in its annual report:

- the organisation's environmental policy
- the capitalisation of environmental expenditures
- any environmental liabilities, such as bringing the organisation into line with new regulations
- disclosure of other anticipated environmental expenditure

The Pearce Report for the British Government would, if it were ever acted upon, require organisations to disclose their man-made, natural and critical capital assets and the costs of maintaining them. Other possibilities are a mandatory environmental audit to monitor observance with environmental standards or a full energy-accounting system.

These are just a taste of the numbers being looked at. As a result of these new numbers, the environment is in danger of consuming more forests through measuring the forests it is saving. The environmental-cleaning business is now thought to be worth over $60 billion in the US alone, and growing. The bigger the problem, the bigger the business. Germany is estimated to have nearly 40 per cent of the Eastern European environmental market. If you turn the problem into a business, the numbers will appear.

Consumer needs are another growing business. Sensible businesses recognise that contented customers are faithful customers and will run surveys, collect data and analyse repeat buys. As more organisations realise that they are businesses even if they don't have shareholders, the practice is spreading. Britain's hospitals have started a customer-response record, to keep track of how satisfied their patients feel with their treatment. So have prisons. Neither hospitals nor prisons want their customers to come back, so they have to turn the repeat-business statistics upside-down. Big numbers are bad. Comparing their non-repeat business with their peer institutions across the country is a valuable benchmark. They have, at the very best, to explain why they are different. The different numbers set different agendas.

For a proper balance, organisations need an audit of their relationships with all their stakeholders, even if some of the details should remain confidential. There would be no damage in publishing details of a firm's involvement with the community, or its investment in its people. One sign of the changing priorities of the times is the number of firms who see some competitive advantage in advertising their activities in this field instead of merely reporting them.

'Join us,' advertised one accounting firm, ' and we will invest at least 10 per cent of your salary in your development each year.' 'We promise every employee the chance to work one day a month in the community at our cost,' declared another. If it is seen as a business opportunity, the numbers emerge. Details of intellectual property or supplier relationships may be more private, although audited general ratios such as an innovation ratio would give nothing away to competitors but would be some indication of the level of investment in the long-term capacity of the organisation. These could and should be public. It should be good business to publish good ratios because shareholders might be impressed.

Many boards of large companies now have separate audit committees for social policy, for ethics, for remuneration and for the environment. Some, such as ICI in Britain, publish a separate environmental report alongside their annual report. This must be a good start. It is another recognition of the hexagon, of the variety of interest groups and of the multiple contradictions involved in charting the path of a business. It will be better still when we can make the data public, on a standard basis. A social audit is required in France as part of the annual report. My guess is that something similar will soon be required of all European companies. They will resent the bureaucracy and the costs involved, they will chafe at the restrictions on their freedom of action, but by counting the invisibles they will better balance the present against the future and the interest groups against each other. Sometimes, it seems, we have to be forced to be sensible. Once the playing-field is level and the rules are known, the game can start.

A Personal Scorecard

'How much money do you earn?' I used to ask my friends in my competitive days. It seemed the best way, then, of comparing progress in life, after aiming off for the fact that I was then an oil executive while some of them were bustling bankers and others exhausted young doctors. I was brought up short by one who replied, 'Enough.' 'What do you mean – enough?' I asked. 'What I say – enough. I work out what I need and that's what I make sure I earn. Why bother to make more? How much sugar do you buy in a year?' he turned and asked me. 'I have no idea,' I said. 'But I bet that there's always sugar in your house when you need it. Money is like sugar, no point in hoarding it, it usually goes bad, or you have to make quite unnecessary cakes to use it up.'

Crazy man, I thought; but as I grew older I realised the sense in what my friend had said. He was never rich but, as he said, 'there was always sugar in the house' and he seemed much less harassed than the rest of us. But then he knew what he wanted out of life. He wasn't using money as a substitute for uncertainty. In a time of materialism most of the numbers are financial ones. The higher we score, the better we do, apparently, but like the sugar we then have to go out and spend it, often on the equivalent of cakes which we don't really need. In the recession, many couples found that they were unable to trade up in the housing market as their families grew along with their income, because they could find no buyer for their current home. 'I was frustrated at first,' one of them told me, 'but then we said – we've been very happy in this place; maybe it's a bit small and a bit un-smart, but that doesn't really matter. Let's go on enjoying what we've got and take the hassle out of life. We've got enough.'

Money is seldom the measure of much, once you have enough. It is only the core of our personal doughnuts. I cannot be the only person to wonder what those people who are paid one million pounds or dollars in a year do with it all. Sugar goes bad if you don't use it. Money isn't even necessarily the sign of success. In Britain the quickest way to get rich is to fail at the top. Sign a three-year contract and then fail in the first six months, walk away with a million pounds for six months' work. As I grew older I realised that my friends were not that impressed by those who had riches, as long as 'there was sugar in the house'.

Some Hints of Change

If money is not the measure of all things, how do we put numbers on the other things – a walk in beautiful country-side, artistic expression, the love of a family, the joy of teaching, watching someone get well, the thrill of dis-covery, the satisfaction of a job well done, the delight of friends? We all know the taste of such things but find it hard to call them success. We need to find a way to list them even if we can't count them. We can learn a lot from our children, particularly when they grow into adults. I once asked my 24-year-old daughter what she thought she was doing with her life, dabbling in this and that, travell-ing, adventuring, socialising. 'When', I said crossly, 'are you going to find a proper career, make a serious contribu-tion to this world?' She looked at me, a little pityingly, I thought. 'There are many people,' she said, 'who rely on me for comfort and for help, who use me as their home. I learn something new each day, I laugh with someone every day and I cook for someone almost every night. Oh, and I do no one any harm. I don't think that's bad for 24.' I went away, wondering how long it would be before I could say the same.

Laurence Shames, in his book *The Hunger for More: Searching for Values in an Age of Greed*, puts the dilemma this way:

The frontier . . . is what has shaped the American way of doing things and the American sense of what's worth doing . . .

More money, more tokens of success – there will always be people for whom these are adequate goals, but those people are no longer setting the tone for all of us. There is a new sort of *more* at hand: more appreciation of good things beyond the marketplace, more insistence on fairness, more attention to purpose, more determination truly to choose a life, and not a lifestyle, for oneself. Dare we suggest that these new forms of *more* comprise a species of frontier?

Measuring more, he goes on to say, is easy, measuring better is hard.

Mickey Kaus, in America, shares my worries of a society increasingly divided because money is the measure of so much. He would like to take more things out of the market so that it did not matter whether you were rich or poor. The National Health Service in Britain does not differentiate between rich and poor. I am always relieved to land at Heathrow Airport after a trip abroad because I know that I can now afford to be seriously ill. Kaus would add the draft, or National Service, all schools and colleges, parks and class-integrated housing. I would add all public transport. His dream that there would ultimately be a society which regarded a janitor as being 'just as good as a banker because he works as hard' must be unrealistic but the notion of taking as many things out of the money economy has much to commend it, expensive though it would be in taxes.

My own hope lies more in the denizens of the Third Age of life. They will not, most of them, have much chance to add more sugar to their store. Enough of that will have to be enough for them. They will then begin to find that there are satisfactions and achievements which cannot be measured by money, that gift work and study work and home work of all types can be richly rewarding. Because there are going to be a lot of such people they will be noticed. They will not be old, as we used to think of old, they will not be retired in the way their parents were retired, and most of them will not be poor. They will establish new sets of case law, some new models for success, some new numbers. How many young people have you coached this year, they may enquire, how many paintings finished, gardens planted, books read or even written? How many school trips did you organise, how many patients driven to the hospital, what moments of quiet beauty did you catch, which fireside chats have you treasured, what special meals, what letters written or photographs framed, friends counselled, feuds settled, loves kindled?

Imagine one of those lambent June evenings in England, when the sun doesn't set until after nine, and the air is still and scented – I was walking along the river-bank in Cambridge, with the immaculate lawns and the hauntingly beautiful chapel of King's College in front of me when a snatch of treble voices in a choir floated over the trees and a young American couple stopped, entranced. 'Remember this, honey,' she said, 'remember it always. This is quality time.' If we are going to find a better balance in our lives and a better justice in our societies, we need to find more examples of quality time, make them more accessible to more people, and make them count. We can do that by celebrating them more, for fashion is a powerful agent of change.

Part Four:
The Search for Meaning
Making Sense of Paradox

The Three Senses

The White Stone

'What is the point of it all?' my friend asked. 'Why should we struggle with these second curves, doughnuts and compromises? In the end, isn't life just a sick joke?' I knew how she felt. I had recently watched my wife's mother dying. One month she was the twinkly, irascible old lady at the heart of the family; the next she was a grey, emaciated shape in a hospital bed, hardly able to smile, let alone talk. After that, nothing – a small pile of ashes in an urn. Could this be all there was to it?

For some there is no point. Chekhov said: 'You ask me what life is? It is like asking what a carrot is. A carrot is a carrot.' Maybe, as Gertrude Stein once said of Oakland, California, 'There is no there there.' We are all accidents in the evolutionary chain. We can lie back and enjoy it, or we can occupy ourselves, as scientists do, in trying to understand more about what is going on. There is, however, nothing which we can do to alter it, even when we understand it. We can only play with it. Man is as the smallest piece of dust in the universe. Descartes thought that animals were machines. Some biologists see no reason to think that humans are any different from animals.

This 'myth of science' so frightened Allan Bloom, when he saw the effect it was having on modern American youth, that he wrote his best-selling book *The Closing of the American Mind*. American college students, he observed, were not only lifeless and ignorant, they were reluctant to offer or to hold any opinions at all. People who thought that they were right in the past did terrible things as a result, therefore it is best to have no opinions at all. The only true knowledge is science. Everything else is wishful thinking. From that it follows that it is wrong to take a position on anything, worse still to try to impose your wishes on your bit of the world. A passive voyeurism will have to suffice, preferably uncritical and politically correct because it would be wrong to suggest that any one way of life was superior to another.

That way lies a moral vacuum, where nothing is right and nothing really wrong. That way also lies inertia, no second curve, with compromises made for the wrong reasons – for a quiet life, not for justice or for progress. Immanuel Kant, then an obscure lecturer in philosophy in an obscure Prussian town in the eighteenth century, disagreed with Descartes. He sat down, wrote his *Critique of Pure Reason* and made the world stop and think, because in it he offered an alternative to the scientific arrogance which then, as maybe now, held sway. Man, he maintained, was not a means to an end, he was himself the end. Man's life was driven and shaped by a moral pressure, which came from within. There is something about the human condition which implies something religious, however we want to describe it. It is God in the human soul, Kant said, not God the architect of the scientific universe, who makes sense of who we are. 'How do you know this?' he was asked. 'Because of the moral force within me,' he replied.

It is as good an answer as I know. Faith has no reasons. If there were reasons, or logic, there would be no need of faith. I cannot prove that there is a point to our existence. I agree with the philosopher Ludwig Wittgenstein, who said that, 'Even when all the possible scientific questions have been answered, the problems of life remain completely untouched.' I also agree with John Updike, who said that existence felt like ecstasy, even if we were not able to describe it or define it. Even if it is a conceit, we feel that we know that we have something like a soul, that we matter, and that we are in some small way unique. There is a haunting passage in the Book of Revelation in the Bible: 'to anyone who prevails, the Spirit says, I will give a white stone, on which is written a new name which no one knows except he who receives it.' I keep a white stone on my desk as a reminder of my uniqueness. Even if there is no point, even if it is all a game of science, we must still believe that there is a point. If we don't believe that, there will be no reason to do anything, believe anything, change anything. The world would then be at the mercy of all those who did believe that they could change things. It is a risk we cannot run.

To find that point, that reason for our doing and our being, it helps to build on three senses – **a sense of continuity**, a **sense of connection** and a **sense of direction**. Without these senses we can feel disoriented, adrift and rudderless. The world is going to be a confusing place for the next few decades. We shall need all the help that we can find to recognise our place and role in it. These senses are the best antidote I know to the feelings of impotence which rapid change induces in us all.

14   A Sense of Continuity

Cathedral Philosophy

A few years before he died my father gave me a dirty brown envelope. 'I'm never going to get round to this now,' he said, 'so you had better have it.' It was a collection of old family papers including one of those family trees going back two or three hundred years. I looked at it and noticed that there was an actual namesake of mine a few generations back, one Charles Handy, who was born in 1765 and died in 1836. He married and had four children of whom two died early. One of the other two was my great-great-grandfather. That was all I knew. The paper told me nothing about where that first Charles Handy lived, what he did, how he looked, how rich he was, or whether he was a nice sort of chap or not – nothing. 'Is that what will become of me?' I wondered, a name on a family tree to be opened 100 years hence by someone I know not of. Is that what it's all about? Why, then, I might as well make merry and die.

It was then that I, by chance, came across the last few verses of the Book of Ruth in the Bible. These are hardly famous verses: they consist entirely of a list of names – 'Pharoz begat Hezron,' it goes, 'and Hezron begat Ram, and Ram begat Amminadab . . .' and so on for another six names, and then, conclusively, 'and Jesse begat David'. But that was the point; David was the point. He was the great king of the Jews, and the link, ultimately, with Jesus. Without all those other people there would have been no David, they were the essential links in the chain. Without that eighteenth-century Charles Handy, I would not be here today.

I realised, then, that I should not have been so arrogant as to think that it was up to me to make a great contribution to the future. Great, if that was how it worked out; but my main task was to ensure the continuity, not just of my family but of the things that I believed in. Forget the literal meaning of 'begetting', treat it metaphorically. It can apply to institutions and ideas as much as to kith and kin. We are links in a chain; it is up to us to keep things going because who knows which generation will be the one to make the big difference. David came nine generations after Ram.

The definition of a wise person in the Book of Proverbs reinforces the importance of continuity – he should ensure 'that there should be an inheritance for his children's children'. Jonathan Rauch, in his insightful book about Japan, *The Outnation*, describes his meeting with Yasunari Hirata, who started a business in 1946 making pushcarts and baby carriages, but is now making industrial robots. Talking of his job, Hirata says, 'I see the company as an infinitely growing child. I will die, but it continues to live, and my responsibility is to see to that. And I want to continue to build better and better robots.' Jonathan Rauch goes on to say that the word 'profit' would not have passed Hirata's lips if he, Rauch, had not brought it up. 'Yasunari Hirata was plainly not particularly interested in profits – not, I mean, in the sense of *taking profits*. He did not live lavishly and he seemed more concerned with immortality than with money.' He was expressing something which Richard Hooker was saying in England at the end of the sixteenth century: 'The Act of a Publick Society, of men done five hundred years sithence, standeth as theirs, who are presently of the same Society, because Corporations are immortal.' These ideas are of long standing.

John Rawls, the philosopher of justice, says, 'Each generation must not only preserve the gains of civilization and culture, and maintain intact those just institutions that may have been established, but it must also put in place a suitable sum of real capital appreciation.' Long before him, Edmund Burke, writing about the French revolution, said: 'Society is indeed a contract . . . not only between those who are living but between those who are living, those who are dead and those who are to be born.'

It is cathedral philosophy, the thinking behind the people who designed and built the great cathedrals, knowing that they would never live long enough to see them finished. The new cathedrals will not be of stone and glass, but of brains and wits. They will take equally long to build and we who must start the building may not live to see the conclusion. They is why we need to look beyond the grave and beyond our generation. It is hard to believe that we will make the sacrifices involved unless we can believe in the long-term existence of our little local world and of the bigger global one. We should, however, remember that there is no need for that continued existence to be in the same form as it is at present. The second curve is different from the first; there has to be change to be continuity. Yasunari Hirata started with push-chairs and moved on to industrial robots. We need to have faith in the future to make sense of the present.

How Big and Far Should We Think?

Some would say that even life itself is now under threat, that Malthus' fears, two centuries ago, that the world would not have the resources to feed its peoples, are now coming true. The numbers do indeed look frightening, and the arguments of people like Paul Kennedy, in his recent book *Preparing for the Twenty-First Century* or Edward Wilson with *The Diversity of Life* are horribly convincing, but the end is not the end if we don't wish it to be. We may need to adopt the sort of measure that Lester Thurow suggests, paying rents to the Third World for their forests. This payment might encourage us to develop the millions of different life forms which Wilson identifies in his book. One way or another, we shall need to have enough faith and interest in the continuity of the world and its peoples to give up some of our present wealth for the unseen benefits of people whom we will never know. It will need a bigger sense of continuity and of cathedral thinking than now exists.

Some people have that sense in their culture. Charles Hampden-Turner argues that Americans see time sequentially, as a straight line, whereas the Oriental races see it as a loop. To many Westerners, time, he says, is a running reaper, waving his sickle. But in the East, time comes round again and again to seek people's engagement in new opportunities. If you take the running-reaper view, then there is no time to lose. Things must be completed before time runs out. In the loop view of things, time never runs out. Therefore what you want to create are self-renewing systems, systems which will still be in place when time, your friend, comes round again, even if you are not there.

We could look at Europe in this light. In one way or another, Europe has to become more integrated. Its separate countries are too small to go it alone in a world of eight billion people. But for Europe to succeed, it must be more than just a convenient arrangement for the exchange of goods. It must, in the end, be a federal unity with all that federalism implies, twin citizenship, separation of powers and proper subsidiarity. Federalism also requires a common law and, ultimately, a common currency. At the moment, the unequal economies of Europe adjust their currencies when they have to, in order to restore their competitiveness and to allow them to sell their goods. Once there is a common currency, devaluation is no longer possible. Europe will then have to do what individual countries do to equalise their regions – make grants, loans and tax concessions to help the weaker catch up with the stronger. For Europe to have the cash to do that adequately, we shall probably have to increase the tax which we all pay to the centre, possibly by a factor of seven or eight. No voters will be prepared to do that unless their sense of history, of continuity backwards and forwards, allows them to see themselves as an integral and continuing part of this place called Europe, a place which has been a part of their heritage and a place which will contain the future of their great-great-grandchildren. There will be no short-term rewards for this sort of sacrifice, no way of justifying it within the lifetime of a parliament.

In a business, quarterly reports and an average lifespan of 40 years for big companies tend to put immortality on the back burner in most boardrooms. Boardrooms always want numbers, but trust no numbers beyond four or five years. It is always safer to put one's money on deposit than to risk building some cathedral of new enterprise. Only family businesses have the urge to think beyond the grave, and even then probably not beyond three generations of graves. The pressures to do it in your own lifetime seem to be mounting, even though the institutions who currently own our public companies are themselves supposed to have a continuing existence, independent of the people who run them. We need to re-emphasise that institutions can be immortal even if we are not. The Mitsui Corporation and my old Oxford college are both over 600 years old, both still going strong and thinking far. You only look ahead as far as you can look back.

Invited to help one large bank think out a statement of its visions and values, I looked, to start with, for their understanding of their purpose. 'Why do you exist?' I asked. 'To make our shareholders seriously rich,' they replied. Their shareholders were mainly other banks, insurance companies and pension funds. Had any of these, I asked, ever made that request of them, or defined for them what their expectations might be? It appeared not. The chairman added that, after announcing their first-ever annual loss, some years back, he had thought it right to call on their principal shareholder, an insurance company, to explain the situation. 'They were noticeably uninterested,' he said. 'They seemed to assume that we would be around for ever and that this was only a temporary hitch which we would put right.' Maybe they were right, I suggested; maybe they wanted to keep their money in a place where it could stay for ever. 'I think that they are very unusual,' he replied, disposing of that suggestion. Immortality as a concept can be frightening. Continuity can, however, be a useful and less scary compromise.

On a more domestic scale, we have to worry about the grandchildren. Now that one in every 2.3 marriages in Britain is ending in divorce, it is not clear who will be thinking about the grandchildren when there will be an abundance of unaccepted step-grandchildren or, looking at it the other way up, many children with grandparents whom they have never known. It is hard to plant trees in your garden if you do not know who will be around to look upon them when they are fully grown. More formally, the concept of justice between the generations will be harder to maintain when the generation after next is semi-detached. Families used to last for ever. It made sense to say 'when I am gone', knowing that much would continue even if subject to change. If families become things of temporary convenience, or inconvenience, time will indeed run out.

My hopes are fragile ones. We should not, for a start, underrate the power of the millennium idea. It will encourage people to look backwards and forwards farther than they have ever done before. The heritage movement is also gathering pace. We don't pull down things so often but refurbish them instead, turning our docks, warehouses and factories into new uses. That is usefully symbolic.

RISC, the International Research Institute for Social Change, reports, from its recent surveys, that 'we can witness an increasing sense of responsibility towards the flux of history, including a greater recognition of the importance of both past and future generations'. That is encouraging. The environmental campaigns, and particularly the idea of Gaia, of earth as a self-renewing system, take us on huge leaps back into history and forward into the future.

If companies, as I hope, rediscover the virtues of membership for their chosen ones, if job-hopping becomes more perilous and if shareholders wield less power, then the corporate world may see a desire for permanence creep in again. Corporate leaders do wield influence, so when 48 executives from the largest corporations in the world come together to form the Business Council for Sustainable Development, governments and others will listen. Carl Hahn, as chairman of Volkswagen a member of that group, wrote in its report: 'If we think of the future – a central part of the obligation to rising generations – we must adopt the cyclical approach on which the whole of nature is based.' In the market-place, fashion, that god of the merchandisers, may be losing some adherents, or rather, the new fashion may be to make do with what you have, or to choose what suits you and not your neighbours' fancy. Home-made, second-hand, good not flashy quality, the stuff that lasts, may become the style.

Now that people live longer and four-generation families, with great-grandchildren, become more common, the idea of continuity in a family may yet re-emerge, when today's footloose parents become tomorrow's grandparents and realise what they are missing – a stake in the future. Because we look forward only as far as we can look back in life, this realisation can only come late in life. The rights of grandparents would then become an issue, with children effectively adopted by their grandparents irrespective of their parents' new arrangements.

Without a sense of continuity there is no point in sacrificing any of the present for the future.

15 A Sense of Connection

We were not meant to stand alone. We need to belong – to something or someone. Only where there is a mutual commitment will you find people prepared to deny themselves for the good of others. We, however, in our belief in liberalism and individualism, are wary of commitments. We look suspiciously at words like 'loyalty' and 'duty' and 'obligation'. Independence, whether we seek it or not, is being thrust upon us. 'Modern society knows no neighbours,' said Disraeli more than a century ago, and it has been no different since. Loneliness may be the real disease of the next century, as we live alone, work alone and play alone, insulated by our modem, our Walkman or our television. The Italians may be wise to use the same word for both alone and lonely, for the first ultimately implies the second. It is no longer clear where we connect or to what we belong. If, however, we belong to nothing, the point of any striving is hard to see.

More crucially, perhaps, if we belong to nothing, there is no reason to make sacrifices for other people. Duty and conscience have no meaning if there is no sense of commitment to others, and of others to us. 'Think of a person,' said Rawls, 'without any sense of justice. He would be without any ties of affection, friendship or mutual trust, incapable of resentment or indignation. He would queue-barge if he could get away with it and expect everyone else to do the same. He would be less than human.' The interesting question is, then, not why some of us are criminals, but why more of us are not, in a world where so many of the connections which underlie that sense of justice are breaking down.

The workplace has been the central community in the lives of many in this century. Lewis Mumford, extolling the virtues of the monastic community, said, 'True leisure is not freedom *from* work but freedom *in* work, and, along with that, the time to converse, to ruminate, to contemplate the meaning of life.' Modern work does not provide too many of those opportunities, even for those in the core. Even so, the lament of the prematurely retired is usually the loss of community, while the loneliness of the long-distance teleworker is well documented.

If the idea of membership becomes more prevalent for those in the core of institutions, then the workplace will remain a central point of connection for many. That 'many', however, is likely to be less than half of the workforce and less than a third of all adults. It is a connection, however, which could be a very isolating one, consuming all its members' time and energy, and insulating them from the surrounding society, unless more attention is paid to the corporate contract with the other stakeholders and more trouble taken to chunk time sensibly.

The New Ghettoes

This has been one unintended consequence of the organisation society; the key place of the organisation in our lives removed from many of us the need to belong to anywhere other than our workplace. As a result, when we leave it we have nowhere. We also substituted the homogeneous communities, which our work provided, for the mixed communities of the old neighbourhoods. We replaced the community of place with the community of common interest. When you do that, there is no longer any need to think of sacrificing anything for your new neighbour because your neighbour is in the same position as you. If we then compound that by turning our communities of place, where we choose to live, into equally homogeneous zones, we shall never need to see, meet or pay heed to anyone different from ourselves.

There were, in 1989, 130,000 community associations in the United States, according to the Community Associations Institute, helping to administer the lives of 30 million Americans, one out of every eight. Some of these are just small condominiums, but 80 per cent of them own land as well and have an average of 543 dwelling-units. More are on their way and are getting more homogeneous; one new development in Newport Beach has even put a limit on the size of residents' dogs.

There is also the Leisure Hills development in Laguna Beach in California – 21,000 people with their own taxes, security force, television station and 12 bus routes. Guards at its gates check the identity of all visitors. It, and the other ghettoes like it, are the equivalent of the walled cities of medieval Italy. They provide their inmates with the security and peace of mind which they cannot find in the mixed community. They should remember, however, said the *Economist* when reporting this, that those walled cities of Italy were the source and cause of endless wars.

The new ghetto communities are too small and too like-minded to be the basis of any new balance of society. They are only connected to themselves. On the other hand the nation is too big and amorphous a concept to count as a connection. We are not easily going to be persuaded to make sacrifices for people whom we never see, to pay to clean streets we never walk, or to mend sewers we shall never use. The rich of Surrey may feel sympathy for the poor of Tyneside in the North but they will not put too much of their money their way, because they will never see the results. The organisation society has gradually become the ghetto society, ghettoes of the rich and ghettoes of the poor. We should remember that it was the enclosure acts of Henry VIII in England, done in order to get better productivity from the better farmers, which forced the poor into poverty and into a new underclass. We need a community which is large enough to be a mixture and small enough to be visible to all its inhabitants. We need to return to the city state or at least to the township.

Civic Pride

There used, in Britain, to be a thing called civic pride. Town hall would compete with town hall in magnificence and in achievement. Central government down the decades has progressively stripped the cities and the towns of their powers, distrustful of how they used those powers and, in some cases, undoubtedly abused them. All that is now left in Britain of this tradition is the city football club.

There was a time when the municipal universities were the pride of the city fathers; businesses competed to see their names inscribed above some new hall or lecture theatre, their sons and daughters studied there, married there, lived and worked there. In the 1950s the British government decided, in a spirit of liberalism, that they would give fees and maintenance grants to allow students to study at any university in the land. The city universities instantly became national universities. They lost their local identity and their local patronage; students roamed freely, made their contacts and their roots far from the city of their birth. It was done in the name of freedom or, say some, because the universities of Oxford and Cambridge wanted to have the pick of all the land. Whichever, it was one more blow against the city state.

The city may, however, be on the rise again. Europe is fast becoming a Europe of the cities. Manchester competes with Barcelona, which competes with Munich, in business and in sport. Airlines fly from city to city, not only from capital to capital. Cities twin with cities. It makes good sense. We can identify and connect with a city, even if we only live in its hinterland. The castle, the cathedral spire and even its tower blocks are a visible reminder of its presence. The city is a community on a human scale, the nation state is not. The only people who wave the Union Jack these days, or the French Tricolor for that matter, are drunken sports fans. As the middle orders disappear in a more integrated Europe, the city is replacing the nation state as the focus of our identity and our way of connecting with society.

But our cities are a mess. They represent the extremes of riches and poverty, of affluence hobnobbing with squalor. They look to be an unlikely basis for community. It is for that reason that they should be given back the responsibility for their futures. In Britain the bulk of the income of the cities comes from central government. The cities are only the delivery agents. Proper subsidiarity requires that they have the right to decide on their own priorities and are given both the authority and the means to deliver these.

Cities, together with their hinterland, are the best basis for the Chinese contracts which are required of a fair society. Only in that size of community will it be possible to harness the talents and the money of the more successful in order to provide the investment in the infrastructure and the help for the less fortunate. Those who give will be able to see the results of their giving or their taxes. In a city you can make some difference in your spare time. At the national level making a difference is a whole career. Giving the cities more responsibility, however, also means giving them the right to raise the money to deliver that responsibility. There lies the rub, because central government in all countries, save perhaps Canada, likes to have the first and largest bite of the tax take. It will require a radical central government to give up its fiscal control to this extent.

America's cities are farther down the road than most European ones, but everywhere there are some encouraging signs. The idea of an annual European City of Culture has begun to catch the imagination. Cities, rather than countries, are promoting themselves as centres for tourism and development. They compete for heritage and environmental awards. Cairo, with its 15 million population, recently received a United Nations award for recycling its rubbish, proving that size need be no drawback to civic pride. Only London, amongst the world's large cities, has no government of its own, no centre for civic pride.

The hard truth is that federations should be both small and big, with the inevitable result that the middle levels fade. Europe will one day be a federation of cities in all but name. When it is, then it will mean more to each of us to be a European because every city will need to rely on Europe and its connections far more than they do today. Reciprocity, too, is easier when there are many different players. It is easier for Glasgow to exchange people or projects with Oporto than with Birmingham, because it is less directly competitive. It is also more fun for both. The idea of twin citizenship is, it seems, easier to foster on a city basis than a national one.

I have long cherished the idea that at age 13 every child in Europe should spend a semester at a school and in a home in another European country. If done universally the only cost would be the travel. This is something which it would be hard to negotiate or to organise on a national basis. It could be much more fruitfully done on a city-to-city scheme. Nothing would do more to heighten a young person's sense of history and of a shared destiny than that connection.

For Europe, read North America, because surely, one day, geography and economic logic will combine to create a new and larger federation there, bringing in Mexico and Canada. That, too, will need to be broken down into cities and large towns rather than nations or even states, if the rich are ever going to be prepared to shell out for the poor. Twinning and swapping will then help to create a sense of shared history and shared destiny. Japan and South-East Asia may, one day, feel the same pulls to be both larger and, at the same time, smaller, if they are to compete with the growing force of China.

Most of the hope for cities, however, rests with the organisation, and particularly with the organisations of business. Businesses need the cities, they need the educational and cultural resources which the city offers in order to attract the quality of people whom they will need in their core. They will need the transport connections which cities alone can offer. They need the plethora of small service businesses and portfolio people who congregate on the edges of cities, in the new-style villages. They need the buzz of cities, the energy and excitement which you find there, the variety of life, the contacts and the political connections. Paradoxically, the trend at present is all the other way. Organisations are fleeing to the countryside or the suburbs, seduced by the dream of the office or factory in a garden, bringing the work to the workers rather than the other way round, relying on telecommunications to give them their link with the outside world. They are creating their own walled cities in the woods.

They may rethink. The new federal dispersed organisation does not have to have many people in any one place. Local work centres and tele-clubs can proliferate in the woods and the suburbs but the city needs part of their action and they need the city, for the stimulus of its connections. Only when the organisations return will they be prepared to invest in making these hubs of humanity civilised once again, because they have the clout, the spending-power and the leadership skills. Compromise may be the way forward. The symbolic analysts will increasingly work in more places than one, live in more places than one, not *rus in urbe*, the classicist's dream of the country in the town, but *rus et urbs*, for they will need them both. It is when the rich as well as the poor live in the cities and the towns again that there will be some chance that the rich will pay towards the education and the transport of the poor, because it will ultimately be in their interest to see their city better educated and therefore richer.

If organisations do not rethink and relocate we shall see the cities declining even faster, those of power and influence retreating still further into their walled villages and insulating themselves from anyone unlike themselves. That way there is no balance, less chance of sacrifice or compromise, less likelihood of turning paradox into progress. It is, therefore, heartening to know that the businesses of London are coming together to create a programme for London, that those of Birmingham are doing likewise, as are the leading citizens of Atlanta, Seattle, Barcelona, Seville, Glasgow and many more. 'Federations,' said Osborne, 'are the laboratories of democracy.' Some of our cities may yet, unexpectedly, find ways to reconnect us with our neighbours. Where they lead others may follow, as long as those who rule in the centre come to appreciate the benefits of federalism.

Virtual Cities

Great cities are made up of small villages. The truth is, as so often, that we need our village and our city. We need both the comfort of friends and the stimulus of strangers. We relax in the company of people like us, but we also need a connection with a bigger and wider society both to keep us from falling asleep, and to make us feel part of something bigger. Only then will conscience prevail over self-interest, and duty over comfort. Villages, even villages of like-minded and like-income people, in the midst of great cities would be a good basis for a fairer society. For most of us it will not happen like that. Our cities will not change fast enough. We must create our own virtual villages and cities, communities which one can describe and can visualise but which do not necessarily belong to any one place.

The family has always been one of our 'villages'. The traditional family is no longer so traditional, but there are still families. They may not be composed of conventional relationships, and there may be more step relations than blood relations, but there are still families. The extended family is now horizontal as well as vertical, covering a wider group of people of the same generation and offering a wider choice of soul mates than the narrower nuclear family of old. These new 'virtual families', which include close friends and partners as well as the blood relations, may well be more comfortable 'villages' than the older model. We should not despair of the family, but redefine it.

Work was another of those villages, often, as I have suggested, a ghetto unconnected with the world outside, but a comfortable way of connecting with like-minded colleagues. The spread of the minimalist organisation is making these connections more difficult, as more people move or are moved outside. Increasingly, the modern-day portfolio workers have to create their own 'virtual organisation' made up of clients and occasional partners or co-workers.

The virtual organisation can be glimpsed in the new 'clubs' for the independent portfolio workers. One of these clubs is provided by the intermediary employers, the employment agencies, who are the brokers for the portfolio workers, just as agents are for actors, writers and models. The intermediary employers, or agents, provide a reference point, a base and an ally, even if it is only at the end of a telephone line. There are also the networks of contacts which any independent soon builds up, the job clubs for the unemployed and the professional associations for those qualified to belong to them. My son, an independent actor, has both an agent and his 'filofax club' of contacts. These are his virtual organisation between engagements. One new development is the tele-club, a building designed to be used by the occasional tele-worker, offering cubicle space, receptionist services, food and drink, and all the necessary communications equipment.

Some of these facilities are hired by organisations for the use of their people, providing them with a local regional office. Others are for hire by individuals by the day, week or month. There are more up-market versions in the city, offering meeting and eating rooms for hire by strangers or more formal clubs which restrict their facilities to members. Hotels, airports and railway stations have seen the commercial potential in the new form of work, and have provided their own tele-clubs for travellers with a gap in their schedule. In time, these places may offer a form of temporary fellowship as well as their facilities, becoming a physical embodiment of the virtual work village.

There are other alternatives, other virtual villages. One study, delightfully called 'Organizing around Enthusiasms', discovered that there were 315 organisations in one Surrey suburb devoted to hobbies, interests, sports and other enthusiasms, all run by volunteers, all doughnuts with a core of organisers and a space full of subscribers and participants, all offering some sort of club to their members. They offer scope for activity, these places, not paid work, but they provide an opportunity to take comfort in the company of friends, a temporary village.

These virtual villages need then to be complemented by virtual cities, opportunities to meet and be challenged by strangers. Mickey Kaus advocates more use of what he calls 'Third Places', places like cinemas, churches, shopping-malls and other common meeting-arenas. More could be done to make these Third Places into opportunities for connecting with strangers. Too often, however, they are made up of lonely crowds. We cannot rely on these, but must do more to build our own connections with strangers. This is more difficult and more challenging but not impossible.

My brother-in-law left his full-time job in business at the start of his Third Age. He looked for part-time work for some four days a week. Four years later he thinks that he might manage to fit in an occasional day. He is far too busy to do more. He is a local magistrate, a governor of a local school, and a member of the parish council; he sits on various committees of the local judiciary and the police authority, runs the local gymkhana and part of the big agricultural shows in that part of the world. In place of one rather monotone business organisation he now belongs to a wide range of groupings. He sees sides of life which were probably undreamt of in his business office. Like him, we can use the new flexibility of work and life to make more connections than we would have in the days when the one organisation kept us fully occupied for most of life.

A portfolio of community activities, be they good works or good 'enthusiasms', is the antidote to ghetto life, be the ghetto a country village, a fenced city in California or a slum tenement in an inner city. You do not have to have my brother-in-law's background to serve the local community. Some of the best school governors, the best tribunal members and the best youth-leaders come from deprived areas. They have an understanding and a grip on reality which outsiders can only envy. Our community organisations promote the connections across the divides, both horizontal and vertical.

'There is no such thing as society,' said Margaret Thatcher, famously. She meant that individuals could not hide behind 'society', looking to it to provide for them or to protect them. 'Individualism,' said John Maynard Keynes, 'if it can be purged of its defects and abuses, is the best safeguard of individual liberty.' But the 'if' in Keynes's statement, the proviso, is important. The sense of connection which you can find in a mixed community is the best means of purging those defects. There can be a beneficial compromise between the individual and a community.

Society does exist and is necessary, but as a supplement to individualism not a substitute. Society is also an outlet for our contributions, a place to give to as well as get from.

We get more local as we get older and often feel the need to give something back to society, in time and expertise rather than money. As long as they don't hide away in their geriatric shrubberies and golf gardens with their size-restricted dogs, the Third Age people have a lot to give, but they will want to do it locally where they can see some of the results. We could see a new corps of para-professionals emerging in the community, individuals basically trained and competent enough to help with the Youth Service in the schools, in the hospitals and clinics as counsellors or drivers or attendants, in the dispensing of benefits and welfare, as researchers for projects or co-ordinators of volunteers. Some of this happens already. More could happen if civic pride were resurrected everywhere. We cannot wait for central government to give away its power, we have to do what we can without it. In the world ahead we shall increasingly have to make our own connections, our own virtual city and our own virtual village.

16   A Sense of Direction

The End of History

In the end, however, a sense of continuity and of mixed connections will not be enough to give point to any striving. Maybe nothing will. Francis Fukuyama, the author of *The End of History and the Last Man*, put it this way:

> The end of history will be a very sad time. The struggle for recognition, the willingness to risk one's life for a purely abstract goal, the worldwide ideological struggle that called forth daring, courage, imagination, and idealism, will be replaced by economic calculation, the endless solving of technological problems, environmental concerns, and the satisfaction of sophisticated consumer demands. In the post-historical period there will be neither art nor philosophy, just the perpetual caretaking of the museum of human history.

Fukuyama's argument is that liberal democracy, the tolerance which it brings with it and the affluence which made it possible, have removed the will to fight great causes. We are slumped in comfort. When we compete it is for the World Cup or gold medals. Such things do not bring forth great art or noble deeds, they don't stir the heart more than momentarily nor do they foster revolutions. Like dogs, if we are well fed we are content. When scientific and economic progress lead more and more societies into the contentment stage we shall see the end of history.

De Tocqueville saw it coming long ago, in America:

The first thing that strikes the observer is an innumerable multitude of men, all equal and alike, incessantly endeavouring to procure the petty and paltry pleasures with which they glut their lives. Each of them, living apart, is as a stranger to the fate of all the rest; his children and his private friends constitute for him the whole of mankind. As for the rest of his fellow-citizens, he is close to them, but he does not see them; he touches them but he does not feel them; he exists only in himself and for himself alone; and if his kindred still remain to him, he may be said at any rate to have lost his country. Above this race of men stands an immense and tutelary power, which takes upon itself alone to secure their gratification and to watch over their fate ... it is well content that the people should rejoice, provided that they think of nothing but rejoicing.

Democratic societies are tolerant; they do not tell their citizens how they should live, or what will make them happy, virtuous or great. It is not an accident that people in democratic societies are preoccupied with material gain and with the myriad small needs of the body. Nietzsche, who deplored this state of being, said that 'the last man' has 'left the regions where it was hard to live, for one needs warmth'.

One still works [he goes on] because work is a form of entertainment. But one is careful lest the entertainment be too harrowing. One no longer becomes rich or poor: both require too much exertion. Who still wants to rule? Who to obey? Both require too much exertion. No shepherd and one herd! Everybody wants the same, everybody is the same: whoever feels different goes voluntarily into a madhouse.

Maybe, says Fukuyama, it was boredom which was the underlying cause of the First World War, too much comfort among the bourgeoisie of Europe. If so, they got more discomfort than they bargained for and would not want that again. In 1989 the citizens of the then West Germany were none too excited by the thought of uniting their country when the Wall came down. It might cost too much. It did. Europe's politicians did not hurry to the defence of Bosnia four years later. They knew that there would be no stomach for that cause among their citizens. Only bloodless wars (bloodless, that is, for the democracies) like that of the Gulf, arouse any enthusiasm.

There are no great causes any more. We fill in our résumés in the hope that they may be the pathways to a style of life to which we feel accustomed. It is hard to detect great, unfulfilled longings or irrational passions just beneath the surface of the average first-year law associate. We have to find our pride in sports or eccentricities instead. It may not be great but it is better than any conceivable alternative. We are all last men now.

On the other hand we may not like the end of history when we see it. Fukuyama again: 'Self-interest rightly understood came to be a broadly understandable principle that laid a low but solid ground for public virtue in the United States . . . But in the long run those values had a corrosive effect on the values . . . necessary to sustain strong communities and thereby on a liberal society's ability to be self-sustaining.' Hegel understood that the need to feel pride in one's humanity would not be satisfied by the peace and prosperity that comes with the 'end of history'. In 1806 he wrote, 'We stand at the gates of an important epoch, a time of ferment . . . when a new phase of the spirit is preparing itself.' Almost 200 years later we are in another time of ferment, another dark wood. It may not yet be the end of history.

Maslow was right when he postulated that there was a hierarchy of needs, that when you had enough material goods you moved your sights to social prestige and then to self-realisation. Perhaps, however, his hierarchy did not reach far enough. There could be a stage beyond self-real-isation, a stage which we might call idealisation, the pursuit of an ideal or a cause which is more than oneself. It is this extra stage which would redeem the self-centred tone of Maslow's thesis which, for all that it rings true of much of our experience, has a rather bitter aftertaste. Maslow himself was to acknowledge this towards the end of his life.

For the Sake of a Cause

If we are not machines, random accidents in the evolution-ary chain, we need to have a sense of direction. Tolstoy, in his confessions, tells how he could find no logical purpose for his existence. He was successful, happily married, rich, yet it all seemed pointless. He came to the conclusion that man only lived because he believed in something. If he didn't believe there was anything there, he would kill him-self. Faith, therefore, was 'the power of life'. Laura Ashley, explaining why she started her country fabrics business, said: 'I sensed that most people wanted to raise families, have gardens and live as nicely as they can.' Her business flourished in the Seventies and into the Eighties because I think she caught the mood of the times, the generation of the last men. Mayor Dinkins, however, at Arthur Ashe's memorial service in 1993, said: 'Service to others is the rent we pay for our space on earth. Arthur Ashe paid his rent in full.'

Mayor Dinkins, in his turn, may have caught the mood of the approaching millennium. The RISC survey, men-tioned before, identified a growing search for meaning and authenticity as the distinguishing element of the mood of the Nineties, in contrast with the 'boring generation' of the Seventies and Eighties – 'people uninterested in ideological

debate and more concerned about themselves'. This new
'ethical' dimension had, they said, several manifestations –
'a sense of purpose, a search for identity, dignity and a
quality of life prior to lifestyle (aesthetics and harmony)'.

It is a search for a cause. The cause, however, to be truly
satisfying must be a 'purpose beyond oneself', because to
be turned in on yourself, said St Augustine, is the greatest
of sins; because we discover ourselves through others, said
Jung; because the immortality, for which we all privately
long, is really immortality through others. This last statement needs some justification because it suggests that most
of the religions have got it wrong. There may be some
future existence after death, for all that we know, but it will
certainly not be expressed in bodily shape, or in time or in
space. It is, therefore, literally inconceivable, and, as a result, not something which I myself can take seriously. My
purpose in this life, as I read the teachings of the sages, is to
so live that others can live better after I have gone, that, if I
live on in any sense, I may live on in the continuing lives of
others. Heaven and hell I see as medieval forms of social
control, along with theories of reincarnation. They are also
rather self-centred theories – pie in the sky by and by, if
you're good.

We do not need to change the world. To nudge a little bit
of it along will be enough. One owner-manager of a bakery
once contacted me. 'I want to make my little company the
best in the country,' he said. 'What do you mean by best?' I
asked. 'Are you talking profits?' 'Only up to a point,' he replied. 'Without some longer-term profitability I won't be
able to keep it going, but that's not really the point – I want
it to be a showcase, the kind of company of which I and all
who work there will be proud to say, "that's my place." '
He had a cause. Art Fury, of Post-It fame, commenting on
entrepreneurial success said once, 'Those who invest only
to get rich will fail. Those who invest to help others will
probably succeed.'

Those who talk about vision as essential for the future of an enterprise are right, but it has to be the sort of vision that others can relate to. Not many in the lower realms of the organisation can get excited by the thought of enriching the shareholders. 'Excellence' and 'quality' are the right sort of words, but they have been tarnished by repetition in too many organisations. They were often synonyms for cost- or people-cutting, or they begged the question – for whom are we doing this? We need to believe in what we are doing if we are to lift ourselves on to a second curve in any enterprise, or if we are going to be prepared to compromise our wishes and our needs for the good of others. Some businesses turn this into a concern for the customer, but we have to wonder whether this concern is not a means rather than an end, a more effective way of doing business.

I once attended a top management seminar arranged by a leading group of hotels. The keynote speech was given by a Benedictine monk who explained St Benedict's view of hospitality. In his monastery, he said, they got many visitors, both men and women, who came for peace and reflection. 'We try to practise St Benedict's command to welcome every man, each man and the whole man.' 'That means,' he explained, ' that we do not discriminate between president and pauper (every man), and we had both last month; we treat each person as an individual (each man), paying attention to their special needs and wishes; lastly, we try to deal with the whole of them, with their deep needs as well as their surface wants, and to enter as fully as they will let us into their lives.' His talk was rapturously received by the executives who saw in it a reason for their hard work, a reason more deeply satisfying than numbers on a balance sheet. When, however, I checked in later to their hotel, I found that every movable item was attached in some way to the walls. Even the toilet-roll in the lavatory was in a locked container. 'We have to,' they explained to me. 'Our visitors will steal anything, given half a chance.' If you can't trust your visitor with the toilet-roll, I reflected, it will be hard to deliver the Benedictine message. Yet for a moment, there, they glimpsed a vision, a direction worth the journey.

As George Bernard Shaw put it, in *Man and Superman*: 'This is the true joy in life, the being used for a purpose recognized by yourself as a mighty one; the being a force of nature instead of a feverish, selfish little clod of ailments and grievances complaining that the world will not devote itself to making you happy.'

Britain will never be 'Great' again, in the sense that she could be a world power or an economic force again, but she could find a new cause and forge a new existence as, for instance, the 'Athens of Europe', meaning the old Athens of learning, culture and the arts. Her great comparative advantage is her language. Everyone, everywhere, wants to learn it. Her universities, theatres, designers, artists, architects, film- and TV-makers, writers and literati, musicians and dancers are world-class. Sadly, she is more likely to be known as a museum than as a cultural centre, but the opportunity is there to find a second curve and to lift her people, to give her a sense of new direction.

Malaysia now boasts a 2020 Vision. The pun is deliberate. It is a 30-year plan outlining the kind of place the country's leaders would like to see it be in 2020. It is underpinned by an optimistic rate of growth – 7.2 per cent, enough to bring it up to American standards of living by 2020 – but that is where it starts, not where it stops. The Vision is full of the ways in which that money will be spent and distributed, on education, on the handicapped, on the old, on the environment (belatedly). Visiting that country I expected cynicism, instead I found excitement. Business leaders had a justification for their efforts. Others had hope. The headlines of the plan were even pinned up in the taxis.

It is hard, in the conditions of comfortable democracy, to find a cause which lifts the efforts of the comfortable ones.

That is why some fear a return to war as a way of putting some energy back into our peoples. Making money not war has turned out to be less inspiring. Another war would be a wasteful way to disprove the end-of-history thesis. It is tempting to call for better leadership, but we probably expect too much from the leaders of the nations. Those nations are too big, the connections not strong enough, the commitment to the future not long enough. It is better to look smaller, to our now-smaller organisations, to local communities and cities, to families and clusters of friends, to small networks of portfolio people with time to give to something bigger than themselves. We have to fashion our own directions in our own places.

A Postscript

Two Stories

My wife's ancestor was Sir Rowland Hill, famed as the inventor of the penny post and the first postage stamps in the 1840s. Until he came on the scene, letters were priced according to their weight and the distance they had travelled, rather logically when you think about it, and were paid for by the recipient. A letter from London to Edinburgh, for instance, might cost one shilling and sixpence, a lot of money in those days, but, then, it was a long distance. Some clever folk used to send an empty envelope to their families, who would then refuse to pay for it on arrival because they had heard what they needed to hear, that their loved one was alive. That put the costs up even more. The result was that only the rich could afford to send real letters to each other. Letter-writing was an élite pastime.

Rowland Hill proposed that we do some upside-down thinking. If every letter cost only one penny, no matter where it went to in Britain, and if it was prepaid by a 'stamp' which you could buy in advance and stick on, he argued that two things would happen: first, the volume of mail would expand hugely, more than compensating for any loss on the cost of the longer deliveries, but, more importantly, everyone would be able to send letters to each other. This would give an enormous boost to education because there would be some practical point in everyone learning to read and write. It would also help the cohesion of the nation because friend would be able to keep in touch with friend, mother with son, wife with distant husband. It would be, he said, not just a commercial success but a significant piece of social reform.

Nobody believed him. It took years of argument and campaigning before he convinced Parliament to make the change. When they did, the results were dramatic. Within 10 years some 50 countries had adopted the idea of pre-bought stamps and the modern postal service was born. Rowland Hill died richly honoured and is remembered to this day as the father of the penny post.

What is interesting about this story, however, is this: when he started his campaigning Rowland Hill was not in the postal service. He was a clerk in the South Australia Commission, having, before that, been a schoolteacher in his father's school. The postal service was nothing to do with him; it was none of his business. He was not rich, nor famous, nor influential, but he cared, he saw something which needed to be done and he decided that he could not live with himself if he didn't do something about it. We can't wait for the mountain to move, we have to climb it ourselves.

We are not, however, all destined to be social reformers. Richard Harries, the Bishop of Oxford, tells another story. There was a rabbi once, called Zuzya of Hannipol. He spent his life lamenting his lack of talent and his failure to be another Moses. One day God comforted him. 'In the coming world,' he said, 'we will not ask you why you were not Moses, but why you were not Zuzya.' We are not gods. We can't do everything, or even very much at all, in the small interval of time we have in this world. It is as much as we can do to be our full selves, full doughnuts and full raincoats.

Fires in the Darkness

There are two photographs on my desk, taken by my wife in South Africa. The first is the head of a small black boy.

He is smiling; everything about his eyes and his face radiates intelligence, enthusiasm, excitement. It is a happy face, full of promise. The second photograph is of the same boy, but this time the photographer has moved back, so that you now see him full-length. You see the shanty hut behind him, his bare feet and the excrement in which he is standing. The two photographs may be a symbol of our challenge today, not only in South Africa. The intelligence and the promise are there, if we can only release them from the chains of their surroundings.

Our people are clever, many of them. Most people are decent, given half a chance. They are not uncaring, if only because they know that a world which crumbles around them will do them no good at all. But first there has to be a general acceptance that the world has changed. The end of communism does not mean that capitalism, in its old form, is therefore the one right way. The triumph of the democracies over totalitarianism does not mean that everything in those democracies is thereby validated. The huge strides made by science in the last decades does not mean that scientists have or could have the answer to everything and that the rest of us need not bother.

It is also the end of the age of the mass organisation, the age when we could all confidently expect to be employed for most our lives if we so wanted, and over 90 per cent did so want. Work will still be central to our lives but we shall now have to rethink what we mean by work and how it might be organised. At first sight, the challenge is daunting, but work in those mass organisations has never been unalloyed bliss for all. The mass organisation has not been with us that long. We should not think of it as a law of nature. Maybe we shall be better off without it.

The hope lies in the unknown, in that second curve, if we can find it. The world is up for reinvention in so many ways. Creativity is born in chaos. What we do, what we belong to, why we do it, when we do it, where we do it –

these may all be different and they could be better. Our societies, however, are built on case law. Change comes from small initiatives which work, initiatives which, imitated, become the fashion. We cannot wait for great visions from great people, for they are in short supply at the end of history. It is up to us to light our own small fires in the darkness.

Bibliography

Abbeglen, James C. and Stalk, George Jun., *Kaisha, the Japanese Corporation*, New York, Basic Books, 1985

Albert, Michel, *Capitalism Against Capitalism*, London, Whurr, 1993

Anderson, Digby (ed.), *The Loss of Virtue*, London, Social Affairs Unit, 1993

Appleyard, Brian, *Understanding the Present*, London, Pan Books, 1991

Baden-Fuller, Charles and Stopford, John, *Rejuvenating the Mature Corporation*, London, Routledge, 1992

Bahrami, Homa, 'The Emerging Flexible Organization', *California Management Review*, Summer 1992

Ball, Christopher, 'The Adelphi Idler', London, *RSA Journal*, May 1993

Bennis, Warren, *An Invented Life*, Reading, Mass., Addison Wesley, 1993

Bishop, Jeff and Hoggett, Paul, *Organizing Around Enthusiasms*, London, Comedia, 1988

Bloom, Allan, *The Closing of the American Mind*, New York, Simon and Schuster, 1987

Commission for Social Justice, *The Justice Gap*, London, IPPR, 1993

Drucker, Peter, *Post-Capitalist Society*, Oxford, Butterworth-Heinemann, 1993

Fukuyama, Francis, *The End of History and the Last Man*, London, Hamish Hamilton, 1992

Galbraith, John K., *The Culture of Contentment*, London, Sinclair Stevenson, 1992

Gorz, P., *A Critique of Economic Reason*, London, Verso, 1989

Goyder, George, *The Just Enterprise*, London, André Deutsch, 1987

Hammer, Michael and Champy, James, *Re-engineering the Corporation*, New York, Harper Collins, 1993

Hampden-Turner, Charles, *Corporate Culture*, London, Hutchinson, 1990

Hampden-Turner, Charles, *The Seven Cultures of Capitalism*, London, Piatkus Books, 1994

Havel, Vaclav, *Disturbing the Peace*, New York, Vintage Books, 1991

Hegel, G., *The Philosophy of History*, London, Dover Publications, 1956

Henzler, H.A., 'Eurocapitalism', Harvard Business Review, Jul/Aug. 1992

Hewitt, Patricia, *About Time*, London, Rivers Oram Press, 1993

Kanter, Rosabeth M., *When Giants Learn to Dance*, London, Simon and Schuster, 1989

Keegan, William, *The Spectre of Capitalism*, London, Radius, 1993

Kennedy, Paul, *Preparing for the Twenty-First Century*, New York, Random House, 1993

Kester, W. Carl, *Japanese Takeovers*, Boston, Harvard Business School Press, 1991

Kraus, Michael, *The End of Equality*, New York, Basic Books, 1992

Leinberger, Paul and Tucker, Bruce, *The New Individualists*, New York, Harper Collins, 1991

Lucas, J.R., *On Justice*, Oxford, Clarendon Press, 1980

Nietzsche, F., *Beyond Good And Evil*, New York, Vintage Books, 1968

O'Neil, John R., *The Paradox of Success*, New York, Putnam, 1993

Osborne, David and Gaebler, Ted, *Re-inventing Government*, Reading, Mass., Addison Wesley, 1992

Peters, Tom, *Liberation Management*, New York, Knopf, 1992

Rauch, Jonathan, *The Outnation*, Boston, Harvard Business School Press, 1992

Reich, Robert, *The Work of Nations*, New York, Knopf, 1991

Sampson, Anthony, *The Essential Anatomy of Britain*, London, Hodder and Stoughton, 1993

Schor, Juliet B., *The Overworked American*, New York, Basic Books, 1992

Schumacher, E.F., *Small is Beautiful*, London, Blond & Briggs Ltd, 1973

Schwartz, Peter, *The Art of the Long View*, New York, Doubleday, 1991

Semler, Ricardo, *Maverick*, London, Hutchinson, 1993

Senge, Peter, *The Fifth Discipline*, New York, Doubleday, 1990

Shames, Laurence, *The Hunger for More*, New York, Times Books, 1989

Stayer, Ralph, 'How I Learnt to Let My Workers Lead', Harvard Business Review, Nov/Dec. 1990

Stewart, Rosemary, *Choices for the Manager*, London, McGraw Hill, 1983

Thurow, Lester, *Head to Head*, New York, William Morrow, 1992

Trompenaars, Alfons, 'The Organization of Meaning and the Meaning of Organizations', doctoral dissertation, Wharton School, 1987

Waldrop, M. Mitchell, *Complexity*, New York, Simon and Schuster, 1992

Watkinson Report, *The Responsibility of the British Public Company*, London, British Institute of Management, 1972

Young, Michael, *The Rise of the Meritocracy*, London, Penguin, 1961

Index

THE HUNGRY SPIRIT
Beyond Capitalism – A Quest for Purpose
in the Modern World

Charles Handy

'Charles Handy has done it again: *The Hungry Spirit* is the distillation of a lifetime's experience, a personal recipe for what we have to do to survive in a capitalist society. Handy's anecdotal style is highly readable, his erudition evident on every page . . . This is an important book.'
People Management

'*The Hungry Spirit* is a wide-ranging examination of business and social problems . . . shrewd, scholarly, thoughtful analysis' – *Modern Management*

'Charles Handy is Britain's only world-class management guru' – *Director*

While one third of the world's workforce has no paid work, more than two thirds of world trade is managed by just 500 corporations – answerable to no one but their investors. Against this picture of division and uncertainty, Charles Handy argues passionately for a future with values more sustaining and enriching than those of free market capitalism.

The Hungry Spirit is an inspiring book – sometimes provocative, always intensely personal, and ultimately full of hope. It is certain to spark controversy and debate wherever it is read.

THE GODS OF MANAGEMENT

Charles Handy

The four gods of the title symbolise the very different styles of management and culture to be found in today's organisations. Zeus is the dynamic entrepreneur who rules over companies of the **club culture**, characterised by speed of decision and rapid, intuitive communication. Apollo, god of order and bureaucracy, is the patron of the **role culture**, based not on personalities but on definition of the jobs to be done. Athena, goddess of craftsmen, recognises only expertise as the basis of power and influence: hers is the **task culture**. Dionysus is the god preferred by artists and professionals within the **existential culture**, people who owe little or no allegiance to a boss.

Under the witty and sparkling allegory Charles Handy, Britain's foremost business guru, makes a serious analysis of the changing patterns of work and business. Management is not a precise science but has aspects of a creative and political process which is influenced by the prevailing culture and traditions of the organisation. His theme is illustrated with a wealth of case studies and examples drawn from business around the world.

This book is a world bestseller which is required reading for managers, business students and everyone who wants to be a survivor in a world of constantly changing organisational culture.

BEYOND CERTAINTY

Charles Handy

'. . . remarkably fresh and stimulating – a radical and articulate call to shape our own futures in uncertain times, without allowing the past to stand in the way'
John Plender, *RSA Journal*

Over the last decade, change has accelerated violently. The Thatcher/Reagan years were a time of certainty, when greed was good, more meant better, and the Western world rejoiced to see George Orwell's dismal prophecy for 1984 confounded. But there is a curvilinear logic in the universe. Prosperity cannot last for ever.

Empires and organisations must flounder. The world must be reinvented. We can now be certain only of uncertainty. Compromise may be the way forward, and organisations must give more freedom to individuals to preserve commitment and creativity.

In this challenging and exhilarating collection of pieces, Charles Handy, Britain's foremost business guru, takes us on an intellectual journey through a changing world, in order to see how we must adapt to make our future work.